Praise for *The Struggle Is Eternal*

"Joseph Fitzgerald's *The Struggle Is Eternal* is the first book to fully examine the Cambridge movement and its leader, Gloria Richardson. In 1963, I saw that unforgettable magazine photograph of Gloria Richardson calmly facing an armed contingent of soldiers who were sent to put down the movement she led in Cambridge, Maryland. Mrs. Richardson evolved into a civil rights leader whom the authorities considered almost as dangerous as Martin Luther King Jr. She remains engaged in the struggle for social justice to this day. I am thrilled that Fitzgerald's work allows a broader audience to know Gloria Richardson, and to enhance their understanding of the civil rights movement, in which she played a significant role."—Kathleen Cleaver, Emory University School of Law, and former communications secretary of the Black Panther Party

"Joseph R. Fitzgerald's *The Struggle Is Eternal: Gloria Richardson and Black Liberation* provides the deepest exploration to date of one of the most significant, complex, and overlooked female leaders of the modern black freedom movement. Gloria Richardson's distinctive activist history brings into sharp relief broader debates over nonviolence and armed self-defense, civil rights and Black Power, models of black political leadership, and the roles of women in the movement, as well as the relationship between local campaigns and national racial change. Fitzgerald's analysis is a part of an important, growing body of historical work that challenges, complicates, and ultimately enriches popular conceptions of the movement era."—Patrick D. Jones, *The Selma of the North: Civil Rights Insurgency in Milwaukee*

"*The Struggle Is Eternal: Gloria Richardson and Black Liberation* is such a necessary and welcome addition to the canon of scholarship that analyzes SNCC, the Black Power movement, and the struggle for racial equity in America. This incredibly detailed book clearly lays out Richardson's dedication to the Cambridge movement, the black radical movement, and the overall fight for black liberation. Richardson is tireless in her efforts and there is finally a book to honor and contextualize her many contributions not just to black history, but to American democracy."—Christina M. Greer, author of *Black Ethnics: Race, Immigration, and the Pursuit of the American Dream*

"Fitzgerald has written the definitive biography of Gloria Richardson, arguably the least-known civil rights activist of the 1960s. By delving deep into available written sources as well as making use of multiple interviews with Richardson, family members, and Richardson's compatriots, he presents a vivid picture of a woman who stood alongside Rosa Parks and four others who were honored at the 1963 March on Washington as the 'Negro Women Fighters for Freedom.' Fitzgerald's biography of Richardson enhances our understanding of the civil rights movement of the 1960s by adding new layers of geographic, gender, and ideological complexity to it. At the same time, Fitzgerald makes it clear that Richardson's life and beliefs remain relevant to anyone who has an interest in the ongoing struggle for human rights today."—Peter B. Levy, author of *Civil War on Race Street: The Civil Rights Movement in Cambridge, Maryland*

The Struggle Is Eternal

The

STRUGGLE

Is

ETERNAL

GLORIA RICHARDSON
AND BLACK LIBERATION

JOSEPH R. FITZGERALD

UNIVERSITY PRESS OF KENTUCKY

Scholarly publisher for the Commonwealth,
serving Bellarmine University, Berea College, Centre
College of Kentucky, Eastern Kentucky University,
The Filson Historical Society, Georgetown College,
Kentucky Historical Society, Kentucky State University,
Morehead State University, Murray State University,
Northern Kentucky University, Transylvania University,
University of Kentucky, University of Louisville,
and Western Kentucky University.
All rights reserved.

Editorial and Sales Offices: The University Press of Kentucky
663 South Limestone Street, Lexington, Kentucky 40508-4008
www.kentuckypress.com

Maps by Dick Gilbreath, independent cartographer.

Library of Congress Cataloging-in-Publication Data

Names: Fitzgerald, Joseph R., 1965– author.
Title: The struggle is eternal : Gloria Richardson and black liberation /
    Joseph R. Fitzgerald.
Description: Lexington, Kentucky : The University Press of Kentucky, [2018] |
Series: Civil Rights and the Struggle for Black Equality in the Twentieth Century |
    Includes bibliographical references and index.
Identifiers: LCCN 2018027368 | ISBN 9780813176499 (hardcover : alk. paper) |
    ISBN 9780813176536 (pdf) | ISBN 9780813176543 (epub)
Subjects: LCSH: Richardson, Gloria, 1922– | African American women civil rights
    workers—Biography. | Cambridge Nonviolent Action Committee (Cambridge,
    Md.)
Classification: LCC E185.97.R535 F58 2018 | DDC 323.092 [B] —dc23
LC record available at https://lccn.loc.gov/2018027368

To the people of
the Student Nonviolent Coordinating Committee.
You made the United States a better place for everyone.

Contents

Introduction

On a cool afternoon in late September 2016 former civil rights activist Gloria Richardson sat with one of her granddaughters outside the National Museum of African American History and Culture, where they were participating in the facility's grand opening ceremony. Her granddaughter took photos throughout the day, some of which show Richardson in deep thought as she surveyed the museum's section on the modern civil rights movement. The visit gave Richardson a surreal feeling because, as she moved through the facility, she encountered displays about people she had known personally and events she had lived through, some of which dated back to the mid-1920s. Interestingly, most of the people at the museum that day had no idea they were in the presence of such an important American, and they had probably never heard about Richardson's role in making the nation a better place to live. They can be excused for not knowing this because many of the people who worked with Richardson after the 1970s were also unaware of her activism, and the same was true of her extended family. Years ago, when Richardson was visiting relatives, her granddaughter's in-laws were talking about the Cambridge movement in Maryland and wondering about its leader. One of them asked, "Whatever happened to that woman in Cambridge?" Richardson's eldest daughter replied, "Why don't you go and ask her? She's downstairs."

It is understandable why so many people are unfamiliar with Richardson, but even among those who have heard of her, she is somewhat of a mysterious historical actor. Not too much has been written about her activism, even though she and the Cambridge movement were front-page news in national papers such as the *New York Times*. Richardson often gets a brief mention in general histories of the civil rights and Black Power waves of the black liberation movement (BLM), but their coverage and analysis rarely go deep. This is due to several factors, one of which was the nature of the Cambridge movement itself: it was a multifaceted liberation campaign to end white people's systemic oppression of black people in the areas of housing, education, health care, and employment. This type of story does not fit easily into histories that focus on black people fighting for voting rights and access to public

1

accommodations. Another factor was the Cambridge movement's support and use of the tactic of armed self-defense; this placed it further outside the master narrative on the black freedom struggle, which privileges nonviolent direct action over all other tactics. Additionally, after 1964, Richardson was not directly involved in human rights activism, and the media's coverage of her ceased; therefore, she was no longer in the public's consciousness when Black Power was on the assent and the press was closely following its leaders' pronouncements and actions. Almost all these leaders were men who used masculinist rhetoric about black freedom and promoted a male-centric agenda. Scholars privileged these men's perspectives in the early histories of Black Power while ignoring women's influences and contributions, including those of Richardson.

Eventually, scholars began to write about Richardson, and while all of them focus on her civil rights activism, only a couple point to her role in the development of Black Power. Another element to these works is that they focus on *what* Richardson did as the leader of the Cambridge movement but not too much on *why* she did those things.[1] I wondered what had motivated her to act. Long before young civil rights activists brought the movement to Cambridge, Richardson could have taken advantage of her family's wealth and left the city for a place less hostile to black people, but she chose to stay there. I also wondered what she thought about the Cambridge movement specifically and the civil rights movement in general, including its metamorphosis into Black Power. I knew that finding the answers to these questions and others would allow me to understand Richardson's importance to our nation's history and how her social, economic, and political philosophies affected her decisions and actions.

The research process was an exciting one because I was the first scholar to take a deep dive into the available sources about Richardson, most of which were newspaper articles pertaining to her childhood in Baltimore and her leadership of the Cambridge movement from 1962 to 1964. Still, it would have been difficult if not impossible to reconstruct her history from these sources, which covered very limited periods of her life and contained little critical information about events and people. Furthermore, Richardson left a meager paper trail consisting of one journal article and a book proposal on race relations in Cambridge. I knew that these gaps could be filled in only by Richardson herself, so I conducted a number of in-person and telephone interviews beginning in the summer of 2002 and ending in 2015. Aiding my research were several excellent biographies and essays on some of Richardson's civil rights comrades, including Septima Clark, Ella Baker, Fannie Lou

Hamer, and Rosa Parks. These and other works allowed me to see points of convergence and divergence between Richardson and other important women of the movement, and my portrait of her adds to the continuously evolving body of scholarship about the modern civil rights movement, which was merely one phase of the multicentury struggle for black liberation.[2]

To tell stories, historians commonly use presentation frameworks that rely on the periodization of time, location, and specific people and events. This framework is efficient for telling some types of history, such as that related to the First and Second Industrial Revolutions, but not for others. A case in point is the black liberation movement, where rigid time frames and historical processes do not lead to a greater understanding of why and how black people fought to free themselves from white supremacy. I subscribe to the viewpoint that the BLM is a "long movement" that occurred everywhere in the United States; it began in the nation's colonial period and continues today. Generally speaking, the BLM consists of four main periods, or waves, characterized by high degrees of advocacy, activism, and protest during which black people worked to exercise their human rights. The BLM is not commonly thought of as a human rights movement, but that is precisely what it is. When the United Nations created its Universal Declaration of Human Rights in 1948, that international body endorsed what activists in the BLM have always argued either explicitly or implicitly: black people's rights *are* human rights. Among the rights enumerated in the UN's declaration are that no one should be enslaved and that everyone has the right to equal protection of the laws of their nation, the right to be free from state harassment and abuse (including torture), the right to vote and travel within their nation, the right to freedom of assembly, and the right to work and receive equal pay for equal work. One of the declaration's implied rights is access to public accommodations.[3]

The earliest wave of the BLM was abolitionism, which sought to end the crime against humanity known as enslavement. This was followed by the Civil War and Reconstruction wave, when black people fought to end enslavement and actively supported the federal government's expansion of political rights initiated by the Reconstruction Amendments to the Constitution. The third wave—the civil rights wave—lasted roughly from the early twentieth century through President Lyndon B. Johnson's signing of the Civil Rights Act of 1964 and the Voting Rights Act of 1965. Activism during this wave focused largely on self-help efforts and exercising the guarantees of the Fourteenth Amendment, specifically equal protection and due process of the law, as well as exercising the right to vote granted through the Fifteenth and

Nineteenth Amendments. Some of the organizations that played critical roles in this wave's activism were the National Association of Colored Women, the National Association for the Advancement of Colored People (NAACP), the Congress of Racial Equality (CORE), and the Student Nonviolent Coordinating Committee (SNCC). The fourth wave ushered in Black Power, whose activists and advocates sought to use the legal victories of the civil rights wave and leverage them to achieve significant social, economic, and political power. There was some overlap between the third and fourth waves, as I discuss later in this book.[4]

Within and between all these waves were the freedom fighters who pushed their communities and the nation to be places of true democratic freedom and opportunity for all. Although activists almost always agreed on the broad goals of their struggle, they did not always agree on the tactics or strategies used to achieve them. Those who promoted incremental and reform-oriented changes to the system, and who considered the white community's perceptions of black people's grievances, are commonly described as *moderates.* In contrast, *radicals* pushed for the quickest and most systemic changes to the US society, economy, and political system. They normally disregarded white people's opinions about what constituted reasonable demands or appropriate methods of protest. Some activists held a combination of moderate and radical views and acted accordingly, based on the situation. Despite their different viewpoints on how to achieve black liberation, collectively these people were challenging white supremacy. Thus, the nature of their work was inherently radical, and it constitutes a sociopolitical tradition within black America.

Gloria Richardson's family belonged to this black radical tradition—one of the many similarities she shares with other prominent female civil rights activists. As a group, these women's families stressed racial pride and advocacy of black people's human rights, and they lived in black communities that supported and appreciated such ideals. Most of them attended historically black colleges and universities that encouraged students to be advocates for their communities. These factors fostered a shared personality trait: racial discrimination was anathema to them. In other words, these women were angered by racial injustice, and that is what motivated them to get involved in human rights activism. Personal belief systems also played a part in their fight for human rights, and for many, this meant living out the Christian ideal of trying to make the world a better place. The woman who is best known for this religiously oriented activism is Fannie Lou Hamer, who was committed to creating a "beloved community" rooted in the Judeo-Christian tradition.

She spoke about the "moral evil of racism," and one of her biographers observes that her activism was tied to her "moral pragmatism," which was rooted in her commitment to satisfying her community's material needs. Hamer worked to fulfill this obligation by championing numerous causes, such as the Mississippi Freedom Labor Union and the Freedom Farm. In contrast, Gloria Richardson's motivation for becoming an activist arose from her secular humanism, based on the tenets of behaving ethically toward one's fellow human beings in ways that affirm their humanity, while working to eliminate structures that create injustice. It was on this bedrock of belief that Richardson formed her social, economic, and political philosophies that affected her decisions and actions throughout her life. Richardson's humanism worked well with other activists' Christian ethics because they agreed on many issues and were working toward the same goals.[5]

These women activists shared other commonalities, including a socioeconomic egalitarianism that stressed the inherent value of all people, irrespective of class and education, and a gender egalitarianism that acknowledged, explicitly or implicitly, women's right to live free and full lives and held that sexism undermined the effectiveness of the black liberation movement. Gender-related issues were especially important to these women's lives and to the civil rights movement because they affected how people viewed the movement and women's places in it, including the type of work that should be done and who should do it. One gender dynamic concerned the "politics of respectability" as it related to women's public behavior, and Richardson and her fellow women activists generally rejected "respectability" as a protest strategy. Additionally, these women had a qualitatively different view from most men their age about how civil rights activism should be organized and executed, as well as who should be leading it. Richardson and the other women all subscribed to a group-centered, member-driven organizing model that encourages local people—including women—to lead their communities' freedom movements.[6]

The nexus between gender and activism has been analyzed extensively over the last two decades. Many women who participated in the civil rights movement belonged to and sustained what Septima Clark's biographer describes as "woman-centered professional and civic organizations" that served as "fertilizer" for the grassroots organizing that took place after World War II and were the soil from which a lot of the movement sprang. Additionally, they and their associates in women's church groups performed what historian Charles M. Payne calls "women's work"—those activities performed by women more often than not, usually done in private rather than in public, and for which they often did not get paid. This work, he adds, was "the everyday maintenance of the movement," and it was a major reason why the movement was successful. Historian Françoise N. Hamlin offers another concept related to gender and activism: "activist mothering." It is, she argues, a "style of political engagement" used by women activists who are "nurturing [the] youth" of their community.[7] Richardson was not actively mentoring Cambridge's youth, so Hamlin's concept does not apply to her; however, Payne's description of "women's work" does encompass some of Richardson's early activism, but not the leadership work she engaged in.

Sociologist Belinda Robnett unpacks the interplay between gender and leadership and writes that during the civil rights movement, people commonly understood a leader to be a person who had an official or "formal" leadership role in a hierarchical civil rights organization. That person wielded real and implied power inside the organization and often served as its public face. At the time, all the leaders of such organizations were men, and Robnett argues that this narrow understanding of leadership has to be broadened to include the women who led local movements. Some of them also served as "bridge leaders," whom she describes as liaisons between local civil rights organizations and those at the national level, and this type of leader also facilitated and articulated her group's goals and concerns. Interestingly, Robnett states that Richardson was a bridge leader, and although she did serve as a spokesperson for the Cambridge Nonviolent Action Committee (CNAC), she did not serve as a bridge between it and national civil rights organizations or their leaders.[8] Richardson did have contact with some of these people, but her purpose was to inform them that CNAC was an autonomous organization that determined its own goals, strategies, and tactics.

As a female leader with national stature, Richardson held an uncommon role during the civil rights movement, and although her work has to be analyzed using a gender framework, it must be one in which she is compared with male leaders of hierarchical organizations that were leader-driven and top-down in their approach to identifying and addressing issues. In this regard, she was quite different from her cohort because she subscribed to an organizing philosophy based on serving the community's needs, as determined by its residents. Furthermore, Richardson had a no-nonsense and straightforward communication style that was polite but not accommodating to people's egos, no matter their race, gender, or class. She rubbed many people the wrong way, especially men, and she made no apologies for that. At the same time, her leadership principles were extensions of her belief that black people's rights were nonnegotiable; thus, she refused to act in ways that she believed would devalue, undermine, or threaten them. The most salient example occurred in October 1963, when she boycotted the referendum vote on black people's access to public accommodations. Many people criticized Richardson for taking this position, but she saw the referendum as representing the tyranny of the white majority over the black community. She believed that if black people participated in the vote, at best it would lead to a short-term gain in a battle for freedom that encompassed much more than being able to patronize a white-owned restaurant.

Her leadership was also on display when she strategized with fellow Cambridge activists to employ a protest strategy she called "creative chaos." It was based on the use of unusual tactics and maneuvers to confuse white politicos and keep them off balance, which ultimately limited their ability to outflank the Cambridge movement. Still, despite being a national civil rights leader, Richardson had less in common with her male counterparts than with the rank-and-file women of the movement, with whom she shared the same group-centered organizing philosophy. Many of them believed, as she did, that the goals of the BLM should include economic justice. When we factor into our analysis these women's belief in black people's right to self-defense, we can see just how radical their political views were.[9]

Geography is another element of Richardson's story because Maryland's location in the mid-Atlantic region of the United States places the Cambridge movement outside commonly understood frameworks of civil rights and Black Power histories. Local movements in the Deep South focused mainly on desegregation and voting rights, whereas northern movements were generally built around access to jobs, quality public education, and housing. The Cambridge movement had some commonalities with each of these regions. Racial segregation was legal in Maryland, so desegregation was part of CNAC's agenda, but voting was not an issue because black people did exercise that right. Richardson and her colleagues in the Cambridge movement focused on obtaining greater job opportunities, access to decent housing and health care, and quality public education for their children. Thus, northern liberation campaigns during the mid-1960s had a lot in common with the Cambridge movement, and many northern activists saw it as a model for improving their communities' economic and political conditions. Significantly, many young activists embraced this agenda when they built their Black Power organizations, and they saw Richardson as a model of Black Power leadership.[10]

Despite being active for only three years—1962 through 1964—Richardson had an important influence on the civil rights and Black Power waves of the BLM, which makes her unique. Almost all her peers (particularly women) had much longer engagements with the BLM that commenced long before the 1960s and continued throughout that decade and into the next. Yet Richardson's activism was not a peculiarity of her life; when she reentered the workforce in the late 1960s, she followed a career path that can be described as social work and in many ways was an extension of her human rights activism.

This biography is important for a number of reasons. For one, it provides a key to understanding a person who is often considered a historical enigma. I discuss in detail Gloria Richardson's human rights activism and her intellectual history, as well as her personal life as a daughter, wife, and mother and her relationships with friends, activists, and coworkers. This book also expands our understanding of the civil rights and Black Power movements by showing how Richardson and the Cambridge movement were integral to both in terms of goals, strategies, and tactics. Additionally, this book positions Richardson as a transitional leader between these waves of activism because she served as a philosophical and strategic model to younger activists in the Black Power movement.

Organized mainly in chronological order, this book begins with the story of Richardson's maternal and paternal families, who built their personal and family wealth and leveraged both to improve their own lives and those of their fellow black people. Additionally, the St. Clairs of Cambridge, Maryland, and the Hayeses of Mecklenburg County, Virginia, stressed formal education and black self-help organizations as a means of uplifting themselves and others. Of special importance was the role played by Richardson's maternal grandfather, Herbert Maynadier St. Clair, in improving black people's lives through his involvement in Maryland's Republican Party and his service as an elected City Council member in Cambridge. Chapter 2 focuses on Richardson's childhood in Baltimore and Cambridge. During these years she displayed a strong sense of justice and a reluctance to accept what she believed was the unfair treatment of herself and other black people. These character traits were encouraged by her parents, especially her father. Richardson's family was also influential in the development of her philosophies on race and class, which would become evident when she began her civil rights activism. Chapter 2 also discusses the earliest indications of Richardson's secular humanism. Chapter 3 continues to detail Richardson's intellectual development during her time at Howard University in Washington, DC. There, she studied under intellectual powerhouses who helped her hone and expand her social, economic, and political philosophies. Of particular importance were the knowledge and research skills imparted by her sociology professors, which she utilized effectively during the civil rights movement.

The focus of chapter 4 is Richardson's life when she moved back to Cambridge and married Harry Richardson in the mid-1940s. In addition to covering her marriage (and subsequent divorce) and the birth of her two daughters, this chapter discusses Richardson's accommodation and rejection of gender norms. Importantly, the activities she engaged in during those years helped prepare Richardson for her civil rights activism, and they provided the first impressions of the type of leader she would become during the Cambridge movement.

Chapters 5 and 6 chronicle the history of the social justice–focused Cambridge movement and analyze Richardson's role as its leader, including her leadership style. Significant attention is paid to how her social, economic, and political philosophies influenced the tenor of that local struggle, particularly who should be involved in it, what their goals should be, and what strategies and tactics they should use to achieve those goals. These chapters are crucial to the history of the black liberation movement of the 1960s because they reveal that the Cambridge movement was an influential source of the Black Power wave, and young radical activists saw Richardson as the type of leader black America needed to achieve its goals.

Chapter 7 concerns one of the most important aspects of Richardson's civil rights work: a boycott of the referendum devised by white Cambridge residents to keep their city's public accommodations racially segregated. There was a backlash against the boycott that highlighted white Americans' frustration with activists like Richardson who used asymmetrical tactics to challenge white supremacy. Many black moderates also criticized the boycott because they believed it undermined other black freedom movements, especially those involving the right to vote. However, Richardson saw voting as a tactical means of advancing the BLM and believed that people should not vote simply for the sake of voting. Both groups realized that Richardson's radicalism, and that of the Cambridge movement in general, not only disrupted Cambridge's racial status quo but also threatened the long-established civil rights grievance process that privileged hierarchical civil rights organizations and their leaders over grassroots groups with their locally based agendas.

Beginning in 1963 Richardson traveled to northern cities to aid local movements there, and in the process, she built a network of radical activists and supporters that helped sustain her spirit and the Cambridge movement. Those journeys, the role of gender dynamics in Richardson's activism, and her decision to exit the Cambridge movement in the summer of 1964 are the focus of chapter 8. Even though she did not stay directly involved in Cambridge's civil rights struggle, Richardson kept engaged in the BLM by participating in ACT, an organization she had cofounded with some of her fellow radical activists. ACT's purpose was to do for northern movements what SNCC had done for the southern freedom struggle: revolutionize how the BLM would be carried out. The history of that organization is the basis of chapter 9, which also discusses Richardson's close personal and working relationship with Malcolm X.

Chapter 10 starts by giving readers an insider's view of Richardson's second marriage and her life in New York City after she left Cambridge. It then moves on to her reinvolvement in Cambridge's ongoing civil rights struggle right around the time she attended the National Conference on Black Power in Newark, New Jersey, in the summer of 1967. Richardson's assessment of Black Power's potential and her final analysis of it, particularly its advocates' goals and strategies, close out the chapter. Chapter 11 takes readers back to Richardson's personal life. She and her husband Frank Dandridge divorced, and Richardson reentered the workforce. Despite some early setbacks, she found jobs that spoke to her secular humanism and were similar to the work she had done during the civil rights movement: advocacy on behalf of people in need of social justice. Throughout the many decades since the 1960s, Richardson has stayed focused on social issues related to racism, and she has maintained her radical posture toward them because she believes that the problem of America's systemic and enduring white supremacy cannot be solved with a moderate and incremental approach to eradicating it. For the solution to work, people must create group-centered grassroots movements that will confront and challenge racism everywhere it exists.

This biography of Gloria Richardson is more than just a story about an individual who used her intellect and skills to work on behalf of black liberation. It is also a story about America. The unjust and oppressive systems she fought more than fifty years ago are still with us today, as evidenced by people's hierarchical relationships based on skin color, gender, sexuality, and financial wealth, among other distinctions. By reading Richardson's story, current and future activists participating in all types of social change movements can learn how to work toward their goals here in the United States and around the world.

A note on sources: Oral histories and interviews were a key source for this biography, and I took the same critical approach to them that I employed when reading written texts. That is, I attempted to verify whatever the sources stated. I did my best to corroborate everything Richardson said by looking for documents and speaking with other people who were knowledgeable about the events, but this was not always possible. In many cases the people who could have shed light on Richardson's claims were no longer living. In a few instances I might have been able to obtain corroboration (or refutation), but the people who possessed the pertinent information were not willing to share it.

1

Foundations

The roots of Gloria Richardson's human rights activism can be found in the legacies of her maternal and paternal families. Her maternal family, the St. Clairs, were descended from a line of free black people in the town of Cambridge on Maryland's Eastern Shore, whereas her paternal family, the Hayeses, came from rural Mecklenburg County, Virginia, and had been enslaved. Yet these families had more in common than not. Both came of age in America's post-Reconstruction period, which saw the rise of racially segregated public spaces, an expanding industrial economy, and a retreat from the racial advancements arising out of the Civil War. The two families also possessed strong entrepreneurial spirits that they cultivated over generations and resulted in significant business and financial success. Another similarity, and perhaps a more important one, was their belief that, as black people living in a white supremacist society, they should take concrete actions to improve the lives of black people. These families worked constantly to bring to fruition a world in which all black people were free from racial oppression. To that end, they emphasized education, using their knowledge, skills, and personal qualities to establish and maintain institutions of racial uplift and progress. These actions constituted a pattern of "race service" that became a family tradition as elders passed it on to their children, including Gloria Richardson's parents.

The St. Clairs

Maryland's racial history dates back to the colonial period, when free and indentured white people from Europe migrated to Maryland's Eastern Shore to grow tobacco. Europeans' insatiable appetite for this addictive plant quickly outpaced the European immigrants' production capacity, so officials in England permitted the colonists to enslave Africans and force them to grow the cash crop, which was steadily spreading throughout the colony. This enslaved labor system began in 1644 when the first Africans were forcibly transported to Maryland, including to the town of Cambridge in Dorchester

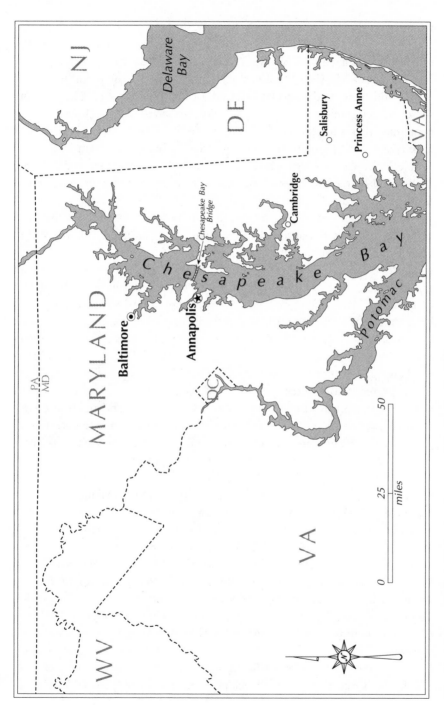

Maryland, home of Gloria Richardson's maternal family, the St. Clairs.

County, on the Chesapeake Bay's Eastern Shore. Early on, white colonists codified the legal status of Africans and Europeans, the result of which was to establish a racialized society where white people ruled over black people. In the mid-1640s Maryland's colonial legislature passed a law permitting black people and their children to be enslaved for life. Free black people lived in a social and economic world where white people viewed them with suspicion or contempt; therefore, some of the former emphasized their Christianity and their mastery of English in the hope of receiving better treatment from white people. A few free black people on the Eastern Shore owned farms during the 1600s, and on rare occasions, a black man from this group was permitted to testify in civil court.[1]

Dorchester County's African population increased throughout the colonial period, and by the outbreak of the Civil War, it numbered almost 9,000. This group was split almost equally between free and enslaved people, with the latter forced to labor on farms, in the local shipping industry, and in skilled trades.[2] Black Marylanders sought to build better lives for themselves by resisting their white oppressors, and two of the best-known champions of black resistance are Frederick Douglass and Harriet Tubman. Both were born into enslavement on the Eastern Shore, and both risked their lives to help free their black brothers and sisters in bondage. While Douglass and Tubman were engaged in direct action tactics to gain black people's freedom, others on the Eastern Shore were taking less confrontational but nevertheless important steps to improve black people's social, economic, and political conditions. Many of them used their business experiences and enterprises as resources for organizing, financing, and building a web of black social, economic, and political connections. Gloria Richardson's great-grandfather, Cyrus St. Clair Sr., was one of those people.

Cyrus was a free man born sometime around 1815, making him a contemporary of Douglass and Tubman. His wife Annetta was also free, and together they had four children: Cyrus Jr. (b. 1849), Martha (b. 1851), Edward (b. 1864), and Herbert Maynadier (b. 1867). The St. Clairs lived on High Street in a home they paid for with money Cyrus Sr. earned from his butcher shop, a trade he probably learned through an apprenticeship program. Importantly, the St. Clairs were literate, and Herbert Maynadier, Gloria Richardson's grandfather, attended school in Cambridge and Morgan College in Baltimore, a black institution that trained men and women to be teachers.[3]

Cyrus Sr. had undoubtedly seen much pain and suffering among Cambridge's free and enslaved black populations before the Civil War, so he made it part of his life's work to serve his race in very public ways. One avenue for this service was the Cambridge African Colonization Society, an organization he helped found in 1851 to promote free black people's emigration to Liberia in West Africa, where they could establish new and self-directed lives free from America's racist oppression. (Many white people also supported emigration, but they did so primarily because they saw free black people as potential rabble-rousers among enslaved black people.) St. Clair himself did not migrate to Africa, probably because he identified as American more than African, and he thought he could do more for black people on the Eastern Shore by staying in the United States. He also participated in the black convention movement, which free black people from around the nation and from various political persuasions (conservative, moderate, radical, and militant) had organized prior to the Civil War to identify and address the social, economic, and political issues affecting black America.[4]

Cyrus Sr.'s race service became a family obligation assumed by his children, especially his sons, who also followed in their father's footsteps in the business world. Both Cyrus Jr. and Edward became successful butchers, and the youngest brother, H. Maynadier, became a successful grocer. These men and their families lived and operated their businesses in Cambridge's black political ward, a geographically and racially defined area separate from the town's all-white political wards. The St. Clair family's businesses were also tied directly to the region's bourgeoning economy, which resulted from the new railroad that connected the Eastern Shore's sandy marshlands and pine forests with southern Delaware, as well as the Army Corps of Engineers' clearing of the nearby Choptank River and improvement of Cambridge's harbor in the late 1880s. These infrastructure projects permitted the Eastern Shore's cash-crop economy of grains, tomatoes, and oysters to be transported to the growing consumer markets in the mid-Atlantic region. Improvements in railroads and shipping also ushered in a phase of industrialization that greatly expanded both black and white residents' opportunities to obtain relatively good-paying jobs in the city's shipbuilding, oystering, and timber industries.[5]

At the dawn of the twentieth century, Cambridge's economy revolved around the town's canning industry, which was dominated by the Phillips Packing Company. William Winterbottom and brothers Albanus and Levi Phillips established the company in 1902, and it employed hundreds of black and white laborers who canned vegetables (particularly tomatoes) and oysters. Black people worked in a variety of other occupations in Cambridge; a significant number of women and girls worked as domestics in white households, and half a dozen men had careers in the skilled trades. These black workers patronized black-owned businesses like the St. Clairs', as well as small restaurants and barbershops.[6]

Cambridge's black ward offered its residents a social atmosphere that encouraged community pride and insulated them from many of the racist indignities in the broader society. That social scene was augmented by routine influxes of visitors from Baltimore's black community, who took daylong excursions across the Chesapeake Bay to shop and enjoy the entertainment at Cambridge's black bars and clubs. The city was also a popular destination for celebrities, such as poet and political activist Alice Dunbar Nelson, world heavyweight boxing champion Jack Johnson, and musicians Fletcher Henderson and Cab Calloway, all of whom made it a point to stop by the home of H. Maynadier St. Clair and his wife Fannie. Gloria Richardson's maternal grandparents and other St. Clair family members also traveled to visit with relatives, friends, and professional associates in Baltimore and points beyond.[7]

Existing side by side with the secular life of black Cambridge was the sacred world of black religiosity, which had served an important role in black people's lives since America's colonial period. There were both small and large congregations within Cambridge's black community, and they were active in revivals and the temperance movement. On rare occasions, black and white churches joined forces to work for a common goal, such as raising funds for Cambridge's hospital. Maynadier and Fannie attended Waugh Methodist Episcopal Church and were two of its most dedicated congregants. He served as trustee, and she was an important part of the church's music program. Together they organized and attended a multitude of church and community events held at Waugh, including those concerning missionary work and the support of black children's education.[8]

Promoting formal education also fell within the scope of the St. Clair family's community service. They helped establish the black school system in Cambridge and stood up for equal educational opportunities when, for example, the white Dorchester County school board decided that the school year for black schools would be three months shorter than that for white schools. Maynadier met with local and state officials to discuss improving black people's access to education from kindergarten through college, and he served as a trustee of Morgan State College. He publicly challenged white politicos who ran the city's separate and unequal school systems by demanding more funding for black teachers, who were paid less than white teachers, as well as more and better school supplies. Inside the schoolhouse, St. Clair taught at and served as principal of the black high school, a role that required him to interview and hire many of the town's black educators.[9]

Gloria Richardson's maternal grandparents were also members of several fraternal and self-help organizations, which were popular at the turn of the twentieth century. Fannie belonged to the Order of the Eastern Star and the National Association of Colored Women, whose motto was "Lifting as We Climb," and Maynadier belonged to the Masons and Order of Knights of Pythias.[10] Pythian conventions gave members the opportunity to telegraph their concerns about black people's social and economic conditions to individuals outside of the order. At the 1931 statewide convention in Hagerstown, Maryland, St. Clair told conferees and their guests, including Hagerstown's white mayor and the white state's attorney, that black men faced considerable odds when it came to providing for their families. He asked the white politicians to go back to their white communities and "kindly tell them that the only way to have us to have peaceful slumber is to give us an opportunity to earn our livelihood."[11] This statement was not out of character for Maynadier, as he had made similar arguments over the years while serving as an elected official in Cambridge.

Because it did not attempt to secede from the Union, Maryland did not experience the tumultuous Reconstruction process that occurred in other southern states. The Fifteenth Amendment gave black men the right to vote, and those in Maryland were able to exercise that right because white men did not attempt to disenfranchise them after Reconstruction ended, as happened throughout much of the South. Cambridge's political landscape was a single-member district system consisting of four all-white wards and the all-black Second Ward. Gloria Richardson's great-uncle Cyrus was elected to the City Council in the late 1880s, and her grandfather was elected a few years later. Maynadier handled various types of city business, including improving the city's infrastructure (streets, streetlights, telephone lines) and approving building permits. With only a couple of defeats in his political career, Maynadier represented the Second Ward until he retired in the late 1930s.[12]

Like most black Americans during this time in the nation's history, Maynadier St. Clair belonged to and supported the Republican Party because of its work in outlawing enslavement, providing equal protection to black citizens, and extending the vote to black men. (When the Nineteenth Amendment was ratified in 1920, Fannie St. Clair joined the party and served as the first vice president of Dorchester County's Colored Woman's Republican Club.) Maynadier attended Grand Old Party (GOP) functions at the state and national levels and served in various appointed roles.[13] In the mid-1920s Maryland's governor appointed him to the state's Inter-racial Commission, which was directed to "consider legislation concerning the welfare" of Maryland's black population. St. Clair recommended raising black schoolteachers' pay to equal that of white teachers, giving black people greater access to health care, increasing the funding for technical and vocational education facilities serving black students, ending the hiring out of black boys incarcerated at the state's reformatory, and repealing the state's 1904 law that legalized racially segregated intrastate railroad travel.[14]

St. Clair must have relished this opportunity to attack Maryland's Jim Crow system because it affected so many parts of his life, including his political work. Less than one month after the Supreme Court handed down its ruling in *Plessy v. Ferguson* (1896), which legally sanctioned racial segregation, St. Clair had to confront it firsthand. He was one of six black men from Maryland's Republican Party to serve as delegate alternates to the Republican National Convention in St. Louis, Missouri, but he did not attend it because white hotel owners refused to rent rooms to black people. This type of racial offense occurred at the local level, too. When Cambridge's City Council held its annual banquet, the white councilmen sent a plate of food to St. Clair's home because they did not want to eat with him.[15]

He was not too concerned about his white colleagues' reluctance to break bread with a black man, but he did object to white politicos' efforts to marginalize black Republicans, and there are numerous examples of his efforts to improve his party's treatment of its black members. In the late 1800s he and a number of others told a large gathering of black Dorchester County Republicans that they intended to inform the party's white officials that black Republicans must be given "equal representation in convention[s] and on all standing committees and delegations."[16] St. Clair took similar action two decades later when he traveled to Washington, DC, with a handful of other black men and women to meet with recently inaugurated President Warren G. Harding. The group was representing the Maryland chapter of the Lincoln League of America, a wing of the Republican Party created in 1919 by black Republicans who felt their party had abandoned its historical commitment to support black citizens' civil and economic rights. During their White House meeting, St. Clair and the others asked for the president's assistance in getting Maryland's Republican Party to hand out patronage jobs to black party members, but the president politely rebuffed them.[17] In spite of their inability to obtain a commitment to patronage equity from the president, the trip was a firm statement that they would not be passive witnesses to white Republicans' racist marginalization of the GOP's most faithful constituency.

Over the course of his lifetime, Herbert Maynadier St. Clair vastly expanded the St. Clair family's social, economic, and political power, and he advocated for black people in ways that he thought would be most productive. Neither an accommodationist nor a revolutionary, St. Clair operated as a forceful gradualist who believed that racial progress would continue over the course of time, although black people would continue to face setbacks and resistance from white people.

The Hayeses

The black presence in Virginia dates to 1619, when Dutch sailors traded twenty indentured black servants in return for supplies provided by British colonists in the village of Jamestown. Within a few decades, the white colonists had begun to codify Africans' enslavement, forcing them to labor on the colony's tobacco farms. Two hundred years later, one-quarter of Virginia's white residents were enslaving black people, and in the Piedmont region, where Mecklenburg County is located, those enslaved people were often the majority of the population.[18] Gloria Richardson's paternal family was among this group.

The earliest evidence of the Hayes family dates to the mid-1820s with the birth of Richardson's great-grandfather Jim and great-grandmother Mary Ann, both of whom were enslaved by a white man named George Hayes. Jim and Mary Ann lived as husband and wife during their enslavement, but it is not known whether their union was voluntary or forced on them by Hayes. After their emancipation in 1865, due to the Thirteenth Amendment, the couple continued to live as husband and wife along with their seven children, one of whom was James Washington Hayes (b. 1857), Richardson's grandfather. It was also around this time that Jim and Mary Ann began using the surname Hayes for themselves and their children.[19]

After the Civil War, Virginians began to improve and fortify their economic, political, and social conditions. Mecklenburg County's black residents engaged in enthusiastic public displays of their newly won political power, such as celebrating Emancipation Day (9 April) and organizing political rallies. They even helped elect a handful of black men to local and state offices, although white residents were less than enthusiastic about this challenge to the racial status quo.[20] The Hayes family and others like them saw their political fortunes take a dramatically bad turn with the Compromise of 1877, which resolved the disputed presidential election of 1876 by handing the South over to former enslavers and their supporters. State legislators from the Democratic Party began to weaken the GOP by instituting a literacy requirement for voters; this had the effect of disenfranchising a significant portion of

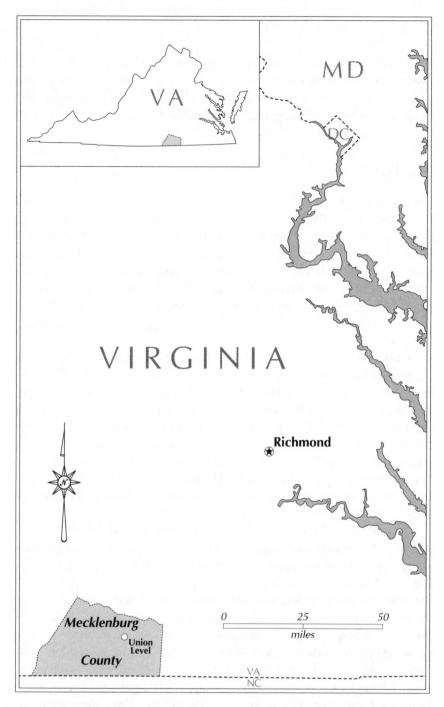

Union Level, Mecklenburg County, Virginia, home of Gloria Richardson's paternal family, the Hayeses.

black men, almost half of whom had never learned to read and write. Black Virginians' economic realities were also tough. The majority of them lived in rural areas where they were engaged in cash-crop farming, usually as either tenant farmers or sharecroppers; a smaller number were landowners who cultivated their own crops. Jim and Mary Ann Hayes were not members of the latter group, but their children's generation—specifically their son James— joined it eventually.[21]

During the first five years of their freedom, Jim and Mary Ann Hayes made strides toward financial independence for themselves and their growing family. They were living in the tiny locale of Union Level, where they began to accumulate property (livestock and a horse) that allowed them to establish a farming enterprise of their own. According to census data from 1880, the Hayes family was still living in Union Level, with Jim working as a farmer and Mary Ann as a homemaker. A marriage document from 1885 describes their son James Washington's nuptials to Bettie Jones; within a year they had their first child, James Mathew, who was followed by John Edward (Richardson's father) and seven other siblings, including Truly Washington, Helen Salene, and Lawrence.[22]

Richardson's grandparents were tenant farmers in the early 1890s, but by the middle of that decade, James had paid $5 for 144 acres of land once owned by George Hayes, his former enslaver. The purchase price raises an interesting question: why did its owner, a surviving daughter of George Hayes, sell the land for so little money? One possibility is that she felt a real or imagined familial connection to James, or perhaps she felt it was the morally right thing to do because her father had unjustly enriched her own family at the expense of the black Hayes family. Irrespective of the reason, the purchase catapulted James W. Hayes and his family into a more secure economic realm, and over the next two decades they built a successful farming business based mainly on growing tobacco and cotton.[23]

In terms of social environments, Union Level was like other rural communities throughout the South, and the Hayes family had to navigate its racialized and increasingly segregated landscape. Black people and white people lived apart from one another; they prayed in separate churches, read different newspapers, and came into contact only when they had business dealings. White people used propaganda and violence to maintain this racial segregation, which fostered an environment in which lynching became common. One example of that terroristic crime occurred in Mecklenburg County when Gloria Richardson's father was just two years old. On Christmas Eve 1890, white people lynched five black men who were accused of murdering a white man. Despite this oppressive social and political climate, Richardson's paternal grandparents worked to improve their community's quality of life. One measure they took was to donate one acre of their farm for the site of the Hayes Grove Baptist Church, built by them and their neighbors.[24]

Richardson's grandparents were also active in a black self-help organization that became popular in the latter part of the nineteenth century: the United Order of True Reformers (UOTR). The UOTR started out as a temperance society in the 1870s, and by the 1880s it had transitioned into a burial society that was tending to the needs of widows and their children. Interestingly, at a time when most self-help organizations segregated men and women, the UOTR was gender integrated, although men occupied all the powerful administrative positions, including leadership of its local chapter, or "fountain." At the beginning of the twentieth century the UOTR had fountains in twenty-four states, mainly along the Eastern Seaboard. Among them was the Hayes Grove True Reformers Club (Fountain #1322), founded in 1905. Located near the Union Level railroad station, the club was situated on a half-acre plot of land purchased by the cofounders, James and Bettie Hayes and other local residents, who allowed the newly established Mecklenburg County Training School to use it for classroom instruction.[25]

Throughout the second half of the nineteenth century, small privately supported primary day schools for black children sprang up around Mecklenburg County. By the early 1870s there were almost twenty such schools that offered basic lessons in reading, writing, and arithmetic. The Hayes children received a primary school education, and many of them attended secondary schools. For example, Helen Salene graduated from the high school department of Hartshorn Memorial College in Richmond, Virginia, and James Mathew attended Boydton Academic and Bible Institute, one of two black boarding schools in Mecklenburg County.[26] Richardson's father, John Edward, and several of his brothers went on to earn degrees at historically black colleges and universities. He attended Virginia Union University in Richmond and later earned a pharmacy degree from Howard University. James Mathew graduated from Howard University's medical program in 1914, Truly earned a carpentry certificate from Hampton Institute in 1914, and Lawrence earned a pharmacy degree from Howard University in the early 1940s.[27]

The Hayes children's academic accomplishments are one indication of how much had changed in the course of 100 years. Whereas Jim and Mary Ann had been enslaved and robbed of their labor, one of their children owned the land on which he and his wife built a successful farming business and raised another generation of Hayes children, including Gloria Richardson's father. As black people living in the post-Reconstruction South, they learned the value of community service, hard work, and an education. All three lessons helped the Hayes children navigate a socially, economically, and politically hostile world for black people. For John Edward Hayes, there was an additional benefit: he became part of a social network where he eventually met Richardson's mother, Mable Pauline St. Clair.

Hayes Meets St. Clair

John E. Hayes arrived in Washington, DC, in 1913, a new student about to enter Howard University's undergraduate pharmacy program. He had just participated in a collective event known as the Great Migration, a massive movement by tens of thousands of rural black people to urban centers in the North and South in the years surrounding the First World War. For most of these migrants, the main impetus pushing them out of the countryside was the lack of economic opportunity, although they were also unhappy with racial segregation and political disenfranchisement. Pulling them toward the urban centers were better economic opportunities in the expanding industrial economy and greater social freedom.[28]

Despite the promise of a better life, Washington was a racially segregated city, and the vast majority of black people who found employment there occupied the stratum of the working poor; they toiled in menial service jobs as laborers, laundry workers, and domestics in wealthier people's homes. The District of Columbia offered greater career opportunities for black people who possessed professional training and skills; a small number from this group obtained political patronage jobs in the federal government, while hundreds more worked as educators in the city's black public schools.[29] Black Washington had a reputation for being a very socially conscious community, which contributed to the development of intragroup segregation patterns based on wealth and skin color. More prosperous black residents had little contact with black working-class people, who, as a group, tended to be darker in color than their wealthier counterparts. The latter constituted the nation's most powerful "aristocracy of color," and its members stood atop black Washington's social, economic, and political ladders. Some of them were so color-conscious that they created social clubs where light skin was the main requirement for membership.[30]

Howard University was black America's premier liberal arts and sciences institution when twenty-four-year-old John Hayes joined his older brother

James Mathew there. John's parents paid for his tuition and expenses, and he worked summers as a waiter in a Pennsylvania Railroad dining car to earn spending money until he graduated in 1918.[31] Besides providing John with career training, Howard afforded him the opportunity to network with other students, establishing and building connections that would help him succeed during and after his schooling. This networking system was one factor that made Washington the center of America's black universe long before Harlem would be ascribed that honor in the 1920s. Anybody who was somebody either had lived in Washington at one time or had ties to the city. One scholar characterized the city's social significance to black America this way: "From Washington radiated a nationwide network of social relationships among individuals and families similar in origins, culture, color, aspirations, and life styles." John integrated into this network by joining Alpha Phi Alpha, the nation's first black fraternity, which had established a chapter at Howard a couple of years earlier. He also befriended fellow pharmacy students Esther and Ruth Fowler, sisters whose parents, Dr. and Mrs. Charles Fowler, were pillars of Baltimore's black community and friends of Maynadier and Fannie St. Clair. John must have made a good impression on the Fowler sisters because they introduced him to Mable St. Clair, who was boarding with their family while she attended school in Baltimore.[32]

Mable graduated from Baltimore's Colored High School in 1915 and studied at Cheyney State Teachers College, a historically black institution in Pennsylvania. She then moved back to Cambridge, honoring her father's request that his children return to Cambridge so they could share their professional training with the town's black community. Mable's brother Frederick opened a law practice in Cambridge after earning his baccalaureate from historically black Lincoln College (also in Pennsylvania) and a law degree from Boston University. Their brother Herbert followed their example, returning to Cambridge to teach at its black high school after also graduating from Lincoln.[33] In no time, Mable had assumed her role as a community servant, just as her parents had done. She was active in Waugh Methodist Episcopal Church's music and outreach programs, and she supported black-initiated improvements of the segregated public school system. Mable also joined Dorchester County's Colored Woman's Republican Club, where she served as its corresponding secretary.[34]

While Mable was making a life in Cambridge, her future husband was doing the same across the Chesapeake Bay. John moved to Baltimore sometime in 1919, after serving as an army medic in France during World War I. He was living with his oldest brother James (now a physician) and his family

Left to right: H. Maynadier St. Clair, Mable St. Clair Hayes, Fannie St. Clair, and John E. Hayes. (Courtesy of Gloria Richardson)

on North Gilmor Street, and John wasted no time securing a place for himself in the city's economy. He opened his own pharmacy on West Lexington Street, where he served a clientele originating in part from James's nearby medical practice.[35]

Since the Federalist Era, Baltimore had been known as the "Queen of the Chesapeake," and that moniker was still accurate when John Hayes moved there. At the center of the city's economy was a web of financial institutions, shipping enterprises, and light and heavy industries that met the energy and consumer needs of America's mid-Atlantic states. McCormick Spice, Procter & Gamble, Western Electric, and Bethlehem Steel, to name a few, manufactured their products in Baltimore and shipped them all over the world from the city's port. Working in those factories were black and white laborers who had come to Baltimore from other parts of the Eastern Seaboard and European immigrants who were part of the massive migration to America lasting from the late 1880s through 1920.[36] In addition to experiencing a population boom, Baltimore was turning into a modern American city; urban planners saw to it that work crews paved over dirt streets, and skyscrapers began to dot Baltimore's skyline—signifying a city entering the modern age. Department stores utilized electricity to offer customers elevator- and escalator-enhanced shopping experiences, and electric lighting permitted businesses to extend their hours into the evening.[37]

Despite having a modernized infrastructure and economy, Baltimore was a typical southern industrial city. Its housing and public accommodations were racially segregated, and its black residents were barred from most occupations that would have allowed them to move up the economic ladder. More than 50 percent of black women worked outside the home (three times the rate of white women), and the vast majority of them were employed as domestic servants or personal assistants. In the predominantly male sphere of industrial work, white managers and business owners discriminated against black men by relegating them to unskilled and menial jobs. Outside the factory, black men worked as laborers and in the service industry at hotels and restaurants. White politicians also imposed a color bar in civil service hiring; one of the few city jobs available to blacks was as teachers in the racially segregated schools, where they were paid less than their white counterparts. Baltimore's black City Council members worked to improve these and other inequities.[38]

The Hayes brothers were active in the professional associations related to their careers, leaving their mark on Baltimore's black community. When John and Mable married in 1921, they settled down in a three-story brownstone on Stricker Street, a gift from Mable's parents. As the newlyweds began their new life together, they also moved forward on a path of professional success. John filed incorporation papers for his pharmacy business, and he worked as a pharmacist at Provident Hospital, which black residents had established to serve their community. Living on Stricker Street meant that the Hayeses were close to the Druid Hill district and Pennsylvania Avenue—the heart of Baltimore's black community. Druid Hill was where many of the city's wealthy, prominent black residents lived, and the area had a black YMCA branch that offered the same types of outreach services offered to white branches' constituents. Black people went to Pennsylvania Avenue to shop and to be entertained. The city was going through a black cultural renaissance much like the one occurring in Harlem, New York. An integral part of Baltimore's cultural scene was its harmony singing groups, which were among the earliest expressions of modern gospel music; they influenced other groups such as the Ink Spots, a Baltimore quartet popular in the 1930s.[39]

Local residents danced and listened to bands at live entertainment venues such as the Royal Theater, a center of black Baltimore culture during the Roaring Twenties. John and Mable Hayes visited the Royal and other Druid Hill attractions, but their socializing consisted mainly of attending parties and participating in various organizations and clubs. John belonged to the Knights of Pythias and the National Medical Association, and he and Mable blended those organizations' activities with race service that focused on community outreach and fund-raising for local causes. Mable's social calendar was far more extensive than her husband's, and it was chronicled extensively in the *Afro-American*'s society page, which described her as a "popular Baltimore matron."[40]

As a married couple, the Hayeses fit easily into Baltimore's elite black social group, and they spent the 1920s earning reputations for being fun yet respectable people known for service to their community. When John and Mable's daughter Gloria came along, they presented her to this social group and, importantly, taught her to carry on the family tradition of race service. By the time Gloria St. Clair Hayes entered elementary school, she was showing signs of having the right personality for that type of work.

2

Get Up, Stand Up

The front page of the 6 May 1922 edition of Cambridge's *Daily Banner* newspaper contained an article critical of Maryland for being the only state that had not passed a law to enforce the Prohibition amendment ratified two years earlier. Maryland, the *Banner* stated, was "on the outside" of American legal norms and "looking in" on the rest of the nation. On the same day across the Chesapeake Bay in Baltimore, a newlywed couple—John and Mable Hayes—welcomed into their family a baby girl named Gloria. No one could have known then that she would grow up to be a fierce human rights activist who played a critical role in showing the nation that, forty years after her birth, her home state of Maryland continued to be a place where parts of the Constitution were not enforced.[1]

Many people who knew Richardson during the formative years of her childhood could see that she had a naturally strong personality and that she bristled at unfairness and injustice, no matter their sources. This trait was nurtured by her parents and maternal grandparents; they permitted Gloria to be her own person, all the while preparing her to carry on the family's tradition of race service. Her home life, together with the culturally and economically dynamic black communities where she lived, helped Richardson develop a strong sense of community, and it was in both spaces that she began to formulate a secular humanist worldview on serious matters, particularly racism, that would become the basis of her human rights activism.

It was a warm and sunny day in Baltimore when Dr. Jay Garland McRae ascended the white marble stoop of 910 Stricker Street to attend to his patient, Mable Hayes, who was in labor. A few minutes before midnight she gave birth to Gloria, whose name had been chosen by Mable's childhood friend and Gloria's godmother, Marie Payne Flagg. The baby was given the middle name St. Clair because, at the time, she was the only maternal grandchild, and her parents wanted her to carry on that family name.[2]

Gloria attended a neighborhood public school and, when not in class, passed the time playing outside with the other children or alone in her family's home. She did not always get along with the other kids, particularly one "girl bully" who beat up Gloria on the way home from school, but that stopped when she "finally got up the nerve [and] punched and knocked [the girl] down." Gloria also socialized with the children of her parents' friends who resided in other neighborhoods in West Baltimore. One such event was a birthday party in the summer of 1929 for Jay Garland McRae (son of the doctor who had delivered Gloria), and it provides a snapshot of the larger social group to which Gloria and her family belonged. More than fifty children and their parents attended the party, which was held at Edgewater Shore, near the black resort of Highland Beach, Maryland. The *Afro-American* newspaper reported, "From the guest list, there were very few children, if any, of Baltimore's elite that were not invited."[3]

Each day Gloria anxiously waited for her father to come home during his dinner break from his pharmacy. He also had a part-time pharmacy job at Provident Hospital, and she sometimes accompanied him there. One particular visit left an especially strong impression on Gloria when she witnessed a head nurse taking charge of the staff. Gloria briefly considered becoming a head nurse herself, attracted to the idea of having that type of command over people. Another big part of Gloria's childhood were the weekly visits with family friends, especially the regularly scheduled bridge games to which Mable "dragged" Gloria.[4] She had connections to both sides of her family, but the distance between Baltimore and Mecklenburg County, Virginia, made it difficult for Gloria to see her paternal relatives. Her grandfather James Washington Hayes died when she was a toddler, and she does not recall ever meeting him; however, she does remember visiting her grandmother Bettie Hayes, and Gloria had routine contact with three of her father's siblings: James, Helen Salene, and Truly. In contrast, Gloria's maternal family was a ubiquitous presence in her life because her grandparents made regular trips to Baltimore to visit the Hayeses, who reciprocated by taking excursions to Cambridge.[5]

Gloria's closest family relationship was with her cousin Sylvia Raven, who lived in Chester, Pennsylvania. The two girls saw each other mainly in Cambridge at large family gatherings and parties, which were often attended by family friends as well (including college classmates of Richardson's uncles). The festivities commonly included musical entertainment provided by family members such as Gloria's uncle Cyrus St. Clair, who was a successful jazz musician. As a side event to these gatherings, the girls often made cigarette runs for their uncles and their friends, but this led to Gloria's own habit when she began smoking on the way back from the store.[6] This was an early display of Richardson's rebellion against her parents' idea of respectable behavior for girls from well-to-do families, and it foreshadowed more substantive rejections of gender expectations when she became an adult.

The Hayes family also relaxed and socialized during summer vacations in Cape May and Wildwood, New Jersey. Even when they could not spend an entire summer at the Jersey shore, the family sometimes traveled there for short visits with their friends Raymond and Sadie Tanner Mossell Alexander, attorneys from Philadelphia. Another popular vacation spot for the Hayes family was Highland Beach, near Annapolis, Maryland, which was frequented by wealthy black people from the Baltimore-Washington area. Gloria also attended summer camp in New England, a practice that became popular among wealthier families in the 1920s.[7]

John and Mable Hayes provided their daughter with indoor activities that stressed her intellectual and cultural development. Gloria recalled sitting with her parents and listening to classical European music, as well as contemporary pieces by artists such as Roland Hayes (no relation). Mable taught Gloria how to play the piano, and her repertoire of talents also included public speaking. Whenever the opportunity arose to talk in front of a group of people, such as at Sunday school programs, Mable made sure her daughter participated. Gloria dreaded these events and was convinced she would never attain the ease and proficiency demonstrated by other family members.[8]

Although Gloria read all types of literature, she found essays, fiction, and poetry most enjoyable, particularly the works of Louisa May Alcott, Rudyard Kipling, Langston Hughes, Edna St. Vincent Millay, and Walt Whitman. Her first encounter with Ralph Waldo Emerson took place when her father gave her a copy of *Compensation*. She also appreciated Victor Hugo's *Les Misérables* and some of Charles Dickens's stories because their subject matter—oppression and poverty—were conditions that black people experienced in America. By the time she entered her teens, Gloria's father had given her the complete works of Shakespeare. Summer trips to Chester expanded her literary background because she pored over her uncle's Harvard Classics series. Later, Gloria's membership in the Book of the Month Club served as a lifeline to the broader literary world because Cambridge's white leaders made the city's public library a white-only facility. Her family's subscription to the NAACP's publication the *Crisis* rounded out Gloria's exposure to stimulating writing and provided her with a comprehensive view and assessment of black life in America.[9]

The Hayes family left Baltimore for the Eastern Shore after the stock market crash of October 1929, which ushered in the decade of economic decline known as the Great Depression. As the economic crisis deepened, Baltimore's unemployment rate rose when industries laid off workers. The unemployment rate for black residents reached nearly 50 percent—much higher than the white unemployment rate—and by the mid-1930s, more than 40 percent of black families were receiving government relief to help them survive the crisis. Baltimore's worsening economy was evident in businesses such as John Hayes's pharmacy, which experienced a drop in sales because his customers had less money to spend on sundries and medicines. In addition, his brother James, the doctor, had recently relocated his family to Newport News, Virginia, which reduced greatly the number of prescriptions being filled at John's pharmacy. The Depression hit Cambridge too, but John saw an opportunity there because the city's Second Ward did not have a black pharmacist to serve its black residents, who were patronizing a white pharmacy in town. Additionally, John could expect a steady stream of customers originating from Gloria's cousin Carroll St. Clair, who had opened a medical practice in Cambridge a few years earlier.[10]

Cambridge's black community had a lot in common with Baltimore's, albeit on a smaller scale. It was vibrant, and its residents patronized dozens of Pine Street businesses that catered to their shopping and entertainment needs. Most of the community also belonged to one of the ward's numerous churches, which provided spiritual guidance to congregants and outreach to community members in need of aid and comfort. Youngsters participated in various school activities, including choirs, bands, and drill teams that displayed their talents at the annual Fourth of July parade. This environment, combined with an extensive family support network there, eased John and Mable Hayes's decision to move to Cambridge with Gloria in March of 1931. Gloria was introduced to her new peer group about six months before the family moved when she joined more than 100 other children for the dedication of a new playground at the corner of Pine and Dobson Streets—right around the corner from her grandparents' large Muir Street home, where the Hayes family would soon be living.[11]

Cambridge had not changed much since Mable had spent her childhood there. It remained a racially segregated one-company town controlled by the Phillips Packing Company. Phillips's fortunes had actually risen significantly since its expansion during World War I, when it sold canned foods to the military. Keeping tabs on the town's activities was the *Daily Banner*, which covered the social, economic, and political issues impacting Dorchester County and the surrounding region. In March 1931, the month the Hayeses moved to Cambridge, the newspaper reported that the crab haul for 1931 was expected to match the previous year's record catch. Other stories attested to the white community's view of its regional and national identities. One front-page story noted

St. Clair family home, Muir Street, Cambridge, Maryland. (Courtesy of Gloria Richardson)

the positive economic impact the proposed Chesapeake Bay Bridge would have throughout Maryland, observing that it would "invariably bring about a closer community interest between the two shores." Another piece—an advertisement for an American Legion membership drive—played on white readers' sense of patriotism and their concern about the spread of international communism and anarchy. They were warned to "Maintain Law and Order," because if they allowed someone in their midst to "CRACK ONE LINK OF LAW," then "THE WHOLE CHAIN IS WEAKENED." When viewed from the vantage point of the twenty-first century, these two pieces foreshadowed the role of the Bay Bridge in bringing Cambridge closer to the outside world during the city's civil rights movement, as well as white Cambridge's attitude about black liberation.[12]

Despite the fact that Baltimore was her birthplace and she missed some of the friends she left behind, Gloria's adjustment to life in Cambridge was uneventful. Her grandparents' home on Muir Street had always been the center of Gloria's universe and the place she really considered home. The only real difference was that she was now living in a multigenerational home in a neighborhood surrounded by extended family members she saw on a daily basis. In addition, a steady stream of guests stopped by Muir Street to visit or to gather before heading out to parties sponsored by social clubs to which Gloria's parents belonged.[13] Individual personalities added an interesting texture to life on

Muir Street. Gloria's father and grandparents were quiet yet strong people, whereas her mother had a more "volatile . . . personality." A trait they all shared was a high degree of self-respect that originated in their racial pride. Richardson recalled her father being someone people "didn't boss . . . [not] even white folks." He signed his name using only the initials of his first and middle names so that white people would not know either one and thus could not address him in an informal manner when they spoke to him.[14]

A hallmark of family life was discussions among the adults and their guests about important subjects and issues. Gloria observed and listened to her elders, learning about the world and how to navigate it. Sometimes she was part of the conversation, such as the time her grandfather gave her a lesson on political leadership. Maynadier St. Clair told Gloria that before politicians take a position on an issue, they must learn what their constituents think about it. "'You have to find out what the people think. Find the key person on that block or in that neighborhood, the person that people look up to, and see what they're thinking,'" he told her.[15] Other lessons centered on the family's relationship to the rest of the Second Ward. Although Gloria's family had little social interaction with the ward's working-class residents, her elders taught her to value people for their actions, not for their socioeconomic status; they reminded her that their family's standard of living was dependent on the working class's patronage of their family businesses. "'If it was not for poor, low-income people supporting these businesses you wouldn't be able to do this, that, and the other,'" they told Gloria, and this created an obligation for her to continue the family tradition of race service. She saw her family live out this philosophy during the Depression, when her mother and grandmother brought donated food and clothing to needy residents, and other family members carried a number of people "on the book[s]" at the family's stores. Richardson recalled that the working-class clientele always paid their bills, while the black middle class were known to charge "a three-cent stamp" and not pay it off until months later. Richardson described the latter's social posture as "kind of phony" and noted that this group was "not sufficiently aware of what they owed their race of people."[16]

In terms of gender, the Hayeses and the St. Clairs both reinscribed and challenged societal norms. Women and girls were expected to know how to play the piano, sew, and run a household that the men ultimately controlled. Despite this gendered environment, Richardson never saw her father or grandfather try to control their wives' thoughts and actions or dictate their goals. Richardson's grandmother and mother never "genuflected or agreed to everything" their husbands said or did, and one particular argument between

Left to right: Gloria Hayes Richardson, Mable St. Clair Hayes, Frederick D. St. Clair, and Joanne St. Clair (a cousin), late 1920s. (Courtesy of Gloria Richardson)

her grandparents illustrates this. Fannie had become tired of Maynadier's "'peeping' in her pots and pans," and she protested his intrusion into her domestic sphere by refusing to prepare the daily meals, so he began to cook for the family, a task he performed for some time. Fannie's decision to go on a cooking strike did not create any strife within the family, a fact that Richardson attributes to the men in her family having gender-egalitarian streaks. On the whole, the gendered lesson Richardson got from her family was that she would be expected to adhere to some gender norms for girls, but those did not include being deferential to men simply because they were men.[17]

When asked whether her parents were proud to be black, Richardson replied that they were, because if they had felt otherwise, "they wouldn't have produced me." They did not go around telling people they were proud to be black, she added; rather, they demonstrated their pride by the way they "carried themselves." Yet there were times when their pride percolated to the surface. For example, John Hayes's response to a case of intraracial color prejudice—known as colorism—showed Gloria that her father accepted blackness in all its shades. When a light-skinned black neighbor in Baltimore asked John whether he thought Gloria was "'a little too dark,'" he replied:

"'She's just the exact color she should be.'" And even though her grandfather did not protest when his fellow City Council members sent his annual banquet meal to his Muir Street home because they did not want to eat with a black man ("'Well, this is just the way the times are,'" Richardson recalled him saying), her grandmother became indignant, teaching Gloria that when an opportunity to fight racism presents itself, she should take it. That lesson was reinforced with a family trip to Harpers Ferry, West Virginia, the site of the 1859 armed revolt against enslavement, and through the stories Gloria's parents told her about Frederick Douglass and Harriet Tubman, both of whom became inspirations to her.[18]

Racial segregation was ubiquitous in Richardson's childhood, and she was conscious of the limitations it placed on her, but with so little real power to change this fact of life, she reconciled herself to it. Despite the obvious oppression that segregation represented and reinforced, Richardson had a happy and "normal childhood." She believed being forced to live in the Second Ward actually "protected" her and the other black people there because it insulated them from a steady stream of overt assaults to their persons and psyches by white people. The protection Richardson felt in her all-black community was the result of *functional segregation*, an unintended consequence of white America's decision to segregate itself from black people. In all-black communities like Cambridge's, residents built their own institutions to provide goods, services, and aid to one another, and this fostered the creation of coping mechanisms and resistance strategies to racial oppression that ultimately stressed community values of self-help and respect.[19]

Richardson's home was an emotionally and intellectually nurturing environment where she learned that any limitations placed on her dreams and goals would almost certainly come from outside her family. Her parents supported her right to express her own beliefs and opinions, and this proved to be a critical factor as Gloria developed her identity and built self-esteem.[20] John and Mable Hayes also taught their daughter about respectability, which, according to one scholar, consisted of a set of "morals and manners" black children needed to learn so that they could become "self-defin[ed]" individuals who would respect themselves and be well-adjusted members of their communities. Respectability included being polite to people and avoiding potentially dangerous confrontations, especially with white children and adults, who commonly maintained white supremacy by enforcing racial etiquette in public settings. To lessen their children's chances of breaching this racial etiquette, black parents—including Gloria's—instructed their children to avoid contact with white people altogether, but when this was not possible, these parents taught their children how to navigate such encounters.[21]

The two most common situations in which black people were likely to encounter white people in public were while shopping and while being engaged by law enforcement officers. Racial etiquette in white-owned department stores generally centered on white employees displaying dismissive attitudes toward black customers or simply ignoring them. Other forms of disrespect included white clerks' refusal to use courtesy titles such as "Ma'am" or "Sir" when addressing black adults and using racist epithets against them. Black customers commonly did not have the "try-on" privilege for clothes and accessories, and a "final sale" rule prevented black customers from returning items they had purchased. Both these restrictive customs were grounded in white people's racist beliefs that black people were inherently dirty and that no white person would want to purchase something a black person had handled or worn. Black parents made conscious efforts and went to great lengths to shelter themselves and their children from these racist and hurtful indignities. For example, Carl Murphy (publisher of the *Afro-American*) sent his daughters to Philadelphia and other northern cities to shop so that they could avoid the racial offenses at Baltimore stores. Gloria, Mable, and Fannie shopped in northern stores for the same reason, but back in Cambridge, there was one exception to the try-on rule. The manager of a white-owned clothing store sent a selection of girl's and women's apparel to the family's home so that they could try on the clothes and choose which articles they wanted to buy.[22]

Concerning law enforcement officers, the local sheriffs, deputies, and police had total control over black people who were rightly or wrongly suspected of committing a crime. These officers routinely stopped, questioned, detained, and interrogated black people of all ages, especially males. Learning how to minimize the possibility of coming into contact with the law vastly improved a black person's chances of getting to work on time and, in more extreme cases, his or her chances of living to see another day. Richardson's parents taught her to avoid eye contact with the police. "'Don't look. You can't look because they are liable to stop us,'" they told her.[23]

Two lynchings occurred on the Eastern Shore within a few years of the Hayes family's move there, providing more evidence that law enforcement officers were not in the habit of protecting and serving black people. White supremacist terrorists lynched a black man named Matthew Williams in nearby Salisbury, Maryland. The lynching was a two-stage process that began with white people attacking and shooting Williams, who was accused of killing his white employer. Dr. A. B. Brown, a black physician and a nephew of

Richardson's grandmother, attended to the suspect and took him to the local hospital after he was shot. Stage two began when his murderers entered the black ward of the hospital, pushed him out the first-floor window, took him to the courthouse, and hanged him in front of a crowd estimated to be as large as 2,000 people. The lynch mob then lowered Williams's body and proceeded to drag it down Main Street, where they set it on fire. The barbaric ritual ended with the terrorists suspending Williams's body from a lamppost in front of a local store. The *Afro-American* reported that Dr. Brown may have known some of the members of the lynching party and feared they would attack him and his family unless he kept quiet. Brown moved his family from their home, and the doctor left Salisbury by car, armed with "a sawed-off shotgun and a revolver." Not long after the lynching, John and Mable Hayes took Gloria to Salisbury to view the scene of the crime so that she would be more conscious of the dangers confronting black people.[24]

Another gruesome attack occurred southeast of Cambridge in Princess Anne, Maryland, less than two years later. George Armwood, a twenty-two-year-old black man, was suspected of attacking an elderly white woman. While he was in police custody, a mob of terrorists used bricks and stones to intimidate the two dozen state police officers who were guarding Armwood at the county jail. The police did not open fire on their attackers, and the mob was able to kidnap Armwood. They proceeded to strip him of his clothing and then dragged him behind a car by the neck. He may have been dead already, but if he had any life left in him it was snuffed out when the murderers cut off one of his ears and hanged him from a tree while more than 1,000 white men, women, and children watched. The lynchers finished their crime when they removed Armwood from the tree (pieces of the rope were handed out as souvenirs) and burned him in the town square, where his body remained until the next morning. Reporting on the lynching for the *Afro-American* was a young man named Clarence Mitchell, who captured the climate of fear that gripped Princess Anne's black community. "Silent groups of our people on their way to work, or with nothing in particular to view, solemnly gazed at the horribly-mangled corpse. . . . There is no adequate description of the mute evidence of gloating on the part of whites who gathered to watch the effect upon our people," he reported.[25]

As a child, Gloria was aware that the justice system was stacked against black people, and one of the most glaring examples of its unfairness was that black people could not serve on Maryland juries until the mid-1930s. Gloria felt that whenever black people were found guilty of crimes, they became marked people who might pay for their offenses with their lives. She recalled a shoot-out between a black ex-convict and white law enforcement officers who were using what she considered a disproportionate response to apprehend him. "I was rooting for him," she said. "And I can remember [I] admired him and hope[d] he gets away. He didn't, but I hoped."[26] That a young child would cheer for an ex-convict in a gunfight with the police shows that Gloria had already concluded that law enforcement stood ready to maintain white supremacy through the use of force.

The health care system also had a double standard for blacks and whites, and Richardson's uncle Fredrick St. Clair (Mable's brother) was a case in point. He died at age thirty-two from typhoid fever because Cambridge's racially segregated hospital system prevented him from obtaining the comprehensive care required to treat the disease. The impact of Frederick's death on the family is something Richardson never forgot. His mother, Fannie, took it hardest, and the family's sense of personal loss was compounded by their knowledge that the Second Ward had lost one of its talented professionals who had served the community through his charitable and educational endeavors. Mourners from around Maryland and the Northeast traveled to Cambridge to pay their respects to Frederick's family, and some of his classmates from Lincoln University, including a Philadelphia civil rights attorney named Maceo Hubbard, served as honorary pallbearers.[27]

Richardson's family openly discussed death and the meaning of life. Her mother and grandmother approached these topics from the perspective of their deeply held religious convictions. When they lived in Baltimore, John and Mable Hayes had attended St. James Episcopal Church, where Gloria had been christened. Mable had been an active member of that parish, known for its prominent membership, and she had served as an organist, worked with the junior choir, and helped run a vacation Bible school. After they moved to Cambridge, the Hayeses became congregants of Waugh Methodist Episcopal Church because the town's Episcopal parish, Christ Church, was a white congregation. Mable and Fannie belonged to Waugh's Woman's Home Missionary Society, where a large portion of the two women's community service originated. Because of his pharmacy business, John did not attend church very often, but he "knew the Bible" and supported the church financially.[28]

In contrast to Mable and Fannie, Gloria and her grandfather held a pessimistic view of religion. Although Maynadier financially supported Waugh and participated in various religious activities, he did not "[believe] that much in church," as evidenced by his irregular attendance and his conversations with Gloria in which he talked about the church's limitations in addressing black people's problems. These talks heavily influenced Richardson's own thinking on religion, and they allowed her "to take a more . . . realistic view of the church at that time." On an intellectual level, the church and Sunday school offered Richardson very little because Waugh's minister "could not explain to [her] anything logical" about "those tales" concerning two of Christianity's basic tenets: Jesus's ability to perform miracles and his birth to a virgin. In hindsight, Richardson thinks she might have stayed in the church if someone could have provided her with better answers to her questions, rather than just telling her to have "faith."[29]

Richardson does not know whether there is a god, but if so, she does not think it is the justice-exacting god of Judaism and Christianity; instead, it is a deity that is "prejudiced" against black people because it made them "[start] out behind the eight-ball . . . and [they] continue to be." An intellectually unsatisfying Christian theology combined with her own experiences of living in a racist society led Richardson to have a "dim" view of religion, and she stopped attending church on a regular basis sometime in her teenage years. It was around that time that she adopted a secular humanist view of the world that rejects the belief that everything good and moral comes from a divine being. Rather, people are the source of goodness because they have the capacity for ethical and rational behavior, and they should use both to make personal and societal progress. Though uncommon, Richardson's view is not unique, and religion scholar Anthony B. Pinn writes that humanism has been embraced by many black Americans over the centuries, including icons Frederick Douglass and W. E. B. Du Bois and Harlem Renaissance writers James Weldon Johnson, Langston Hughes, Zora Neale Hurston, and Claude McKay. They and other humanists believe that religion cannot solve all the problems caused by "moral evil," and people have the "responsibility for reorienting human destiny and fostering equality."[30]

Richardson also showed signs of nonconformity at school. She "always had [her] own ideas" about things and was not afraid to stand up for them— or, in one case, stay seated. While attending kindergarten in Baltimore, Gloria refused to stand and recite the Pledge of Allegiance because, to her, the pledge and the flag were symbols of white people. In the seventh grade she defended herself when a male classmate took one of her books and refused to give it back. She told their teacher what the boy had done, but the teacher dismissed Gloria's complaint, and when Gloria began to chase the boy around the classroom, the teacher stepped in and stopped her. Indignant that the teacher had not mediated the situation from the start, Gloria threw a book at her and rationalized it by saying: "I figured she was just totally wrong and she was violating me and my rights." The teacher reported the incident to Gloria's uncle Herbert, who was also a teacher at the school, and he intended to punish his niece by paddling her. She informed him that her "father wasn't going to let him get away with that" and refused to be punished. Herbert deferred to Gloria's father, who "chastised" her, but that was all he did. Another book-throwing incident occurred in high school after one of Richardson's teachers made an insulting comment about the shape of her nose. Just as before, the teacher wanted Gloria to be paddled for insubordination, but her father intervened, and this time he did not even reprimand her.[31]

These stories raise a number of questions. First, how *could* Richardson refuse her teachers' discipline? One reason was the teachers' perception of their own place in the school system; they relied on Maynadier St. Clair's support for their continued employment, so they did not aggressively pursue disciplinary action against his granddaughter. Second, why *would* a child in the early 1930s refuse her teachers' discipline? Some people might interpret Richardson's behavior as signs that she had anger management issues and problems with authority, but she generally did not resist her parents' authority, and on the rare occasion when Gloria was insubordinate, her parents disciplined her. The real cause of Gloria's outbursts was her expectation that she should be treated with fairness and respect by adults, behaviors that her parents demonstrated often. For example, during one disagreement between Gloria and her grandmother, John Hayes told his mother-in-law that while she may not agree with her granddaughter, she had to respect Gloria's right to have her own views on the issue.[32] Richardson's parents may have not been pleased with how she responded to her teachers, but they supported her rationale for standing up for herself.

Despite these occasional classroom issues, Richardson has fond memories of her education. After she finished elementary school at Jenifer Hall (a small building attached to Waugh Methodist Episcopal Church), she moved on to Frederick Douglass St. Clair High School, which had been named after her deceased uncle. Richardson was impressed by her high school teachers because they were good instructors and good role models. John and Mable Hayes taught Gloria that she needed to excel in school and reach her full potential, and she challenged herself by becoming a member of the school's debate team, which gave her valuable public-speaking experience. Although she did not find high school all that challenging, she thought her courses were interesting, and she earned high grades across the board. Of all the subjects she studied, Gloria especially enjoyed history—particularly black history. Her interest in the subject was piqued when her father gave her a black history book. Although black history was incorporated into civics courses in her primary and secondary schools, one of her high school courses was dedicated to the subject. With these resources and instruction, Gloria learned more about famous black Americans such as Frederick Douglass, Harriet Tubman, and W. E. B. Du Bois and their efforts on behalf of black liberation. This knowledge increased her racial pride, as well as making her more aware of white people's oppression. It also contributed to Gloria's sense of frustration and anger toward her country because it raised her awareness of white America's hypocrisy regarding equality.[33]

Gloria graduated from high school in the spring of 1938, and her parents threw a graduation party in the backyard of their Muir Street home. Family and friends feted Gloria and shared in her excitement at being accepted into the fall class at her father's alma mater, Howard University. Not long after the party, John took Gloria on a trip to New York City and the Jersey shore. The New York trip was strictly social in nature, and it included an afternoon visit to the home of essayist George Schuyler, whose daughter Philippa treated the Cambridge guests to a piano recital. The purpose of visiting New Jersey was to give Gloria some experience at navigating the nightlife she would be exposed to in Washington, DC. John Hayes took his daughter to an upscale nightclub in Atlantic City, where he advised her how to conduct herself in such establishments.[34]

Gloria Richardson's parents and maternal grandparents formed the nucleus of her family, and they taught her about self-respect, respect for family, and respect for and service to her black community. In recent years Richardson has looked back at her childhood and thought about the impact her relatives and their friends had on her development. She acknowledges that she stood on their shoulders and that the examples they set for advancing their race made her into the person she became.[35] Yet it would take the faculty of Howard University—some of America's most eminent intellectuals—to teach Richardson how to apply her education to challenge America's racial hierarchy. The time she spent studying at Howard would be the most important phase of Richardson's intellectual development, and it helped prepare her for her role in the civil rights movement.

3

Capital Gains

Reflecting on her years at Howard University, Gloria Richardson said, "The whole educational experience led you, probably, into civil disobedience." The professors' course materials and teaching methods were not explicitly political in nature, but they "may have laid the groundwork" for the type of activism Richardson engaged in during the civil rights movement. This assessment of her education is insightful because it points to a shared agenda among the professors at Howard, who worked toward the goal of making the world a better place for people of African descent by integrating black people's contributions to science, history, art, and politics into their curricula. This also had the effect of validating students' racial pride and self-esteem, something that Richardson acknowledged when she said: "I don't care what white folks thought, you did not think you were inferior."[1] This was a common feeling among black students who attended historically black colleges and universities (HBCUs), whose supportive faculty and climate helped Richardson and many of her fellow civil rights activists see themselves as carrying on a long tradition of race service, even if these institutions did not overtly claim this as their purpose.

Howard's environment also stimulated students' activist streaks, including Richardson's. It would be hard to overstate the impact her professors had on her intellectual development and, by extension, her activism in the civil rights movement. Their coursework expanded her understanding of the world and undergirded her already established beliefs, including the importance of race service, the value of black culture, and the right of working-class people to improve their lives. Additionally and critically, the knowledge and skills she obtained in specific courses became vital components of Richardson's leadership capabilities during Cambridge's civil rights movement two decades later.[2]

There was never any question that Richardson would attend college. Her parents had the financial means to pay for her education, and they wanted her to earn a degree that she could use to serve black people. She considered Wellesley College and Vassar College, but her parents warned that if she attended one of those predominantly white institutions, she would have to contend with some amount of racism. John and Mable felt that Howard University was the most logical choice for their sixteen-year-old daughter, who had never been away from home for very long. Howard was fairly close to Cambridge, in case Gloria needed her family. In addition, two of her cousins, Sylvia and Celestine Raven, were already enrolled there, and they could help her adjust.[3]

A nondenominational liberal arts institution established just after the Civil War, Howard University eventually became the nation's premier black institution for higher learning, thanks to the efforts of its administrators and professors. By the 1930s, they had expanded the institution's curriculum to include the "scientific study of black life and culture." Integral to this change in curriculum and mission was Dr. Mordecai W. Johnson, who had become Howard's first black president in 1926. He spearheaded the adoption of curricula intended to meet the needs of a race that was facing assaults from every corner of American society. Aiding his efforts was a solution-oriented, world-class faculty, which allowed Howard to promote itself as "National and International in Scope and Influence." The list of faculty members who would become major influences in American scholarship on race is impressive, and five of them—Ralph Bunche, Sterling Brown, E. Franklin Frazier, Rayford Logan, and Alain Locke—were among Richardson's professors.[4]

In terms of size and structure, Howard was different from most other HBCUs created after the Civil War. It had a large enrollment and was nonsectarian. The latter allowed it to be relatively independent from outside influences, unlike institutions that were formally associated with the white Protestant denominations that had helped establish them and continued to exert a significant influence on their curricula and culture. Thus, it is not surprising that so many of those HBCUs tended to be politically conservative on issues of race and economics. Additionally, many of those institutions emphasized industrial or vocational training, an educational model championed by Booker T. Washington, a graduate of Hampton Institute and founder of Tuskegee Institute. He believed black people should focus on building an economic base that would allow them to become financially successful; this would convince white people that black people were worthy of respect and first-class citizenship. Many black people supported Washington's vision, and so did many white people, including northern white industrialists who wanted a technically trained workforce for the growing industrial economy. Another reason for white people's support was that industrial education programs did not challenge the racial and economic status quo; as such, they were considered a safer alternative to liberal arts programs like Howard's, which were graduating people who sought to improve the social and political lives of the masses.[5]

Black critics of the Hampton-Tuskegee model, such as sociologist E. Franklin Frazier, highlighted this issue. He wrote, "A landmark in Negro education, so far as the white man was concerned, was reached when a type of education was discovered that concerned itself with this world and at the same time did not disturb the Negro as a worker. Tuskegee has stood in the white man's imagination as such a reconciliation." He also argued that black liberal arts institutions did not prepare students to be active agents for societal change and proposed the establishment of cutting-edge scholarly programs in which black people were at the center of research and were viewed as innately capable of participating in civic life and, more importantly, were expected to do so. Within a decade, a small number of activist-intellectuals (including Carter G. Woodson and W. E. B. Du Bois) had contributed their own assessments of black education, and together their works served as a sort of *Federalist Papers* that argued for the creation of an educational model grounded in the scholarly treatment of the black experience. Their vision would eventually be institutionalized in higher education as the field of black studies. In the meantime, Howard University operated as *the* laboratory in which the scientific study of black life was conducted, and Richardson became an acolyte in her professors' problem-driven and solution-oriented educational program.[6]

Richardson's first semester consisted of a hodgepodge of courses that included a political science class taught by Ralph Bunche. He had produced a handful of important essays assessing Europeans' colonization of African societies and had concluded that colonization was a symptom of capitalism (which he was morally opposed to), and its supporters privileged greed over all else. Bunche further argued that white people's racism was a by-product of this exploitative system. Through his writings and advocacy, Bunche worked to end colonization and imperialism, and he urged black people to challenge the United States' racial and economic status quo. Richardson described him as "a fine man" who reminded her of her grandfather Maynadier St. Clair because, as one scholar has noted, Bunche was "neither a fervently committed radical nor a mere tool of the establishment." One highlight of Bunche's course, Richardson recalled, was a guest lecture delivered by Kwame Nkrumah, a student from West Africa who, two decades later, became the first president of Ghana (formerly the Gold Coast) when it gained its independence from British colonial rule.[7]

Howard University faculty. Left to right: James Nabrit, Charles Drew, Sterling Brown, E. Franklin Frazier, Rayford Logan, and Alain Locke. (Courtesy of the Moorland-Spingarn Research Center, Howard University Archives, Washington, DC)

By her sophomore year, Richardson's courses brought her into contact with other esteemed academics, such as her European history professor Rayford Logan. He had arrived at Howard after holding professorships at Virginia Union University and Atlanta University, where he had earned a reputation both on and off campus for his militant advocacy of black liberation. The black newspaper the *Chicago Defender* once described Logan as a "Bad Negro with a Ph.D." because of his radical scholarship that challenged the ideology of white supremacy. Whereas some of his Howard colleagues emphasized a class analysis when analyzing black America's problems, Logan always viewed racism as the overarching system of the oppression of black people. He was a good fit for Howard's intellectual and political environment because his teaching philosophy encouraged students to "serve both their race and the United States." Richardson said that Logan routinely challenged his students, and his lectures were the best part of his courses because he would "enthrall" the class with his "down-to-earth" presentation style. He "was not in awe of all these kings and queens," Richardson remembered with amazement, and he spoke of them "just as if they were ordinary people no matter what their accomplishments were." These lectures "had a great effect" on her, and they were the main reason she did not automatically have respect for "highly placed people."[8]

As luck would have it, Richardson's one and only philosophy course was taught by Alain L. Locke, a Philadelphia native who had already made a name for himself as an influential scholar on philosophy and the black aesthetic. Locke's essay "The New Negro" defined the artistic and political spirit percolating among black artists and intellectuals of the Harlem Renaissance. He believed in the transformative power of art—literature, painting, and sculpture—and his biographers wrote that he "challenged his students to expand their cultural horizons and discover their own history," especially their black history as represented in African sculpture. A colleague of Locke's who also worked to increase his students' cultural literacy was Sterling Brown. Born on Howard's campus at the beginning of the twentieth century (his father taught in the university's Theology Department), Brown returned to Howard in 1929 and began an illustrious career as a literary scholar and professor concerned with racism. His essay "The American Race Problem as Reflected in American Literature" assessed how black and white writers have touched on America's racialized landscape. He also coedited an anthology of black literature to which he contributed an important chapter on folk literature that included his analysis of spirituals and blues music.[9]

Brown was Richardson's professor for four English courses, and they spoke to her creativity as well as her secular humanism. She found his novel and poetry selections artistically exciting, and the essays he assigned commonly had themes that Richardson connected with because of her own experience of being black in America. One that stood out was Henry David Thoreau's "Civil Disobedience," in which he argues that citizens should resist being passive participants in their government's unjust actions. In the course American Prose and Poetry of Negro Life, Brown assigned Claude McKay's poem "If We Must Die." McKay was a Harlem Renaissance writer who had penned the piece as an angry and reflective response to the Red Summer of 1919, when white supremacists had started race riots and viciously attacked black Americans. The poem resonated deeply with Richardson, especially the lines "If we must die—let it not be like hogs / Hunted and penned in an inglorious spot, / Like men we'll face the murderous, cowardly pack, / Pressed to the wall, dying, but fighting back!" Brown also showed students the richness of black American art by playing blues and jazz musicians' recordings in class and assigning black vernacular (black dialect) poetry. He encouraged students to be proud of these art forms and taught them how to use literary criticism to analyze them.[10]

An interesting set of occurrences factored into Richardson's decision to major in sociology. Her grandfather Maynadier St. Clair had hoped she would become a pharmacist or a doctor, and she was agreeable to pursuing either of those professions; however, because she had received a liberal arts scholarship from the Maryland Commission on Scholarships for Colored People (almost certainly secured by her grandfather), Richardson was unable to major in a professional degree program. After briefly testing the waters as a journalism major, Richardson decided to switch to sociology after taking Introduction to Sociology, which captured her attention because it focused on individuals' contact with one another and society. The following semester she took two more sociology courses, one of which was taught by E. Franklin Frazier.[11]

As Howard's foremost sociologist, Frazier was in a unique position to drive his department's agenda, which had been his goal since joining the university's faculty. Using the force of his personality and the culture of intellectual freedom established by university president Mordecai Johnson, Frazier embarked on a journey to understand and alleviate black people's suffering in America. He had earned a baccalaureate from Howard in 1916 and later a doctorate in sociology from the University of Chicago. His essay "The Pathology of Race Prejudice" (1927) unpacked the effects of racism on black people, but his most important contribution to sociology prior to the 1950s was his book *The Negro Family in Chicago*.[12]

Frazier was a self-assured intellectual who did not care what anyone thought of his research or himself, with one exception to the latter. He had apparently never gotten over Mable St. Clair's rebuff of his romantic overtures when the two were students at Baltimore's Colored High School about twenty-five years earlier. On Richardson's first day in Frazier's class, he told everyone that her mother "thought she was too good for [him]" and had called him a "thug." Richardson recalled that he initially "treated me like this little elite, know-nothing snob," the type of person Frazier skewered years later in his book *The Black Bourgeoisie*, but she later realized the professor had only been ribbing her.[13]

Richardson remembered Frazier fondly and described him as "an excellent teacher," noting that "people liked to go to his class." A tribute printed shortly after his death corroborates her claim: "Frazier was a dynamic and inspiring teacher. His lectures tended to be a steady stream of biting or pointed or amusing anecdotes to illustrate the issues on which he talked." Richardson also respected his intellect, adding, he "probably was one of the people that really described the anatomy of racism and how it operates in this country—both in the urban and rural areas," and she credits him with being "a significant person in shaping [her] views and attitudes" about the nexus between race and class. Richardson took Frazier's class Methods of Social Research, a graduate-level course that taught the students how to design surveys. Other sociology professors taught her two favorite courses at Howard: Introduction to Social Psychology and Collective Behavior. The former focused on how individuals are affected by their contact with society, and the latter covered (according to the course description) "mass behavior, public opinion, propaganda, social movements, revolutions and reform."[14] Together, these two courses helped Richardson process and make sense of some of her earlier experiences, especially one event that took place in Cambridge a year before she left for Howard.

The nation's laboring class had made tremendous strides in unionizing during President Franklin D. Roosevelt's second term, although their efforts were challenged by company owners and their supporters. In the summer of 1937 Cambridge was one of the locales where company owners fought workers' attempts to unionize, a battle depicted in an article from the *Afro-American*. The unsigned piece read like a paid advertisement for Cambridge's largest employer, Phillips Packing Company, because its overt message was that a non-union workforce would be better for Phillips and thus better for Cambridge. It also described Richardson's grandfather Maynadier St. Clair as an "outstanding business man" who talked in exceptionally positive terms about the climate at the plant, even saying that the town's entire economy would come to an end if Phillips did not exist. The article accurately characterized St. Clair's belief about what would happen to Cambridge if the workers unionized, and that was why he stood on the porch of his Muir Street home and discouraged hundreds of black workers from doing so. Richardson witnessed this event, and it made a huge impression on her. She was amazed by her grandfather's confidence and his ability to place himself "in the middle of that, and whether rightly or wrongly, just speak to that group and to that problem." Her sociology courses helped her

Sylvia Raven Batipps and Gloria Hayes Richardson, Howard University, circa 1939. (Courtesy of Christina Batipps)

understand how her grandfather was able to leverage his political reputation and oratory skills to convince black workers not to unionize.[15]

Despite having an appreciation for her grandfather's skills in mass persuasion, Richardson disagreed with his position on unionizing, and that became one of the subjects of their "ongoing arguments, and debates, and discussions" when she returned home on breaks from Howard. The university's extracurricular activities were partially responsible for Richardson's willingness to debate the merits of organized labor and capitalism; she had attended a number of campus forums on communism, where she learned that people around the world were attempting to reform their way of life so that no one had to live hand to mouth. Richardson did not know whether communism was the best economic system for black people in America, but she was unwilling to simply dismiss it as an illogical way to alleviate black people's economic problems. She believed that capitalism was one of the causes of black people's exploitation, and many communists and their supporters were promoting an interracial and humanistic response to rid the nation of white supremacy.[16]

Outside the classroom, the social scenes Richardson encountered at the university and out and about in Washington were exciting and occasionally challenging. One of her safe spaces was her tight social circle consisting of her cousin Sylvia and friends Margaret Willis Reynolds, Johnnie Upshaw, and Eunice "Tootie" Joyner. Richardson was especially impressed by Joyner's intellect and her politics, calling her both "bright" and "very radical for those times." Together, these young women formed a band of sisters that eased Richardson's transition into the Howard social scene, which included on-campus dances and concerts as well as trips to off-campus venues to see popular entertainers such as William Henry "Chick" Webb and Jackie "Moms" Mabley. Edward Brooke was another friend of Richardson's, and they shared a special bond. A Washingtonian who was a year ahead of her at school, Brooke was the "big brother" Richardson never had. He saw her as a "quiet and reserved" little sister who smiled a lot and was liked by many students because "she was fun to be around." They behaved like siblings, too. Richardson "always argued" with Brooke about his membership in the Republican Party, and he teased her for being from a small town. He also inserted himself into her dating life: "You can't give her a drink," Brooke told her suitors. It was a warning she found unnecessary, considering her father had taken her to Atlantic City to teach her how to handle her liquor.[17]

The Hayes and St. Clair families had their own opinions about the other college students Gloria spent time with. They thought she should date men from families they knew, but her father's only real requirement was that they be "nice young men." Richardson had only two criteria: anyone she dated had to have a good sense of humor and be a "sharp dresser." She was not always considerate to her boyfriends, as illustrated by the time she scheduled back-to-back visits to Cambridge with two men she was dating at the same time. She justified her behavior by saying, "If I'm going to have a full holiday, you know, [I'll] have two different [dates]." Both men stayed at her uncle Herbert's home, where they crossed paths—something Richardson had not considered when arranging their visits. "Annoyed" by her cavalier attitude, both men broke up with Richardson not long afterward.[18]

She dated only a couple of other men during her college days. One was a Howard University librarian who was the younger brother of Howard sociology professor Hyland Lewis. Richardson had mixed feelings about him and admits she "treat[ed] him pretty badly." Until they stopped dating and he "all of a sudden upped and got married," Richardson was not that interested, but once he was unavailable, she realized she had feelings for him and nursed a broken heart for a while. She was most serious about W. Beverly Carter Jr., a tall Philadelphian who went on to become publisher of the *Pittsburgh Courier* as well as US ambassador to Tanzania and Liberia. He was attending

Lincoln University at the time and traveled to Washington for weekend visits with Richardson. They dated for more than a year before drifting apart and breaking up for reasons she never really understood. Carter's family was friends with Richardson's cousins the Ravens, and the two families traveled in the same Philadelphia social circle. Mable Hayes had apparently told Gloria's uncle and aunt that Carter "was too dark" for her daughter, and the remark made its way back to Carter. Richardson did not learn this until some thirty years after the fact, as her mother had never said or done anything to indicate she wanted Richardson to choose a lighter-skinned man over someone who was darker.[19]

Richardson's social life also included visits back to the Eastern Shore for holidays. Thanksgiving weekend of 1939 was especially noteworthy because her family entertained Mary McLeod Bethune, the director of Negro affairs for the National Youth Administration, a component of the federal government's Works Progress Administration. Generally, however, Richardson stayed in Washington, where there were always exciting things to do with her friends. An open invitation to stay at the home of Roy and Ida Ellis—family friends of the St. Clairs—helped fill in those weekends when Richardson wanted a break from campus life. She also attended teas and parties thrown by other friends of the St. Clairs, and those events provided networking opportunities for her.[20]

Life in Washington challenged Richardson's social dexterity because she came into contact with people from all over the country, and like her, they had brought their own habits and assumptions to the nation's capital. This confluence of ideas and attitudes forced Richardson to expand her cultural literacy so that she could make the most of her interactions with people. At the same time, many Howard students were from the District of Columbia's "old families," and they tended to exhibit a form of elitism based on deportment and manners. Washingtonians were also known for their colorism, which Richardson experienced firsthand at a debutante party when one of the girls asked her, "'Aren't you a little dark to be here?'" The question threw Richardson for a loop: "I can't believe this. I simply cannot believe this! . . . What the hell does that mean?!" Critiques of colorism homed in on the absurdity of the premise that lighter is better and that this intraracial color prejudice had negative consequences for black America. Specifically, it prevented racial unity at a time when black Americans could least afford it. When Richardson pledged Alpha Kappa Alpha sorority, she learned how destructive and divisive colorism can be.[21]

Founded by Howard students in 1908, Alpha Kappa Alpha (AKA) is the oldest black sorority in the nation. Women who were recruited to join AKA were first invited to join the Ivy Leaf Club, the sorority's interest group. Richardson and her friends Johnny Upshaw and Margaret Willis joined the club in the spring semester of 1939, and all three women eventually became members of the sorority, but not at the same time. Upshaw and Willis were inducted in the fall of 1940, and Richardson was inducted the following year. The delay was caused by Richardson herself, who "walk[ed] off the line" during her probationary period. She did this for two reasons: she was beaten by AKA members during a hazing ritual, and she discovered that Upshaw had previously been rejected by AKA because she was considered too dark. This had happened prior to Richardson's arrival at Howard, and Upshaw had been so demoralized that she took a year off from Howard. Oddly, once Richardson walked off probation, a number of sorority sisters pleaded with her to return, but she refused. AKA leaders inducted Richardson anyway, possibly to prevent the involvement of university officials or students' families.[22]

Off campus, Richardson and her classmates faced the same color bar her father had encountered when he attended Howard two decades earlier. Theaters were segregated, and black people were refused try-on privileges at clothing stores. They could not eat at lunch counters in the city's ubiquitous drugstores, and white business owners and managers refused to hire black people for all types of jobs in the city's service industry. Some positive changes had taken place in Washington since the dawn of the New Deal; for instance, federal facilities were desegregated, and Catholic University (a white institution) accepted a black student into its social work program in 1936. Black people welcomed these efforts, but they wanted the pace of progress to speed up. The NAACP used boycotts in the mid-1930s to bring attention to the racially discriminatory hiring practices of small mom-and-pop businesses and major grocery store chains.[23]

Near the end of the decade, the city's New Negro Alliance initiated a "Don't Buy Where You Can't Clerk" campaign. Protesters targeted two locations of the People's drugstore chain in black neighborhoods; these demonstrations continued for more than a year and spread to dozens of People's drugstores around Washington. Among the protesters was a contingent of Howard University students who had been organized largely through the efforts of Walter Washington, an activist student who chaired the university's Youth Committee. Washington enlisted his friend and classmate Edward Brooke to walk the picket line outside the People's drugstore at Fourteenth and U Streets, which was a little more than a mile from campus.[24] Richardson eventually joined Brooke on the picket line after her friend Tootie Joyner told her about the protests. Brooke was not surprised by Richardson's decision to demonstrate because he knew she was highly conscious of the nation's race problems and willing to work for black people's freedom. Richardson's own experiences with Washington's color line drove her toward this activist stance.[25] Once she had gone into a department store to purchase a pair of gloves, but the white clerk would not allow her to try them on. When she asked why, the clerk responded: "'Because you all are colored. We don't allow you all to try on gloves.'" It was Richardson's first experience with overt racial discrimination, and it bothered her very much. Another painful incident occurred on a city streetcar. Although Washington's public transportation system was not legally segregated, that did not deter some white people from trying to maintain a de facto color line. Richardson and her friend Joyner were riding together in a streetcar one day when a couple of white people asked Joyner, a light-skinned black woman who could pass for white, why she was "'sitting with that nigger.'"[26] Offenses like these, which Richardson described as "psychic abuse," took a toll on her and reminded her that white America did not consider black people first-class citizens.[27]

Back on campus, Richardson confronted other types of issues. She participated in a campus-wide protest so large and full of drama that the *Afro-American* and *Chicago Defender* ran stories about it. The issue involved the dean of women's restrictive policies concerning students' dress, weekend passes, curfews, and arbitrary rules that were not written down. Joyner was one of the protest's organizers, and Richardson joined her for a sit-in at the dean's office. Interestingly, Richardson was not opposed to the clothing restrictions because she was used to wearing a uniform of sorts on campus, as were all Howard students (women wore skirts or dresses, and men wore jackets and ties). Nor was she bothered by the gendered nature of the curfew, which restricted female students more than male students; however, she took issue with the curfew because it made no distinction between first-year female students and those in their junior or senior year. If these older students were going to be graduating soon and moving out into the world, the university's administrators should recognize their maturity and start treating them like responsible women, she reasoned. Her parents seemingly agreed, because they did not admonish Richardson for protesting.[28]

The final semester of college is a time of both promise and uncertainty for many students because they usually have to decide on a career. Richardson faced that challenge in the spring of 1942, when she was about to graduate. Initially, she saw herself using her sociology degree to become a social worker, but she speculated that racist hiring practices on the Eastern Shore would prevent her from getting employment. The Second World War added to her uncertainty, because campus blackout drills reminded her that graduation might be little more than a day of celebration with no future beyond it. Nevertheless, Richardson focused on finishing her coursework and feeding a passion of hers: directing theater productions.[29]

Richardson's love of theater had begun at summer camp, where she had participated in various drama activities. It was cultivated further when she joined the Howard Players, the university's theater group, in her sophomore year. In the spring of 1941 she played the role of Ada in Edward Chodorov's melodramatic three-act play *Kind Lady*, but she was much better behind the scenes. In her senior year Richardson's classmates elected her president of the Howard Players, and she oversaw the group's production of James Thurber and Elliott Nugent's comedy *The Male Animal*. The experience allowed Richardson to hone her directorial skills under the tutelage of James W. "Beanie" Butcher, an outstanding professor of theater art from whom she took the course Play Directing.[30]

Richardson's fondness for Butcher had an unintended consequence in her final days of college. A conflict arose when the final exams for Butcher's course and Richardson's Spanish course were scheduled for the same time. Richardson spoke with both professors, trying to find a solution acceptable to everyone, but neither was willing to reschedule his exam. Richardson decided to take Butcher's exam because she "liked [him] better" than her Spanish instructor. Faced with a failing grade in Spanish, Richardson appealed to E. Franklin Frazier, who tried unsuccessfully to intervene on her behalf. As a result, Richardson did not graduate in the spring of 1942. "Furious" at her Spanish professor's intransigence, Richardson refused to attend the graduation ceremony and requested that the university mail her diploma to her after she passed Spanish during the summer session.[31]

One of Gloria Richardson's last activities at Howard University was helping to direct 100 students in the "tableaux" portion of the institution's annual May festival. The theme was Howard's past, present, and future, and in many ways, Richardson personified these stages. Her father was an alumnus, tying Richardson to Howard's early history of educating the formerly enslaved and their children. As a student, Richardson was immersed in the institution's problem-driven and solution-oriented curriculum, which fortified her secular humanism. Her professors prepared Richardson for her future as a human rights activist by teaching her how to analyze white supremacy and understand how it operates. In some of those courses she learned the research methods and group-management skills she would use to assess and guide black Cambridge residents as they fought against the racist system that oppressed them all.[32] Richardson's use of those skills was still way off in the future, and in the meantime, she would experience a multitude of other important events in her life, including marriage, the births of her daughters, and the deaths of many loved ones. In one way or another, racial oppression touched all these events and prompted her to become socially active in Cambridge.

4

Dreams Deferred

On the morning of her wedding day, Gloria Richardson confided in her father that she was having second thoughts. John Hayes told his daughter it was too late to change her mind, so she went ahead with the ceremony.[1] This was but one decision Richardson made in the first half of her life that adhered to societal norms for women. As she got older and experienced numerous personal losses, Richardson felt she had attained the social and personal freedom to make choices that reflected her own desires, including the uncommon decision to get a divorce.

Richardson had other considerations as well. When she looked out on the midpoint of the twentieth century, she saw a future for her children that, at least in terms of race, looked a lot like the one she and her parents and grandparents had already lived. Everything in Cambridge was still racially segregated and oppressive, and Richardson decided to do something that would, she hoped, improve her daughters' future and that of all Cambridge's black residents. Richardson did not know whether her race service would bring about tangible change, but she was determined to take on a public role and rely on the tactic of public confrontation to push for change—something her family members had avoided in the past. By the end of the 1950s, Richardson's life was very different from the one she had known during the previous decade, and she was evolving into the person who would captivate the nation in the 1960s.

After her graduation from Howard University, Richardson asked herself two important questions: what career would she have, and what type of job would she get in the meantime? An invitation from Johnnie Upshaw to visit her home in East Chicago, Indiana, gave Richardson a good place to sort out her options, so with the help of her father's old Pullman Porter connections, she traveled by train to the Midwest.[2]

In between sightseeing trips, Richardson and Upshaw talked about their futures. One option Richardson may have discussed was joining the army, which had been on her mind since the Japanese attack on Pearl Harbor in

Gloria Hayes Richardson's senior portrait, Howard University, 1942. (Courtesy of the Moorland-Spingarn Research
Center, Howard University Archives,
Washington, DC)

December 1941. Americans from all walks of life threw their support behind
the war effort, including those in college. Only male students were subject to
the draft, but many of them were planning to join the armed forces anyway.
For their part, female students joined organizations that provided training in
"first aid, motor mechanics," and other useful pursuits. Richardson supported the war effort by volunteering for the black United Service Organizations (USO) and working with other women to host various morale-boosting
events for the troops.[3]

When the federal government established the Women's Army Auxiliary
Corps (WAAC) in May 1942, women like Gloria Richardson had another
avenue to support the war effort. Like the all-male army, the WAAC was
racially segregated, but this did not deter black women living in the nation's
capital from inquiring about enlisting. Volunteers had to be at least twenty-
one years old and meet minimum height and weight standards. Combat duty
was off limits to women recruits, but the WAAC provided workers for a variety of fields, such as clerical, bookkeeping, pharmacy, food service, and
machine operators. Within weeks of its creation, thousands of women had
applied to join the WAAC. Despite the fact that the United States was no
haven of democracy for black people or other minority groups (including
Japanese Americans, who were being sent to internment camps), Richardson

considered joining. She had no immediate career plans, and it seemed like a viable option for her and her peers; her friend Edward Brooke was already serving in the army. Even with all its racial contradictions, Richardson felt that joining the WAAC "sounded like something great to do." It also would have afforded her an opportunity to participate in the double-V (double-victory) campaign started by black Americans to strike a crushing blow against tyranny and oppression overseas as well as at home in the United States.[4]

John Hayes had a vastly different take on his daughter's intentions. "He almost had a fit," Richardson recalled. During his time in the army during World War I, John had witnessed the military culture's inherent hostility toward women (sexual harassment and assaults), and he was worried for her safety. She thought this was the only reason for her father's opposition to her plan, but it seems reasonable to assume that he might have thought her well-known reluctance to follow unfair and unjust rules made her a poor candidate for the military. This was one of the rare occasions in Richardson's life when she took her father's advice and decided not to enlist.[5]

With military service no longer an option, Richardson focused on a career path. One of her long-term goals was to earn a graduate degree in social psychology from the University of Chicago, but she was uncomfortable with the idea of moving so far away to an unfamiliar city. For the time being, Richardson was content to stay in Washington and seek employment in the city's civil service sector, which had expanded since the war began. Mable Hayes supported this plan, which she saw as an opportunity for her daughter to learn how to be a responsible adult by getting a job and living on her own. Richardson's mother instructed her to ask family friends Roy and Ida Ellis if she could rent a room from them, and they agreed. The arrangement worked out well. Once Richardson passed the civil servant exam and started working as a clerk, Roy Ellis (a career civil servant) mentored her, teaching her the ins and outs of being a black worker in the federal government. She found the work itself rewarding, and she liked her coworkers, but one of the tough lessons Richardson learned was that despite having college degrees or "any degree of intelligence," black workers did not progress through the civil service ranks as quickly as white workers did.[6]

Richardson worked for the government for approximately two years, until her mother's illness caused Richardson to reexamine her own future. Her relatives implored her to move back to Cambridge. One of the most vocal was her grandfather, who had always wanted his children and grand-children to return to the Eastern Shore. Now he was seizing on Richardson's sense of family obligation to convince her to move back there. Richardson saw little reason to do so: her family employed housekeepers who could take care of the household while her mother was ill, and she was unlikely to find a job in Cambridge that would put her college education to good use, such as social work. The one person who did not push Richardson to return to Cambridge was her father. He knew firsthand how liberating it could be to leave home and create a life of one's own in a new city. He watched as his in-laws forced his daughter to choose between her career aspirations and her family, a decision that weighed heavily on Richardson. Ultimately, she decided to take "the line of least resistance." She quit her job and gave up her life in Washington to move back to Cambridge.[7]

A little over a year after Richardson returned home, the *Baltimore Sun* ran a story about Cambridge's past and present. It portrayed the city as a booming business town where the modern food-packing industry peacefully coexisted with the old farming world populated by day laborers who picked tomatoes and other cash crops on land owned by gentlemen farmers. Cambridge, the article implied, was a typical American town that charmed visitors with its scenic gardens and friendly, slow-paced social scene. But viewed through the lens of race, Cambridge was not the land of opportunity the *Sun* claimed it was.[8]

Richardson easily settled back into her pre-Howard life. Most people would have found it difficult to move from a big city to a tiny locale on the Eastern Shore, but Richardson was not one of them. To her, the change in location was primarily one of geography because both places were segregated spaces that restricted black people's movements and opportunities. Still, the move allowed Richardson to resume her debates with her grandfather, an idealistic pragmatist whom she described as "a vocal admirer of Frederick Douglass and [W. E. B.] Du Bois but tied to the philosophy of Booker T. Washington."[9]

Richardson planned to stay in Cambridge only until her mother finished convalescing. Then she hoped to attend graduate school in Chicago. However, another family obligation—this time to her maternal grandmother— kept her on the Eastern Shore. Fannie St. Clair wanted to see her granddaughter married as soon as possible, but with the exception of Beverly Carter, Richardson had not had any serious relationships. Harry Richardson was a newly hired teacher at Frederick Douglass St. Clair High School, and Gloria's family thought he was a promising candidate. He was a college graduate with a respectable career, and he had a preexisting medical issue that exempted him from the draft, so he would not be called up for military service.[10]

Gloria found Harry "attractive" and pleasant, but the details of how they met and their six-month courtship were, by her account, unmemorable. For Gloria, at least, it seems their relationship lacked a spark of passion, but she went ahead and married him anyway to make her family happy.[11] Fannie St. Clair had made it clear that before she passed away she wanted her granddaughter to be married with children, and Gloria felt the need to please her. Furthermore, she feared being labeled an "old maid," which seemed more likely as she entered her mid-twenties. This was an interesting paradox: the person who sat during the Pledge of Allegiance, protested Howard's treatment of women students, and protested at a pharmacy chain that discriminated against black people felt compelled to conform to others' expectations when it came to marriage. Richardson attributed this mainly to gender socialization, noting that she had been so thoroughly "inculcated" that she was not even aware of it.[12]

Mild temperatures and a rising sun greeted Gloria when she awoke in her family's Muir Street home on the last Sunday of February 1945. Despite the good weather, she was getting a case of cold feet concerning the wedding ceremony that was about to take place downstairs. As she got dressed in her blue suit (no formal gown for the occasion because of the family's wartime cutbacks), she kept wishing she could go back in time and at least postpone what was about to happen because she was not certain she was in love with Harry Richardson. She shared her feelings with her father, but he told her it was too late to back out, and he walked his daughter downstairs to her future husband. Less than six weeks later, her grandmother passed away.[13] Harry moved into his in-laws' home, and the following year he and Gloria added a fourth generation to the St. Clair household when their first child, Donna, was born in Baltimore's Provident Hospital. Richardson had been traveling to Baltimore for monthly checkups with her black obstetrician because medical services for pregnant black women were deficient in Cambridge; however, she gave birth to her second child, Tamara, at Cambridge's hospital, and they were attended by a white doctor.[14]

As a newlywed and then a new mother, Richardson had to alter her domestic life. Prior to marriage, she had not been expected to cook or clean because her family had employed housekeepers and cooks. Now Richardson was expected to perform those tasks herself, and the household staff taught her how to do them. Learning the ropes of household management was just one of Richardson's new responsibilities; another was parenting. She felt she had limited leverage over what she could get her daughters to do because "they had wills of their own." Donna characterized her mother as a strict disciplinarian, whereas Tamara recalled that she was not too stern. Where the sisters' views converged was on their parents' personalities: Gloria was "very strong," even "domineering," while Harry was "quiet" and "very subdued." Both instilled in their daughters the same ideals Gloria's parents had taught her, such as how to behave in public and to be respectful of people both inside and outside the family. Gloria's and Harry's conversations with other adults showed their daughters the importance of being aware of current events and politics. Added to this mix was Gloria's mother Mable, who taught Donna and Tamara that it was fine to be both female and strong. Their elders' lessons fit a mold of black parentage described by Charlayne Hunter Gault, one of two black students who integrated the University of Georgia in 1961. "Where black parents . . . could not give us first-class citizenship, they labored instead to give us a first-class sense of ourselves."[15]

When Gloria and Harry were not spending time with their family, they could be found attending Second Ward social club events or music shows in town. The couple also entertained relatives and neighborhood friends with parties that featured dancing and card playing. These friends included James and Jacqueline "Jackie" Fassett. He was a primary care physician who opened a practice in Cambridge in the late 1940s, and she was a homemaker raising the couple's two children. Jackie and Gloria shared similar interests, such as politics and modern fashion, and they organized fashion shows for the Second Ward.[16]

As Gloria was enjoying this vibrant social life and experiencing the joys of raising her daughters, she suffered a number of personal losses that rocked her sense of security. It began in 1946 with the death of her father, Richardson's biggest emotional supporter throughout her life. John Hayes suffered a heart attack that left him bedridden for six months until he died at home in early December. Her cousin Dr. Carroll St. Clair had treated John and arranged for a heart specialist to see him, but Cambridge's hospital was segregated, which prevented him from obtaining the timely and comprehensive care he needed to improve his chances of surviving. This angered Richardson and brought back memories of her uncle Frederick St. Clair, who had died of typhoid fever due to a lack of adequate health care. Even though both men had been financially prosperous and enjoyed more than a fair amount of social standing, neither factor could mitigate the disadvantages of living in a racially segregated community in which white people restricted their access to health care. "I internalized [my father's death]," Richardson said, and "as I got older I began to realize what that meant. That this was pure racism and segregation. They didn't let not only my father but any blacks in [the hospital]." These deaths, along with her own experiences with racism in Washington, collected in Richardson's psyche and were "translated into something else once" when she reached her thirties.[17]

Death continued to thin the ranks of Richardson's family. Fifteen months after her father passed away, Carroll St. Clair died. A little more than a year later, her grandfather died from a serious head injury he suffered when the car he was riding in, driven by Harry Richardson, collided with a truck. Speaking on behalf of Cambridge's city government, Second Ward councilman Charles Cornish expressed sympathy to the family and presented them with a resolution praising Maynadier St. Clair's political work. This did not sooth Richardson's pain, nor did it evaporate her unspoken anger at her husband, whom she blamed for the accident "at some level." Compounding Richardson's sense of loss was her mother's marriage to Methodist minister Theodore Boothe and her relocation to Wilmington, Delaware, where he was leading a congregation. Richardson saw Boothe as a hustler who had married her mother for her money. Gloria's disdain for him increased over the years, and she felt he exacerbated disagreements she had with her mother.[18]

Other painful issues pertained to Gloria's own marriage. She believed Harry was being unfaithful, but when she shared her suspicions with her mother, Mable advised her that an affair was insufficient grounds for divorce. In fact, the message she got from her family was that divorce in general was not "the appropriate thing to do," so she stayed married. However, Gloria's breaking point came when the couple began to have finance issues. Since Mable's move to Delaware, Gloria and Harry assumed financial responsibility for the upkeep of the Muir Street home (although Mable still retained ownership of it). Gloria had also inherited her father's pharmacy, and she was trying to keep it open and viable. She hired black pharmacists to work there, but when she did not have an in-house pharmacist, the owners of Craig's Drug Store in Cambridge filled prescriptions at no cost to Richardson, a favor she appreciated greatly.[19] Harry helped run the Hayes pharmacy, but Gloria never felt that he was fully committed to its success; she also alleged that he mismanaged their household money and did not pull his weight in supporting their daughters. The girls had allergies that required treatment, which became an additional household expense. Donna and Tamara were aware of the strife between their parents, and it was painful to witness. On one particular night, it became frightening: "I just remember a big argument at the dinner table," Tamara said, "where she threw a glass at him—across the table." Gloria Richardson could not recall this event, which she attributed to an unconscious decision to block out the parts of her marriage she would rather not remember.[20] Gloria initiated the divorce in the summer of 1959, and she and Harry separated for eighteen months, during which time the couple made an unsuccessful attempt at reconciliation. Harry did not contest the divorce, which was finalized in July 1960. He was ordered to pay child support to Gloria, who had been granted custody of their daughters. While she was supportive of her daughters having close relationships with their father, Gloria was never close with Harry after they broke up because, in her words, "I don't believe in being friends with ex-husbands."[21]

After the divorce, Richardson still had to raise two girls in the same racist society that had plagued generations of St. Clairs. Her friend Jackie Fassett was shocked by Cambridge's racial climate. A native of Long Island, New York, Fassett had attended college in Baltimore, where she found white people's overt racial prejudice appalling. But if anything, Cambridge's white residents were even less welcoming than Baltimore's. Sometime in the early 1950s, white community leaders invited Fassett and Gloria Richardson to attend a fund-raising event for Cambridge's segregated hospital. The event included a sit-down meal, but Richardson and Fassett left in protest when they learned that the white organizers had set up a separate table for them.[22]

Another event involved the most segregated hour of the week in America—the Sunday church service. When Gloria was living in Washington, she had attended St. Luke's Episcopal Church, which is where she was confirmed.[23] Upon her return to Cambridge, Richardson occasionally attended Waugh Methodist Episcopal Church, but Harry Richardson was an Episcopalian who "felt that he could go to" Christ Church (the white Episcopal church in town), "so I went with him." Their daughter Donna was baptized into the faith the following year in a ceremony held at the family's Muir Street home.[24] Christ Church's white congregants did not show any signs of disrespect to Richardson's family when they attended services because that type of behavior would have been "beneath" their social status. But when it became apparent that the Richardsons intended to make Christ Church their permanent house of worship, some white members did "everything they could to discourage [it]." This was happening right around the time the Fassetts—also Episcopalians—tried to join Christ Church. Jackie, Gloria, and a few other people confronted the church's leadership about its reluctance to open membership to black people. Pressed into a corner, church leaders created a separate-but-equal solution to their dilemma by providing funds to establish an all-black "mission" congregation in the Second Ward, ministered by a black priest who presided over a congregation that consisted of the Richardsons, the Fassetts, and a handful of other people. The experiment lasted only a few years before it closed down. Richardson said many years later that she should have just stopped going to church altogether rather than attend a segregated house of worship, and it was at this point that she ceased any personal association with organized religion. Gloria and Harry also stopped taking their daughters to church, and although Donna and Tamara did attend services at Waugh with other family members, religion was never a significant part of their family life.[25]

Christ Church was but one example of Cambridge's unwelcoming spaces for black people. A few positive changes did take place, such as the elimination of segregated waiting areas in the local Trailways bus station in 1952. And although the opening of the Chesapeake Bay Bridge increased the city's contact with the Western Shore, it had little effect on white people's racial attitudes. For example, the white chapter of the American Legion continued to hold minstrel shows throughout the 1950s.[26] Racist attitudes like these permeated Maryland's white communities, and their members fought black politicians' attempts to dismantle the state's Jim Crow system in schooling and public accommodations. When change did come, it was through the judicial branch of the federal government. Early in the spring of 1954, the Fourth Circuit Court of Appeals ruled that a Maryland law requiring racial segregation on public beaches was in violation of the Fourteenth Amendment's equal protection clause. Two months later, the US Supreme Court handed down its decision in *Brown v. Board of Education of Topeka, Kansas*, ruling that racially separate public education systems are inherently unequal.[27]

Gloria Richardson found an entirely different racial climate north of the border when she took a vacation to Montreal with her mother and Dorothy Banton (a friend of Mable's who had babysat Gloria when she was a child in Baltimore). The ten-day driving vacation first took them through New England, after which they headed to the province of Québec. "The farther north we got, the less racist pressure we felt," Richardson recalled. "When we hit Canada, whatever that thing about color was seemed to disappear. . . . I realized that at some point, in certain little spaces in the world there probably were situations where black people were not looked upon as pariahs, or left to wait, or treated discourteously." During the early 1960s Richardson spoke to reporters about this trip and its impact on her ability to assess America's racial landscape: "It was the first experience of feeling perfectly normal and human. It was as if a big burden was lifted off my shoulders." Her reflection was an indictment of the United States, because she had to leave her own country to experience such a feeling. Many black military veterans reported similar feelings after serving in Europe during both world wars. However, unlike the black veterans who had served overseas, Richardson's trip to Canada did not raise her expectations of what life in America could be like. She already knew her homeland could be a great place for black people to live if white people would only reject racism and act in accordance with democratic and humanistic principles.[28]

Richardson decided in the mid-1950s to participate in her family's tradition of race service and try to make a positive impact on Cambridge. She and Jackie Fassett began working to mitigate the negative effects of white supremacy on black children by challenging the segregated school system that ultimately limited black people's ability to obtain better job opportunities that could improve their quality of life.[29] Despite the Supreme Court's *Brown* ruling, white officials throughout Maryland resisted integrating the state's public school systems (a tactic employed by countless other officials throughout the South). A special committee of the State Board of Education studied how Maryland could go about implementing *Brown*, but it concluded that the Supreme Court's decision actually "created a new right" for black people while "abrogat[ing] the right" of white people.[30] Though legally meaningless, the State Board of Education's finding provided political cover for white people who were resisting school integration.

Back on the Eastern Shore, Dorchester County's white power brokers initially seemed willing to abide by the *Brown* decision. They appointed local businessperson Helen Waters to the Dorchester County Board of Education, the first black person to serve in that role in the entire Eastern Shore (at the time of her appointment, Waters had been serving on Dorchester County's advisory board concerning public school integration). In time, Dorchester County began its official school desegregation process by opening up white high schools to black twelfth graders whose parents requested that they be transferred. No black parents made such requests, likely due to their knowledge of white parents' opposition to integration and the possibility of white violence against black students. Consequently, three years after *Brown*, Dorchester's classrooms remained segregated, although small steps toward integration had taken place. For example, the county's schoolchildren had begun to attend integrated music programs and athletic events, and faculty and staff attended integrated meetings.[31]

One measure of Dorchester County's racial inequality in education was the amount expended on white versus black students. For the school year 1955–1956, the county spent $205.04 per white student but only $138.06 per black student. Richardson and Fassett knew they had to apply pressure to county officials to get them to do right by black students, so these women attended parent-teacher association (PTA) and school board meetings, where they advocated for black students' right to an equal education. This type of challenge to the racial status quo was uncommon in Cambridge, and it concerned some officials. Fassett recalled one PTA meeting where she stood up to "speak [her] mind" about the inferior education black children were receiving, and the superintendent "cautioned the people about listening to people like [Fassett] because it would cause trouble."[32]

Richardson and Fassett also brought their community's concerns to the City Council, where they sought resources to improve black residents' quality of life. The Cambridge city government was a logical place for black people to seek assistance because, as early as 1950, the councilmen had approved the allocation of public land and monies for recreational activities and facilities for the Second Ward. Eventually, a small number of residents established the Second Ward Recreational League (SWRL) to manage these resources and organize community outreach programs. Members included Gloria and Harry Richardson, her cousin Frederick St. Clair, councilman Charles Cornish, and numerous others who had ties to important community businesses, churches, and fraternal societies. Richardson and Fassett collaborated on a needs-based community action plan whose goal was to expand SWRL's recreation programs; it also included an educational component to augment services being provided by the city. Informally called Ed/Rec (for education and recreation), the program would rely on volunteers from within the Second Ward to donate their time and skills to help their fellow residents improve their literacy, as well as to provide scholastic tutoring, music instruction, and coaching for organized sports. All these activities and programs would take place throughout the year at various Second Ward churches and in public places such as parks and schools. On the evening of 12 May 1958 Richardson and Fassett presented their plan (which included a request for funding) to the Cambridge City Council, but Cornish's colleagues declined to fund or otherwise support it. With little money and limited space, the Ed/Rec program never took off.[33]

White officials' failure to finance and support Ed/Rec was a defeat for all the residents of the Second Ward. As Richardson said some years later, Cambridge's racial caste system and its concomitant lack of economic opportunities "kills ambition at an early age," potentially leading to high dropout rates among black students. The picture was rosier for college-educated Blacks who entered the fields of medicine, law, and teaching, but Richardson's attempts to find employment failed. When she applied for a position as a social worker, city officials told her that she did not need the job because her family was wealthy, and they hired another college-educated black woman. Richardson also tried to get work sewing at a local garment factory, but she failed the manual dexterity exam. Richardson knew firsthand that in a place like Cambridge, economic opportunities for black people were largely limited to jobs where, in her words, they "skin tomatoes and shuck oysters."[34]

When a fire destroyed Frederick Douglass St. Clair High School in the winter of 1952, the Second Ward lost an important repository of its history. Strewn among the ashes of the building were students' records, photographs, and awards earned by the school's athletic teams. Although they were devastated by the fire, black residents immediately secured alternative sites around the Second Ward where students could continue their education until a new high school could be built. In one way, the fire was an informal marker in Gloria Richardson's life. Since the death of her grandfather H. Maynadier St. Clair, the school had been the most visible symbol of Richardson's maternal family and its importance and prominence in Cambridge. Now that the school was gone, Richardson had one less thing keeping her connected to her past. Her father, her grandparents, and her cousin Carroll had all died within the half dozen years preceding the fire, and her mother had remarried and moved to another state. These personal losses were one reason why Richardson's life was less than happy. Another factor was her unsatisfying marriage, but she assumed much of the blame for that. "I don't think I really should have been married. I don't think I was . . . probably, emotionally ready for it."[35] The decision to divorce was not an easy one, and it came with its own risks. Yet it shows that Richardson had rejected at least one tenet of social conformity. We will never know, however, if Richardson would have taken this step if her grandparents and father had still been alive and her mother had not moved away.

Despite her personal losses and challenges, Richardson moved forward, just as the black community moved forward after St. Clair High School burned down. She focused more of her energy on her daughters and their needs and worked to improve the lives of all the black residents of Cambridge. Interestingly, her actions were part of a broader postwar movement among American women who engaged in a variety of causes focused on improving their communities. Some of these women were involved in advocacy and activism related to gender issues, while others, like Richardson, addressed racism.[36]

The time Richardson spent advocating for the Second Ward by attending PTA meetings and working with the SWRL was not wasted. SWRL's Ed/Rec proposal became a prototype for programs implemented a handful of years later by Cambridge's civil rights activists. Additionally, Richardson's very public and firm advocacy for the black community helped establish her credibility as a race servant. Her activities also made her aware of the political fault lines in the Second Ward between racial progressives like herself and the community's gradualists, such as Helen Waters and Charles Cornish. This split became more obvious when William Downs, one of the black workers who led the labor strike against Phillips Packing Company in 1937, twice challenged Cornish for his City Council seat during the 1950s. Downs lost both contests, but the fact that his vote total increased significantly on his second run indicated that a growing number of Cornish's constituents were disillusioned by his type of politics and lack of forward thinking. This was one of many dynamics Richardson would capitalize on during the civil rights movement.[37]

Unbeknownst to Richardson, in just a few years college students would arrive in Cambridge as part of the larger desegregation movement taking place in the American South. These students brought attributes that Richardson felt were lacking in Cambridge's black community: energy, enthusiasm, and creative thinking about how to advance black liberation.

5

Shock Therapy, Round One

At the close of 1961, Cambridge's *Daily Banner* newspaper ran two pieces that predicted, unintentionally perhaps, what lay ahead for the city. The first was a front-page article that told of two dozen Freedom Riders who had traveled from Baltimore to the Eastern Shore town of Crisfield in December to desegregate a couple of lunch counters. These rides were similar to those organized by the Congress of Racial Equality (CORE) earlier in the year in which racially integrated groups of young men and women left Washington, DC, and headed to New Orleans to test public accommodations along bus routes through the South; on several occasions, white supremacist terrorists attacked the riders. Maryland's Freedom Rides were initiated by Baltimore's Civic Interest Group (CIG), a student organization consisting primarily of members from two historically black Maryland colleges: Morgan State and Coppin State. They decided on Crisfield because it was the hometown of Maryland's governor J. Millard Tawes, and the student-activists wanted to create a very public connection between the governor and racial segregation. In the months preceding the Maryland Freedom Rides, Tawes had been forced to address his state's segregated public accommodations after African diplomats traveling by car from New York to Washington, DC, had been denied service at various restaurants along the stretch of Route 40 between Baltimore and the Delaware state line. The governor did little more than criticize the treatment these Africans had received, so the Freedom Riders were hoping their demonstration in Crisfield would force him to take concrete action.[1]

The other *Daily Banner* piece was an editorial that touted Dorchester County's economic progress, as evidenced by an increase in jobs and industry, a rise in merchants' sales, and the county government's establishment of a Housing Authority to address residents' housing needs. All these developments showed that "as 1961 drew to a close the prospect of exciting growth faced the community." There would be "other problems to be met and mastered," the editors warned, but plenty of residents were prepared for the challenge because "after years spent watching the rest of the world go by, this area was ready to swing out into the mainstream." The editorial avoided mentioning that those same residents would have to decide whether to join a growing list of white communities (including Crisfield's) that were abandoning racial segregation, a main element of the South's racialized capitalist-democratic institutions. White Cambridge's decision on this issue was just two weeks away.[2]

Driving the push for desegregation in Cambridge were youths who were reluctant to live in the same type of world their parents and grandparents had inhabited. Those children were about to confront a white community that wanted to keep Cambridge as it always had been, but black parents, including Gloria Richardson, would step into the breach and lead the black community along the path to freedom their children had blazed. She had her own reasons for entering Cambridge's civil rights struggle, known as the Cambridge movement. Foremost among them were her dissatisfaction at living in a segregated society and her desire to serve the black community that had supported her family's businesses. In many ways, the events that transpired over the first half of 1962, and the black community's push for racial equality and freedom over that entire year, were similar to what was happening in dozens of other southern locales in states such as Virginia, Georgia, and Mississippi. That is, local people, with the aid of a recently created civil rights organization, were taking it upon themselves to make their communities places of racial equality and freedom. A common element in these movements was the development of local leaders.[3]

Gloria Richardson became one of those leaders when she used her knowledge and skills to advance the cause of black liberation in Cambridge. Her activism was essentially the same as the advocacy work she had done in the 1950s, except that this time around, it was more public and much more confrontational. Underpinning her work were Richardson's philosophies concerning the organizing of a broad-based social change movement and the goals, strategies, and tactics that should be part of such a movement. Of particular importance was the role of voting and whether it could move black Cambridge one step closer to freedom. Significantly, the debate about participating in electoral politics would eventually bring the Cambridge movement into direct conflict with civil rights organizations with different agendas.

Saturday, 13 January 1962, is viewed by some as the beginning of Cambridge's civil rights movement because on that day the city's black community held its first civil rights demonstration of the 1960s. Dozens of black high school students, including Richardson's daughter Donna, joined a number of young men and women from Baltimore's CIG and CORE and two members of the Student Nonviolent Coordinating Committee (SNCC) as they moved on Cambridge that Saturday afternoon. However, it would be a mistake to read that day's protest as a stand-alone event because it took weeks of coordinated planning by Cambridge's black youths and their allies from outside the city to pull off the unprecedented action.[4]

Those non-Cambridge participants were just the first of many young people from Maryland and around the Northeast who would travel to that quiet and socially isolated part of the mid-Atlantic region over the next two years. Most of them were students at either HBCUs located in and around Maryland or predominantly white colleges in the North, and as a group, they shared an idealistic view of an America in which all citizens, irrespective of race, were treated equally before the law and had equal social and economic opportunities. The students' quest for racial progress had begun years earlier when most of them were teenagers. Their teachers and the mass media had fed them a narrative that touted the United States as a nation of god-fearing free people who were the opposite of those enslaved to the godless communists who ruled eastern Europe and parts of Asia. This propaganda raised the expectations of many young Americans of all religious faiths (especially those who were white) that their government would champion the ideals of democratic freedom. But because there had been so little progress on racial matters since the *Brown* decision in 1954, these students had grown tired of waiting for their parents' generation to make changes, and they decided to take matters into their own hands.

For many of these black students, the lynching of Emmett Till was an additional reason—and in some cases *the* reason—for getting involved in the black liberation struggle. The fourteen-year-old black boy had been kidnapped and murdered in Mississippi by white terrorists for whistling at a white woman. The black-owned magazine *Jet* covered Till's funeral and printed a horrific photograph of his battered body. That image was seared into the collective consciousness of the southern black youths who would later be known as the "Emmett Till generation," and they were determined to transform the nation into a place where no black child had to live in fear of being lynched.[5] Four men of this generation were students at the historically black North Carolina Agricultural and Technical State University in Greensboro, and after talking one night about what they could do to challenge racism, they decided to try to desegregate the local Woolworth's lunch counter on 1 February 1960. They were not successful, but their action that day altered the country's history. News of their protest reached students at HBCUs throughout the South, and many of them held their own sit-ins at restaurants and lunch counters. Representatives of civil rights organizations attempted to channel these students' autonomous local efforts into an organized movement, and in the spring of that year, more than 100 students gathered at Shaw University in Raleigh, North Carolina, to strategize about the next steps in this student-led phase of the black liberation movement.

The outcome of this conference was the creation of SNCC, an independent and interracial organization. The pillar of SNCC's philosophy was participatory democracy, which meant that local people would lead their own movements and determine their own goals and how to achieve them. As a member-driven and group-centered organization, SNCC was qualitatively different from centralized, hierarchical, leader-driven organizations such as CORE, the National Association for the Advancement of Colored People (NAACP), and the Southern Christian Leadership Conference (SCLC). Historian and civil rights activist Howard Zinn was fully aware of SNCC's importance to the movement and wrote that its members "are radical, but not dogmatic; thoughtful, but not ideological. Their thinking is undisciplined; it is fresh, and it is new." These "shock troops"—as SNCC field members were called—fanned out across the South to provide moral and strategic assistance to local people who were working to organize or expand direct action projects (such as desegregation) or voter registration projects.[6] The moniker was appropriate because SNCC members' community presence, work, and dedication to black liberation gave local people a much needed jolt of energy. Additionally, SNCC workers' activism and organizing tactics forced white people to realize that the southern way of life built by their ancestors was receding into the past, just as the mechanical cotton picker had forever changed the South's economy.

The SNCC contingent on the ground in Cambridge on 13 January consisted of Bill Hansen and Reginald "Reggie" Robinson. A white Cincinnati native, Hansen had been one of CORE's Freedom Riders the previous spring. He was then sent to Baltimore as part of CORE's desegregation efforts in Maryland, which was where he met Robinson. A black college student from the Washington area, Robinson had left his studies to work with CIG. Then, while working with SNCC as a field secretary, Robinson had helped people in McComb, Mississippi, organize their own movement. Gloria Richardson's cousin, local bail bondsman Freddie St. Clair, was one of the Cambridge residents who welcomed Hansen and Robinson to town. St. Clair had contacted them some weeks earlier, after learning about the Eastern Shore Freedom Rides, and asked them to help kick-start a desegregation drive in Cambridge. Both men worked with St. Clair and local youths ahead of the January protest to pick targets for their demonstration and to gather resources and support.[7]

After a short meet and greet, the demonstrators assembled, picked up their signs (one read "We are hungry for civil rights"), and marched to local establishments to protest segregation. Twenty activists were arrested and charged with trespassing or disorderly conduct, including a nineteen-year-old local woman named Enez Grubb. St. Clair bailed out the activists, and the NAACP hired Baltimore attorney Juanita Jackson Mitchell to represent them. The ready involvement of the NAACP indicates the multiorganization coordination that went into planning and supporting the protest. At the end of the day, 300 people—including Gloria Richardson and Second Ward councilman Charles Cornish—joined the activists at Waugh Methodist Episcopal Church for a mass meeting where they sang freedom songs and listened to speakers discuss the next steps of Cambridge's liberation struggle.[8]

Also in attendance that night was Philip "Phil" Savage, the NAACP's field secretary for New Jersey, Pennsylvania, and Delaware. He advised residents to start a letter-writing campaign to local politicians, requesting that they outlaw racial segregation in public accommodations, and to demand that their state legislators pass an open accommodations law; he also encouraged people to boycott Cambridge's white-owned businesses. Then Reggie Robinson spoke about his voter registration work in Mississippi and observed that, based on what he had witnessed in Cambridge, there was little difference between the two locations. The struggle in Cambridge, Robinson said, would be centered on equality "not only in restaurants but in schools and in employment." Acting on SNCC's organizing philosophy of supporting local people, he told the residents, "We can come into your community and give you a shot in the arm but the real job is up to you." The meeting ended with an announcement that there would be another desegregation protest the following weekend.[9]

Over the next couple of weeks, the pace of events steadily increased as Cambridge entered the early phase of its freedom movement. On 18 January students from the city's black Mace's Lane High School initiated and led their own demonstration when they picketed Collins' Drugstore. A few days later, with the help of a handful of younger black children, they targeted the Dizzyland restaurant. That same week, a few adults from the Second Ward established the Cambridge Nonviolent Action Committee (CNAC) and selected Freddie St. Clair and Enez Grubb as its cochairs.[10] Both were respected members of the Second Ward and brought something important to their roles. St. Clair was financially independent from the white community, which meant he could not be bullied into submission. Furthermore, he had already shown a high degree of interest in moving the city forward by contacting Hansen and

Robinson. Grubb was idealistic and energetic, qualities that were invaluable for a local movement that would likely run up against older residents' reluctance to embrace change. The fact that she was a woman also showed the community's forward-thinking attitude: whoever was capable and willing to do the work was the right person for it, regardless of gender.

Operating just like SNCC, CNAC would provide black Cambridge students with assistance and moral support as they worked to desegregate their city. The task would be a daunting one in light of the Eastern Shore's racial history, and early on, the *Daily Banner* printed stories that said as much. On the day CNAC was formed, the paper ran an article about a telegram sent by the Maryland branch of the NAACP to Cambridge's mayor Calvin Mowbray, Governor Tawes, and US attorney general Robert F. Kennedy. NAACP officials expressed "grave concern" about the safety of demonstrators during the upcoming protests on the Eastern Shore, and they sought assurances that the protesters would have adequate law enforcement protection from potential white assailants. The newspaper's editors echoed the NAACP's concerns, but only because they were worried that white "extremists" could create major problems for the county's image. "There are elements in the world that would like nothing better than to lump Cambridge with Little Rock as cities where the rights of American citizens are not respected." The white people of Cambridge needed to embrace a culture of law and order and reject mob violence as a means of maintaining segregation, and if they failed to support black citizens' right to seek redress for their grievances, Cambridge's allegedly progressive record on race would be tarnished, and the county's economic investment and growth would suffer.[11] Implicit in the editorial was an assumption that the white community of Cambridge would never behave like the white people of Little Rock, who had tried to block nine black children from integrating the city's white high school; by extension, there would be no need for a military presence in Cambridge to keep the peace between the races. Of course, what happened over the next eighteen months showed just how badly the editors missed the mark in their assessment of the white community.

From the beginning of the demonstrations, white people resisted any attempt to change the racial status quo, and stories circulated in the press about the intimidation of activists and their supporters. One such allegation was levied at James G. Busick, the white superintendent of Dorchester County's public schools. Some students from Mace's Lane High School claimed that Busick had forbidden them from "us[ing] the word 'freedom' in any shape or form," something the superintendent refused to confirm or deny. Local activists sent a telegram to President John F. Kennedy, Attorney General Robert F.

Kennedy, and Governor Tawes, claiming that federal intervention was necessary because law enforcement officers had failed to provide even minimal protection to the demonstrators, as evidenced by their being menaced and attacked by white people during the latest protests. The telegram also alleged that white law enforcement officers had been among the assailants.[12]

While some Cambridge residents were out in public jostling one another during the protests, others were writing letters to the editors of the *Daily Banner* to express their own opinions about race relations in the city. Second Ward resident Mrs. Joseph Saunders said race relations were pitiful and were based on white people's racial prejudice, which allowed them to rationalize the city's employment structure that privileged themselves over black people, who suffered further indignities when they were prevented from spending their money freely because businesses were segregated. The Reverend John W. Ringold (vice president of Dorchester County's recently reactivated NAACP chapter) and CNAC's Freddie St. Clair also framed recent events as an organic development. They told white readers that the "outsiders" who came to Cambridge served only as a catalyst for local black people's desire to free themselves from racial oppression.[13]

White people's view on the matter was the inverse. One wrote that the black liberation movement was an "integration disorder"—a sign that America was moving away from the principle of "free and private enterprise" that guaranteed a business owner the "right to select his customers." The origins of this cultural shift allegedly stemmed from the "octopus of communism," which had gotten its arms into every aspect of American society and disguised communist ideals as democratic freedoms and Judeo-Christian ethics such as "the golden rule, [and] the ten commandments." The *Banner* noted claims made by white politicians, including Dorchester County's Democratic state senator Frederick C. Malkus and its state's attorney C. Burnham Mace, who said that race relations in Cambridge were good but were threatened by black people's protests.[14]

The *Daily Banner*'s editorials and stories revealed a perception gap between the white and black communities. Editors acknowledged that Dorchester County was not a perfect place, but it was a "community [that] has a long list of accomplishments in the area of race relations." More work needed to be done in this area, the editors acknowledged, but this would best be accomplished by local people working on their own initiatives through biracial committees. They were certain that nothing would change in Cambridge as long as white people felt they were being coerced into change by "freedom raids" conducted by an "invasion" of nonlocal college students.

The *Banner*'s view of race relations and how to improve them reflected what historian William Chafe describes as the "progressive mystique." Its subscribers "believe that conflict is inherently bad, that disagreement means personal dislike, and that consensus offers the only way to preserve a genteel and civilized way of life." According to Chafe, "The underlying assumption [about the progressive mystique] is that conflict over any issue, whether it be labor unions, race relations, or political ideology, will permanently rend the fragile fabric of internal harmony. Hence, progress can occur only when everyone is able to agree—voluntarily—on an appropriate course of action." In other words, white people will permit societal change only when it is based on "consensus, voluntarism, and the preservation of civility."[15]

For the next two months, black and white people engaged in a tug-of-war over CNAC's demands. *Banner* editors were the most vociferous promoters of the narrative that white people were being reasonable and should discuss racial grievances only with "responsible" black people who did not "[fall] for the racial propaganda" espoused by CIG, CORE, and SNCC. These organizations were accused of blinding black residents to Cambridge's racial progress and to the "opportunities now unfolding for them." Despite black people's alleged confusion about their own situation, the editors found "some evidence that our colored citizens are beginning to see the need for a sense of responsibility. This," they added condescendingly, "is the first mark of good citizenship." The recent reactivation of Dorchester's NAACP chapter had shown that "responsible local leadership" was arising in the Second Ward, and that organization would serve as "an important point of contact" between black Cambridge and the city's white power structure. "The chapter needs to develop a program and a timetable for progress. With this in hand," the editors continued, "the community can begin that careful negotiation which alone will lead to solid improvement in the community." Editorials like this were unvarnished attempts by white opinion makers to privilege the NAACP and so-called moderate black leaders over CNAC and its members, who were characterized as "local extremists." Since its founding in 1909, the NAACP used the court system as its primary means of achieving societal change, whereas CIG, CORE, and SNCC applied pressure on the system from outside. Interestingly, these editorials did not name CNAC, which may have been an attempt to avoid legitimizing it. However, no one in the Second Ward was confused about what CNAC meant to the black community; it was a critical support system for black children working to improve their own lives.[16]

Some members of the Second Ward agreed with the *Banner*'s viewpoints. On the morning after Cambridge's first civil rights demonstration, the

Reverend Richard C. Hubbard, chairman of the newly established Housing Authority and pastor of Grace Methodist Church, told his congregants that black Cambridge had "gotten all confused with two words—Integration and Equality"—which made it hard for people to be "certain as to what they want to believe." When Edythe Jolley, the principal of Mace's Lane High School, reportedly said that "Freedom Riders are not needed in Cambridge," some of her students responded by picketing her home, and an unknown vandal threw a brick through one of its windows. The black community's conservative element had been downplaying the extent of the city's racial issues for many years. Jackie Fassett recalled one instance in the 1950s when she had been scolded by some black people for being vocal about Cambridge's race problems.[17] Yet inside the Second Ward, the mood was hopeful that change would come. Pushback against councilman Charles Cornish was beginning to originate from within the ward. Mrs. Joseph Saunders had argued in her *Daily Banner* letter that he was part of the city's race problem rather than part of its solution. As an elected official, Cornish benefited directly from his constituents' tax dollars, so he should be doing more on residents' behalf. "Instead of staying at home or siding with the whites," Mrs. Saunders wrote, "he should be at the front of the (C.I.G.) helping his own people."[18]

Gloria Richardson was also dissatisfied with Cornish. The political system rewarded racial gradualists like Cornish and his predecessor, Richardson's grandfather Maynadier St. Clair, but she saw an important distinction between the two politicians. St. Clair had lived through black America's lowest points since the end of Reconstruction, which included terrible social, economic, and political realities and the ever-present threat of lynchings. She did not extend this understanding to Cornish. So much had changed in white America since her grandfather's time in office, and because of those changes, a gradualist strategy was no longer necessary. For example, white people had rejected European fascism, and the federal government had joined the United Nations, a body that included a Commission on Human Rights. The US military became fully integrated after the Korean War, and legal mechanisms of white supremacy, including the white political primary (1944) and segregated education, had fallen. On the ground, black liberation movements had been percolating in the South since the Montgomery, Alabama, bus boycott in the mid-1950s. The southern student movement exemplified by CORE's Freedom Rides and SNCC's grassroots organizing was further evidence that the nation was ripe for a much more aggressive assault on white supremacy. As such, black leaders' gradualism seemed passé to Richardson, and it meant that black liberation would take hundreds of years to achieve, an unacceptable strategy for people who wanted their freedom *now*. Black leaders' gradualism was also called into question when it was perceived, rightly or wrongly, that they had a personal interest in maintaining the racial status quo. Cornish was a case in point; he owned a bus company that had a contract to transport black students to black schools, and he would have lost money if the school district was integrated.[19]

When Richardson first heard about Freedom Riders coming to the Eastern Shore in December 1961, it seemed to her as if all that activity was happening thousands of miles away, "like in Europe, . . . and I was so busy that it kind of went in one ear and out the other." It was only after activists came to Cambridge that she realized the freedom movement was occurring all around her. Richardson's first contact with those activists occurred when they stopped by her family's pharmacy to inquire about local "guides" who could show them around town while they planned protests. She suggested her teenage daughter Donna, who was eager to join them. Richardson explained her reasons for allowing her daughter to participate: "It would give the kids something constructive to do." In addition, she thought that "somebody should help [the civil rights movement] locally," for which "there would be hell to pay." In those early months of 1962, Richardson joined other adult observers on the sidelines, where they watched their children engage in "disciplined and courageous" actions.[20]

It was at this point that Richardson realized these young people were leading the adults in the black community toward greater involvement in the black liberation struggle. Wanting to do more than simply observe, Richardson walked the picket line with her daughter a couple of times, but she got in trouble for trying to trip white onlookers she accused of being belligerent toward the demonstrators. Richardson was only protecting her daughter and the other teenagers, but the students were in charge of the demonstrations, and Donna sent her mother home until she could guarantee that she would demonstrate nonviolently, as they had been trained to do. It was a commitment Richardson could not make at the time, but her behavior gained her respect in the black community: it showed she was ready for a fight with white people. Instead, she focused her energies on working with the black community's secretive and highly efficient intelligence-sharing network, known as the "grapevine." Operating from within her family's drugstore, Richardson provided information to CIG and SNCC about how Cambridge's political system operated, as well as "what the black community was thinking or saying."[21]

White Cambridge believed it was approaching the city's racial issues with the best of intentions. Its leaders created an Equal Opportunities Commission (EOC) that sponsored interracial "seminars," which identified three areas Cambridge needed to focus on: interracial relations, employment opportunities for black people, and open accommodations in restaurants. With regard to jobs, the EOC stated that employment opportunities existed for black residents, and their ability to obtain such jobs would be driven largely by their qualifications. Additionally, after the EOC failed to convince white restaurant owners to voluntarily desegregate their establishments, it suggested that the mayor and City Council members should take the lead and try to change owners' minds.[22]

As the demonstrations became more frequent, white leaders expressed concern about their effect on the city's image, as well as the possibility of violence breaking out between black people and white people. White leaders therefore demanded an end to the demonstrations before they would take any steps to address the students' demands. A few prominent members of the black community supported this approach, including Councilman Cornish and several ministers. They promised the student-activists that if they ceased protesting, white politicians and business owners would negotiate an end to segregated public accommodations. Taking them at their word, the students stopped demonstrating, but the white leaders and business owners failed to make good on their promise. As a result, black students' enthusiasm was replaced by a feeling of discouragement. According to Richardson, white leaders' foot-dragging was predictable because, in her words, Cambridge was a "one-company town," and the owners and operators of Phillips Packing Company behaved paternalistically toward all residents, irrespective of race.[23] In practice, this meant that the white men who controlled the city thought they knew how black people and white people felt about racial issues, and they calculated that a hands-off, wait-and-see strategy was their best course of action.

With the student movement stymied, CNAC modified its mission from one of student support to one of adult assumption of responsibility for restarting Cambridge's liberation struggle. This coincided with a change in CNAC's leadership. In April, Freddie St. Clair resigned as cochair because he felt that being a bail bondsman for arrested activists created a conflict of interest. CNAC's executive committee asked Richardson to replace him. The committee's rationale was that Richardson belonged to the same well-respected St. Clair family, and she had earned social credibility through her community advocacy work in the 1950s. Additionally, she was completely immune to white Cambridge's financial pressures. Richardson was initially reluctant to accept the position because it would take up a lot of time, and she was already dedicated to raising her children and running a business. Up to this point, she had not really been involved with CNAC, even though the activists had been "bugging" her to attend meetings.[24]

When she considered CNAC's request, Richardson came away with a positive impression of the organization. It was based on SNCC's grassroots and group-centered model of social change, and it was an independent organization that answered to its own members and not to a regional or national office. Among other things, this meant that no one else could veto CNAC's goals, strategies, and tactics. This was especially important to activists who needed to respond immediately in a "fluid situation," because quick decision making would allow them to make the most of circumstances and events. Richardson also found the composition of CNAC's executive committee conducive to meeting the community's needs; it consisted of "key" persons from the Second Ward who were respected by their neighbors and worked together to coordinate the Cambridge movement's daily operations.[25]

CNAC welcomed people from all walks of life into its fold, and the organization made a conscious effort not to privilege one person's sexuality, political or economic philosophy, or religion over another's. This approach to community outreach was in alignment with SNCC's, whose founding statement includes both religious and humanist elements that stress cooperation and understanding among people. Richardson saw CNAC's organizing philosophy as one of its keys strengths, along with the fact that there were no clergymen on its executive committee. The latter vastly improved its chances of building a community-wide movement because it avoided dividing people along denominational lines, which would have undermined the community's cohesion. This is not to say that CNAC ignored people's faith and religiosity—quite the contrary. Cambridge's movement was grounded in part in black Christian liberation theology, which holds that the god of the Bible is a just god who wants black people to be free in this world, not just in the next one. This type of faith led many people in Cambridge to join and support the movement, and they prayed before and after demonstrations and meetings and sang freedom songs, many of which have their roots in black Christianity. Yet CNAC successfully presented the Cambridge movement as an all-for-one and one-for-all movement that was big enough for the believers and their humanist neighbors like Richardson.[26]

At a public meeting held in Bethel African Methodist Episcopal (AME) Church, CNAC formally asked Richardson to join the organization and serve as its cochair with Enez Grubb, and she agreed. The opportunity to give back to the Second Ward was important to Richardson. "I had lived well because my father and grandfather had been able to make a living [from] this community, and . . . I needed to give something back to my community." SNCC's Bill Hansen welcomed the change in CNAC's leadership because Richardson was the type of person SNCC had in mind when it talked about cultivating local leaders. "She was clearly quite intelligent with a dry wit, more than a little candor, especially for a woman in those days and a level of analysis that was clearly far more sophisticated than that of most people (including Reggie and myself) who were involved. In our minds Gloria became essential for any sort of long-term movement and progress in Cambridge." And in Cambridge's forward-thinking black community, no one objected to two women being at the helm of CNAC.[27]

Another change came when CNAC established a formal relationship with SNCC and aligned with its direct action wing. With this affiliation, the Cambridge group hoped to obtain continued logistical support and ideas about how to employ the organizing strategies and tactics SNCC had implemented in other local movements in the South. Using donations collected in the Second Ward, Richardson and Yolanda St. Clair (wife of Freddie) flew to Atlanta in April to attend SNCC's annual conference, the first of a handful of such gatherings Richardson would attend over the next two years. Wearing summer dresses and white gloves, the two women stood out among the crowd of more than 200 conferees wearing the de facto uniform of SNCC: jeans and white shirts.[28]

The conference was a lively event where the attendees shared their experiences and ideas about organizing and used their time together to bond and build camaraderie. The latter was an especially important aspect of these gatherings because activists were often stationed in small, geographically isolated towns and villages around the South. Some of the civil rights movement's most important movers and shakers attended SNCC conferences, and they made lasting impressions on Richardson. Few people at the April conference were more highly esteemed than Ella Baker. Addressed by everyone as "Miss Baker," she had a long history of human rights activism dating back to the 1920s. Richardson described her as "very laid back [and] very ordinary," but Baker was a radical humanist who had worked as an organizer for the NAACP and SCLC. SNCC would not have existed without Baker's vision or influence. She had recognized the student sit-in movement as the most promising development in civil rights activism in her lifetime, and she helped secure a donation from the SCLC to sponsor the student conference where

SNCC was born. The SCLC's leader, Martin Luther King Jr., had envisioned these students as a youth wing of his group, but Baker knew that the SCLC's leader-driven and hierarchical structure would discourage the students' creative thinking and sap their energy. Working behind the scenes, Baker encouraged the students to remain independent and focus their energy on establishing a group-centered, member-driven organization of their own.[29]

Julian Bond, a founding member of SNCC, interrupted his senior year at Atlanta's Morehouse College to become the organization's communications director. Ruby Doris Smith Robinson put her studies at Spelman College on hold so that she could work for SNCC. The Atlanta native was known for her pleasant yet no-nonsense personality and for being highly astute. The latter was a virtual necessity for her eventual role as SNCC's executive secretary, which required her to administer large parts of SNCC's operations, including its fleet of vehicles. Sisters Dorie and Joyce Ladner had begun their human rights activism years earlier when they joined an NAACP youth council in Hattiesburg, Mississippi. Their work in that organization brought them into contact with Medgar Evers, who took an interest in the sisters and mentored and groomed them for race service. While attending historically black Jackson State College in Mississippi, the Ladners joined up with SNCC and worked on local projects in the state.[30]

Richardson was "in awe" of these and other SNCC activists, and many of them had strong feelings about her as well. Dorie Ladner recalled meeting the "soft-spoken" and "very, very strong-willed" Richardson at the spring 1962 conference. Ladner felt an immediate connection to the Cambridge activist, who reminded the young Mississippian of her own mother, who "was very straightforward with blacks and whites and she taught us to be straightforward and not to back down." Her sister Joyce remarked that Richardson was "approachable and easy to talk to," and as time went on, the younger SNCC activists viewed her as "an older person to be looked up to . . . because she had proven herself. [Richardson] had just tremendous credibility."[31]

That conference was an important experience for Richardson, and she learned some salient lessons there. One was that for the Cambridge movement to be effective, CNAC had to operate in ways that brought it closer to its goals and reduced the chance that members could be played against one another by their opponents. Upon Richardson's return from the conference, CNAC began to hold closed-door strategy meetings. When meeting with white leaders, CNAC made sure there were at least two members of its executive committee present, so no one could claim that someone had cut a deal with white leaders behind CNAC's back. The SNCC conference also reiter-ated a lesson Richardson had learned from her grandfather: take a reading of the black community to learn how its members feel about important issues to ensure that your goals are those of the community. To achieve this, CNAC conducted a needs assessment in the Second Ward to identify residents' primary concerns. This was achieved through a formal survey designed by Richardson—a skill she had learned at Howard University—and administered by local residents door-to-door.[32]

The survey revealed that 42 percent of residents considered jobs the most pressing issue, followed by housing (26 percent), improved schools (21 percent), open accommodations (6 percent), and police brutality (5 percent). The results surprised Richardson, who had expected public accommodations to be black residents' biggest concern because it had been the focus of their protests. But as one respondent pointed out: "You can't eat in those restaurants if you don't have the money."[33] Enlightened by these findings, CNAC began a multipronged campaign to encourage black voter registration, increase employment opportunities for black workers, and end racially segregated education by having black parents apply to transfer their children to white schools. CNAC continued to hold protests at various white-owned businesses, which were relatively easy to attack. The demonstrations also drew media attention, which allowed the black community's grievances to be telegraphed outside of Cambridge. All these goals were more likely to be attained if the civil rights organizations operating on the Eastern Shore coordinated their work. Since its creation, CNAC had been open to working in coalition with others who supported black people's right to self-determination. For example, CNAC collaborated with Baltimore's Civic Interest Group and students involved in the predominantly white northern student movement in planning and executing Project Eastern Shore, which took place in the summer of 1962. The project focused heavily on community organizing for voter education and registration, educating factory workers about the benefits of unionization, and providing tutoring services to improve students' performance so they could be academically successful at all-white schools if they chose to transfer to them.[34]

Richardson was one of the parents who led the drive to desegregate the schools. She and other members of CNAC believed it was important for black parents to apply for school transfers so that white residents could see how serious they were about desegregation. Tamara Richardson was initially reluctant to be part of the desegregation process, but she agreed when her mother told her that she would be lending support to the movement. Tamara and a couple of other black children desegregated the fourth grade at Academy School, while Donna and three other black teenagers desegregated Cambridge High School's eleventh grade. White parents and their children did not try to prevent the black students from attending these schools, and there were no dramatic scenes like those in Little Rock, Arkansas. Tamara's teacher treated her no differently from the white students, and she became friends with a few of them; she stayed in the class for the entire school year. Donna and the other black students left the white high school after three weeks and transferred back to Mace's Lane. The *Daily Banner* reported that although the black students had no issues with their teachers, the white students gave them the "silent treatment," making their experience unbearable. Actually, there was more to the story. The silent treatment did not bother Donna, but she recalled that there was plenty of open "hostility, mainly name calling from the students," which created a "stressful situation." Gloria Richardson supported Donna's decision to leave the school, and she alleged publicly that the teachers had played a role in creating a hostile environment because they "didn't do too good a job of maintaining classroom discipline."[35]

Voting became a focal point of CNAC's community organizing. It conducted a voter education program and voter registration drives that activists promoted through announcements in churches and halls. The intent of such activities, done in collaboration with SNCC activists and the local NAACP chapter, was to raise citizens' consciousness about politics. As a result of CNAC's political organizing work, people developed a greater awareness of public officials' statements and actions, and the process itself dispelled the myth that all politicians are alike. Richardson doubted that having more black voters would actually improve life in the Second Ward because gerrymandering favored white voters. "For me [voting] was a chance to organize throughout the county and to prove that it didn't help," said Richardson, although she would have been happy if she had been proved wrong. When election time came a few months later, the increase in black voters helped send a strong message of dissatisfaction to local and state politicians who opposed a public housing project and a statewide open accommodations law. However, the election validated her assessment that voting within racially gerrymandered districts left white people's political power intact.[36] In the very near future the topic of voting would distinguish the Cambridge movement from other local movements in the Deep South where people were fighting to obtain the right to vote. Furthermore, CNAC's eventual position on voting would place it at odds with almost all national civil rights organizations, including the NAACP, and result in an irreconcilable rift between them.

Richardson's support of voter education and registration tells us a lot about her nonelitist view of social activism. She fully endorsed CNAC's use of the democratic principle whereby each member of its executive committee had one vote and everyone worked at building consensus among the group. When they gathered to talk about strategy or tactical moves, everyone participated, and even though "everybody [on the executive committee] had a strong personality," no one tried to dominate. There were occasions when those meetings turned into "stomping down fights" about tactics or timing, but no one engaged in personal attacks. For example, Sally Garrison, a working-class woman who was receiving public assistance, had suggested the voter education program. When all was said and done, Richardson realized that Garrison had been right all along about its value, illustrating that "nobody has all the answers." CNAC was a strong organization because it drew on the opinions and perspectives of people with different experiences and backgrounds.[37]

Another early collaborative effort between CNAC and the NAACP took place when they invited Martin Luther King Jr. to a mass rally in June 1962 to increase publicity for the Cambridge movement. The president of Dorchester County's NAACP chapter, the Reverend T. M. Murray, asked King to come to Cambridge and deliver a speech that would serve as a "stimulus . . . to motivate, enlighten, and encourage the group in [their] efforts toward freedom." King's other commitments prevented him from speaking in Cambridge, which Richardson actually found advantageous for the Cambridge movement: rather than relying on a dynamic speaker to draw people to the movement, CNAC did "basic community organizing" that resulted in residents' being more invested in their own freedom struggle.[38]

As important as school desegregation and voter education were to black people, the majority of them were more concerned with the bread-and-butter issues of housing and jobs. Almost 75 percent of black residents rented rather than owned their homes, whereas approximately 45 percent of white families lived in rental properties. Black and white homes also differed in basic amenities: more than 80 percent of residences in the Second Ward lacked adequate plumbing, versus less than 20 percent of residences in the city's white wards.[39] Adequate housing was such an important issue to black residents that hundreds of congregants from Waugh Methodist Episcopal Church sent a letter to the Dorchester County commissioners asking them to support the proposed public housing project consisting of 100 family units. The letter, which was read during the commissioners' meeting, lamented the public comments emanating from business and political leaders. Although these people mentioned "progress and development" as desirable goals for

Dorchester County, they failed to consider residents' quality of life, specifically with regard to available housing, as an essential ingredient of that progress and development. "Ours is a Christian demand for *social justice* for all the people," the letter read, and without an increase in affordable housing, city residents would find it difficult to adjust to the changing world.[40]

On the employment front, CNAC moved to desegregate local industries, some of which were part of the nation's growing military-industrial complex supported by the federal government's increased spending on the Cold War. Despite the presence of a high-tech sector in the area, Cambridge lagged behind other Eastern Shore towns because of white business and political leaders' antiunion sentiment, something that dated back to the early twentieth century. The most visible labor conflict had been the strike of 1937, when some strike leaders had been imprisoned on dubious charges. However, one of the most telling examples of business leaders' power was their ability to create purportedly independent unions of canning workers that were actually pro–Phillips Packing Company unions. This neutralized any chance of a real labor movement in Cambridge—and an interracial one at that. Since the end of World War II, white leaders had maintained this posture against independent unions as they tried to attract businesses to replace the canning industry, which was on the decline.[41]

Five months of negotiations between CNAC and local merchants failed to secure black workers equal pay for equal work or greater opportunities for blue- and white-collar jobs. CNAC thus initiated a "selective buying" campaign to pressure the white community into compliance. Reverend Murray and the NAACP gave "moral approval" to CNAC's campaign because the two groups "stand on the same principles." The head of the city's Equal Opportunities Committee called the campaign "ill advised" because the boycott would set back the racial progress allegedly made in Cambridge. A late-August editorial in the *Daily Banner* reiterated the divided view of Cambridge's social, economic, and political climates, providing another example of white people's belief that black people needed to prove that they were mature enough to be treated as full-fledged citizens. The editors claimed that black residents had plenty of employment opportunities but lacked the necessary skills to fill these positions. Black workers who found jobs could either pave a positive path for others or pave a path of hardship if they "abuse[d] their new opportunities."[42]

White residents' protests against and condemnations of the selective buying campaign fell on deaf ears in the Second Ward. The black community knew too well that the city's workforce was racially stratified; generations of white business owners had privileged white workers over black workers, with the former gaining access to better-paying skilled and semiskilled jobs while the latter were relegated to menial labor on farms and in factories. Adding to black residents' economic woes was the fact that most of them were able to work only seasonally. The selective buying campaign was one way they could leverage the power of their purses to force local businesses to create real job opportunities rather than symbolic or token ones.[43]

When 1962 came to a close, Cambridge's white leaders assessed where the city had been and where it was going. They considered the expansion of the city's port the year's top story, and they expected it to dominate the news in the coming months. They also mentioned the city's "civil rights issue [that] simmered like an uncertain volcano." Despite this uncertainty, the *Daily Banner*'s editors were optimistic that Cambridge would continue to make racial progress. Black people were much less optimistic. Over the last twelve months, the white community had demonstrated that it did not have the will to dismantle the social and economic structures of its racial privilege. Having been mobilized and motivated to transform those structures themselves, black residents would soon show the world how they were going to change their own lives. Ironically, months earlier the *Daily Banner* had given its readership an indication of what might happen in Cambridge. The title of the paper's story about a sixteen-year-old human rights activist in Albany, Georgia—"Albany Girl Would Give up Her Life for Freedom"—showed how far some black people were willing to go to liberate themselves from white supremacy. The Second Ward was home to many people who felt the same way, including Gloria Richardson.[44]

6

Shock Therapy, Round Two

The year 1963 was an important one for the modern civil rights movement because a number of events occurred that affected the tenor of the black liberation movement for the remainder of the decade. Cambridge's local struggle and the ones in Birmingham, Alabama, and throughout Mississippi—and white people's responses to them—pulled back the curtain and exposed the depth of racial resentment in white communities from the mid-Atlantic to the Mississippi Delta. Activists in all these movements used demonstrations to execute their strategy of overwhelming local governments with mass arrests, but the movements differed with respect to their specific goals and the degree to which the federal government responded to them. Activists in the Deep South continued to focus on desegregation and the right to vote, whereas in Cambridge the focus was jobs, housing, and education. Officials in Washington kept the more southern movements at arm's length, but they fully engaged the Cambridge movement.

Gloria Richardson played a big role in the Kennedy administration's decision to work with the Cambridge Nonviolent Action Committee. By the summer of 1963, she was living her egalitarian philosophies concerning community organizing and democracy, and she was willing to risk her family's standing among the black elite to achieve CNAC's goals. For these reasons, Cambridge's black community easily acknowledged her as its leader, making her one of few women to achieve that position during the entire civil rights movement. She used creative means to keep the Cambridge movement viable, specifically by relying on family connections to sustain activists' momentum and by developing a leadership style that was confident, steadfast, focused, and impervious to co-optation. The Kennedy administration could not ignore the political reality on the ground in Cambridge, so it invited Richardson to the bargaining table where a solution could be hammered out. These were some of the main reasons why CNAC achieved in 1963 what had been out of reach since the early days of the Cambridge movement: the white community's formal agreement to take concrete steps to end the oppression of the black community.

Demonstrations and Demands; Threats and Arrests

Throughout the winter of 1962–1963 Cambridge's public accommodations remained segregated, black workers' job opportunities continued to lag behind those of white workers, and county officials failed to act on the proposed housing project. Undeterred, CNAC continued to focus on building a grassroots movement by holding meetings in the Second Ward, usually at churches. At first these meetings attracted no more than a few people, but as CNAC expanded its outreach efforts, more residents started to turn out. Besides holding meetings, Richardson and her cochair Enez Grubb spoke at City Council meetings and presented officials with demands that reinforced their goals of obtaining social and economic justice.[1] Jobs continued to be at the forefront of CNAC's agenda, and near the end of 1962 Richardson told the recently reelected Dorchester County sheriff that racial issues at the jail (such as black prisoners' claims of mistreatment by white staff members) might be defused if he hired a black man as a deputy sheriff and a black woman as a jail matron. She also reminded the sheriff that without the Second Ward's support he would not have been reelected, so he owed it to the black community to hire black civil servants.[2]

Not long afterward, black and white workers from the Rob Roy garment factory in Cambridge asked CNAC to attend a meeting of their labor union, the International Ladies' Garment Workers Union (ILGWU), where they were going to discuss the wage differential between themselves and garment workers in New York City, who were getting paid more money to do the same work. (This was one of the rare cases of an independent and interracial union operating in Cambridge.) The ILGWU sent two representatives, who defended the pay differential. This was not surprising, considering the organization's notorious history of showing favoritism to various locals, as well as engaging in outright racial discrimination. What followed became the first of numerous power moves by people trying to control Richardson specifically and the Cambridge movement in general. Richardson stood up for the Cambridge workers, which angered the ILGWU representatives, who verbally attacked her and accused her of being a communist. They also tried to have Richardson ejected from the meeting, but the workers defended her presence. The ILGWU representatives stopped by Richardson's home a few days later and told her to stop "interfering with union business." They threatened to contact SNCC and get it to silence her, and they warned of unnamed consequences if she stayed involved in the local workers' pay grievance. Richardson scoffed at their scare tactics and informed them that CNAC was an independent organization, and she had been living with threats on her life since joining the Cambridge movement, and they had not deterred her.[3]

It is unclear why the union representatives were so aggressive toward Richardson, but they may have seen the Cambridge dispute as similar to recent grievances by black and Puerto Rican workers in New York City's textile industry. Importantly, those internal challenges to the ILGWU were fortified by external ones coming from government officials. For example, at the time (early 1963), New York State was investigating the ILGWU for violation of state antidiscrimination laws, and Harlem's US congressman Adam Clayton Powell Jr. had recently concluded hearings about the organization's racial discrimination.[4] Throughout the remainder of the decade, organized labor in general would be pushed from both inside and outside its ranks to expand its membership and job opportunities for people of color. Civil rights activists, including Gloria Richardson, supported these challenges because they knew that an integrated labor movement based on equity benefited everyone.

Near the end of March 1963, CNAC increased its pressure on Cambridge's white officials. At the City Council meeting on 25 March, Richardson, Grubb, and CIG's Clarence Logan presented a two-page list of demands to the mayor and councilmen. Logan's presence shows that CNAC's executive committee was continuing to work in coalition with other civil rights organizations, as it did throughout the Cambridge movement. The demands included hiring a black civil servant in the Department of Employment Security, training and hiring black workers in local industries (specifically, in defense contractors' factories), and achievement of a hiring goal whereby black workers constituted 30 percent of the county's industrial workforce. CNAC's other demands focused on housing issues, specifically, expanding the city's sewer system throughout the entire Second Ward, getting local government to pass a public housing law, and creating federal housing projects. CNAC also demanded the complete desegregation of the school system and the busing of all students to the schools closest to their homes. Desegregation of public accommodations and entertainment sites (including the Dorset Theater, bowling alleys, and the roller rink at the Rescue and Fire Company arena) rounded out the organization's demands, which CNAC considered time sensitive because "our children are growing up and we wish to leave them more than hope." Richardson and Grubb told the white leaders they should use their political capital to convince the white community to change, and if they failed to show "concrete proof" that they were addressing CNAC's demands, the organization was prepared to take further action because it had "to fulfill [its] obligations to the Negro community."[5]

Threatening to demonstrate was only one tactic Richardson used to get white leaders to do the right thing. She also stroked their egos by paying them compliments she did not believe, and she challenged white people to rise to the occasion confronting them. "We do not think that Cambridge is less progressive than Salisbury," she said, referring to the nearby Eastern Shore town where white politicos had recently desegregated public accommodations. Mayor Calvin Mowbray may have agreed with Richardson on that point, but he and other city officials claimed they did not have the power to change everything in Cambridge (for example, the county government controlled the schools), and they noted that black workers did have employment opportunities. A terse entry in the City Council's minutes show just how unconcerned local government was about the black community's demands: "A delegation was present relative to equal opportunities."[6] Downplaying CNAC's grievances and demands played well among these politicians' white constituents, but it told CNAC that white leaders had to undergo another round of shock therapy to force them to cease their oppression of the black community.

The first event was a day of protests organized by CNAC in coalition with CIG and students from Maryland State College at Princess Anne and other regional colleges. Just as it had done prior to other protests, CNAC's executive committee organized nonviolent direct action training sessions that introduced new activists to the movement and reinforced experienced activists' preparation. Because white people had attacked activists during previous demonstrations, CNAC asked for state police protection, but local officials refused and claimed they could handle any potential violence. CNAC's request was another attempt to draw a higher level of government into Cambridge's racial problems so that it could apply pressure on local officials.

On 30 March protesters gathered at Mount Sinai Baptist Church before moving on to four locations: the Dorset Theater, the offices of the Maryland State Employment Service, Airpax Electronics Corporation (a defense contractor), and the Rescue and Fire Company (RFC) arena, which housed a roller rink. Richardson and more than a dozen other activists headed to the RFC arena, where they attempted to gain admission to the racially segregated facility. She told the fire chief that the arena was public property, and they should have access to it. The fire chief called the police to have the demonstrators removed, and when police chief Brice G. Kinnamon showed up, he began to argue with Richardson. The *Baltimore Sun* reported that he arrested her after first "seiz[ing] her roughly by the left arm and jerk[ing] her down the three steps." Richardson's actions that day showed just how fully she had embraced the tactic of nonviolent direct action. She calmly stood up to men who represented the city's white power structure, and she did so with dignity and determination. It was one of the many times over the course of the Cambridge movement that Richardson led her fellow activists by example. While Richardson was being arrested by the chief, other officers were doing the same to more than a dozen activists, including John "Johnnie" Wilson of Maryland State College and Mariam "Mimi" Feingold of Swarthmore College. Police charged everyone with refusal to obey a police officer, disorderly conduct, and tending to incite a riot. The rest of the demonstrators moved to a small park next to the jail and sang "We Shall Overcome" before gathering for a silent prayer. When the demonstrators began to parade through the city streets, white people verbally harassed and "shoved . . . and threw pennies and pebbles at them."[7] Richardson was bailed out a short time later and proceeded to Mount Sinai Baptist Church, where she was welcomed by a group of approximately eighty people. She encouraged them to engage in a "full-scale boycott of the downtown area," which was "the only way we are going to break Cambridge." CIG's Clarence Logan spoke briefly to the group about the next steps in building a stronger social change movement in Cambridge, and he noted that to do so, they had to "stick with Gloria," an acknowledgment that the black community already considered Richardson one of its leaders.[8]

Throughout the month of April, CNAC orchestrated more direct action demonstrations at which dozens of activists were arrested. These events brought more public attention to the plight of black people in Cambridge, and they helped build support in the Second Ward because of the culture they created around the movement itself. CNAC held mass meetings where Richardson and her colleagues discussed demonstration plans and delivered speeches to build up people's excitement and courage, which would fortify them when they encountered white people's verbal and physical opposition. Ministers delivered sermons that tended to activists' spiritual and religious needs, and these meetings usually ended with the singing of freedom songs, which bound people together even more. The fact that almost all the activists from SNCC, CIG, and CORE were put up in homes in the Second Ward added to the communal aspect of the movement. Sharing meals and living quarters with people who sought the same goal of black liberation was a powerful binding agent, and it resulted in a camaraderie more commonly seen among military personnel. The military comparison is an apt one because CNAC had established a highly organized command system that it operated from two posts within the Second Ward—Richardson's Muir Street home and her pharmacy—and they utilized a "walkie-talkie brigade" managed by a local high school student.[9]

The "Penny Trial"

The arrests of Richardson and other activists during the March and April demonstrations resulted in a large caseload for the local court system, so officials decided to try all the defendants together. Richardson was one of more than fifty people who stood trial in early May on charges of disorderly conduct in a proceeding that became known as the "Penny Trial." This judicial proceeding was a snapshot of how the Cambridge movement disrupted white elites' racial comfort zones, and it showcased Richardson's self-assurance in the face of government power, adding to her stature as a community leader. Presiding over the trial was Judge W. Laird Henry Jr., who, interestingly, had also presided over Richardson's divorce. A Princeton graduate, Henry hailed from an old and powerful Dorchester County family, and he knew Richardson's family. He had attended St. Clair family members' funerals, where he and his white relatives would "sit in the front row," and he had addressed Maynadier St. Clair as "cousin." Richardson found this odd, and she suspected that their families may have been related, a matter of conjecture among other residents as well.[10]

The defense team added an element of theater to the four-hour trial. Representing the defendants were two legal heavy hitters: Fred Weisgal of the American Civil Liberties Union, and Louis Redding, a family friend of the St. Clairs. After graduating from Harvard Law School, Redding opened a practice in Wilmington, Delaware, becoming the first black attorney in the state's history. He was the legal counsel for the black students who successfully desegregated the University of Delaware in 1950, and he served as a member of the NAACP's famed legal team that defeated public school segregation in the *Brown* case.[11] Redding's work on the Penny Trial was the first of many times during the Cambridge movement that Richardson's network of family friends and associates would intersect with her civil rights activities.

After the attorneys delivered their closing arguments, Judge Henry found the defendants guilty, levied a symbolic fine of one penny on each of them, and suspended their payments. Henry argued that the media coverage of the trial had unfairly maligned Cambridge's white community as incorrigible racists who were resistant to the winds of change pushing America toward integration. He cited an article by Ruth Van D. Todd, a white newspaper reporter for the *Sun*, as proof of the unbalanced reporting on Cambridge's race problem. She had written about the "stalemate in the cold war of integration grip[ping] Dorchester county," whose battle line separated black residents, who had rising expectations that their Eastern Shore community would soon have the same types of freedom western Europeans were experiencing—and that black military personnel had helped them obtain during World War II—from white residents, who lacked the political and social will to confront that aspect of society that "brings about the demonstrations." Todd also argued that white people were in denial that black citizens had legitimate grievances—namely, that they had a right to employment, housing, and educational opportunities—and she debunked the idea that the demonstrations were caused by "outsiders," as some white people claimed.[12]

College students made up a large portion of the defendant pool, and the judge scolded them for "traveling around to strange communities and making nuisances of [themselves]," rather than focusing on their studies. Henry then singled out Richardson and declared he had never known "a finer gentleman" than her grandfather Maynadier St. Clair, and he asked rhetorically if it was "fair" for her to criticize Cambridge's white residents, who were "trying so hard to do what is good for you and your people." He cited a few examples of integration in educational institutions and the police force, but that only showed how differently he and Richardson viewed things: what he saw as progress, she saw as token efforts intended to sap the Cambridge movement's momentum. The judge probably expected her to nod her head in agreement with his positive view of Cambridge's racial climate, and that may have been why he asked her: "[do you] know of any other community in this area making greater strides in integration than Cambridge?" The judge broke a cardinal rule of the legal profession: never ask a witness a question unless you know how she will answer it. "You are not going to like this," Richardson began, "but I think far greater progress is being made in Salisbury."[13]

One can speculate why Henry asked Richardson such a loaded question. Historian Peter Levy argues that it was because Henry expected Richardson to play along with white leaders' gradualist agenda, which is what her grandfather had done. Or perhaps Henry expected Richardson to defer to him because of his age (he was of her mother's generation) or because of some unspoken familial connection that would compel her to close ranks with him during this tumultuous time. Last, one cannot ignore the likelihood that the judge's race and gender did not allow him to even consider the possibility that a black woman would disagree with him.

The ramifications of the Penny Trial were significant for the white community and its leaders. Richardson's refusal to accommodate Judge Henry increased her social and political standing within the black community, and it highlighted the shifting power dynamic within the Second Ward. Councilman Charles Cornish was the formally elected leader of the black community, but he no longer possessed the political power to speak on its behalf because Richardson had supplanted him in that role. This was a major blow to white leaders' strategy of laissez-faire gradualism, because Richardson eschewed any type of compromise on issues concerning black people's rights. In addition, white leaders no longer had a small cadre of financially secure black residents of the Second Ward who could channel their working-class neighbors' rage into actions that white leaders found socially and politically acceptable. White leaders were entering uncharted political territory; they had to deal with an organization operating from outside the political system and a leader with no interest in pacifying the black community.

The trial itself and Richardson's testimony highlighted CNAC's rejection of the politics of respectability, which had been a large part of the protest strategy of civil rights activism since the 1950s. That strategy was employed by black people who were concerned about white people's perception of the black liberation struggle. To garner support from the white community, those activists argued, demonstrators should be seen as "respectable" members of their community. They could create this impression during demonstrations by wearing church attire, not arguing with counter-demonstrators, and not retaliating if attacked.[14] CNAC's uniform of choice was the same as SNCC's—jeans, white shirts, and sneakers—and Richardson (as well as some others) did not shy away from verbally challenging white people who harassed them. The composition of CNAC's executive committee also showed the organization's unwillingness to engage in the politics of respectability. The committee had approximately fifteen members drawn from throughout the Second Ward, including one person who received public assistance. Richardson reinforced CNAC's egalitarian philosophy when she took a stand in support of a local black man who had a reputation for public intoxication. He had every right to be involved in the Cambridge movement, Richardson argued, and it did not matter to her whether anyone believed his presence reflected poorly on CNAC.[15]

There is no hard evidence that the Penny Trial had anything to do with it, but Judge Henry was hospitalized for a serious "circulatory ailment" just three weeks later and spent the summer convalescing. In April of the following year (1964), he abruptly resigned his judgeship, a position he had held for more than twenty years. Henry's resignation letter did not include his reason for leaving the bench, but Richardson and others thought the stress of the trial might have been a contributing factor to his poor health. On a symbolic level, his illness and retirement pointed to the possibility that Cambridge's white community could be broken by CNAC, but the white community showed little indication that it was willing to bend. In fact, Henry's handling of the Penny Trial actually buttressed the white community's resistance to CNAC's goal of open public accommodations because many saw his ruling as an insult to the white community's standards of law and order. Not surprisingly, the white community seethed when CNAC resumed mass demonstrations one week after the trial.[16]

Conflict Escalates and Power Shifts

The events of 14 May 1963 turned into something of a family affair for three generations of St. Clairs when they were arrested and sent to the Dorchester County jail in Cambridge. It started when Richardson's mother Mable (who had moved back to Cambridge to take care of her granddaughters) told Gloria she would not be refused service at a "greasy spoon" restaurant in Cambridge, even though it was only for white people. Almost as a dare, Richardson told her mother to go ahead and try, which is exactly what Mable did. Gloria accompanied her mother as she headed over to the Dizzyland restaurant, where, to Mable's surprise, employees refused to serve them. When they refused to leave, Mable and Gloria were arrested and charged with trespass and failing to obey an officer. Later that day Richardson's daughter Donna was arrested while participating in a lay-in at the Dorset Theater. The black community was infuriated when it learned that police officers had roughed up many of the dozen or so teenaged demonstrators, so hundreds of black people, some of them armed with guns and knives, marched to the jail. There, they were greeted by police officers, who watched the protesters sing and shout as they circled the jail three times. Police charged some of the demonstrators with disorderly conduct, but many of them had to be released because the jail could not accommodate such a large number of arrestees.[17]

The night of the Dorset Theater arrests was a watershed event in the Cambridge movement. Up to that point, the black community's support for the movement had been gradually increasing, but the police's brutalization of the child protesters actually worked against white leaders because it convinced the remaining holdouts in the Second Ward to support CNAC. Prior to this time, white leaders had always claimed that CNAC did not speak for the Second Ward and that only a small fraction of black residents supported it. White residents believed this because most black residents did not participate in demonstrations: either they could not afford to take time off from work or their employers threatened to fire them if they did. Instead, those black residents supported the movement in less visible or nonpublic ways such as holding fund-raising suppers and dances, housing and feeding activists from out of town, and chipping in money to bail demonstrators out of jail. This community support was so widespread that it even extended to some of the Second Ward's ministers, who opened their facilities to movement activities—something they had declined to do for most of the previous year.[18]

The mass arrests also realigned the Second Ward's power dynamics. Charles Cornish, Edith Jolly, Helen Waters, and every other black person the city's white politicos had dealt with in the past were no longer relevant because black residents no longer supported them. Realizing this, Judge Henry ordered all those arrested on 14 May to be released from jail with the charges dropped, and he and other white leaders decided to confer with Gloria Richardson and other representatives of CNAC "to explore the situation and see if we can find a settlement." The problem for these white leaders was that their white constituents thought they could intimidate the black community into submission.[19]

The stage for increased conflict between black and white residents was set when Judge Henry and five other white men established the Committee for Interracial Understanding (CIU), a working group of attorneys and businesspeople whose goal was to end the city's racial crisis. They hoped to convince restaurant owners to voluntarily desegregate their establishments—a tall order, considering that no owner would agree to do so unless *all* the restaurant owners agreed to it. The CIU had another problem: its members saw the city's racial realities from the viewpoint of Cambridge's other white politicos. A CIU press release reiterated the same old boilerplate rhetoric coming from white elected officials: progress was being made in race relations, and there was ample evidence to prove it. The CIU stated that black residents' "requests have generally been met insofar as they have been within the authority of the city government and compatible with the general welfare." This statement was telling because it showed that the men were ignoring the fact that federal laws, policies implemented by federal bodies such as the Interstate Commerce Commission, and Supreme Court rulings had already nullified the segregation laws and customs still being enforced by Cambridge officials.[20]

Despite the CIU's position, CNAC agreed to suspend demonstrations for one week as a sign of good faith and to give the CIU a chance to gain some traction within the white business and political communities. During this lull in protests, CNAC held a mass meeting at which members of the black community expressed a desire to resume picketing as well as the boycott of local white-owned businesses. Two days later, twelve black students were arrested while picketing the Board of Education, but it was too soon to tell if those arrests would cause CNAC to change its decision about holding demonstrations.[21]

Racial tensions escalated at the end of May after two teenagers, Dwight Cromwell and Dinez White, were arrested while praying at the town's segregated bowling alley. Richardson used their arrests to deliver a sharp critique of white leaders' faith. She "wonder[ed]" whether black people were "dealing with Christians or 'heathens,'" because if white officials were in fact members of that faith, it seemed they "[did] not take the principles of Christianity with them into office." Religious persuasion aside, Richardson was actually more concerned about white leaders' laissez-faire attitude toward police officers' treatment of child protesters, which increased the possibility of violent retaliation by black residents. "It is difficult enough to fight prejudice," Richardson said, "but when it is coupled with stupidity, it becomes dangerous for CNAC and the total community. . . . It is becoming more and more difficult to contain violence here in the Second Ward among those persons not committed and not believing in the effectiveness of a non-violent approach."[22] She was referring to the fact that more than a few Second Ward residents did not subscribe to a nonviolent approach to events such as the arrest of teenagers. Richardson's words proved to be prophetic when a judge meted out Cromwell's and White's punishment a few weeks later.

The judge, E. McMaster Duer, already had a bad reputation among the Eastern Shore's black communities because of his role in getting murder charges dismissed against four white men accused of lynching a black man in Princess Anne back in 1933. Three decades later, he had the lives of two black children in his hands, and Cambridge's black community believed he was about to commit another miscarriage of justice. To start, Duer had Dinez White held without bail in the local jail, a decision so punitive that Richardson sent a telegram to US Attorney General Robert F. Kennedy and the US Civil Rights Commission, warning both that they should intervene in the teenagers' cases because the black community was about to explode in anger. "Failure to act may bring about the very violence we are trying to prevent," she wrote. This had the desired effect, and White was quickly released into her mother's custody. However, the decrease in tension was short-lived.[23] On 10 June, Duer sentenced White and Cromwell to indefinite terms of detention at the state reformatory, and black residents picketed outside the courthouse and sang freedom songs. Twenty of them were arrested for disorderly conduct, and once they were inside the jail, they destroyed their cells' plumbing and spit on corrections officers. Outside the jail, a few black residents smashed the windows of four businesses, and others menaced white automobile drivers. These clashes occurred while Richardson and other CNAC members were meeting with representatives from various racial reconciliation organizations, who informed CNAC that white business owners were not going to desegregate and school desegregation would be done incrementally. CNAC found this unacceptable and informed the press that demonstrations would resume immediately.[24]

Over the next three days, Cambridge experienced a racial conflagration that the *Afro-American* newspaper described as "guerilla warfare." On 11 June, two white people were shot by unidentified individuals; that same night, people threw bricks and Molotov cocktails at one another on and around Race Street, the main dividing line between black and white Cambridge. The following day, a shed behind Helen Waters's Second Ward home was set on fire by an unknown arsonist. Earlier in the week, someone had thrown bricks through the front windows of her home. Both actions were likely the work of residents angered by her vote at a school board meeting to retain the current desegregation plan rather than adopt an expedited one. Elsewhere in the city, someone set a fire at a black-owned bakery located in a predominantly white business section, but it was quickly extinguished.[25]

The bakery fire came at the end of an evening that saw hundreds of black residents and a small number of their white supporters march from Bethel AME Church to the Dorchester County jail in Cambridge in a show of support for the youths arrested on 10 June. Many of these demonstrators knelt in prayer and then broke out into a round of singing "We Shall Overcome." Its refrain "black and white together, we are not afraid," was an expression of their hope that they could force the city to end segregation. Afterward, the demonstrators moved on to the county courthouse for more praying and singing. They were replaced at the jail by yet another wave of demonstrators who were confronted by a few dozen white youths, but the police kept the two groups separated. Shortly thereafter, all the demonstrators returned to Bethel Church, where Richardson spoke about the growing threat of white violence and the possibility that it would goad black residents into a race war that would derail the Cambridge movement. "We must control our emotions," she said. "Retaliation is no good. This is not for one or two nights. I ask you not to attempt retaliation for any of the things that come from the white community or will come from the white community." The meeting ended with another rendition of "We Shall Overcome," and Richardson informed attendees that there would be another mass meeting and demonstration the following evening.[26]

That same day, Richardson asked Robert Kennedy to provide federal protection for Cambridge's black residents. They needed protection from both white menacers and the state police, which had been dispatched to Cambridge to back up local law enforcement. "The State police have proven as intolerable and prejudiced as local police. They are no longer neutral arms of the law," she wrote in her telegram. Emphasizing her concern about the potential for violence between the races, she informed Kennedy that federal involvement in Cambridge might be the only thing that could keep the peace between them.[27] Richardson's telegram to the attorney general was couched in logic that he could not simply dismiss as hyperbole; if local and state law enforcement officers failed to protect citizens, the federal government had a legal and moral responsibility to step in and assume that role.

The situation became more complicated on 12 June when the Maryland Commission on Interracial Problems and Relations (MCIPR) withdrew from its mediation role in Cambridge. "The basic difficulty in the situation in Cambridge is that [white people] believe that they are a law unto themselves and that Dorchester County can be treated as an island apart from the rest of Maryland and the United States." The report continued, "The attitude of the white people is one of granting rights to Negroes, instead of recognizing that these rights are given to all citizens by the Constitution of the United States and are not within the power of the citizens of Cambridge to bestow or withhold." Almost at the same time, Judge Henry disbanded the city's Committee for Interracial Understanding because its members believed that fruitful negotiations were impossible in Cambridge's hostile climate. A final sign that white leaders were unwilling to expend any political capital to end the crisis was Mayor Mowbray's announcement that the city's Equal Opportunities Committee (the CIU's predecessor) would not be resurrected.[28] Together, these actions created a leadership and power vacuum that permitted the volatility level to rise and, in all probability, would prompt the federal government's intervention in Cambridge's affairs.

The next day was essentially a replay of the previous one. Early on 13 June, Richardson, Phil Savage (tristate NAACP director), Reverend Murray (local NAACP chapter president), and the Reverend Charles N. Bourne sent Governor Tawes a telegram asking him to intervene personally in Cambridge, but the governor maintained a hands-off approach to the problem. That night, CNAC held a mass meeting at Bethel Church and decided to march to the courthouse in Cambridge to protest Judge Duer's treatment of Cromwell and White. The demonstrators, which included members of CORE chapters from Baltimore and Brooklyn, New York, marched in waves to the building, where they were greeted by hundreds of white people who heckled both the protesters and the police. The fact that white civilians were turning on white law enforcement officers showed just how badly the city's racial crisis had spun out of white leaders' control. The white crowd proceeded to chant, "Two, four, six, eight, we don't want to integrate." Spliced into their shouts was a white woman's call to carry out a ritual not seen on the Eastern Shore in a generation: "Let's lynch Mrs. Richardson." When black residents began their return march to Bethel, they were followed on foot by hundreds of white people. The police worked feverishly and successfully to prevent them from attacking black residents and from following them into the Second Ward.[29]

Threats of violence, including murder, against CNAC members and their supporters were common. A Howard University student named Stokely Carmichael had been in Cambridge lending his support to the movement when he heard that Richardson was receiving "abusive phone calls and death threats nightly." The murder of Medgar Evers in the driveway of his Jackson, Mississippi, home on the night of 12 June heightened Richardson's awareness that she too could be cut down by an assailant's bullet. But she learned to live with the fear because, "once I'd made the commitment to be active, I couldn't stop simply because I was afraid. Otherwise, the racists would win, and it would be a waste of people's energy to stop."[30]

On the morning of 14 June, Cambridge's mayor and the City Council asked Governor Tawes to declare martial law. He complied immediately and dispatched 500 National Guardsmen to Cambridge, where they patrolled the streets, imposed a curfew, and banned the sale of alcohol. That same day, the governor met with Richardson, SNCC's Reggie Robinson, the NAACP's Phil Savage, and a number of Cambridge's white leaders at the statehouse. By inviting CNAC and its allies to the meeting, the governor was telling Cambridge's white leaders that CNAC did in fact represent the city's black community and that Richardson was its spokesperson. (Sometime before June, Enez Grubb had left CNAC, leaving Richardson as its sole chair.) Tawes characterized this meeting as "a very full and frank discussion of the issues," and by the end of it, he believed the two sides could engage in productive negotiations. Richardson declined to speak with the press because she first had to consult CNAC's executive committee.[31]

Over the years, Richardson has described that meeting with the governor as having a gendered dynamic. When she and her male civil rights colleagues arrived, Richardson was put off by Robinson's and Savage's glad-handing with the white men. "I was just simply amazed how all these men were . . .

smiling and so agreeable," she said. She found this male bonding unseemly because these white men were responsible for maintaining the racial caste system that oppressed black people. Richardson did not shake the governor's hand because she felt the gesture would have implied that she was going to make a "commitment" at that meeting. She added, "If I didn't like somebody I wasn't going to shake their hands simply because they were in a conference room." Richardson did not think the governor noticed her slight, but because she was a woman, "it really didn't matter to them whether I shook hands or not."[32]

When the time came to get down to the business of negotiating, Richardson's male colleagues continued their masculine behavior by posturing as the representatives of the Cambridge movement. "You know they wanted to do the talking. I sat there and let them do the talking," she said. Richardson's decision to be silent added an interesting element to the meeting. Anthropologist Susan Gal states that in many cultures, silence is viewed as a "symbol of passivity and powerlessness." However, in other contexts, "silence can also be a strategic defense against the powerful . . . to baffle, disconcert, and exclude" them from information. When Richardson sat silently, she was engaged in an act of exclusion that kept the governor and Cambridge officials from knowing that no matter what Robinson and Savage said, they were all completely powerless to stop CNAC from organizing and conducting protests. Richardson continued to use silence after the meeting when she declined to give a statement to the press. This left the *New York Times* reporter covering the event with only the governor's perspective that "fruitful negotiations" could now occur between the parties.[33] Richardson's actions at the meeting raise the legitimate question of why she attended. The answer is that she saw the meeting as a necessary "exercise" CNAC needed to go through to get the federal government involved in Cambridge's racial problems. Her strategy was ultimately successful because the failure to make progress at the governor's meeting and in subsequent negotiations showed the federal government—specifically, the Justice Department—that local and state officials were not truly interested in eliminating the city's racial caste system; they just wanted to end the demonstrations.[34]

Back in Cambridge, people were adjusting to life under martial law. Despite this militarization of the city, CNAC was pleased the National Guard had arrived because it brought a semblance of security for black residents. Originally suspicious of Brigadier General George M. Gelston, the officer in charge of the National Guard contingent, Richardson soon learned that "he was honest and he was fair." He gained a lot of credibility in the black community when he stationed a number of troops at the local jail to ensure that black residents were not abused while in custody. The Guardsmen's presence also reduced the possibility of violence breaking out between the black and white communities. From a strategy perspective, CNAC found the National Guard's presence advantageous because it gave Governor Tawes a greater stake in finding a solution to Cambridge's problems. In fact, Richardson believed Tawes sent in the National Guard partly because of the negative publicity his state was receiving in national newspapers such as the *Washington Post* and the *New York Times*. Yet she considered the press a necessary presence in Cambridge because it spread the word about the city's severe racial problems and offered a degree of safety to black people because, in her words, "we figured [white people] wouldn't kill you in front of a camera." With the Guardsmen encamped in town and patrolling its streets around the clock, CNAC began casting a wider net for outside involvement in its movement.[35]

On Sunday, 16 June, Mayor Mowbray broke off talks with CNAC, accusing Richardson and her allies of a "breach of faith" because, the previous day, Savage had told reporters he could swamp Cambridge with 10,000 protesters. Richardson responded by leveling a charge of religious hypocrisy against the mayor and other white leaders, painting them as duplicitous, self-serving, morally bankrupt people whose behavior jeopardized the safety and well-being of all Cambridge residents. "We note with irony that the white political leaders who have attempted to portray themselves to the public as men of peace and good will, would abruptly break off negotiations on Sunday, a day on which all men should have turned to God in this crisis." "We find instead," she added, "the city fathers were plotting like Judases and resorting to political manipulations on a grave moral issue. We feel they demonstrated lack of faith in reaching a real solution to the problems faced by the total community during the past few days."[36]

White leaders continued to strategize about how to end the crisis, and on Thursday, 20 June, the mayor and the City Council met in private to discuss a desegregation plan for the city's public accommodations. One option was to pass an ordinance, something Maryland's attorney general Thomas Finan said was permissible under the state constitution. They seemed inclined to do this, but only in exchange for CNAC's promise to cease demonstrating for one year. The organization rejected this offer, just as it had on previous occasions, because "past experience showed that no progress toward ending segregation is made in the vacuum that results" when black people stop applying pressure on the white power structure. Richardson also pointed out that demonstrations worked as a pressure release valve for the black community's frustration with having to live in a white supremacist society. Another option for white leaders was to pass an amendment to the city's charter. This would achieve the goal of desegregating the city's public accommodations, but it would also provide white politicians with cover at reelection time because a charter amendment could be challenged by a referendum initiated by Cambridge voters. For this reason, Richardson and other activists rejected this option and demanded that the City Council pass an ordinance.[37]

Midway through the third week of June, the Kennedy administration began its public immersion in the Cambridge crisis, an unusual but understandable move on its part. Located just a few hours by car from Washington, Cambridge and its racial problems were getting national press coverage. Any escalation there threatened to embarrass the administration because it would imply that the president did not have control over events taking place in his own backyard. Attorney General Robert Kennedy directed Burke Marshall, an assistant attorney general in the Civil Rights Division of the Department of Justice (DOJ), to call a meeting at his office on 18 June. It would be the first of numerous meetings Marshall and other DOJ officials held with CNAC and Cambridge's white leaders in an attempt to mediate an end to the racial stalemate. At that first meeting, Gloria Richardson was joined by fellow CNAC executive committee member Betty Jews, the NAACP's Phil Savage, and SNCC's Reggie Robinson and John Lewis. Lewis was an experienced activist who had been involved in Nashville's desegregation movement, and he had made the trek through the South in 1961 as a Freedom Rider. He was elected SNCC's chairman in 1963 and was a rising force within that organization and the civil rights movement at large. This group of activists met with a representative of Governor Tawes to discuss the two sides' demands.[38]

The fact that this meeting even occurred was no small victory for CNAC. Since the early months of the Cambridge movement, it had wanted some form of federal involvement in the city's problems. In contrast, white segregationists saw Washington's involvement as federal overreach, similar to what had happened in Little Rock in 1957. The Kennedy administration's decision to mediate Cambridge's racial problems gave Richardson a sense of optimism, and she told reporters that "progress is being made" and, "for the first time," she was "hopeful that the problems will be settled by the people of Cambridge." Richardson shared this outlook at a mass meeting back in Cambridge the following night. Speaking to more than 300 people who had crowded into the Bethel Church sanctuary, Richardson told them: "We should walk in peace and tranquility until everything that we have asked for is accomplished. I think it will be."[39]

That same week, Marshall oversaw two other meetings between CNAC and white leaders. In one of those meetings, the governor's executive assistant, Edmund C. Mester, floated a multipart proposal: creation of a biracial committee to convince white business owners to voluntarily desegregate their establishments, resumption of the building of public housing in the Second Ward, the hiring of one black person at the city's employment agency, desegregation of the public schools, and an amendment to the city's charter that would desegregate public accommodations. In return, CNAC would agree to stop demonstrating for eighty days. SNCC's Robinson told the press that this proposal was "the best we can get at this time." His statement gave the impression that CNAC would agree to the proposal in its entirety, and a rumor spread that an agreement had been reached. What white leaders did not understand was that Robinson's statement carried no weight; only Richardson could speak on behalf of CNAC, and that would occur only after its executive committee had voted on the proposal. CNAC was in favor of many of its elements, but it was never going to agree to a moratorium on demonstrating or a charter amendment. Believing that city officials had started the rumor of an agreement, CNAC broke off negotiations. Mester placed the burden for progress on Richardson and CNAC by telling the press that "the Mayor and City Council were fair, generous, and legally went as far as they could go. The next move is up to the Negro leaders."[40]

White politicos' attempts to undermine CNAC's authority were commonplace and dated to the beginning of the Cambridge movement, but they escalated in the summer of 1963. At an early June meeting between CNAC and white leaders, the latter openly challenged CNAC's claim that it was the legitimate voice of the black community. One member of the MCIPR expressed suspicion that CNAC was speaking for the entire Second Ward, and he suggested polling the non-CNAC-affiliated black people present at the meeting to better gauge the black community's attitude about demonstrations. CNAC rejected this suggestion and informed those present that CNAC's right to speak for the black community derived from the fact that the organization was open to all Second Ward residents, and CNAC's executive committee only conveyed the liberation agenda determined by those residents.[41] The white community tried to undermine CNAC's leadership position by supporting black residents who seemed to be amenable to white leaders' goals and tactics. When white leaders demanded that Charles Cornish be included in any group of black negotiators, Richardson's response was swift and left no doubt that CNAC called the shots in the Second Ward. "We wish to make it unalterably clear, it is we, and not the political structure of the city, who shall speak for the Negro community. The day has ended in America when any white person can determine our leaders and spokesman. No Negro, except those selected by us, will act as intermediary or negotiator." Richardson dismissed these moves as throwbacks to the time before the Cambridge movement began. "Here in Cambridge race relations have always been based on the 'slave and master' attitude. Our ancestors and our 'leaders' of yesterday and today have always been happy to accept it. We are not."[42]

Although her statement automatically included her grandfather Maynadier St. Clair and other black elected officials from the nineteenth and early twentieth centuries, Richardson was not actually condemning them as "happy" sell-outs. She knew the conditions they had had to endure. However, she did include Cornish in that category, and her rhetorical flourish about him and the city's racial politics served as notice that the sun had set on Cambridge's standard operating procedure for race relations. A new day was dawning in which the black community would lead itself to freedom on its own terms. Cambridge was not unique in this regard. In many places in the South, particularly where there was a SNCC presence, black people were rejecting gradualist and moderate black leadership.[43]

When their attempts to outmaneuver CNAC did not work, white leaders tried to co-opt Richardson with the prospect of employment opportunities. In one case, the minister of Bethel AME Church conveyed a message from local white leaders offering her a job as a social worker; she was also offered the directorship of a jobs training program that was under consideration. Promises of political fortune followed. Governor Tawes sent recently elected black state senator Verda Welcome to Cambridge to deliver a message: Tawes would support Richardson's candidacy for the state senate if she removed herself from the Cambridge movement. Richardson alleged that after she rejected these proposals, people within the federal government tried to intimidate her into resigning from CNAC. According to her ex-husband, the FBI had contacted him and said that because Gloria was a communist, he could get custody of their daughters. Richardson told Harry to "go back and just tell [the FBI] I said to go to hell, and you, too."[44]

Richardson also claimed that people working for the Kennedy administration tried to intimidate her into leaving the movement by threatening to reveal embarrassing gossip about her. When Gloria was separated from Harry but not yet divorced from him, she had an affair, and the administration threatened to leak the story to reporters. Richardson sent word to the administration that if the press ran that story, she would indeed resign from CNAC, but she would not go without a fight. For generations, the St. Clair family had had friends and associates in Washington's black community, and Richardson was prepared to mine this extensive network of contacts, which included current and former black employees at the White House who could provide all sorts of stories about the activities of President Kennedy. Richardson's threat to share these stories with the press was a weighty one, and in light of later revelations about Kennedy's personal life, it was clearly too risky to call her bluff.[45]

The stalemate between CNAC and Cambridge's white leaders continued for the remainder of June, but they kept an open dialogue with Marshall at the DOJ. After a meeting there on 24 June, Richardson spoke with reporters and indicated that she had lost her earlier optimism. In all probability, she said, CNAC would resume demonstrations because "only a miracle" could prevent them from occurring. Three days later, Richardson met one-on-one with Mayor Mowbray to discuss the stalemate and their respective demands. This was significant because, since the spring of 1962, CNAC had always required that at least two activists be present when meeting with white leaders. But by the summer of 1963, Richardson's CNAC colleagues were confident that she could go head-to-head with white leaders and not get played by them. Richardson followed up with Mowbray by telegram, asking him to schedule another meeting to discuss CNAC's demands and telling him that the organization was interested in getting back to the negotiating table. The telegram was pure public relations management on Richardson's part. She knew the mayor and the City Council would never meet CNAC's demands, but the telegram provided proof to the public and the Kennedy administration that CNAC was not being strident.[46]

The "Treaty of Cambridge"

Cambridge's City Council meeting on the night of 1 July 1963 was an important marker in the city's racial history. That was when politicians moved their city to the edge of armed conflict. On that hot and humid evening, more than two dozen people crowded into the City Council's chambers to watch the proceedings, including Richardson, CNAC executive committee members Betty Jews and Fred Jackson, SNCC's Reggie Robinson, the NAACP's Phil Savage, and General Gelston of the National Guard. Council members were considering whether to pass a desegregation ordinance or a charter amendment. Second Ward representative Charles Cornish proposed an ordinance, but none of his colleagues seconded his motion. They voted instead to adopt a charter amendment that would go into effect on 20 August 1963. Businesses explicitly affected by the amendment were hotels, motels, inns, and restaurants, whereas taverns, bars, and cocktail lounges were exempt. Interestingly, other types of public facilities were not specifically listed in the amendment; thus, those sites could reasonably be considered exempt from it. Two of these were the Dorset Theater and the Rescue and Fire Company arena and swimming pool. Cornish abstained from voting on the amendment because his constituents were against it.[47]

During the public feedback portion of the meeting, Richardson spoke on behalf of the black community. Alluding to the likelihood that the amendment would be challenged and defeated by white voters through a referendum, Richardson invoked the concept of tyranny of the majority. It was not "morally right," she argued, "that such a question should be put up to vote, when that question deals with the minority group alone." She then informed white leaders that demonstrations would continue that week "unless 'tangible gains' toward meeting their demands were made." Afterward, black religious leaders, including Cambridge's Reverend Murray and others from around Maryland, concurred with Richardson's argument that white voters should not have a say in black people's rights. Calling the charter amendment "ridiculous," these members of the clergy told the *Pittsburgh Courier*: "We feel that the Negro civil rights leaders are correct in their refusal to accept this type of Un-American legislation."[48]

Governor Tawes saw the City Council's action as a step forward, so he decided to end martial law the following week. His motivations for doing so were twofold. First, it was costing the state more than $20,000 a week to keep almost 500 troops stationed in Cambridge. Second, he was encouraged by Richardson's statement that CNAC would "wait and see how the situation develops" after the troops left town. What he did not know was that her statement was a tactical move to lull him into a false sense of security by implying that the demonstrations might not resume. In fact, once the troops were gone, CNAC could restart the demonstrations and reapply pressure on the white community. National Guardsmen pulled out of Cambridge at midday on Monday, 8 July, ending three weeks of martial law. The night before the troops left, CNAC met behind closed doors to discuss its next steps. First on CNAC's agenda was to resume demonstrations, which it did by targeting the Dizzyland restaurant immediately. The event received national exposure when the *New York Times* ran an article that included a photograph of the restaurant owner cracking an egg over the head of a white activist.[49]

Aware that the situation in Cambridge was volatile and unlikely to improve, the Kennedy administration invited Richardson for a one-on-one meeting with Maceo Hubbard, an attorney in the DOJ's Civil Rights Division, on 9 July. Richardson already knew Hubbard, who had attended Lincoln University with her cousin Carroll and her uncle Frederick and had visited the family in Cambridge. Hubbard and Richardson had a cordial meeting that lasted ninety minutes, although she found it a little strange to be having such an important discussion with someone she had looked up to as a child. The two talked about the Cambridge movement and other topics related to civil rights, such as the proposed civil rights bill being considered by Congress. Hubbard gave Richardson a copy of the bill, and they made plans to see each other the following day in Cambridge, where Hubbard was going to assess its racial climate and to meet with CNAC. Hubbard met with CNAC's executive committee and then stopped by Richardson's home to visit with her mother. According to Richardson, he tried to enlist Mable in his efforts to get Richardson to stop demonstrating, and he reiterated the federal government's offer of the directorship of a jobs training program if she removed herself from the movement.[50]

Shortly after Hubbard left Cambridge, local activists held another protest inside the Dizzyland restaurant, where two of them were beaten. Police officers eventually gained access to the restaurant and forced everyone to clear out. The following afternoon (11 July), more activists tried to desegregate Dizzyland, but white patrons inside the restaurant assaulted them. Once law enforcement officers convinced the restaurant owner to open the door, the segregationist thugs threw the activists out of the building. Later on, hundreds of black residents and their white supporters marched to the county courthouse to hold a rally, where they were met by dozens of white people who heckled and yelled obscenities at them. Officers kept the two crowds separated, and they finally dispersed and went back to their respective neighborhoods.[51] The calm did not last long. By ten o'clock that evening, two carloads of armed white people had entered the Second Ward, firing guns as they raced around the neighborhoods. The *Afro-American* reporter covering Cambridge described the black community's response to this invasion by white terrorists. Close to 100 black males, young and old, positioned themselves "behind cars, buildings and in windows and on rooftops" and engaged the terrorists in "an hour-long gun battle." For the remainder of the night and into the early hours of the next morning, unidentified people peppered Race Street and nearby blocks with small-arms fire. A state police commander said the shooting was "almost on the scale of warfare." When the gun smoke finally dissipated, there were a dozen casualties, including three National Guardsmen. "Only an act of God," the *Afro-American* reporter wrote with amazement, "could have stayed the hand of death during the long night when bullets literally rained on the county seat of Dorchester County." Determined "to preserve order" in Cambridge and prevent violence from spreading to other parts of the state, Governor Tawes ordered the National Guard back to Cambridge on Friday morning, 12 July.[52]

Editors at the *Daily Banner* believed they knew who was responsible for the spate of racial clashes. In a front-page editorial printed the day after the National Guard returned, they told readers that "twice within the past month the Negro civil rights movement in Cambridge has gotten out of control and produced civil disorder and bloodshed." Although not explicitly named, Richardson was certainly on the editors' minds when they wrote of "extremist integrationists" whose actions allegedly provoked the "opposition," who then responded in ways that created "riotous disorder." To combat the city's slouch toward anarchy, the editors proposed that the federal judiciary impose an injunction on future demonstrations so that Cambridge's residents could get back to their lives grounded in "law and order." Because of this editorial and the *Banner*'s generally unfavorable reporting of the Cambridge movement, CNAC initiated a boycott of the newspaper and continued to boycott white-owned businesses. This, combined with armed troops patrolling the city's commercial district, caused white business owners' profits to plummet.[53]

Hubbard called Richardson the following week and invited her back to Washington to discuss the crisis, but she declined, observing, "There's no point in going up there and hearing them tell us what they cannot do." Her decision reflected CNAC's growing frustration with the Kennedy administration, which Richardson and others held partly to blame for the lack of progress in Cambridge. She believed the administration was unwilling to use the full power of the federal government to force Cambridge's white leaders to dismantle the city's system of racial segregation. Richardson was also incredulous that the Kennedy administration was touting its support of human rights around the globe while Cambridge was in a state of civil unrest because black people were fighting for their rights. So when Hubbard called Richardson and informed her that the president wanted to speak with her, she replied that he should "tell those Kennedy brothers they both can go to hell."[54]

Richardson's disgust with President Kennedy increased when he commented on the Cambridge movement during one of his press conferences. "They've almost lost sight of what the demonstration is about. . . . I'm concerned about those demonstrations. I think they go beyond information—

they go beyond protest and they get into a very bad situation where you get violence, and I think the cause of advancing equal opportunities only loses." Richardson sent the president a telegram in which she instructed him on the particulars of the Cambridge movement and what its activists faced on a daily basis. "The only solution to the racial crisis in Cambridge is the achievement of equal rights for the 4000 Negroes of the community," she wrote. This meant equal access to jobs, affordable housing, and desegregated education and public accommodations. Richardson also informed him that CNAC relied solely on nonviolent direct action tactics when demonstrating, and when black people did use force, they did so only in self-defense against white attackers after the demonstrations had concluded.[55]

On Friday, 19 July, Richardson told reporters that CNAC would "temporarily suspend" demonstrations to give a recently formed race relations committee an opportunity to break Cambridge's racial impasse. But on Saturday evening, CNAC did not seem overly concerned about holding to its decision. Richardson, Reggie Robinson, Stanley Branche, Phil Savage, and Clarence Logan were in a shoeshine shop near the corner of Pine and Elm Streets in the Second Ward talking with General Gelston about the possibility of holding a demonstration, which the general said would violate his ban. As they talked, a tense situation was developing outside the shop, and the National Guard was in the middle of it. On one side were black residents awaiting Richardson's decision on the demonstration, and on the other side were hundreds of white people protesting the Guardsmen's presence. The latter's hostility toward the Guardsmen mainly took the form of verbal abuse, and one white man grabbed a soldier's rifle and tossed it to the ground. Interestingly, the Guardsmen did not respond with force to these provocations.[56]

An *Afro-American* reporter witnessed the Guardsmen being ordered to charge the crowd of black residents after a black man had come into physical contact with one soldier and provoked him and others. During the charge, one soldier told a black man, "Get back nigger," which "sent the man and his friends into a frenzy." Believing that the situation was getting out of control, an officer threw a canister of tear gas into the crowd of black people, which caused "screaming and scuffling among" them. Richardson and the other activists noticed what was happening and rushed out of the shop in an attempt to defuse the situation. But just as they moved in, one of the Guardsmen advanced toward Richardson, leading with his bayoneted rifle. Shocked, she immediately reacted with a defensive maneuver and pushed the rifle out of her way. Guardsmen set off another canister of tear gas before General Gelston ordered them to leave the scene and relocate to another part of town. CNAC sent word to the black community that it would not hold any more demonstrations because, in Richardson's words, "the people are too upset and they need time to cool off."[57]

That same weekend, Richardson forecast a terrible outcome for Cambridge if the violence between black and white residents continued. Speaking at a Sunday evening event at Campbell AME Church in Washington, DC, she told a packed audience that President Kennedy had an obligation to demonstrate leadership on civil rights issues and should spend some of his political capital to ensure that black people did not have to endure racist treatment in society and in the economy. If he failed to rise to this important challenge, Cambridge might have a "civil war," she warned, because no one had control over the black residents, who would no longer put up with segregation and indignities, and no one had a handle on the "uncontrollable white mobs" who were menacing them.[58]

In an attempt to prevent another melee, Attorney General Robert Kennedy called a meeting at the Department of Justice for the afternoon of Monday, 22 July, where he and his staff would try to help CNAC and white leaders find common ground. It was highly unusual for such a high-ranking official to get personally involved in a local civil rights struggle, indicating how desperately the Kennedy administration wanted to contain the Cambridge crisis. It also proved to Cambridge's white community once and for all that CNAC was the black community's political arm. Representing CNAC were Richardson and Betty Jews, who presented the attorney general with a report based on CNAC's community survey conducted the previous summer. Accompanying them were John Lewis, Reggie Robinson, Stanley Branche, and Phil Savage. Representing the Maryland state government were Attorney General Thomas B. Finan, Deputy Attorney General Robert C. Murphy, Edward Mester (Governor Tawes's executive secretary), and General Gelston. Not invited to the meeting were local Cambridge officials, whom Robert Kennedy and Burke Marshall believed would not "be the most useful" for the meeting's purpose.[59]

In his memoir *Walking with the Wind*, John Lewis wrote about how the attendees' personalities affected this meeting. Richardson did not want to be there; "she felt it was an empty ritual" intended to improve the president's image on civil rights, and it was obvious to everyone in the room that the absence of progress in Cambridge "was written all over [Richardson's] face." Kennedy attempted to break the ice by asking her: "'Mrs. Richardson, do you know how to smile?'" Lewis recalled that Richardson responded with a smile, "but it was a weak one."[60] Cambridge City Council member William "Bill"

Wright heard about Kennedy's question and remarked decades later that Richardson "was always either . . . nasty looking, or disrespectful looking, certainly to me as a member of the City Council and to the mayor." Recent research on facial expressions illuminates why Wright and Kennedy may have been more comfortable if Richardson had smiled: people "appear less power-ful" when they smile, and "a scarcity of smiles is associated with aggression." These men may have interpreted Richardson's serious facial expression as threatening, or they may have found her sternness unladylike. They appar-ently did not consider that Richardson was a human rights activist fighting for freedom from racial oppression, which gave her nothing to smile about.[61]

Once the introductions were over, Richardson and Kennedy highlighted what they considered the most important elements of the Cambridge crisis. She reiterated what she had said the previous evening: if the National Guards-men were unable to prevent white people from entering the Second Ward, black residents would be forced into "defending their homes," and a "civil war" could occur. Kennedy chastised CNAC for destroying Cambridge's economy, but Richardson informed him that the white community had cre-ated the problems, and "if they had done like other places on the Eastern Shore," the situation would not have escalated to civil unrest. The initial meeting with Kennedy lasted about an hour, after which everyone headed over to Marshall's office, where he began the delicate job of facilitating a mar-athon round of negotiations to end the stalemate.[62]

Richardson and the other activists took a break from that meeting to visit Robert C. Weaver, an administrator with the federal government's Housing and Home Finance Office. For the second time that month, Richardson found herself in a high-profile meeting with a civil servant who had ties to her family. Weaver was from a prominent Washington family whose roots in the capital dated back to Reconstruction. He and Richardson's mother were childhood friends who had spent vacations together at Maryland's Highland Beach. Richardson and Weaver discussed the possibility of getting a public housing project built in Cambridge, but like Hubbard, Weaver tried to con-vince her to stop CNAC from demonstrating. When that did not work, he tried playing hardball and told Richardson he would see to it "that [not] a shovel of dirt [was] dug on" the proposed public housing units in Cambridge "until [CNAC] stopped demonstrating." She calmly replied that if that was the case, the black community would "have to wait a lot longer" for housing to be built.[63]

Richardson always believed the Kennedy administration tried to exploit Weaver's and Hubbard's relationships with her family to influence the

Cambridge movement. Both men likely interpreted her behavior as violations of their social group's norms and respectability politics. In fact, a few of Mable Hayes's "upper-class" friends actually asked her why her daughter was "in the streets smoking" and "what did [Richardson] think [she] was doing?" Mable only increased their confusion when she defended her daughter's activism.[64] If anything, Richardson's willingness to engage in political brinksmanship with Weaver and Hubbard proved that she would not compromise on CNAC's goals, which caused her to be identified even more with Cambridge's working-class community.

After her meeting with Weaver, Richardson and the others regrouped at Marshall's office to resume negotiations. Richardson delegated this task to Savage, Branche, and Robinson because she was not interested in sitting in a room for hours talking endlessly about the same issues she had been discussing for months. Even so, she was CNAC's main representative at the meeting and could veto anything the others had agreed to. "I just sat in the office with the secretaries and told [the men] 'You all do whatever you want in there. Let me see the final copy and what I don't like I will mark through.' And that's what I did for about four or five hours."[65]

Shortly before midnight, Richardson agreed to a set of action items that would become known as the "Treaty of Cambridge." The agreement was essentially the same offer the city had made to CNAC four weeks earlier, but this time the terms were in writing. Cambridge officials would create a biracial committee and address the key issues important to the black community, as revealed by CNAC's survey. A black resident would be hired to work at the state's employment office in town, and officials would begin desegregating Dorchester County's school system. Additionally, officials would file an application with the Federal Housing Administration for "a low-rent public housing project, which will materially benefit the Negro community."[66] The agreement was essentially a list of actions white officials were supposed to carry out to address the city's racial problems. It did not require any action by CNAC, but it stipulated that CNAC would not engage in demonstrations "for an indefinite period hereafter." The question naturally arises: why did Richardson sign off on an agreement that prohibited CNAC from demonstrating and left the charter amendment in effect rather than replacing it with an ordinance? Richardson said that despite these terms, the overall agreement was important because it memorialized and legitimized CNAC's grievances against Cambridge's white power structure. Additionally, Richardson never believed that Cambridge's white leaders and their constituents would live up to the terms of the agreement. This would effectively nullify the moratorium

Gloria Richardson, US attorney general Robert F. Kennedy, and Cambridge mayor Calvin Mowbray, 23 July 1963. (Getty Images)

on demonstrations, and the Kennedy administration would get a wake-up call that its power of persuasion was ineffective in a racially hostile place like Cambridge.[67]

The following morning, 23 July, Mayor Mowbray joined Richardson for a press conference at the attorney general's office, where they and members of the negotiating teams signed the agreement while Robert Kennedy and Burke Marshall looked on. Recognizing the importance of the event—it was front-page news in the *New York Times* and other papers—and being sensitive to how it would be interpreted, Kennedy said the agreement signaled "a step forward" for Cambridge, but it was "not a victory or defeat for anybody." Governor Tawes, who received news of the agreement while on vacation in Miami Beach, said he "hope[d] that the city of Cambridge can now return to normal conditions." Cambridge's white community agreed with the governor. It saw the agreement as its first chance since 1962 of controlling the city's trajectory and steering it back to the course it had been on before black youths started the Cambridge movement. The *Banner*'s editors hoped the city could "return to [the] civilized living" it had enjoyed prior to the summer's racial clashes, and politicians and business leaders expected

Cambridge's status as a pariah community on the Eastern Shore to end. Most of them would be supporting desegregation not by actively campaigning for it but by hoping that their constituents did not challenge the charter amendment with a referendum.[68]

The feeling among many black residents was that the agreement was a major victory against a recalcitrant white political system. During a mass meeting back in Cambridge later on the day of its signing, the NAACP's Phil Savage addressed a crowd of more than 300 black residents. CNAC's ability to obtain such concessions, he told the overflowing crowd, was an uncommon achievement when compared with the concessions obtained by activists in places like Birmingham, Alabama, and Jackson, Mississippi. And the person who made this success possible was the leader of the Cambridge movement. "Nobody in this community should ever forget Gloria Richardson," he said. "I think you all know you owe her a debt of gratitude." They responded with a standing ovation, a display of respect and appreciation that moved her to tears.[69]

Richardson's work on behalf of Cambridge had been getting a lot of ink in the black press. For example, the editors of Chicago's *Daily Defender* said the Cambridge movement would walk Dorchester County into the twentieth century, even though it would likely be with a limp. At the head of that movement was Gloria Richardson, who had been providing "resolute" leadership to make black liberation more than just a dream; this was something her "spiritual ancestor" and Eastern Shore native Harriet Tubman had also done. Back on the East Coast, New York City resident Joseph C. Thomason was so impressed by Richardson's leadership that he penned a letter to the *Amsterdam News*. "Women make the best mothers," he wrote, "and now it looks as though they are also the best negotiators." Thomason felt that, given Richardson's success at leading the Cambridge movement, she might be able to "slip a non-violent suggestion" to Attorney General Robert Kennedy to pass along to his brother: namely, that there were plenty of black judges who could be nominated to the US Supreme Court when the opportunity presented itself. Thomason closed his letter by thanking Richardson for her "noble contribution on the altar of freedom" and noting that her "name must belong among those garlanded by the smile of the Almighty."[70]

Right before the "treaty" negotiations took place, the *Washington Post* ran a story about the dire future facing Cambridge. Since the racial strife began, no progress had been made in terms of black workers' employment opportunities, and that trend would probably continue for some years. This was because the National Guard's presence, black residents' boycott of white businesses, and the absence of tourists caused Cambridge's economy to collapse. The city had become a place that businesspeople drove by when looking to expand their companies, and the "treaty" was not going to change that perception.[71] White residents did not share the *Washington Post*'s stark outlook; they believed the agreement positioned them for a better future, and although they continued to live under martial law, the cessation of demonstrating had decreased tensions between the city's black and white residents. In this less volatile environment, residents throughout the city were taking steps to exert more control over their lives. For many white residents, this meant putting the brakes on desegregation by initiating the referendum process to overturn the charter amendment. For Richardson and most other black residents, this meant carrying on the fight against their social and economic marginalization. CNAC continued to boycott local white-owned businesses, and the organization encouraged parents to enroll their children in its summer Freedom School. This student-centered education program was run by two white sisters, Rachel and Connie Brown, who were attending colleges outside of Philadelphia. They and a handful of other volunteers provided remedial instruction in reading and arithmetic to more than 100 black schoolchildren. The program's other goal was to raise black students' consciousness about their lives and how to transform them. Students responded well to the volunteers' innovative pedagogy, which included a "relaxed discipline" that fostered "discussions" among the students.[72]

Gloria Richardson also began a new phase in her human rights activism. The media coverage of the Cambridge movement had thrust her into the national spotlight, which led to invitations to deliver speeches and attend events that raised her public profile even further. Cambridge would also be receiving a lot more media coverage because of how Richardson responded to white voters' attempt to prevent their city from desegregating.

7

A Nonnegotiable Right

Although Maryland is a southern state, it resides in the upper portion of the South, and during the civil rights movement that geographic distinction meant it was both similar to and different from the rest of the region. In terms of society, Maryland was as racially segregated as the rest of the South, but in terms of politics, it was very different. Since the end of Reconstruction, Maryland had never taken away its black population's right to vote, as other southern states had. These common and different realities meant that the Cambridge Nonviolent Action Committee's goals would sometimes intersect with the broader goals of the Deep South's civil rights movement and sometimes diverge from them.

The most salient example of divergent interests occurred when Cambridge's white community forced a referendum on public accommodations and CNAC boycotted the referendum because it objected to putting black people's constitutional right to equal protection up for popular vote. CNAC's position distinguished it from national civil rights groups, particularly the NAACP, which was fighting for black southerners' right to vote and believed that once they obtained it, they should always exercise that right. These organizations' differing views about the meaning of voting, and what it could and could not achieve, caused friction between them and illustrated that local groups and national organizations sometimes had competing agendas. Additionally, CNAC's uncompromising political position was almost unheard of in the United States at that time, and many people found it outlandish.

At the center of this boycott was Gloria Richardson, who had led CNAC through the historic summer of 1963 that saw Cambridge's white leaders accede to the organization's demands and sign the "Treaty of Cambridge." That agreement and the events leading up to it garnered national media attention, bringing Cambridge and Richardson into countless homes across America. It also forced national civil rights leaders to acknowledge the magnitude of what had been achieved in Cambridge and Richardson's instrumental role. That was why they invited her to participate in the March on Washington. But because those leaders were uncomfortable with Richardson's style of leadership and her radical views on how to achieve black liberation, they took steps to counteract her influence with the civil rights community that showed up en masse to march that August day. Those efforts—unknown to the public for almost fifty years—reveal another instance of moderates and radicals competing for control of the civil rights movement's agenda and its posture toward white America.

If there was anything to be learned from the summer of 1963, it was that the Cambridge movement and its leader were committed to their long-term strategy to liberate the city's black community from the systemic racism that reduced their opportunities to live as first-class citizens. No amount of criticism or intimidation would convince CNAC and Richardson to forgo their strategy in favor of one that would bring only short-term gains.

Gloria Richardson's meeting with Maceo Hubbard on 9 July at the Department of Justice was the first of two events she attended in Washington that day. The second took place in the East Room of the White House with President Kennedy, who was soliciting women's help to implement his program for improving the nation's gender and racial climates. More than 300 women attended this meeting, and they represented a wide range of groups and interests, including the National Council of Jewish Women, the United Daughters of the Confederacy, and the anti–nuclear weapons organization Women Strike for Peace. Richardson was one of approximately fifty black women invited to the event, and among this group was Diane Nash, who had traveled to Washington from Mississippi. A student leader of the Nashville movement and a founding member of SNCC, Nash had a reputation as a tenacious human rights activist. When CORE's Freedom Riders were attacked by white supremacist terrorists near Anniston, Alabama, in 1961, the organization's national director, James Farmer, had called off the event because he feared for the riders' safety. When Nash learned of Farmer's decision, she called to "get his blessing" for students from the Nashville movement to continue the rides. Farmer agreed to let the Nashville students step into the breach, and they completed the journey.[1]

The White House affair began with brief statements by President Kennedy and Vice President Johnson, after which the women were able to voice their concerns about civil rights issues. Richardson and Nash kicked off a lively question-and-answer session when they asked "what could be done in the friction-torn areas" of the nation. Overall, Richardson was displeased with the meeting; she had expected it to be a policy discussion concerning the problems of living in a racialized democracy. Instead, the majority of her fellow attendees seemed more interested in shaking hands and mingling with some of the world's most powerful politicians.[2]

Finding themselves out of step with the rest of the group, Richardson and Nash huddled together and assessed the president's proposed civil rights bill, a copy of which Richardson had obtained from Hubbard earlier that day. Nash recalled the scene: "We found a corner, sat down and read through it together. We circled the sentence or paragraph in each section that took the 'teeth' out of each measure; some of the sections did not mention enforcement at all. . . . The bill had virtually no enforcement power." This meant that white citizens would have to enforce the provisions voluntarily, which Richardson found bizarre: if white people had been inclined to treat black people as first-class citizens, there would have been no need for protests in Cambridge or elsewhere in the United States. At that point she began to move around the room, talking with the other attendees about the bill's severe limitations. "I was trying to show how it wasn't worth a hill of beans because there was no enforcement power, all of it was voluntary. And so that just meant we would be tied up fighting another battle." Richardson found that few shared her concern, and after the event she told the press the meeting "was not particularly worthwhile." Although she "commend[ed] the President's attempts to do something about civil rights . . . that is not enough. People are being shot and killed just because they try to register to vote."[3]

This Washington trip was the first of four Richardson took during the next seven weeks. In late July she traveled to San Francisco, California, to attend meetings and deliver a speech to a local civil rights group. Accompanying her was Paul Cowan, a young white man who was active in the northern student movement and had met Richardson the previous year during his participation in Project Eastern Shore. He would be serving as her public relations manager during this West Coast trip.[4] In the Bay Area, Richardson met with members of a Japanese American group who shared their experiences of being interned during World War II. She was also the featured guest speaker at the inaugural meeting of the United San Francisco Freedom Movement, an organization created by members of the city's various civil rights groups. Held at the Greater Gethsemane Church of God in Christ on Haight Street, the gathering was attended by a racially integrated crowd of 1,400 people who swelled the church's sanctuary and sang freedom songs that aligned with the evening's theme of "Freedom Immediately, Yesterday." They greeted Richardson with a standing ovation and then sat down to listen attentively as she talked about Cambridge's freedom struggle. She told them

Left to right: Gloria Richardson, Rosa L. Gragg of the National Association of Colored Woman's Clubs, and Diane Nash at the White House, Washington, DC, 9 July 1963. (Associated Press)

about the white leaders who refused to work in good faith with CNAC and forced it to employ mass demonstrations to keep the pressure on them. The remainder of Richardson's speech was not intended for the people warming up the sanctuary's seats. Richardson addressed San Francisco's white leaders and asked whether they would dig in their heels and resist black people's efforts to liberate themselves from social, economic, and political marginalization. "The question is now, as it has been all along, whether the white leaders, political and business men, can bring themselves to understand that we are absolutely serious in all of our demands" and "whether they can comprehend what we mean when we insist that 'we want freedom and we want it now.'" Astute listeners heard Richardson's words as a clear warning to San

Francisco's white politicos that the cost of doing nothing would be much higher than the cost of allowing black people to live as first-class citizens.[5]

When she finished her California itinerary, Richardson headed back home to Cambridge, where she spent a few weeks visiting with family and catching up on the latest news about the Cambridge movement. Afterward she traveled to New York City for some rest and relaxation at the Park Avenue home of Paul Cowan's parents. The break was exactly what Richardson needed; although the trip out west had been exciting and interesting, it had come at the end of a stressful eighteen-month period. The Cowans' comfortable surroundings on New York's Upper East Side were a huge contrast to the life she had been living in Cambridge since the movement began, and interestingly, Richardson missed the action. So when she was asked to be a guest speaker at one of SNCC's New York City fund-raisers, she gladly accepted.[6]

Billed as a "Freedom Now" rally, the evening fund-raiser on 23 August was held at Harlem's Salem Methodist Church. New York City attorney Percy Sutton served as emcee and introduced Richardson as the keynote speaker. A few of her SNCC associates—Avon Rollins from the Danville movement in Virginia and Dorie Ladner—shared stories about their own work in the civil rights movement, and Ladner introduced the premiere of the SNCC film *We'll Never Turn Back*.[7] In terms of style and substance, Richardson's address that night was essentially the same as the one she had delivered in San Francisco, but this time, the Socialist Party's newspaper *New America* reprinted her speech in its entirety. This was an important development in Richardson's intellectual history. It was the first printed text that clearly displayed her secular humanism and detailed some of her key social, economic, and political philosophies. Up to that point, these concepts had been presented almost exclusively through newspaper and magazine articles that discussed her actions but not the motivation behind her activism. Additionally, her speech outlined the main issues that would become a large part of the northern civil rights movement the following year.

Just as she had in San Francisco, Richardson educated her racially integrated New York audience about Cambridge's racial problems. White politicos, she said, were playing a dangerous game with black people's existence by manipulating the political process through gerrymandering and the economic system through discriminatory employment quotas that favored white workers over black workers. The latter was the most important issue, Richardson argued, because the lack of job opportunities was the root cause of Cambridge's racial problems, and any plan to break the city's racial impasse had to address this issue. "Desegregated schools are irrelevant to families who cannot afford to buy their children school books, or provide them with enough space at home to study. An opening of public places is irrelevant to people who cannot spend money in them. Federal housing projects are irrelevant if the rest of the ghetto conditions—faulty education and lack of employment—are maintained. The only way to break this vicious circle is to ensure better jobs." Richardson felt compelled to not only identify the source of Cambridge's problems but also propose a solution to them: "The entire community must work together harmoniously; each race must learn to trust the other, and more important, both races must learn to trust their common future."[8]

She warned her audience that white leaders could not be relied on to act in their constituents' best interest. "I no longer fool myself by saying that the economic and political progress will be achieved because men are moral." "If it [progress] comes in Cambridge," she added, "it will be because the white leaders have decided that for them to sacrifice a portion of their power is a lesser evil than for them to sacrifice an entire town." Richardson's statement was a critique of civil rights activists' reliance on appeals to white people's sense of morality, which history had shown to be effective only if the white people were receptive to such appeals, as they had been during the abolition movement. She was fully aware that the vast majority of white Americans were not experiencing a crisis of conscience because their fellow black citizens were suffering from disenfranchisement, grinding poverty, and social ostracism. In Cambridge, this fact was complicated by white residents' refusal to see that they were being exploited economically by the white power structure. "White people really will have to examine their way of life—and much more profoundly than if I happen to sit next to one of them at a lunch counter. They will have to accept the risk of an uncertain future, where the white masses as well as the Negroes begin to question the pattern of jobs and schooling that has so long constricted them." Richardson expressed hope that the white masses would reject their leaders and replace them with people from within their own ranks, just as Cambridge's black community had rejected its own gradualists. "[Whites] will, ultimately, have to accept the basic premise of democracy: that the people as a whole really do have more intelligence than a few of their leaders and that they know what is best for themselves."[9]

She finished by telling her audience that Cambridge was essentially a microcosm of America, and there were countless communities around the nation where residents faced a dire future because of racism. They still had time to embark on a course of action that ensured everyone's survival and prosperity, Richardson said, but white people would have to believe that they had as much to gain from the journey as black people did. "The choice that Cambridge and the rest of the nation faces is, finally, between progress and anarchy, between witnessing change and experiencing destruction. The status quo is now intolerable to the majority of Negroes and will soon be intolerable to the majority of whites. People have called our movement the Negro Revolution. They are right; the changes for America that will flow from what Negroes throughout the country are doing shall be truly revolutionary. And we can only hope and work, and work some more, to make that revolution creative—and not spattered with blood."[10]

The next morning Richardson said good-bye to the Cowan family and headed back to Cambridge, where she spent a couple of days with her family before leaving for her next engagement, which was in Washington, DC. That event would be the largest one she ever attended.[11]

The March on Washington

The March on Washington for Jobs and Freedom was held on 28 August 1963, and it became one of the most symbolic and important events in US history. Seven men and two women had primary responsibility for organizing it. The two women were Dorothy Height of the National Council of Negro Women and Anna Arnold Hedgeman, who had spent decades working in a variety of civil rights organizations. The men included a group of black power brokers informally called the "Big Six": labor leader A. Philip Randolph, who had proposed the same type of march in 1941; Martin Luther King Jr., head of the SCLC; James Farmer, head of CORE; Roy Wilkins, head of the NAACP; Whitney Young, head of the Urban League; and SNCC chairman John Lewis. Operating from behind the scenes was the seventh man—Bayard Rustin—the person most responsible for the march's success. As a gay man and a former communist, Rustin was considered controversial by some within both the black and white communities, and they were reluctant to support the event if he played a highly visible role in it. A pragmatist, Rustin agreed to keep a low profile to avoid becoming a lightning rod for the march's detractors, of which there were many.

Richardson initially supported the march because of its theme of jobs and freedom—the goals she and her colleagues in CNAC had been working toward for more than a year. Additionally, she liked an idea floated by some of her colleagues on SNCC's executive committee (Richardson had been elected four months earlier): use the march as an opportunity to ratchet up the pressure on the Kennedy administration by holding direct action demonstrations around the nation's capital the same day. With the exception of Lewis, the rest of the Big Six opposed any type of civil disobedience and demanded that marchers utilize the politics of respectability to appeal to the millions of white Americans who would be watching, listening, and reading about the event. SNCC eventually agreed, a decision based on its belief that it was more important for Lewis to give his planned speech critiquing American democracy. Once the direct action demonstrations were nixed, Richardson had no interest in attending the march, and other SNCC activists had reservations about the event. Staff member Mary King felt that a huge sum of money was "being poured into what we regarded as a symbolic gesture"— funds that could have been better spent purchasing vehicles and communications equipment for ongoing and future projects throughout the South.[12]

Courtland Cox had the task of reaching out to SNCC members, including Richardson, and encouraging them to participate. She finally agreed to attend because she felt the need to demonstrate solidarity with her comrades. Richardson, Daisy Bates (an NAACP official from Little Rock, Arkansas, who mentored the students who desegregated the city's white high school), Diane Nash, Myrlie Evers (widow of Medgar Evers), Prince E. Lee (widow of a slain Mississippi civil rights activist), and Rosa Parks were being honored in the portion of the march called "Tribute to Negro Women Fighters for Freedom."[13] The march's stakeholders believed that the politics of respectability could be successfully employed if they kept tight control over the event's messaging and imaging, which included how much time guests would be allowed to speak and what they should wear. Someone from the NAACP told Richardson she would have "one minute to speak and that it was not appropriate for [her] to wear jeans to the march instead of the hat, gloves, and dress they expected [her] to wear." She had been planning to wear an outfit just like the one the organizer described, but she found the directive so insulting that she wore a jean skirt, white blouse, and leather sandals instead. Organizers' decision to have the Lincoln Memorial serve as the event's focal point also bothered Richardson. In an interview with Robert Penn Warren in March 1964, she told him the Big Six had agreed to the site because they wanted to be legitimized by President Kennedy, a claim all of them would have disputed. She also thought the Lincoln Memorial would be a powerful marketing tool for the Kennedy administration because "Lincoln was the myth of America." Kennedy, she alleged, hoped to parlay that to improve his own public image on civil rights, even though he had done so little to make democracy a reality for black Americans.[14]

Countless white people were uncomfortable with the march itself. One concern among politically and socially conservative white people was that the marchers would trash the city and violence would be rampant. A few white liberals also predicted catastrophe for Washington. Agnes E. Meyer of the National Advisory Committee on Equal Opportunity in Apprenticeship and Training wrote to the *New York Times:* "None would be more disastrous than the march of thousands of Negroes upon Washington in August to urge the passage of the Administration's civil rights bill. Democratic government itself is imperiled when any group seeks to intimidate the members of Congress."[15] Concerns about violence permeated Washington from the White House to the thousands of municipal employees who worked in the city. Bruce Smith, a white nineteen-year-old college student, had a summer job at the DC Highway Department, and he recalled his coworkers' expectation that black people would be violent. His bosses fanned the flames of fear with their instructions for the day of the march. "Officially," said Smith, "those of us who came to work were supposed to work as emergency 'ambulance drivers' and be available to haul the dead and wounded out of the fray after the riot. We came in at dawn and emptied out our trucks so they would be available to be loaded with bodies." At the time of the march, Lewis Flagg Jr., a childhood playmate of Richardson's and the son of her godmother, Marie Flagg, was an attorney for the Department of the Interior (the federal agency responsible for managing the march). Some of his white colleagues had called Richardson a "whore" and accused her of intending to incite violence at the march. Flagg confronted his colleagues and defended his childhood friend's reputation. The incident bothered him so much that he shared it with Richardson at the time.[16]

On the afternoon before the march, Richardson arrived at Washington's Statler Hilton Hotel, which was serving as headquarters for the event's leadership. It was also where attendees obtained their credentials to access the platform at the Lincoln Memorial. Richardson's SNCC colleagues invited her to visit with them, but she had to decline because she had dinner plans with Charles Evers, brother of Medgar. The next morning Richardson left the hotel and headed to the parade route, where she joined hundreds of thousands of "spirited but serious" marchers who had arrived in Washington by airplane, train, bus, car, motorcycle, scooter, and bicycle. CNAC and Dorchester County's NAACP chapter had organized transportation for the 200 county residents who attended the event (Donna Richardson was one of them). In all, approximately 8,000 Marylanders were in the capital that Wednesday morning. A reporter for the *Baltimore Sun* noted that "some

30 youngsters from Cambridge put on a 'demonstration'" for hundreds of onlookers while they awaited their march along Constitution and Independence Avenues. Another reporter wrote that the highly orchestrated event kicked off unexpectedly when a large group of people got out in front of the march's official leaders and began moving toward the Lincoln Memorial. "Some observers," the reporter wrote, "saw this as symbolic of the Negro movement for civil rights today: That some of the Negroes are in front of their leaders."[17]

Richardson did not arrive in time to join the women of the "Tribute" portion as they led a throng of marchers down Independence Avenue to the Lincoln Memorial. Recently, a few scholars and journalists have claimed that this stream of marchers was distinct from the one led by men and was the result of the Big Six's sexist decision to relegate the women to a secondary position within the march itself. Joyce Ladner, who was on Bayard Rustin's march staff, rejected this characterization of events. "There was a lot of confusion that day," but to her knowledge there was no calculated move to separate male and female leaders and have them each lead their own group of marchers. What is not in dispute is the march's gendered list of speakers. Initially, none of the Big Six even considered having any women speak at the event, but they finally relented and scheduled Myrlie Evers to address the marchers. When she could not attend, they asked Daisy Bates to replace her.[18]

When Richardson finally arrived at the Lincoln Memorial, she joined politicians, dignitaries, entertainers, and everyday people who had traveled far and wide to take part in the historic day. Ralph Bunche was there to address the crowd, and he must have been filled with pride knowing that one of his former students was helping America become more democratic. Richardson was introduced to Josephine Baker and Lena Horne, who were among a large group of celebrities milling around the stage. Joan Baez, Bob Dylan, and the folk trio Peter, Paul, and Mary sang songs that lent a "very festive" tone to the event, which Richardson found "surreal," considering the serious nature of the problems that had driven a quarter of a million people to attend the march.[19]

Richardson was speaking with the international press as she awaited the signal to move to the stage along with the other women taking part in the "Tribute" portion of events. That was when Rustin hurriedly approached her and told her the others were already up there. It may have been a simple misunderstanding among the marshals that resulted in Richardson being left behind, but she became suspicious when she joined them on stage and had no place to sit because someone had removed her seat. She was "seething inside" as she walked over to Chicago civil rights lawyer W. Robert Ming and began discussing some legal questions. A few moments later someone called her back to the front. "I said well I guess I'll go up. So I went up and when I said 'Hello' they took the mic away."[20]

When viewed individually, these incidents might be interpreted as examples of poor execution and time management by march personnel, but Richardson believed they were intentional; she believed the organizers wanted to marginalize her because they were afraid of what she might say. If she was correct, their fears were well founded because Richardson planned to encourage the crowd to do exactly what organizers and the Kennedy administration wanted to avoid: engage in mass civil disobedience in the capital. "I was gonna tell the people, 'You sit here until this no good [civil rights bill] passes.'" She was not the only activist march organizers were concerned about. Washington's Catholic archbishop Patrick A. O'Boyle had gotten hold of a copy of John Lewis's planned speech and informed A. Philip Randolph that he would not give the invocation unless Lewis changed the "inflammatory" passages that "conveyed a bitterness not at all [in] keeping with the high moral theme of the occasion or with the religious fervor that the likes of Dr. Martin Luther King Jr. have tried to infuse into the civil rights movement." Randolph and other organizers buttonholed Lewis at the march and pressed him to change his speech, which he ended up doing. However, to SNCC, the incident was a salient display of the limits of white liberalism.[21]

As the march wound down, the crowd began chanting "Pass the bill! Pass the bill!" at the 150 members of Congress seated at the Lincoln Memorial who would soon be voting on the pending civil rights legislation. After King delivered his "I Have a Dream" speech, Rustin proceeded to call out a list of civil rights demands, which the interracial crowd affirmed. Then, to close the event, everyone accompanied Marian Anderson in singing "We Shall Overcome," the anthem of the civil rights movement.[22]

The Referendum

Cambridge spent the month of August working its way through a simple legal process. Just as CNAC had expected, white voters were planning to challenge the charter amendment passed on 1 July. The first step was to get more than 700 registered voters to sign a petition to put the amendment up for a referendum vote. A major sponsor of that effort was local business leader Levi B. Phillips Jr., who believed the charter amendment would deny business owners the right to choose their customers. He was joined by other white voters who opposed the amendment because they believed racial segregation was sanctioned by the Bible. Importantly, Cambridge's white community was not monolithic in its thoughts about racial segregation and the charter amendment. Some white people (including private citizens, politicians, and businesspeople) believed that segregation was a violation of their Christian faith, while others believed it was breaking the city apart and driving businesses away. They wanted the charter amendment to take effect because they thought it would help the city heal and move it forward.[23]

Cambridge's City Council president said that he and his fellow council members would use "moral suasion" to convince voters not to sign the petition. The *Banner*'s editors advised readers not to sign the petition and pointed out the possible consequences if the charter amendment were defeated: federal intervention in Cambridge, a delayed or canceled school year for public school students, industries' refusal to invest in Dorchester County or a downsizing of their operations, and "the loss of [Cambridge's] reputation as a progressive community." This last item weighed heavily on the editors, and they asked rhetorically: "Can anyone deny that if disorder returns we will be standing alone?" Political isolation was not a concern shared by a significant portion of Cambridge's white voters, who signed the petition and thus forced a referendum vote, which city officials scheduled for Tuesday, 1 October 1963.[24]

White people's tactical use of a referendum to limit black people's rights was nothing new. In fact, voters from around the nation had been using referenda to restrict citizens' rights as far back as the mid-nineteenth century. White men in Wisconsin (1857) and New York (1860) used referenda to restrict black men's access to the vote, and white men in Kansas and Ohio did the same to black men just after the Civil War. Prior to ratification of the Nineteenth Amendment in 1920, predominantly white male electorates around the nation used referenda to determine whether women should be given the right to vote in various types of elections. During the mid-1910s a majority of white male voters in St. Louis, Missouri, used a referendum to require housing segregation in that city. In the late 1950s white voters in Little Rock, Arkansas, sought to circumvent the Supreme Court's *Brown* decision with a referendum to maintain racially segregated schools. Interestingly, Cambridge's 1963 referendum was the third such ballot measure initiated by white voters that year, and all three became part of the civil rights landscape. There was a statewide measure in Maryland whereby white voters tried to nullify a recently passed state law that desegregated certain public accommodations, and earlier in the year white voters in Berkeley, California, used a referendum to reject an open housing ordinance.[25]

The Cambridge Nonviolent Action Committee had opposed the charter amendment from the beginning. As Richardson said, black residents "don't want to vote on something that is already their right." With the referendum vote a foregone conclusion, she informed reporters that CNAC would not be supporting a get-out-the-vote campaign in the Second Ward—at least not at that time. This seemed to leave the door open for CNAC to support such an effort if black residents changed their minds about voting in the referendum, but if that did not happen, CNAC was fine with watching the white community take on the issue all by itself.[26]

Some black residents did not want to let the white community determine the outcome of the referendum vote. The Reverend T. M. Murray, leader of the local NAACP, did not believe black people's rights should be put up for a popular vote, but he thought black residents should vote to uphold the amendment, and his organization would be encouraging them to register to vote so they could do so. His position was in alignment with that of the Maryland branch of the NAACP. Councilman Charles Cornish also encouraged his constituents to vote, noting that "it would be a reflection on our intelligence if we do not exercise our right of franchise at all times." Cornish's position was a curious one in light of his actions during the City Council's vote on the charter amendment on 1 July: he had abstained. Practically speaking, Cornish's abstention amounted to a boycott of the vote, which was an odd position for a legislator—even at the municipal level—because a legislator's primary responsibility is to cast votes. Now he was urging his constituents to go to the polls and vote on their rights when he had refused to do so in his job as councilman.[27]

As the voter registration deadline of 30 August approached, Richardson realized that she was not registered to vote. Although she never intended to vote on the referendum, she registered so that no one could criticize her for being someone who held a position on the referendum but ultimately could have no say in its outcome. In other words, she had to join the electoral process before she could refuse to participate in it. For the remainder of August, the black community continued to debate the merits of voting in the referendum. Bethel AME's pastor, the Reverend C. N. Bourne, told reporters there was "a mixed feeling" among residents concerning whether they should vote, but the Second Ward's "ministers are doing their best to encourage the people to vote" for the charter amendment. CNAC reiterated its position that the referendum was a mechanism by which the white majority would determine the rights of the black minority; therefore, CNAC would not, as Richardson said, "go out and beat people over the head and tell them to vote."[28] The

NAACP's decision to support a get-out-the-vote effort in Cambridge angered Richardson. She saw it as an attempt to gain control of the Cambridge movement and use it to buttress the NAACP's voting rights agenda in the Deep South. Because of this, CNAC switched from passively opposing the referendum vote to actively opposing it.

Throughout September the battle over the referendum continued. City residents attended mass meetings where they were encouraged to either defeat or uphold the charter amendment. A meeting by pro-amendment voters in the Second Ward on 25 September played a role in a major but short-lived controversy within CNAC. A day earlier, Gloria Richardson had abruptly resigned as the organization's chair. Reporters speculated that the NAACP was winning the argument over whether black residents should vote in the referendum, and this may have been an "indirect cause" of Richardson's resignation. The *Baltimore Sun* wrote that this turn of events appeared to catch Reggie Robinson "by surprise," and the *New York Times* reported that white residents "were elated" upon hearing the news, but their elation was short-lived because, within twenty-four hours, Richardson had withdrawn her resignation. The *Times* stated that during this brief period, the tide of opinion within the ranks of the Cambridge movement had swung toward Richardson's position on the referendum. Allegedly buoyed by this support, Richardson stated that, "after careful consideration," she had concluded that her resignation would be "a detriment to the movement in Cambridge and across the nation."[29]

Richardson has spoken and written about the events leading up to this episode. It began on the evening of 24 September, when members of CNAC's executive committee and numerous other Second Ward residents confronted her at her uncle Herbert's home. They were angry with Richardson because SNCC's Reggie Robinson had informed them that she would be supporting a vote to uphold the charter amendment. Richardson was blindsided by this accusation and the implication that she was "a betrayer" of CNAC. She denied changing her mind about the referendum and found it "insulting" that these people would believe Robinson's false story without even attempting to verify it. According to Richardson, the members of CNAC's executive committee asked her to rescind her resignation when they realized Robinson had misled them in an attempt to influence "local people's determination." Looking back on the event, Richardson was not surprised that CNAC experienced this "blow up," given the high stress levels associated with the high-stakes and dangerous work in which they were engaged.[30]

Pressure from outside CNAC added to Richardson's stress. In the middle of September, Democratic state senator Frederick C. Malkus appeared at

Baltimore's Goucher College for a televised conference on race relations. He was joined by Mayor Mowbray and Alabama governor George Wallace, who was rumored to be considering a run for the presidency the following year. When the topic of media coverage of racial issues came up, the state senator went on the attack and accused CNAC of using violence in its attempts to change Cambridge's customs and laws. This was "the same [tactic] used by Hitler," Malkus said, adding that Richardson was nothing more than a media-hungry agitator. Cambridge's mayor concurred and claimed that Richardson was on a slash-and-burn mission that would destroy the city's image for good and ruin its chance for economic survival. "In sowing her bitter seeds of hatred, Gloria Richardson expects to reap a harvest of violence. For it is only through violent action that she can project herself in the image of a modern day Joan of Arc."[31]

There was a wide gulf between her white detractors' portrayal of Richardson's character and the image held by those people who knew her intimately. Few family members and friends were surprised that she had joined the civil rights movement, but almost all of them were surprised by her level and type of involvement because they knew her to be a private person who avoided standing out in a crowd. Therefore, the allegations that Richardson was interested in attracting media attention and promoting herself rang hollow to them.[32] With the exception of the white members of SNCC and CORE, few white people understood that anger had motivated Richardson to become active in the Cambridge movement. She was angry that she had grown up in and continued to live in a nation whose white community's rituals, customs, and laws privileged itself over the black community. Black feminist intellectual Audre Lorde wrote about the value of using anger to transform society: "Focused with precision [anger] can become a powerful source of energy serving progress and change. And when I speak of change, I do not mean a simple switch of positions or a temporary lessening of tensions, nor the ability to smile or feel good. I am speaking of a basic and radical alteration in all those assumptions underlining our lives." Richardson was not alone in using anger to bring about societal change. SNCC member Fannie Lou Hamer and antilynching crusader Ida B. Wells-Barnett also cited anger as a motivation for fighting for black liberation. Richardson had channeled her own anger to help achieve the "Treaty of Cambridge," which was one of the more consequential victories of the civil rights movement in 1963.[33]

Mayor Mowbray and Senator Malkus may have believed that Richardson was interested in notoriety and power rather than public service. Since the

1930s, numerous politicians (Joseph McCarthy) and Hollywood entertainers (Marilyn Monroe) had built cults of celebrity to further their own agendas and careers. Mowbray and Malkus may have thought that Richardson was doing the same, but it is more likely that they were threatened by her acquisition of real political power, especially because it occurred outside the system in which they held authority. These men had traveled the socially and politically accepted path to power, which required them to operate according to certain predetermined rules and within an accepted framework of activities, such as political party nominations, primaries, and general elections. The fact that they no longer had a monopoly on political power worried these politicians. This political reality was compounded by a disturbing social reality: these men had no control over a black woman who followed her own rules of engagement.

Another reason Richardson became a focal point for criticism was an early decision by CNAC's executive committee that only one spokesperson would disseminate information to the press and answer questions, "so there wouldn't be confusion in the statements." Richardson had never been told that she might be expected to fulfill this role when she was asked to join CNAC, and she probably would have declined because she was not comfortable speaking in public. The first time the subject came up was in 1962, when reporters had gathered in front of Richardson's Muir Street home during a meeting of CNAC. Richardson recalled that "most of [CNAC's] committee did not want to deal with the press," so they had no intention of leaving the house. A quick discussion ensued about who would go outside to speak with the reporters, and some of Richardson's colleagues began gently pushing her toward the door and telling her that she would do fine. Before she knew it, she was out on the front porch, and a feeling of anxiousness came over her, just like she was a child in Sunday school performing recitations. In the end, Richardson thought that day's press conference went well, and as she held more of them, she became more comfortable being the public face of CNAC, but she never enjoyed the role.[34]

Because she served as CNAC's spokesperson, many people concluded that Richardson was also the organization's decision maker. This was based on a misunderstanding of CNAC's group-centered and member-driven nature, whereby each member had a vote in the decision-making process. One example of this misperception about Richardson's power involved a local black clergyman's decision not to allow CNAC to use his church's sanctuary for a boycott-the-vote rally in late September. The Reverend Charles Bourne of Bethel Church had initially agreed to let CNAC use the site, but he rescinded the offer after Richardson allegedly "went back on her word" and called for a boycott of the referendum.[35] The Second Ward's Elks Club saved the day when it permitted CNAC to hold its rally at the Elks' Pine Street meeting hall. Acknowledging that CNAC and its supporters were outnumbered by white residents and opposed by the NAACP and black ministers, Richardson told the attendees they would "have to go it alone." As Richardson discussed her rationale for boycotting the vote, she was "continually interrupted . . . with shouts of 'Right,' 'Good,' [and] 'We will not go to the polls.'" Then she took a swipe at the NAACP, which had scheduled a high-profile visit to Cambridge by Juanita Jackson Mitchell, its Maryland state conference chairperson, and Gloster B. Current, the national director of branches. Richardson implied that they wanted to impose an agenda on black Cambridge that its residents did not want or need. Richardson read from a telegram she had received from Mitchell, who stated it was "unfortunate" that Richardson was "attempt[ing] to divide the colored community, particularly in view of the national and local support by NAACP of [CNAC's] demonstrations."[36]

Richardson was dismayed by Mitchell's assessment of the NAACP's role in the Cambridge movement, given that the NAACP provided no funding to CNAC. The NAACP's contribution to the Cambridge movement consisted mainly of the work done by two of its dedicated staff members, Stanley Branche and Phil Savage. Mitchell undoubtedly felt that these men's work in Cambridge entitled the NAACP to a quid pro quo from CNAC in the form of supporting its decision to encourage black residents to vote on their constitutional rights. A casual observer of the NAACP's actions over the previous four weeks might have concluded that if anyone was trying to divide Cambridge's black community, it was the NAACP. That organization was actively working to achieve a goal that residents did not want and that CNAC had argued was a losing proposition for them.[37]

Military veterans were especially offended by the referendum, and Richardson conveyed their feelings when she stated, "I think [the referendum] creates a hurt and a disappointment that after 300 years here we are going to have to go to the polls and vote" on our human rights. "But people can come here from Europe," she observed, "and [they] can go anyplace they wish—people who have not been here for generation after generation and have not fought for America." Richardson could have added that in many cases, those Europeans were recent arrivals from Germany and Italy and had actually fought against the United States in World War II.[38] The political reality of being a racial minority in a gerrymandered municipality reinforced the black community's sense of offense. Black voters had engaged in electoral politics since obtaining the right to vote, but "it did not help improve our situation," Richardson noted. Furthermore, white leaders and their constituents had never cared about black residents before, but now the city's entire white community wanted to lay responsibility for Cambridge's reputation and survival at the entrance to the Second Ward. Richardson rejected this and defined the entire referendum—from its initiation through the vote itself—as "a white man's problem and a test of good faith" with regard to the white community's commitment to building a racially egalitarian society.[39]

Projections about black voter turnout started appearing in the press a few days before the vote. Richardson said that approximately 400 voters from the Second Ward would head to the polls, but Savage of the NAACP said he expected a "tremendous" turnout. He linked the referendum vote to black people's past and current struggles elsewhere in the nation, especially in the South, and he claimed that a large black voter turnout in Cambridge would demonstrate the Second Ward's solidarity with southern black Americans who were still fighting for that right. He added, "Negroes who do not vote or vote against (the amendment) will injure the cause in Cambridge and elsewhere," and that would force black America to take "a backward step" in the fight for liberation. Councilman Charles Cornish had made the same argument back in August, when he had drawn a straight line from Cambridge's Second Ward to the entire South and its multitude of local struggles to obtain voting rights. "In the great fight on civil rights," he said, "we are reminded that we are not free until our brothers in the South are free." The best way for Cambridge's blacks to show solidarity with their more southern counterparts was to vote to uphold the charter amendment, according to Cornish.[40] The argument that Cambridge's referendum vote was tied to other local struggles was a faulty one, in that it was based on a political strategy that ignored the real political consequences for black citizens who participated in a process rigged by and in favor of the white majority. It was absurd for Savage to imply that white supremacists inside and outside of southern state governments would change their minds about denying black people voting rights simply because those in Cambridge decided to exercise that right. And if attracting moderate white people to the cause of civil rights was a reason for having black Cambridge residents vote in the referendum, they would be right to question whether those white people would be true allies in the struggle. Furthermore, CNAC could have used Savage's logic against the NAACP. For instance, CNAC could have expected the NAACP to initiate sympathy protests in black communities *everywhere* on CNAC's behalf, even if those protests did not advance communities' local movements. Another flaw in Savage's and the NAACP's logic was that if the black community voted in the referendum, it would legitimize the white majority's inherent claim that the black minority's rights could be subjected to a popular vote.

Since the end of Reconstruction, most black human rights activists believed the vote was the most important right they were fighting for. Ida B. Wells-Barnett, Martin Luther King Jr., John Lewis, and Fannie Lou Hamer were some of the most prominent twentieth-century activists who believed that once the right to vote was obtained, black citizens had a sacred obligation to exercise it. Richardson did not subscribe to this philosophy; instead, she shared Ella Baker's view that voting was just one of many tools black people needed to bring about societal change. Specifically, Richardson viewed voting as a purely tactical move that people could use (or not) when they thought it would result in concrete benefits. She did not believe in voting for the sake of voting. "I value the right to vote," she said, "but I also value my conscience." By boycotting the referendum vote, Richardson could occupy a political space unavailable to her if she had cast a ballot; she could criticize and denounce the referendum as a fundamentally illegitimate process. Nineteenth-century English political radical Herbert Spencer stated as much when he wrote that, of the two choices citizens have on election day—to vote or to abstain from voting—the citizens who abstain are in fact the only ones who have a right to protest the election's outcome because they have not given their consent to that political process.[41]

One subject that was apparently never publicly discussed was the possibility of white retaliatory violence if the charter amendment was upheld. Local and state officials' actions indicate that they at least considered this possibility because, in addition to having plainclothes officers at polling places to look out for voter intimidation, state police officers were on hand to augment National Guard troops in the case of public disorder. Richardson was also concerned that segregationists might react violently against black residents, especially if a black swing vote was the deciding factor in the outcome. Her concern was well founded because white people had been using violence to try to stop the desegregation of various locations in and around Cambridge since 1962. Richardson's fear of white violence increased when, two weeks before the referendum vote, white terrorists bombed Birmingham's Sixteenth Street Baptist Church, killing four black girls. The church had been the staging ground for student-led liberation activities in the spring that had been partially responsible for forcing the city to desegregate public accommodations and stores. Richardson believed it was entirely possible that Cambridge's white community might do something along the same lines, and avoiding the polls was a practical way to stay out of harm's way. Yet no matter which way the vote went, CNAC had made it clear that the white community would be held responsible for its response to the outcome. "It is not we but the whites in this community that must show that they want to settle our problems peacefully," Richardson said.[42]

The day before the vote, *Banner* editors implicitly acknowledged that the amendment would fail if a critical mass of black voters boycotted the polls. Frustrated with CNAC's position, editors asked why the organization could not understand that voting in the referendum was a natural part of the nation's democratic tradition. "Compromise is woven into the fabric of American democracy. . . . The Federal Constitution was built on compromise," they wrote. One can sense the editors' disbelief that CNAC—which, according to the *Banner*, had never proved that it spoke for the Second Ward—was winning the messaging war about the referendum. Despite the likely defeat of the amendment, they expressed hope that it would survive but noted that this could happen only if the black community and the white community supported "responsible, moderate leaders" who would "keep Cambridge in the mainstream of American life."[43] The *Baltimore Sun*'s editors were of the same mind-set. They tied the charter amendment's survival to Cambridge's future, even though they considered the referendum itself an absurdity. "Mrs. Richardson and others know that Negroes should not be required to submit to a public vote on whether they are to be accorded equal treatment as American citizens." Nevertheless, blacks should vote in the referendum because, according to the editors' flawed understanding of federalism (that is, federal laws and court decisions trump those of the states), an affirmative vote for the charter amendment would provide a "firm legal basis for desegregation in Cambridge." Additionally, according to the *Sun*, the white politicians who supported the charter amendment were actually doing black residents a favor, and as such, they had "a right to expect a large Negro turnout" to ensure that the amendment survived.[44]

Cambridge was abuzz with nervous excitement on the day of the referendum, as steady streams of voters visited polling stations all around the city to cast their ballots. The only exception was in the Second Ward, where less than half of all registered black voters went to the polls. Those who did show up were greeted by a campaign sign sponsored by black ministers and white politicians who promoted the referendum vote as a means of advancing black liberation: "You must vote! Your vote is your blow for freedom now!" Outside its headquarters at the Hayes pharmacy, CNAC hung its own signage that pointed out the electorate's lack of voting rights on other important issues. "DID YOU VOTE TO GO TO WAR? CNAC SAYS: DON'T VOTE." At the end of the day, officials tallied the votes and informed the public that 1,994 people had voted against the charter amendment and 1,720 in favor of it—a difference of 274 votes. The city's four white wards voted against the amendment, while the black Second Ward voted in favor of it.[45]

A blame game immediately ensued, with black and white people around the nation criticizing Cambridge's black community and, specifically, Gloria Richardson. Their condemnations were similar to those written by the *Boston Herald*'s George Frazier earlier in the summer. He had framed Cambridge's racial problems as the logical outcome of incompetent black leadership, and his writings drew broad and long-term conclusions about Richardson and the civil rights movement in general. Cambridge's black community certainly "has many grievances against" the white community, Frazier wrote, but black citizens' greatest "grievance—if only [they] would realize it—is against such irresponsible spokesmen as Mrs. Gloria Richardson." Her "demagoguery" resulted in "alienating even the moderates who devoutly wish an end to strife." He singled out Councilman Charles Cornish as the type of leader black residents should be following, but instead they marginalized him for not pushing for faster change. Frazier warned his readers, "As long as the Negro has not Ralph Bunche or Thurgood Marshall or Edward Kennedy ["Duke"] Ellington, but a Gloria Richardson as its spokesman, he is forfeiting his right to be respected." The columnist was not optimistic that black Cambridge would reject Richardson, but he believed history would not treat her well. "All demagogues are defeated—Hitler and Mussolini and Joe McCarthy," he wrote, and Frazier was confident that it was only a matter of time before she too would be reviled and ridiculed.[46]

Editors of the *Baltimore Evening Sun* wrote that if black people had turned out and voted for the amendment, "as was their right and obligation," it would have been upheld, but "Mrs. Gloria H. Richardson . . . bears a heavy burden this morning." The *Christian Science Monitor* lectured the black residents who had stayed away from the polls: "It has never done any harm to have constitutional rights *reinforced* by local recognition. . . . But in this instance," the paper concluded, black people's "preoccupation with a *legal nicety* has been the enemy of a possible community good." *Time* magazine compared Richardson to the Israelites who used armed rebellion to resist their Roman oppressors. The "gaunt, fierce-eyed leader of Cambridge's Negroes" was a "Zealot" who demonstrated "a strange brand of leadership" with her refusal to support the referendum vote, considering that black citizens elsewhere were fighting and dying for the right to vote.[47]

Pulitzer Prize–winning author and syndicated columnist William S. White presented Cambridge's racial problem as a battle between people who believe that business owners had the right to choose their customers and those who believed owners should accommodate everyone. White agreed with the former position and stated that the solution to this problem was not a judicial one because morality cannot be dictated by the courts. He told his readers he was opposed to extremism from any corner of American society, and that included the white extremism behind the terrorist bombing of Birmingham's Sixteenth Street Baptist Church, as well as the alleged extremism of black people like Richardson. Her boycott "deliver[ed] a cruel blow to the hopes of all moderates for a reasonable accommodation of the racial problems of this country." Ringing the same alarm bell that Frazier had rung four months earlier, White wrote that the referendum boycott was a telltale sign that "extremism" was taking root in black America and that "Negro militants" like Gloria Richardson were largely responsible for its spread. He presented her as a legitimate threat to the nation's well-being and then employed the Cold War concept of the domino theory to suggest that her "extremism" must be contained by the Kennedy administration, just as it was working to contain communism in Southeast Asia. "The history of this sad racial conflict is full of instances where one day's single extremism by one Negro leader has led to tomorrow's extremism among many Negro leaders—a fact that is well known to the Administration itself and privately deplored."[48]

Joining these white opinion makers in expressing their frustration with Cambridge's black voters were a number of black editors and columnists. "Strife-torn Cambridge, Md., paid the price of Negro misleadership" is how the *Pittsburgh Courier*'s editors framed the referendum's outcome. Richardson and the Dorchester County chapter of the NAACP were "responsible for this debacle" because she took "the absurd position that Negroes should not vote for something that was their right already," and the NAACP failed to mobilize enough black voters because the chapter's leaders were afraid of losing influence by appearing to be "moderates." "More sensible Negroes elsewhere in the nation would have been delighted to have had the chance to vote" on their right to public accommodations, "but not in Cambridge, where foolish Negroes misled them." An opinion piece in the *Los Angeles Sentinel* agreed with Richardson's "academic" rationale for boycotting the vote but noted that it had a negative effect on the Cambridge movement because it prevented "an opportunity for serious and sincere communication" between Richardson and white politicos, not to mention that black residents still could not patronize white-owned businesses.[49]

Letters to the *Baltimore Sun* revealed differences of opinion about the boycott. One Baltimorean said that Richardson had "rendered a terrible disservice to her people and struck a crippling blow to her community," adding that her actions were one example of the incompetent black leadership with which black communities were all too familiar. An Ohio resident who wrote to express his disappointment with the referendum vote said that he was "speak[ing] for millions of moderates across the land." The results were a lost "opportunity to redeem the reputation of the city and the State . . . and with it a chance to set an example for the whole South." Cambridge's white voters would have to live with the "heavy stigma" associated with their role in the amendment's failure, but he believed "the greater blame lies with the radical Negro leadership" of Gloria Richardson. Sandwiched in between these missives was one from Eugene L. King Sr., secretary of Baltimore County's Human Relations Commission, who stated that Richardson and her Second Ward neighbors had been "absolutely right" to boycott the referendum.[50]

Another rare voice of support for Richardson came from within the federal government. Oregon senator Wayne Morse gave his legislative colleagues a civics lesson grounded in part on Federalist Paper No. 51, which warned of the tyranny of the majority. "What Mrs. Richardson taught the colored people was that it is not possible to compromise a principle and have any principle left. It is that simple. A basic principle of civil liberties was involved. . . . It is not possible to solve the civil liberties problem" using a popular referendum, he said. If Cambridge's referendum was a politically legitimate process, then it would follow that referenda could be used by racists throughout the nation to curb black citizens' constitutional rights. Perhaps the most important part of Morse's message was its implication that the nation's system of federalism was undermined by white Cambridge's use of the referendum. "The equal protection clause of the 14th Amendment is a constitutional right of all citizens everywhere in the United States. . . . But it is not subject to popular vote, and I commend Mrs. Richardson for her recognition of that fact." The senator was aware of the direct and indirect pressure applied by the Kennedy administration to convince Richardson not to boycott the vote, and he admired her for not succumbing to it. He called her a "great libertarian" who had shown a lot of "courage" by standing by her political principle that "the enjoyment of constitutional rights must not be made subject to popular referendum."[51] *Liberator* magazine was an important publication for the black Left in New York City in the 1960s, and its editor in chief Dan Watts wholly supported Richardson's boycott. To him, the critical aspect of the debate surrounding whether to vote in the referendum was that it revealed a problem between black militants such as Richardson, who wanted "freedom at any cost," and black moderates and white liberals, who were willing to settle for "peace at the lowest cost possible."[52]

With the referendum vote behind them, Cambridge's residents began to assess its impact on the city. Mayor Mowbray reiterated his belief that the amendment's defeat would mean "economic suicide" for Cambridge, but despite that gloomy forecast, he was unwilling to ask the City Council to pass a desegregation ordinance; nor would the mayor spend any political capital by taking the lead and trying to convince business owners to desegregate their establishments. *Daily Banner* editor Maurice Rimpo agreed with the mayor's economic assessment. "So far as I can see now, there is no possibility of a solution. I think the town has had it, economically and otherwise."[53] The referendum's outcome had no bearing on CNAC's agenda. A month before the vote, Richardson had reminded the public that racially segregated public accommodations were the least of the black community's problems. CNAC "would feel more encouraged if progress was being made in other areas," such as improved job opportunities and better housing. Thus, during a press conference on the day after the vote, Richardson said CNAC would continue to push for a faster and more complete school integration process, improved job opportunities, a uniform pay scale for black and white workers, and an increase in the minimum wage. CNAC was prepared to "resort to any tactic" to achieve these goals.[54]

In late October, Cambridge's Human Relations Committee (HRC) met to discuss the creation of a community action plan to move the city forward and prevent racial strife. Richardson warned members of the HRC that "if they did not come out with an active program," CNAC was prepared to resume demonstrations.[55] This was not an empty threat. She felt that Cambridge's racial climate was still very bad and that white people had to make a sincere effort to dismantle segregation. Speaking at Washington's Presbyterian Church of the Redeemer, Richardson stated that all levels of government were responsible for black residents' pessimistic attitude about racial progress, and politicians should be aware of the possible consequences if they chose not to take action. Federal officials did not work hard enough to help blacks obtain first-class citizenship status, and local officials had tried to strong-arm black residents into voting on their constitutional rights. Aggravating this climate were white people who menaced black protesters during demonstrations, and Richardson warned her audience that these factors were causing Cambridge's black residents to develop "an attitude of violence" that some of them might act on.[56]

A CNAC press release drove home that point. Titled "Cambridge, Maryland: Background Information," the document was officially CNAC's, but

Richardson's influence was evident in the tone and wording of the warning that some black residents might use violence to express their frustration with the city's white supremacist system. She had given this same warning back in the summer during her speaking engagements, but this time, Richardson went to great lengths to show her white audience the black community's psyche and the potential for a civil revolt if nothing was done to improve their lives. "In many respects, things in Cambridge are as they have always been, but for one new factor. This is the awareness on the part of the Negro that he does not have to allow himself to endure these conditions passively. There is a new Negro militance and determination" originating in racial oppression and its concomitant economic poverty. The most vulnerable victims were the children, "who are being just as surely destroyed . . . by the system that will not allow their parents to work so that they might be fed." This environment caused "a ground swell of opinion to the effect that the system will only respect force. That it is better to die than to live like this." The text warned white politicos that if they refused to make "concessions to those of us who council nonviolence they will have to deal, one day with those who do not, because our people are determined to improve the conditions under which they live."[57]

Another test of black residents' patience came in early November when a white man accused of molesting an eight-year-old black girl was found not guilty by an all-white jury of ten women and two men, despite multiple black eyewitnesses who testified at the trial, including one man who claimed he had seen the defendant assaulting the girl. The black community must have considered the possibility of a not-guilty verdict, given the low value of black females in American society. White males had used sexualized violence against black girls and women for hundreds of years, partly to act out their sexual perversions and partly to maintain white supremacy through terror. In the mid-twentieth century a number of black communities began well-organized campaigns to bring these types of racist perpetrators to justice, and those efforts inevitably became part of broader civil rights campaigns.[58] Richardson had attended the trial, and she spoke with the press after the verdict. Incensed that the jury could ignore eyewitness testimony, she said, "The conclusion is now inescapable that our last vestige of hope, trial by jury, has been removed from our protection whether we be prosecuting witness or defendant." Richardson then called for Dorchester County's black residents to engage in a total economic boycott of Cambridge's "bigoted white community." Richardson's statement highlighted the hypocritical nature of Cambridge's white community, which claimed to be racially progressive but failed to punish the molester of a black child.[59]

The assassination of President John F. Kennedy two weeks later provided CNAC with a unique opportunity to solidify its claim to the moral high ground in Cambridge's racial crisis. CNAC would continue its self-imposed moratorium on demonstrations until the end of the nation's month-long mourning period, but that decision, Richardson noted, was not because conditions had improved; rather, the Second Ward was expressing its "bereavement" for a politician who "had personally tried his utmost, in the face of strong resistance from Congress, to make American democracy more than an ideal."[60] This statement contradicted others Richardson had made about Kennedy in the summer, when she had accused him of not doing enough to bridge the gap between America's promise of democracy and its realization. Nothing had occurred since then to change her mind, but now that Kennedy had been assassinated, Richardson became engaged, albeit briefly, in the mythmaking that inflated his record on civil rights.

Richardson's reasons for speaking so favorably about President Kennedy appear to be due to a mix of emotions about what had just happened, as well as her concern about what lay ahead for black Americans. In an interview she gave a few months after the assassination, Richardson talked about being "extremely sorry about President Kennedy's death" and "extremely upset about it." She told the interviewer that Kennedy's murder in a segregationist hotbed like Dallas should be, if nothing else, a wake-up call to his brother Robert because the same thing was happening to black people all the time in the South. She mentioned that while meeting with Robert Kennedy at the Department of Justice, she had told him that if he and his brother "came to Dorchester County they might be shot" by a white supremacist. "This man simply did not understand this. He thought [my warning] was sort of a joke." The tone of Richardson's voice and the way she delivered her sentences revealed her exasperation with the attorney general for not taking her warning seriously.[61] Tactically speaking, Richardson's praise of President Kennedy allowed her to draw a stark contrast between him and his replacement, Lyndon B. Johnson, whom Richardson saw as a masterful political operative who would position himself to appear sympathetic to black citizens' needs and rights but give only lip service to them. Furthermore, she expected Johnson to use the machinery of congressional committees to prevent real legislative change from occurring, just as he had in the Senate when he helped water down the Civil Rights Act of 1957.[62]

As 1963 came to a close, the *Banner* ran articles that acknowledged the year's racial challenges, but the paper claimed the city seemed to be moving forward. Cambridge's Human Relations Committee praised the recent hiring of hundreds of local residents (half of whom were black) by city industries, and at least some people were noticing a "better atmosphere" between black and white residents.[63] The Cambridge movement itself was the city's main story of 1963, but plenty of ink was used to cover its leader. Indicative of this was the *Banner*'s end-of-year article titled "Racial Story Is Dominated by Woman Leader"—a timeline of the Cambridge movement and an analysis of how Richardson proved to be a tenacious but flawed leader who used demonstrations to disrupt the city's peace and bring unfair racial criticism upon the white community and its leaders.[64]

Regional and national media also made the Cambridge movement and Richardson a story of the year. Unlike the *Banner*, however, the story told by the national media centered on a black community's struggle for freedom against a white community that seemed ready to go to any lengths to resist becoming a racially egalitarian society. The *Afro-American* included Richardson in its pictorial review of the year's most important events, which also featured President Kennedy's assassination and the March on Washington. Chicago's black newspaper the *Daily Defender* cited Richardson's bravery and "Gibraltar rock of courage" as the reasons for her selection to the paper's Honor Roll for 1963. She and the other nine honorees—a group of men that included Supreme Court Justice Earl Warren, Martin Luther King Jr., Robert F. Kennedy, and comedian and human rights activist Dick Gregory—were cited for "beating on the anvil of freedom and equality with greater verve and determination to secure those rights that the Constitution had conferred."[65] While these accolades were nice, they mattered little to Richardson. She had to stay focused on the task at hand, which was to work with CNAC to plan for another winter of protests.

8

Creative Chaos

January 1964 was the two-year anniversary of the Cambridge movement, and even though the "Treaty of Cambridge" had been signed the previous summer, not much had actually changed. The National Guard still patrolled the city, and its racially discriminatory society and economy were about to get support from white supremacists from outside the Eastern Shore, such as Alabama governor George Wallace. Gloria Richardson continued to lead the Cambridge Nonviolent Action Committee's resistance efforts, employing the same basic tactics and strategies she had used over the past eighteen months. She continued to speak with the press so that CNAC's message of job opportunities, decent housing, and equal education for children were telegraphed as broadly as possible, and she attended government meetings and presented officials with CNAC's demands and suggestions for meeting them. Also unchanged was the NAACP's disagreement with the tactics CNAC used to achieve its goals. This time, it was CNAC's boycott of Dorchester County's school system that the NAACP opposed. This disagreement reminded grassroots activists that they and national civil rights organizations continued to have competing agendas, which would produce even more conflict within the movement over the coming years.

One new development was that Richardson started traveling outside of Cambridge to lend her organizational expertise to people engaged in other local struggles for freedom. Changes were on the horizon for the Cambridge movement, too. As the summer of 1964 came to a close, passage of the Civil Rights Act would alter Cambridge's racial terrain, and Richardson would resign from CNAC. Both events would bring important changes to the Cambridge movement, but until that time came, Richardson carried on black Cambridge's struggle to achieve "freedom now." Her impact on that struggle and the broader civil rights movement was significant. Both her leadership style and her vision for achieving black liberation were key elements to her success as a human rights leader. And although she never saw her activism as a means of expanding women's rights or opportunities, she helped young women see that they could and should assume leadership of their own local projects and expand the meaning of freedom to include women's liberation.

Gloria Richardson started the year in Atlanta, Georgia, where she was involved in two movement events: a desegregation effort at the chain restaurant Toddle House, and an executive committee meeting of SNCC. The Toddle House demonstrations were initiated by Dick Gregory and his wife Lillian, who owned stock in the large corporation that owned the restaurant, which did not serve black people. By early January, Richardson, John Lewis, and SNCC's executive secretary James "Jim" Forman had successfully negotiated with the company's representatives for the restaurants to be desegregated.[1]

The SNCC executive committee meeting took place on the last day of the organization's five-day staff meeting. In addition to general organizational matters, SNCC staff discussed more substantive issues such as their economic and political goals. Up to that point, SNCC had not created economic programs for the local projects run by its staff members. In contrast, CNAC had been focused on economics and other social justice issues for almost two years, and that provided SNCC with an operational model for moving in that direction.[2] Some staff members, including Courtland Cox, were attracted to CNAC's focus on economics and criticized members of the executive committee for SNCC's lack of an economic agenda. Robert "Bob" Moses was one of their targets. A field secretary from Harlem and a Hamilton College graduate, Moses was known throughout the organization as a quiet intellectual who did not shy away from debates about important issues. Responding to their criticism, Moses pointed out that they did not have the experience or specialized training required to reform the nation's economic system, let alone revolutionize it to help southern black workers. He suggested that everyone take time in the coming year to fill in their knowledge gaps. The debate about SNCC's economic agenda reflected an expansion of its original goals from desegregation and voter registration to bread-and-butter issues. By the spring of 1964, John Lewis was telling people outside of SNCC that its agenda for that year would include the development of social justice projects.[3]

Back in Cambridge, the focus on economics continued. CNAC planned to ask the Department of Agriculture to provide emergency relief to hundreds of Dorchester County families. "We want some Federal government people sent in here to help people organize their farms, we want the Department of Agriculture to send in surplus food. Our people are really hard-pressed. It's been a rough winter," Richardson said. The hard winter had exacerbated an already difficult time for the area's working poor, and poverty was so extensive that it shocked civil rights activists from the North. In January the *Washington Post* ran an investigative piece on poverty in Maryland, and its findings refuted the commonly held assumption that "a jobholder cannot be a pauper." The journalist had traveled to various places around the state—including Cambridge—where he found people living in grinding poverty and hard-pressed to find a way out of it. Low-paid seasonal workers in agriculturally based economies like Dorchester County's were at the greatest disadvantage; automation had reduced the need for these workers, and many of them lacked the skill required to operate the high-tech industry's sophisticated machinery.[4]

When race was factored into the employment equation, the forecast for black people was even worse. A group called the Maryland Advisory Committee submitted a report to the US Commission on Civil Rights that painted a bleak economic picture of Cambridge. Black workers constituted 67 percent of the city's unemployed, even though they accounted for only 35 percent of its labor force, an unemployment rate four times greater than that of the white workforce. When black workers did find jobs, they experienced the same racist employment structure that had always been present on the Eastern Shore. "It has become apparent that all skilled or semiskilled jobs are reserved by precedence or by outright discrimination for the whites," the report's authors stated. Consequently, "ninety-five percent of the working Negroes earn only $1.17 per hour picking beans, tomatoes, cracking oysters, or picking crabs." Higher education did not always translate into greater economic opportunities for black residents (which Gloria Richardson could attest to): of the city's seventy-five black residents who had earned degrees, twenty were working at manual labor jobs. In addition, the city's racial strife stifled business expansion and discouraged new industries from moving into Cambridge. A small number of job training programs had been initiated or proposed, and some business owners had promised to expand employment opportunities for black workers, but it was impossible to predict the social and economic impact of such efforts on the city.[5]

In the last week of January, Richardson traveled to Washington to attend a conference at the office of Senator Daniel Brewster, a Maryland Democrat who had arranged the gathering to discuss the importance of pressing fellow members of Congress to pass President Kennedy's civil rights legislation. The meeting also gave the Reverend T. M. Murray, leader of Dorchester County's NAACP chapter and a member of Cambridge's Human Relations Committee (HRC), the opportunity to update members of Congress and representatives of federal agencies about the committee's progress. Before the meeting began, Richardson presented Brewster with a copy of CNAC's fall press release, which charged white politicos with continuing their laissez-faire gradualism. City councilmen had refused to pass "a decent building code governing the maintenance of rented houses," and CNAC alleged that members of the Industrial Development Committee were parlaying their positions to enrich themselves rather than to promote long-term employment opportunities for residents. Accompanying the document was a list of three broad demands. First, there should be a minimum wage of $2 an hour, and all time worked in excess of forty hours a week should be paid at time and a half. Second, all levels of government should be involved in the creation of jobs for local residents, which included preventing migrant laborers from working locally during harvest season. "We are not against the well being of migrant laborers," CNAC wrote, but excluding them from the local unskilled labor force at harvest time was necessary because the black unemployment rate was near 40 percent, and migrant workers "are obviously used by the bosses of the town to keep wages low and to break strikes." The third demand focused on the need for Cambridge to have "an *overall economic development plan.*" Black residents should have a voice in creating the plan, which must "be made public" so that the entire community was aware of it. Additionally, black workers must receive training to be competitive for the jobs resulting from the plan. After the meeting, Richardson told the press it was "a waste of time," due in part to Murray's and the HRC's "wrong attitude" about Cambridge's problems, as evidenced by their failure to create "a definite program to garner Federal aid."[6]

CNAC resumed its efforts to move Cambridge forward when it kicked off its winter offensive with a handful of demonstrations, the first in almost six months. They consisted of new targets and at least one new tactic: a school boycott. Richardson called for black parents to keep their children home for one day, 11 February, to draw attention to Dorchester County's broken education system. Reverend Murray spoke out against the boycott and asked his fellow black clergymen to do the same in their upcoming Sunday services. Dorchester County school superintendent James Busick also opposed the boycott and warned that the parents of boycotting students would be guilty of a misdemeanor—the crime of encouraging a student to be absent from school. Even so, a significant number of students did not attend school that day.[7]

Some positive economic development occurred in February when twenty black women started a sewing training program and a handful of other residents initiated an auto mechanics course. In addition, a training program for forty nurses' aides and orderlies was scheduled to start in the spring if the federal and state governments allocated the necessary funds. These developments did not convince CNAC that it should cease demonstrating, so it targeted Cambridge's Welfare Board and State Unemployment Security Commission offices for protests on 25 February. "Spotters" carrying walkie-talkies kept tabs on the white people who showed up at the protests, as CNAC pressured local government officials to expand employment opportunities and distribute food to Cambridge's hungry residents. Fifteen black demonstrators were arrested by National Guardsmen outside the offices, and they were bused to the National Guard armory in Pikesville, Maryland, outside of Baltimore.[8]

The community's hunger problem could have been easily remedied because surplus food was available, but few local white politicos believed the problem was as extensive as CNAC claimed. Dorchester County commissioners declined an opportunity "to participate in the [food surplus] program, saying the County could meet local needs." That decision angered CNAC, which responded by planning a "hunger protest." Possibly concerned that such a protest would result in violence, Cambridge's HRC created a subcommittee to "determine" whether such a program was needed. While the HRC was dithering on the subject, CNAC approached the federal government directly and asked it to establish a surplus food distribution program in the county.[9] The program finally got up and running when Governor Tawes and Senator Brewster made the same request. Curiously, this angered Dorchester County commissioners and Cambridge's HRC. According to the former, the county needed no such program, and the HRC believed that any benefits from the program would be offset by the costs of administering it and the logistical problems of handing out food to hungry residents. As the month of March arrived, the ranks of naysayers thinned when seasonal layoffs in the canning industry and a decrease in farm work "swelled relief rolls." Hundreds of local residents—both black and white—lined up at the Welfare Board office in Cambridge for free surplus food provided by the Department of Agriculture. The HRC ended up switching its position and supporting the program, which, according to one angry county commissioner, it did only "to keep Gloria from demonstrating again."[10]

Around the time CNAC resumed its demonstrations in Cambridge, a number of students at Maryland State College in Princess Anne were preparing an attack on that town's racially segregated public spaces. Calling themselves Students Appeal for Equality (SAFE), the activists planned multiday demonstrations that commenced in the last week of February. However, the most memorable event took place on Wednesday afternoon, 26 February, when 300 students attempted to desegregate two local restaurants. Driving in from Cambridge to assist the students were Gloria Richardson, Stanley Branche, and Reggie Robinson. Richardson was repaying SAFE's leaders James "Jim" Boardley and Johnnie Wilson for their work in the Cambridge movement over the previous two years.[11]

Just before three that afternoon, approximately 300 students left campus and began marching toward town. When they were prevented from entering the restaurants, they sat down in the middle of Route 13, a major thoroughfare. A melee broke out when state troopers attempted to pick up and remove the demonstrators using dogs and nightsticks, and firefighters turned water hoses on the students to force them back to campus. The students responded by throwing broken bottles and bricks, and one person tossed sulfuric acid at a trooper's legs, requiring medical treatment. Richardson, Branche, and Robinson tried to convince the students to return to the college, but they regrouped on campus and made another attempt to reach town. Again, they were thwarted by troopers and firefighters. For the remainder of the evening, the students stayed on campus as troopers patrolled the town in cars and on foot. They witnessed a group of white youths raising the Confederate flag outside the courthouse but did nothing to prevent it.[12]

When it was all over, dozens of students had been arrested, and Richardson was being sought for assaulting a trooper. She had punched a trooper in the back while he held a male student bent over the hood of a car, but she got away during the commotion. When Richardson heard a rumor that the president of the college wanted her to be handed over to the state police, she hid in the men's dormitory and then slipped off campus sometime after midnight by hiding on the floorboard of a car.[13] Many students suffered injuries during the conflict, which Richardson described as "pretty awful." United Press International (UPI) reporter John Kady concurred, describing white people's behavior as "very, very vicious." Some residents thought the town was on the verge of a race war, a perception fueled by the rumor that local stores had sold out of firearm ammunition. Maryland NAACP leader Juanita Mitchell chastised the governor for his lack of leadership during the racial flare-up, which she compared with events in Birmingham, Alabama, the year before, where police had used attack dogs against demonstrators and firefighters had blasted them with water.[14]

Five weeks later, Richardson headed north to Chester, Pennsylvania, to lend her support to Stanley Branche and the Chester Committee for Freedom Now, which was engaged in multiday protests against the city's segregated education system. Located in the southeast corner of Pennsylvania, Chester had a volatile history of race relations during the twentieth century. For example, in July 1917 the city experienced a race riot started by white residents after they learned that a twenty-one-year-old white man had been killed by a sixteen-year-old black boy. The riot lasted five days, during which gangs of white people attacked black residents and attempted to raze some of their homes; seven people died from injuries sustained in the mayhem. At the beginning of the 1960s, civil rights activists began pressuring Chester's white power structure to end de facto segregated public education.[15] Richardson arrived in the city on 1 April to protest police officers' treatment of demonstrators arrested during earlier protests. She and approximately 250 others marched to Chester's police headquarters and sat down in the street. The police arrested Richardson, Branche, and Savage and more than 100 other protesters. She was charged with "unlawful assembly, public nuisance, disorderly conduct, and affray." A magistrate began adjudicating their cases shortly after midnight. He offered all the arrestees the choice of paying a $350 fine or posting $1,500 bond. No one opted to pay the fine, so they were all bused to the Delaware County prison at Broadmeadows. Richardson was finally bailed out on 4 April.[16]

For some time, George Wallace had been wanting to run for president. The Democratic governor of Alabama had promised to put a brake on racial integration and to promote states' rights—two goals he achieved, albeit temporarily, the previous summer when he blocked two black people from enrolling in the University of Alabama. After submitting the necessary paperwork to appear on Maryland's primary ballot, Wallace headed to Cambridge on 11 May for a rally at the Rescue and Fire Company arena.[17]

Daily Banner editors decried Wallace's visit because they believed it would worsen the city's image. In an editorial that read a lot like the ones published two years earlier during the Freedom Rides, the editors congratulated the white community for "weather[ing] the storm" created by extremists and outside agitators. However, they could do little to prevent the seemingly inevitable racial confrontation that would be provoked by Wallace's visit because Gloria Richardson was "a militant leader whose goal appears to be a continuation of conflict, not a genuine search for solutions." Outside journalists were viewed as adding more fuel to an already smoldering racial fire. When UPI reporter John Kady arrived in Cambridge to cover Wallace's speech, he and another white reporter signed in with the National

Guard (a requirement of all press personnel). During this formality, a soldier on duty let them know they were not welcome: "I'll remember your faces tonight, you fucking nigger lovers."[18]

Wallace addressed more than 1,500 cheering white admirers and predicted that Maryland's upcoming Democratic primary would be even more successful in rattling the party's racial moderates and liberals than the others he had participated in that year. While Wallace was promoting his racist agenda, across town, CNAC held a "Freedom Rally" at the Elks Lodge on Pine Street to let the white community know that its support of Wallace was an affront to the city's black community. Wallace had political support not only from individual white supremacists but also from organizations hostile to black people's human rights, including the John Birch Society and the National States Rights Party. This angered Richardson and other black residents because if Wallace became the Democratic Party's nominee for president, he might actually win the election, and then he and his supporters would usher in another nadir for black America.[19]

CNAC's rally began shortly after six o'clock in the evening and was attended by at least 300 people who participated in a round of freedom songs before a long list of presenters took turns addressing the audience. A Catholic priest named James "Peter" Hinde noted that the "strong" speeches included "many prophecies of a 'long, hot summer' if there was no action on the part of the government to improve things in Cambridge." If there was a weak link in the chain of speakers, that distinction belonged to Lonnie 3X Cross, a member of the all-black and racially separatist Nation of Islam. After he "wandered through fantastic interpretations of history, cosmology and women's apparel," his uninspiring talk "drew faint applause." Richardson thought Cross's speech "deadened the whole rally," but the audience's energy level increased as the remaining speakers gave their presentations. In her address, Richardson encouraged black residents to "insist on freedom—now," but she also reminded them of a core tenet of black liberation philosophy: black people were responsible for freeing themselves from oppression. The rally concluded about an hour later with attendees singing a rendition of "We Shall Overcome" that, as a *Banner* reporter wrote, "had the ring of a simple statement of fact."[20]

As people exited the Elks Lodge, they lined up to march over to the Rescue and Fire Company arena. Among them were Stokely Carmichael and Cleveland Sellers, who belonged to a SNCC affiliate at Howard University called the Nonviolent Action Group. The two had answered CNAC's call for outside reinforcements for its anti-Wallace rally. CNAC's decision to hold a march came as a bit of a surprise, because Richardson had informed the National Guard that her group would not be demonstrating that evening. John Kady had heard Richardson make that statement, and when he asked her about it, she said: "I lied. How can we not [march] with that racist son of a bitch down at the other end of the street?" SNCC's John Lewis was also at the rally, and he expressed concern that a march risked a violent confrontation between demonstrators and the National Guard. Richardson recalled that Lewis asked her a series of questions to try to understand the logic behind her decision to go ahead with it. "What is your position? Are you just carrying people up to the edge of violence? Then what do you do?" Richardson was unable to answer Lewis's questions. "I didn't think I could've explained it to him. I was doing creative chaos," she said—a reference to the strategy of using various tactics to keep opponents off balance and confused during any given situation.[21]

Since the National Guard's deployment to Cambridge, Richardson had been acutely aware of the inherent danger in any confrontation between demonstrators and armed soldiers. But she felt that dealing with the National Guard was actually less dangerous than dealing with mobs of armed and angry white people. Two factors led to Richardson's decision to march that night: her relationship with the demonstrators and her leadership skills. She knew the black community intimately, and she understood how far its members were willing to go to make a statement against Wallace. Additionally, given Richardson's background in sociology—specifically, with regard to collective behavior—she knew what she could do and how far she could go in leading hundreds of demonstrators into a volatile situation. The black community's trust in Richardson was another reason why she was able to lead this mass demonstration. In Cleveland Sellers's autobiography *The River of No Return*, he describes the scene as Richardson moved toward the Guardsmen: "It was a crucial moment, the kind that can make or break a movement. We all understood that Gloria was the only one who could decide its outcome. If she had told us to return to the lodge, we would have done so, even though we would not have wanted to. 'I'm going through,' she said. Without waiting to find out how we would respond, she headed straight for the armed guardsmen." With Richardson in the lead, the marchers headed toward the arena, but unbeknownst to them, Wallace had already left town and was on his way to Baltimore. They got only a few blocks before National Guardsmen halted them, and with that, Richardson's desire for a confrontation had been realized. She started to recite to herself Harlem Renaissance writer Claude McKay's poem, which helped her push forward: "If we must die—let it not be like hogs."[22]

Richardson and the other marchers sat down in the street and began singing, but they stopped when Colonel Maurice D. Tawes drove up in a jeep. A distant relative of the governor, Colonel Tawes was the officer in charge of the National Guard that evening. Carrying a riding crop in one hand, he exited the vehicle and approached Richardson, who stood up. The colonel asked her: "You want 'em all to be arrested? Just say so and we'll be glad to accommodate you." Richardson replied affirmatively, and with that, Tawes barked out the command to arrest the demonstrators and herd them into trucks to be driven to Pikesville, Maryland, where they would be detained. As it turned out, Tawes could not "accommodate" Richardson's request for mass arrests because he did not have enough trucks to haul all the protesters away, so he gave them five minutes to disperse. None of the demonstrators budged. A local man named John Battiste told Tawes: "If [Richardson] goes, I go, too." Battiste's declaration was immediately followed by the crowd shouting, "We all go!" Just then, some people behind the demonstrators started pelting the Guardsmen with "bottles, rocks, bricks, [and] sticks," and the soldiers moved into the crowd of marchers to arrest them. Demonstrators piled on to each other and locked their arms together to complicate the soldiers' efforts. While this was going on, John Lewis was trying to gather demonstrators for a prayer circle, and Richardson recalled "stop[ping] him, profanely," because it would have diverted attention from the volatile situation. She was arrested and led away just before the Guardsmen used tear gas to disperse the crowd. The march finally broke up as hundreds of demonstrators scattered to escape the poisonous fumes.[23]

Trucked off to Pikesville that night were Richardson, Battiste, Sellers, Howard University student Stanley Wise, and nine other demonstrators. From inside the detention site, they spoke with reporters about CNAC's intention to keep up the pressure on the white community. Richardson said CNAC would be encouraging black residents to start a rent strike against their slumlords to further weaken the white economy (a tactic she had learned from Jesse Gray, a new associate who had been organizing rent strikes in New York City). On Wednesday morning Richardson and the others were bused to court in Cambridge to face a magistrate, who charged them with disorderly conduct. Their attorney entered not-guilty pleas on their behalf, after which they were released on bail.[24]

Activists held two more demonstrations that week. The next one occurred the night after Wallace's speech and ended without incident when, at General Gelston's request, John Lewis led the hundreds of demonstrators in a prayer, after which they returned to their homes. Two days later, the National Guard again used tear gas to disperse a small group of black demonstrators who had marched toward the troops. Because of this heightened tension, CNAC suspended demonstrations for an unspecified period. Another clash occurred eleven days later when soldiers surrounded a car driven by a black person who had initially failed to yield when ordered to do so. After the car drove away, black residents pelted the troops with rocks and bottles. Four Guardsmen were injured during the melee, including one who was shot in the arm by an unknown assailant. Once again, the black residents were dispersed by tear gas.[25]

With racial tensions so high, Richardson thought the black community could benefit from a cathartic experience, so she invited Dick Gregory to Cambridge to lighten the mood. The two had met in January in Atlanta and had seen each other again in February at the student-led desegregation effort in Princess Anne. Since then, they had been in regular contact because of Gregory's role as a consultant to ACT, a human rights organization cofounded by Richardson in mid-March (see chapter 9). Richardson noted that during the Cambridge movement, she and other activists "laughed a lot, but [they] stayed at a high level of rage also." Gregory's incisive political humor expressed the black community's anger and frustration against the white people who stood in the way of racial progress.[26]

On 27 May Gregory appeared at the Elks Lodge, where close to 300 people paid a penny admission fee to hear one of the nation's best comedians. The audience opened Gregory's show for him by singing freedom songs. Then he stepped up to the microphone and began a performance that, according to one reporter, "injected biting humor . . . into the tense civil rights situation here."[27] The show was a welcome diversion for the black community, but it was sandwiched between CNAC's efforts to bring about meaningful change in Cambridge. Prior to Gregory's performance, CNAC had shared with the public a series of rhetorical questions that served as an assessment of the city's job and housing opportunities. It asked why white politicos were dragging their feet on the creation of public housing and why they had not established a housing code that would force "slum lords" to repair their rental properties. With regard to employment, CNAC asked why black workers had not been hired by the telephone company in line crews and as clerks and operators, and why no bank managers had hired black tellers. CNAC recommended to school officials, business owners, and politicians that they create apprenticeship programs for high school students to prepare them to meet the increasing demand for skilled workers. Another way to expand employment opportunities, according to CNAC, would be Dorchester County's participation in the federal government's antipoverty programs.

Left to right: Elaine Adams, Stanley Branche, Dick Gregory, and Gloria Richardson at the Elks Lodge, Second Ward, Cambridge, Maryland, 27 May 1964. (Associated Press)

Appealing to politicos' concerns about Cambridge's future, CNAC pointed out a benefit of taking action on its demands: "If our grievances were met in some of these areas it would help to relieve some of the tension, which presently keeps new industries . . . away from Cambridge."[28]

Two weeks after Gregory's show, Richardson and American Civil Liberties Union lawyer Fred Weisgal attended a closed-door meeting with the state school superintendent in Baltimore, where Richardson voiced her concern about the lack of jobs available to black residents. She also provided the superintendent with a report that listed four areas in need of attention in

Dorchester County: improve housing conditions, revamp school board rules, add more recreation spots, and divert more government contracts to Cambridge businesses. Interestingly, people working on behalf of Governor Tawes made those same proposals less than a month later.[29]

In an attempt to avoid another summer of strife and violence and more bad press for his state, Tawes established a biracial committee of five "eminent" Marylanders and tasked them with developing a racial reconciliation process in Cambridge. Known as the Miles Committee after its chairman, attorney Clarence W. Miles (a Cambridge native and former president of the Baltimore Orioles baseball team), this body held public and private meetings with citizens to determine how to break the stalemate in Cambridge. Miles met personally with Richardson at his Easton home, where she no doubt reiterated CNAC's position that jobs for black workers had to be at the center of any plan. It was a point underscored by the *Pittsburgh Courier*, which argued "that peace can come to Cambridge, not simply with the effecting of desegregation in public accommodations, but when equal opportunities are made available to all in the more vital fields of employment, housing and health facilities."[30]

When the Miles Committee submitted its findings to the governor, one of them was something CNAC had been arguing for almost two years: the state and federal governments should be involved in addressing Cambridge's social and economic problems. "There are much needed aids to the economy and social welfare of the community," specifically with regard to "job training and procurement," housing, and recreation for youth, the committee wrote. Additionally, local officials would have to play a key role in ensuring that aid was available and accessible to residents. The committee also made two recommendations to the governor, the first of which involved life in Cambridge and had two parts: (1) "restore [the] dignity and normal way of life of a cultured and changing community," which meant removing the National Guard; and (2) discourage black people's use of "riotous street demonstrations" to apply pressure on white politicians. Repeating a refrain expressed by both *Banner* editors and white leaders throughout the Cambridge movement, the Miles Committee stated that such demonstrations and other "mob action" would hinder economic progress. The committee's second recommendation was that Dorchester County officials administer the federal government's surplus food distribution program at least until the fall (it was currently being administered by the National Guard). If county officials refused to administer the program, that responsibility should be assumed by the state of Maryland.[31]

CNAC's executive committee believed the Miles report legitimized CNAC's assessment of the black community's problems and affirmed the organization's proposed solutions, much as the "Treaty of Cambridge" had done twelve months earlier. One part of the Miles report that CNAC disagreed with was its claim that demonstrations would hinder the city's economic life. Richardson and her colleagues believed that their constant and occasionally dramatic demonstrations had actually pushed the private sector and the state government to establish jobs training programs for almost 500 people from Cambridge and the surrounding area.[32]

Immediately after receiving the Miles Committee's report, Governor Tawes ordered the National Guard to leave Cambridge on 11 July, thus ending one of its longest deployments in the nation's history. Coinciding with the end of military occupation were changes in the white power structure. In July's municipal elections, white residents sent two new members to the City Council, and Osvrey Pritchett was elected to replace Mayor Calvin Mowbray, who did not seek reelection. All three of these newly elected officials had supported the defeat of the charter amendment in the previous referendum, and Pritchett had run on a platform of "law and order"—a mainstay of conservative politics for the rest of the decade. Interestingly, a split vote for City Council president propelled Charles Cornish into that position—a first in Cambridge's and Maryland's history.[33]

In the days following the election, the *Banner*'s editors declared that the city's racial crisis was over and that newly elected officials and their constituents should approach the future with a commitment to unity. By joining together and working on behalf of all residents, Cambridge could move forward with economic expansion and development. The editors' argument that business expansion equaled real progress was one they had made numerous times over the years, but what they still failed to grasp was that the white community's definition of progress was a significant obstacle to achieving unity. Cambridge would continue to travel its well-worn path of separate and unequal until the white community's definition came into alignment with the black community's.[34]

The Civil Rights Act was also passed at the beginning of July, and with it came the historical transformation of the South's racial customs. Even though President Lyndon B. Johnson and countless Washington legislators would not admit it publicly, the Cambridge movement and other local struggles—such as those in Birmingham, Alabama, and Danville, Virginia—had created so much political pressure that they were forced to pass the most significant piece of civil rights legislation since Reconstruction. The black press gave accolades to

Gloria Richardson and other national leaders for their efforts in getting Congress to pass the law, which was a much stronger version of the bill Richardson had critiqued at the White House a year earlier. In a piece titled "A Giant First Step," the editors of the *Afro-American* thanked the "old-line warriors" Roy Wilkins, Whitney Young, James Farmer, Martin Luther King Jr., and John Lewis for their roles getting the act signed into law. The radical activists of the civil rights movement—described by the editors as "the Gloria Richardsons"—also deserved thanks because they had forced white Americans to realize the high price of maintaining separate and unequal worlds.[35] Within two days of its passage, black residents of Cambridge tested the new law on their own (CNAC was not involved), and although a few white owners turned away black customers, others served everyone who entered, irrespective of their race. Establishments on Race Street were among the handful of early adherents to the new law, including Dizzyland restaurant, but other facets of residents' lives were still divided by the color line, such as housing, jobs, education, and recreational facilities like those of the Rescue and Fire Company. It would take years for those aspects of life in Cambridge to be altered.[36]

Of course, some white people resisted the change. A *Pittsburgh Courier* writer astutely noted that many white people thought that integration "mean[t] the beginning of compulsory association." A white resident of Cambridge said as much in her letter to the *Banner:* "Does the Negro really think that by the passing of the Civil Rights Bill that people will actually want to associate with them?" What that resident failed to grasp was that black people wanted the actual (de facto) right to patronize public accommodations, but most of them, Richardson included, did not want to integrate, let alone assimilate, into white America because they did not find it a desirable destination. That viewpoint was based on their belief that white America was collapsing under the weight of its own racial hypocrisy. James Baldwin pointed this out in his book *The Fire Next Time* when he asked: "Do I really want to be integrated into a burning house?"[37]

The opening of public spaces by the Civil Rights Act was only one of the significant developments in Cambridge that summer. The other was Gloria Richardson's decision to relocate to New York City. Freelance photographer Frank Dandridge had covered the previous summer's protests in Cambridge, where he met Richardson. She soon fell in love with the handsome photographer, whose base of operations was New York City. By the following spring, they were planning to marry but tried to keep their relationship a secret. Somehow, word got out, and media outlets began writing about them. At first, the couple denied they had wedding plans (as did members of the Cambridge movement). They wanted to keep CNAC's opponents off guard and prevent them from leveraging the information to their benefit—especially the news that no one would be replacing Richardson as chair of the organization.[38]

CNAC's decision not to replace Richardson illustrates the nature of the organization and its members' experiences over the previous two years. Richardson and CNAC's executive committee did not discuss who might replace her because doing so would have violated the organization's ethos. If the community had wanted to replace Richardson, it would have raised the issue with the executive committee, which would have held a mass meeting where everyone could discuss candidates for the position, as well as CNAC's agenda for the future. However, no such meeting ever took place. Richardson speculated that "people were probably just exhausted," and the movement had reached a "plateau" of sorts. Public accommodations were now open, and there had been small but appreciable progress on the economic front with the jobs training programs. Furthermore, elected officials at the federal and state levels had expressed support for the affordable housing project. The challenge for residents would be to keep attention focused on those areas and be prepared to take action if the white power structure started dragging its feet.[39] Assisting them in this effort would be a small number of SNCC staff members who would be staying in Cambridge.

Early in the summer Richardson had hinted at her departure, as well as who would be running point for the Cambridge movement after she left for New York. During one of her last press briefings as leader of the Cambridge movement, she told reporters about a telegram she had sent to Governor Tawes. Richardson had asked him to consider expanding the state's park system to include the Choptank riverfront area, where three black children had recently drowned while swimming without lifeguard supervision. (The area had always been a popular spot for black people because white residents had prevented them from using the taxpayer-supported Rescue and Fire Company pool.) The telegram was, she told the press, a "polite suggestion, not a demand. *I'm not making demands now, just pointing out our goals that are primary.*" Shortly thereafter, Richardson and a handful of young activists from the Cambridge movement traveled to Washington to talk with members of the House Labor and Educational Committee, headed by Harlem congressman Adam Clayton Powell Jr. The meeting focused on implementing the recently approved hiring and training programs for the Eastern Shore. When operational duties for the Cambridge movement were transferred to members of SNCC, they pledged to continue to fight for jobs, housing, and education. Richardson moved to New York shortly thereafter.[40]

Generally speaking, people either welcomed Richardson's exit from the Cambridge movement or were disappointed by it. The white power structure was happy to see her go because she had led a successful grassroots movement that had stopped white leaders from operating their system of white supremacy with impunity. National Guard troops embraced Richardson's departure because they likely believed it would mean fewer civil rights demonstrations and thus less likelihood of confrontations between black and white residents. Putting a suggestive spin on these changes was Captain William A. Harris, one of the few black officers in the Maryland National Guard and one of those deployed to Cambridge during George Wallace's visit. Speaking with a reporter from the *Sun*, Harris acknowledged that "the Gloria Richardsons and Martin Luther Kings" made white Americans pay attention to racial problems, and he believed racial peace would soon arrive in Cambridge now that the Civil Rights Act had been passed and the Miles Committee had issued its report. With such an optimistic outlook, it was no wonder Harris concluded that "[there was] no need for demonstrations."[41]

For Cambridge's black residents, the loss of their movement's charismatic leader was a setback. Almost immediately it became obvious that the white power structure thought it would be dealing with a seriously weakened Cambridge movement. Stanley Wise, one of the SNCC field secretaries who had stayed on in Cambridge, was frustrated by white officials who "seem[ed] to ignore" CNAC's demands. It is easy to imagine why white leaders saw Richardson's departure as causing a dramatic realignment of power in Cambridge. For almost two and a half years, Richardson had used traditional and asymmetrical tactics to wage war for black liberation, confusing white leaders at every turn. Stokely Carmichael observed the psychological effect Richardson's activism had on these people: "She drove the politicians crazy." Cambridge's city attorney C. Awdry Thompson admitted as much in an interview with Murray Kempton of the *New Republic*. Thompson and other white leaders had never been able to get Richardson to budge on any of CNAC's demands, and they finally reached the point of exacerbation when they failed to convince her to support the referendum vote to save the charter amendment. "We can't deal with her and we can't deal without her," he told Kempton.[42] That had been white leaders' political reality for two full years, but with Richardson out of the picture, they realized the pendulum of power was swinging back toward them, and they behaved accordingly.

While Richardson was fraying politicians' nerves, some journalists were writing about her in ways that might lead readers to question her mental stability.

Time implied she was crazed ("gaunt, hot-eyed"), and a *New York Times* profile accused her of changing her mind so often because she was "a captive" of the men in the Cambridge movement. This assessment seemed to be supported by Richardson's own words: "'When I get on the platform and the men are all there, I just feel there is nothing more to say.'"[43] What the *New York Times* did not understand was that Richardson did not speak unless she felt the need to do so. Furthermore, she was not in competition with anyone, so she felt no need to challenge people, even those who behaved as if they were entitled to speak on behalf of CNAC and the Cambridge movement.

Boston Herald columnist George Frazier took issue with the *New York Times* profile not because of its gendered treatment of Richardson but because he thought it cast her in a positive light, giving readers the idea that she was "a kind of colored Jean d'Arc." It is interesting that Frazier compared Richardson with the fifteenth-century French freedom fighter, because Joan of Arc was an iconoclast who shattered notions of masculinity and femininity. She dressed in pants, led men into battle, and spoke publicly about the right of the French to be free from their English oppressors. Joan claimed she heard the voices of Saints Catherine and Margaret and that they guided her during her struggle against the English. To the English nobility and their French collaborators, this was evidence that Joan suffered from gender confusion, a condition many thought was caused by demonic influence or possession. They also believed that if she had been in a right state of mind, she never would have undermined their patriarchal social order, and consequently, they would not have put her on trial for heresy, convicted her of that crime, and burned her at the stake.[44]

At the time of Frazier's column about Richardson, she had already burnished her reputation as a race iconoclast. She sometimes did the same with regard to gender. In a meeting with the Miles Committee, Richardson was rebuked by its only female member—Sara Whitehurst—for not showing deference to the white men on the committee. Whitehurst "verbally upbraided me for being impolite to men," Richardson recalled, because she had spoken up before the men addressed her first. Richardson initially attributed Whitehurst's rebuke solely to her racist attitude, but then it occurred to her that gender also factored into Whitehurst's reaction. "You know, 'You're a woman and these are men.' And I was really mostly unaware of that" dynamic, Richardson said, because she had been raised in a family and a community that expected women to be assertive and strong.[45] Whitehurst's reaction highlights one aspect of the class-based gender socialization that developed in southern white America after the Civil War. "The prevailing image of middle-

and upper-class white southern womanhood in the postbellum period," wrote one historian of gender and race, "devalued . . . outspokenness among young women." This does not mean that patriarchy was absent in black America; it was present and had negative effects on all black people. Still, patriarchy as a social institution was not as strong in black America as it was in white America because black women had always been critical to their racial group's social and economic survival. It was within this cultural context that black women like Gloria Richardson generally had greater latitude to display their racial assertiveness, strength, and confidence in gender-integrated settings, without fear of being rebuked, shamed, or ridiculed by black men.[46]

Interestingly, the black men of CNAC believed Richardson's gender actually worked to the group's advantage because white leaders were essentially unprepared to deal with a woman. Richardson said, "I heard talk that other men didn't know how to deal with women anyhow so it's best to send them in there [negotiating] because [women] were so completely, you know, unorthodoxed [sic] and [white men] would never know how to deal with the women around a conference table because they wouldn't know whether [the women] were crazy or whether they were making sense."[47] Murray Kempton believed this gender dynamic was at play in Cambridge, but he also believed Richardson's race was another factor that put white men at a disadvantage when dealing with her. She "is a stranger and cannot be engaged, because she is both a Negro and a woman and thus represents the two largest figures in Southern myth and the two smallest in Southern reality." *Baltimore Sun* reporter Ruth Van D. Todd hit on this intersection of race and gender when she told Richardson, "'[White men] don't know whether they hate you worse as a woman or as a Negro.'"[48]

White politicians did not call for Richardson to suffer the same fate as Joan of Arc, but some of them did consider a drastic measure to neutralize her: having her forcibly committed to a psychiatric hospital. It was unusual for a person's mental health to be questioned just because he or she was involved in human rights activism, but it did happen. When a white Cambridge man named Eddie Dickerson had a change of heart about racial segregation and decided to join CORE, he left town and moved to Baltimore after learning that someone planned to have him involuntarily committed to a psychiatric hospital. Dickerson was wrong to think that he would be safe in Baltimore. Two civil rights activists who were arrested there were committed to a state psychiatric hospital by the magistrate who adjudicated their cases. Richardson learned from General Gelston that at one point in the 1960s, Maryland officials intended to do the same to her. When a sympathetic doctor learned of the plan, he called Richardson and told her if officials tried to institutionalize her, she should say that he was her doctor, which would give him access to her and allow him to advocate for her.[49] Luckily for Richardson, she never had to take the physician up on his offer. But it was a reminder that white people would consider any means to contain her power and influence, which had grown and spread over the course of the Cambridge movement.

Evidence of Richardson's expanding influence came to light during an event in the Bronzeville section of Chicago's South Side on 4 July 1964. Community organizers there held a freedom-themed pageant and parade to honor black figures from the past and present. Local actors portrayed the likes of Revolutionary War martyr Crispus Attucks, abolitionists Frederick Douglass and Harriet Tubman, W. E. B. Du Bois, and contemporary figures A. Philip Randolph, James Farmer, Martin Luther King Jr., and Gloria Richardson. The Chicago pageant was just the latest of numerous awards and honors Richardson had received since the beginning of the Cambridge movement. She was praised by the Maryland State Conference of the NAACP for "valiant efforts to bring freedom to the people of the Eastern Shore . . . and for courage in upholding the tradition of a family long distinguished in public service." The Tri-State Association of Elks presented Richardson with a Freedom Award, which she accepted on behalf of "all those in Maryland who have given up their property, their lives and their honor to obtain liberty." The Second Episcopal District of the African Methodist Episcopal Church presented Richardson with its Richard Allen Foundation Award for her "distinguished and meritorious service in awakening the moral conscience of America on behalf of human rights."[50]

According to one of Fannie Lou Hamer's biographers, Richardson's influence on Maryland's civil rights movement was attributable to two factors that propelled a number of women to significant roles in the movement: "historical circumstance and personal qualities." The circumstance in Richardson's case was the political vacuum that occurred in the Second Ward when Councilman Charles Cornish lost the support of his constituents, which was initiated by the actions of black high school students who wanted to improve their lives by ending segregation. In the words of an Associated Press reporter, "it was the young people who gave the movement its impetus," a fact Richardson has always acknowledged and has stated countless times over the decades.[51] We will never know if Cambridge would have had its own local freedom struggle if those students had not stood up for themselves and their community, but we do know that their activism created a political space that Richardson stepped into and from which she did her best to improve her community.

Richardson's personal qualities were the other factor in her rise to power in the Cambridge movement. She lived and worked according to ethical humanistic principles that recognized people's inherent value and their obligation to try to improve their society. Furthermore, she displayed strong character and leadership traits and an unwavering commitment to black liberation. In turn, these traits fostered support, loyalty, and trust from men and women both within the Second Ward and outside it. Cambridge residents Dwight Cromwell and brothers Lemuel and Larry Chester appreciated Richardson's work on behalf of their community.[52] Sharing their sentiment was Howard University student William "Winkie" Hall, who said Richardson could be relied on to carry out CNAC's decisions. Her decisiveness was reassuring to Hall and other activists because social change movements are inherently mercurial, and they constantly challenge activists' commitment. Hall added that Richardson possessed a good sense of humor (vital to every good leader, he believed) and exceptional political intelligence, and these traits made her an "extremely dynamic" leader.[53]

Cleveland Sellers and Joyce Ladner concurred with Hall's observation about Richardson's intellect. She was "very bright—insightful—combined with courage and tenacity," Ladner said. Richardson also impressed some of the journalists who covered the Cambridge movement. John Britton was a writer for *Ebony* and *Jet* during the 1960s. He observed Richardson in action and came away with the impression that she was "a very sharp lady—sharp in the sense that she had some political instincts about her, [which] . . . is not all that common among people who . . . are driven by some kind of ideology. But she had a political instinct and seemed to know when to do whatever and when not to do whatever and yet still get her way."[54] Mark Suckle, a Swarthmore student active in the Cambridge movement, provided an interesting explanation of why Richardson was able to do that: Because her college education was not grounded in the legal profession or some other field that would have taught her to be amenable to making concessions, she felt no need to cede anything to white leaders. Additionally, her work experience since college had not required her to compromise on anything important, such as black people's rights. Suckle believed that type of background made Richardson perfect for the role of leader of the Cambridge movement. Her uncompromising approach gave white politicos the impression that the woman *Ebony* had described as the "lady general of civil rights" was presenting her white adversaries with the terms of their surrender to the Cambridge movement.[55]

Ebony's use of the word "lady" indicates that Richardson's gender distinguished her from the movement's other "generals," and it is but one example of journalists' gendered interpretation of her activism. Throughout her time leading the Cambridge movement, journalists for both the black and white media mentioned Richardson's gender, her divorce, and her two children; some reporters even mentioned her physique and weight.[56] It was logical for journalists to highlight Richardson's gender because most national leaders were men, and she challenged gendered concepts of leadership and power. She was, therefore, an interesting anomaly within the movement's leadership cadre, and Britton described her as "a very, very strong standup woman, kind of rare for those days. There were a few women like her who stood up even more so than men in the movement. Fannie Lou Hamer was one down in Mississippi, and [Richardson] was another." Reporter John Kady assessed Richardson's position in the movement by comparing her to some of the men he covered, such as Martin Luther King Jr., Bayard Rustin, and Stokely Carmichael. "She was tough. Just plain tough. I think she was tougher than most."[57]

Activists noticed Richardson's distinctiveness, too. More than a decade after her work in Cambridge, Dick Gregory wrote that she was "undoubtedly the strongest woman to emerge in the civil rights movement." He developed that opinion by observing firsthand her humanistic approach to black liberation. "She didn't take nothing off of [white people] and [she] didn't have a gun, and [she] wasn't talking about killing. She was talking about human dignity. And it took me a while to get used to that 'cause I never seen a black woman with that type of persistence on liberation."[58] Singer and human rights activist Paul Robeson knew that someone like Richardson would arise in the 1960s because, ever since the Montgomery bus boycott, he had noticed that women like her were expanding the meaning of black liberation, as well as its chances of being achieved. In 1958 he wrote: "Negro womanhood today is giving us many inspiring examples of steadfast devotion, cool courage under fire, and brilliant generalship in our people's struggles; and here is a major source for new strength and militancy in Negro leadership on every level." The Reverend C. T. Vivian of the SCLC thought the same. He knew the civil rights movement's viability was tied to its ability to recruit people from a wide cross section of black America to rise up and become leaders, and women were a core source of that leadership. "I wanted [Richardson] to be highly successful because I wanted other women to come up and be highly successful," Vivian said.[59]

Gender was on Richardson's mind during the movement. In May 1964 she delivered a Sunday morning speech titled "The Role of Women in the

Civil Rights Struggle" at Baltimore's Trinity Presbyterian Church. There is no transcript of that speech, but she likely discussed her own work and that of other women in the Cambridge movement, and she probably did so in a matter-of-fact manner. Women and girls had been among the Cambridge movement's instigators, and they were the ones who kept it going (notably, Donna Richardson, Enez Grubb, and Sally Garrison). Men of the Cambridge movement treated Richardson with respect, so she was shocked when a couple of women from SNCC asked her, "'Are you having trouble as a woman?'" The question seemed bizarre to Richardson because she and her comrades "lived on a day-to-day basis . . . in a life-and-death, just about, situation, . . . [and] gender considerations were not there."[60]

Up to that point, Richardson had been aware only of SNCC's success stories about women who were leading local projects and achieving self-actualization in the process. SNCC's culture made this possible because it stressed the principle fostered by Ella Baker that members should think creatively about liberating themselves from all the problems afflicting them. Consequently, when SNCC members strategized about freedom, some of them critically interrogated gender constructions and envisioned what a world free from sexism would look like. Furthermore, SNCC's organizational model fostered women's full participation in the movement. Sociologist Belinda Robnett's research on SNCC explains why: "Organizations built on an ideology of a participatory democracy that discourages the centralization of leadership, seek consensus and are anti-hierarchical, empower women even in the absence of an explicit feminist doctrine or in the presence of gender bias." There are many examples of this, but one of the more well known is the case of Bernice Johnson Reagon, who saw SNCC forcing men and women to push themselves to become the best they could be as both individuals and members of the organization. "My whole world was expanded in terms of what I could do as a person," she said. "I never experienced being held back. I only experienced being challenged and searching within myself to see if I had the courage to do what came up in my mind."[61]

Whereas Richardson and Reagon felt that SNCC did not restrict women, other women disagreed. They found that many of their male comrades were as blind to gender bias as white people were to racial bias. This is because SNCC's members brought their assumptions and attitudes about gender with them when they joined the movement. Ruby Doris Smith Robinson's biographer writes, "Even though many of the young SNCC activists saw themselves as equals regardless of gender, most still had definite expectations regarding male ways of acting and female reactions. Men within the organization would often assume a macho persona. There were variations of this persona, but essentially men flirted, flattered, and swaggered. In return, they expected women to be compliant and agreeable." Sexism within SNCC was enough of a concern for two white members—Casey Hayden and Mary King—to write "Sex and Caste: A Kind of Memo" to start a conversation with their male and female comrades about the need to dismantle patriarchy as they battled racism. Their memo was not well received because many thought a discussion of gender discrimination distracted from the battle to end racism. Still, Hayden and King's treatise was an important event in initiating the second wave of the women's liberation movement, and it primed SNCC to address the issue of patriarchy, which it formally did in 1968 when Frances Beal founded the organization's Black Women's Liberation Committee. A few years later she authored the groundbreaking essay "Double Jeopardy: To Be Black and Female," which raised awareness among countless women about the nexus between racial and gender oppression.[62]

SNCC's goal of facilitating and developing local leadership was epitomized by Gloria Richardson. Through its adult affiliate, CNAC, she lent her organizing and leadership skills to the nascent Cambridge movement and was instrumental in helping it crystallize and withstand constant and concerted opposition. Richardson also learned from her comrades in both organizations. She and others of her generation learned to be passionate about black liberation and to think creatively about how to achieve it, specifically by employing democratic principles of consultation and consensus to determine their collective future.

Young people of the movement, whether in Cambridge or in the multitude of other communities in the South, gained a lot from Richardson's participation in the struggle. With her strong and unwavering leadership, Richardson became a role model to many of them as they continued their work elsewhere, such as in Mississippi and the 1964 voter registration project that became known as Freedom Summer. White people also found inspiration from Richardson. Cathy Wilkerson was part of the Swarthmore College contingent that participated in the Cambridge movement, and she recalled that after hearing Richardson give a speech at a mass meeting, she was not the same person. Richardson "made the [ideas] accessible. She made [me] feel like [I] mattered, that everybody was welcomed, not just men in the movement. My attitude was it was a tremendous honor to participate in this work, and you had to be good enough to do it. [Richardson] made me feel like it was okay, and that gave me the ability to then, the next year, look at the group at Swarthmore and have some consciousness that when the men made you feel unwanted that there was something wrong with that."[63]

Richardson was also admired for her socioeconomic egalitarianism. This philosophy was an inherent element of CNAC's community outreach program that encouraged residents to see themselves as agents of change with the ability to transform their own lives. "The one thing we did," Richardson said, "was to emphasize that while you should be educated, that education, degrees, college degrees were not essential [in Cambridge]. If you could articulate the need, if you knew what the need was, if you were aware of the kinds of games that white folk play, *that was the real thing.*" Joyce Ladner believed this attitude distinguished Richardson from almost everyone else in her socioeconomic group. "[Richardson] didn't give a damn about anyone else's status. . . . And I always felt that it was not the wrong characterization at all to say that she bore the privilege of her class in a very positive way for the movement. She was about the first black person I had ever known who came from such privilege. There weren't many people in SNCC like that. . . . Gloria was fighting in the movement by choice."[64]

This egalitarianism was also evident in Richardson's decision to create the needs assessment survey for the Second Ward. She knew her neighbors had to identify their own concerns and that CNAC had to help them address those concerns. By working hand in hand with residents, CNAC created a viable social change movement that positively affected the community but also influenced one particular politician: Robert F. Kennedy. Richardson presented the attorney general with a copy of CNAC's survey findings at the time of the "Treaty of Cambridge," and this raised his consciousness about the roots of poverty and people's efforts to climb out of it. A little more than a year later, during his campaign for New York's Senate seat, Kennedy stressed the amelioration of poverty and promoted President Johnson's Great Society legislation. Kennedy continued to champion antipoverty programs after he won the election and throughout his career in the Senate, until his life was ended by an assassin's bullet in 1968.[65]

On a broader level, CNAC's emphasis on economics steered the movement's direction. "Cambridge was crucial, really, a turning point in the struggle. The issues were segregation, bad housing, and unemployment," remarked Stokely Carmichael. Reverend Vivian also believed that the black liberation movement's next phase would focus on social justice issues, and Richardson's leadership of the Cambridge movement was a working model for communities throughout the nation. "I saw that what [Richardson] was doing there was clearly going to be our agenda one time, or the other," and the Cambridge movement "really gave hope for what could happen later," he said. CNAC's social justice focus also piqued the interest of Vivian's SCLC colleague, Martin Luther King Jr. Sometime in the weeks before the referendum vote in Cambridge, King sent his friend and speechwriter Lawrence D. Reddick to meet with Richardson at her home, where he spoke "earnestly" about learning her thoughts on economic matters. Five months later, King revealed that one of the SCLC's top three agenda items for 1964 was to increase job opportunities for black workers.[66] Journalist Relman Morin also noticed this change in the movement's focus and goals. No stranger to the civil rights movement, Morin had earned a Pulitzer Prize for his coverage of the school desegregation crisis in Little Rock, Arkansas, in 1957. His February 1964 story "Civil Rights '64 . . . Fight or Freedom" told of the movement's rise in northern urban centers, where its focus would be open housing, jobs, and desegregated schools.[67]

A couple of weeks before Morin's article was published, a young black man named Sam Cooke walked onto the stage of the *Tonight Show* to perform his soon-to-be-hit song "A Change Is Gonna Come," which alludes to the end of segregation in the near future.[68] Yet because segregation was only one concern in black America, Cooke's song could also be read as a signal that much more would be changing in the United States when black people expanded their liberation agenda. This was already happening in the urban North, where black activists were using tactics and strategies that would ultimately transform the black liberation movement. This change was taking place because of Black Power. Under Gloria Richardson's leadership and vision, it had developed organically in Cambridge, and she was one of the key catalysts for its spread around the nation.

9

Vanguard

For the first four decades of her life, Gloria Richardson moved in a social universe created by generations of St. Clairs through their business dealings, educational experiences, and philanthropic works. There were times when family friends and associates aided the Cambridge movement, yet during that entire time, Richardson was developing a network of her own that eventually consisted of some of the movement's more radical activists. A few of them partnered with her to create a new northern organization called ACT (not an acronym), which intended to give local movements the assistance they needed to reach their goal of black liberation. Geography was a factor in why ACT was founded and what its goals were. Richardson's focus in the Cambridge movement had been to expand black people's access to jobs, housing, quality public education, and health care—the same basic issues that concerned black city dwellers in the Northeast and Midwest, and on the West Coast. Young activists there were looking for ways they could, in essence, replicate the Cambridge movement's comprehensive social justice program. Black people in these locales could already vote, which distinguished them from most of their southern counterparts. This meant that instead of fighting for voting rights, ACT could concentrate on leveraging black people's electoral power to gain the most from the political system.

ACT's main base of operations was New York City, where most of its members lived. Richardson had been traveling there routinely since she started dating Frank Dandridge, which allowed her to build strong friendships with two other New Yorkers: Congressman Adam Clayton Powell Jr. and Malcolm X. She asked them both to serve as consultants to ACT. In practical terms, ACT's agenda, strategies, and tactics constituted one of the earliest examples of the radical mid-1960s organizing that served as a foundation for the Black Power wave of the black liberation movement. Specifically, ACT challenged moderate civil rights organizations, their leaders, and their white allies, especially when the latter continued to seek incremental changes to the racial status quo rather than expedited structural adjustments to the nation's economic and political systems.

Richardson spent about one year working with ACT, and during that brief period, she left an important and lasting mark on both the organization and the northern black activists who were exploring new ways to achieve the economic and political changes they desired. To gain a greater understanding of how and why these young people embraced Black Power—and why black moderates and white liberals feared it—one must know the individuals responsible for its development. Gloria Richardson, through her activism in Cambridge and the creation of ACT, was one of the key founders of Black Power.

In the first week of November 1963, Gloria Richardson headed to Detroit to attend the weekend meeting of the Northern Negro Leadership Conference (NNLC). The Reverend C. L. Franklin of the Detroit Council for Human Rights had invited her and other "leading names in the nationwide civil rights struggle" to the Motor City to participate in panel discussions and workshops related to black people's civil rights struggles in the North. Of particular concern were housing and public school issues and activists' tactics to foster change. NNLC organizers also intended for the event to build ties between northern organizations and the Southern Christian Leadership Conference (SCLC), which was hoping to expand its sphere of operation and influence beyond the South.[1]

The conference closed on Sunday afternoon with a rally at Cobo Hall, the city's downtown convention center, where 3,000 conferees listened to speeches and were entertained by gospel singer Mahalia Jackson and soul singer Aretha Franklin (daughter of the Reverend C. L. Franklin). Congressman Adam Clayton Powell Jr. delivered the keynote address in which he told his audience that black people needed to be the principal financiers of their liberation struggle because they could not fully define and control their destiny if white people controlled the movement's purse strings. He also warned the black community not to fall victim to colorism and class prejudice and stressed that it needed to support "black leaders . . . and black unity."[2] The latter was an acknowledgment of the controversy that had arisen during the conference's planning, which resulted in some activists holding a separate conference across town at the same time. A main point of contention between the two groups was the NNLC's agenda, which emphasized racial integration as a desirable goal but did not allow debate on the subject. Another sticking point was Reverend Franklin's decision not to allow Black Nationalists to be delegates to the NNLC. This alienated many of Detroit's grassroots activists, including attorney Milton Henry, who, along with other discontented activists, organized the Northern Grassroots Leadership Conference (NGLC) to run concurrently with Franklin's.[3]

On the day prior to the Cobo Hall rally, Richardson attended NNLC workshops at the Henrose Hotel. She found them disappointing because they did not focus on building a grassroots urban movement that addressed the needs of the black masses. In Richardson's opinion, the conference facilitators were stifling creative thinking and refusing to discuss economic issues, and she began to wonder whether she could learn or accomplish anything at the conference. Particularly troubling, "there was this big fight" every time someone raised the problem of racism in unions. This was a significant issue for Detroit's black workers who belonged to the United Auto Workers, and racial discrimination limited the number who could join their ranks. In fact, racism was systemic in America's labor unions in the mid-1960s, and it could be found in various facets of the economy as well, including import-export services on sea and river ports, the steel industry, and the skilled building trades. Efforts to open unions and their leadership positions to black workers were met with tremendous resistance by white workers, and these battles showed the latter's lack of interest in building an interracial labor force.[4]

During a break between workshops, a couple of fellow conferees approached Richardson and told her, "'You're in the wrong place. You should be over [at the NGLC],'" where Malcolm X of the Nation of Islam was scheduled to appear. Richardson had been familiar with Malcolm X for some years prior to her Detroit trip. Her cousin in Philadelphia had mentioned the charismatic Muslim minister to her, and media reports and an occasional reading of the Nation of Islam's newspaper *Muhammad Speaks* kept Richardson informed about his activities.[5] Interestingly, the two had narrowly missed crossing paths at the Statler Hilton Hotel during the March on Washington. This time around, they would finally meet, and it would be very consequential for the black liberation movement.

At the conclusion of the NNLC's Sunday rally, Richardson headed across town to King Solomon Baptist Church for the mass meeting that would serve as the capstone of the NGLC's event. Accompanying her was Bob Bennett, a Detroit physician and family friend who had paid for her trip and, along with his wife, had hosted Richardson during her stay. The focus and feel of the NGLC were qualitatively different from Reverend Franklin's conference. Members from all sectors of the black community—militants and moderates alike—were welcomed by the NGLC, which offered workshops on various topics such as union discrimination against black industrial workers, self-defense tactics, the use of boycotts, and the "feasibility" of the Freedom Now

Party, an all-black political party. The NGLC's internationalism was revealed when conferees passed a resolution acknowledging that black Americans and other peoples of color were locked in a global struggle against white supremacy.[6]

Richardson and Bennett joined 2,000 other people at the evening rally, a group that included *Liberator* editor Dan Watts and Detroit activists James and Grace Lee Boggs. Various speakers primed the audience for Malcolm X's keynote address. One of them was the Reverend Albert B. Cleage, a conference organizer and an influential proponent of black liberation theology. He discussed the connection between racial identity and faith-based social activism and the effectiveness of passive resistance and self-defense. Regarding the latter, the "wildly cheering crowd" approved of Cleage's statement that the recent terrorist bombing of Birmingham's Sixteenth Street Baptist Church "shows . . . you just can't change the white man by letting him beat you over the head everyday." A more effective method, he argued, was for black people to defend themselves when attacked.[7] He and the other speakers reinforced the conference's spirit of positive black identity and an unwavering commitment to critique the tactics and goals of the civil rights movement, but none of them could match Malcolm X's skill in that regard.

Known as "Message to Grassroots," Malcolm's presentation would become one of the 1960s' most important speeches about black liberation. In part, this was because of his astute analysis of the problems confronting the movement itself, but the speech also indicated his willingness to work with people from outside the Nation of Islam (NOI). Malcolm told his audience they had to come together in a unified movement to increase their chances of survival. On this issue, the stakes were so high that Malcolm felt the need to define the "Negro Revolution" versus the less commonly discussed "black Revolution." The former was no revolution at all because its participants—"the house Negroes," as Malcolm called them—lacked the commitment to free black people, as evidenced by their willingness to "bleed" in white America's wars in Europe and Asia but their refusal to shed blood in defense of black lives back home. "The field Negroes," in contrast, were the black revolutionaries who were ready to push the liberation struggle forward and would not hesitate to sacrifice themselves in defense of black people. "And if it is right for America to draft us, and teach us how to be violent in defense of her, then it is right for you and me to do whatever is necessary to defend our own people right here in this country," he said.[8]

Malcolm also spoke about the power shift under way within the black activist community, one that involved moving away from leaders of the old guard civil rights organizations and toward radicals like Richardson. Malcolm had been following Richardson in the news, and he cited her to make his point: "When Martin Luther King failed to desegregate Albany, Georgia, the civil-rights struggle in America reached its low point. King became bankrupt almost, as a leader. . . . Other Negro civil-rights leaders of so-called national stature became fallen idols. As they became fallen idols, began to lose their prestige and influence, local Negro leaders began to stir up the masses. In Cambridge, Maryland, Gloria Richardson; in Danville, Virginia, and other parts of the country, local leaders began to stir up our people at the grassroots level."[9]

After Malcolm was finished, Richardson was invited to say a few words to the audience, and the moment was caught by a *Jet* photographer. The smile on Richardson's face conveys the delight she felt at having witnessed Malcolm's speech, as well as getting the opportunity to meet him. Afterward they had a semiprivate talk, and Richardson observed that the NOI's most recognizable member was quite different in a one-on-one setting than the man who had held the audience's rapt attention; Malcolm was reserved and exuded a personal strength that impressed her. They exchanged contact information, and Richardson expressed the desire to see him again. Her excitement about Malcolm X's potential to advance the struggle was tempered by her belief that his greatness could be fully realized only if he separated himself from the "sectarian" NOI.[10]

Richardson stayed in Detroit for almost a full week after the conferences wrapped up to get some rest and a checkup from Dr. Bennett. However, the Bennetts' residence was a busy place that week. They hosted a dinner attended by Reverend Vivian and other people from the SCLC. Actor Lincoln Perry (who played the character Stepin Fetchit) and former heavyweight boxing champion Joe Louis also stopped by to meet Richardson. She accepted the latter's invitation to join him at the Elmwood Casino and Hotel in Windsor, Ontario, where he was performing with Pearl Bailey. Richardson and Bennett attended the opening weekend of Redd Foxx's ten-day engagement at Detroit's Club Alamo, where she met the up-and-coming comedian.[11]

In the months following her Detroit trip, Richardson spoke at events hosted by a variety of organizations. In January she addressed the political action workshop of the National Alliance of Postal Employees in Washington, DC, and a couple of weeks later she spoke at the Women's International League for Peace and Freedom (WILPF) convention in Washington. Richardson told the WILPF conventioneers that a major source of conflict around the world was Western nations' oppression and exploitation of peoples of color, and she cited Cambridge, Maryland, as an example of that global problem.

"We (the non-whites of the world) live in one homogenous ghetto, economically, socially, educationally, and politically," and the way out of this ghetto was to end its very existence. Youths in America were leading the way in bringing down white society's system of segregation, and Cambridge was a case study of the effectiveness of that youth movement. Young people were demonstrating the "courage, dogged determination . . . , spontaneity and creativity of non-violence" that would move the nation forward, she said, and when the conventioneers returned to their communities and resumed their peace and freedom work, they needed to remember that youths were key to reaching their goals. Importantly, Richardson advised her audience to evaluate whether their own vision of freedom was better than that of the youths. "If you are no longer able to think and act as radically as they do then do not try to lead but follow."[12]

Subsequent engagements brought Richardson north to New York, where the United Packinghouse Workers of America honored her efforts to unionize Cambridge's workforce. She promised delegates she would keep working with their union, which she saw as a means of improving workers' lives. Harlem's Abyssinian Baptist Church (where Congressman Powell was the minister) invited Richardson to speak at its Women's Day program on the morning of Sunday, 8 March. Immediately following that engagement, she sat for an interview with William Worthy, a special correspondent for the *Afro-American* newspaper. Worthy belonged to the breed of black journalists that saw no conflict of interest between their reporting of the news and their participation in the freedom struggle. Years earlier he had joined the Freedom Rides in the Deep South, and he had addressed the NGLC on the same day as his associate and ally Malcolm X.[13]

Worthy's write-up of the interview did not include any new insights into Richardson's philosophies or her thoughts about the movement. However, it was notable for announcing that Richardson was "the first civil rights leader to accept an offer of cooperation from" Malcolm X, whom she viewed as a viable leader in the human rights struggle because he articulated insightful analyses of America's racial caste system in ways that could change skeptics' minds about the movement's tactics and goals.[14] After the interview wrapped up, Richardson's day got a lot more interesting. While she and Frank Dandridge were having dinner at the popular Harlem restaurant Twenty-Two West, Malcolm X stopped by their table to tell them to watch the evening news because they were going to like what they heard. Upon the couple's return to Dandridge's apartment, they learned that Malcolm X had broken from the Nation of Islam earlier in the day.[15]

The news shocked many Americans, but not Richardson. She had been aware of Malcolm's marginalization within the NOI since its leader Elijah Muhammad had silenced him for commenting that President Kennedy's assassination was a case of the "chickens coming home to roost." She found it interesting that Muhammad had punished Malcolm for making a statement that, in Richardson's words, did not contradict the NOI's "iron-clad position about the 'white devil.'" Malcolm's break with the NOI confirmed a suspicion Richardson first had in Detroit. Malcolm had ended his NGLC speech with a boilerplate statement about the Nation of Islam, which, according to Richardson, he delivered "like his heart really wasn't in it . . . like he was just repeating something." She thought at the time that he might be considering breaking from the organization.[16]

Malcolm X told the press that although he was no longer a member of the NOI, he was still a Muslim and he remained committed to the black liberation struggle. Working toward that end, he announced the creation of a Black Nationalist organization called Muslim Mosque Incorporated, which would conduct political education in northern black communities in anticipation of the upcoming presidential election. "We must make [white politicians] understand that Negro voters have it in their power to decide next November whether Johnson stays in the White House or goes back to his Texas cotton patch." Rejecting the isolationism of the NOI, Malcolm told reporters that he was looking forward to working with locally based human rights activists like Gloria Richardson and aiding their efforts on social justice issues. "Good education, housing and jobs are imperatives for the Negroes, and I shall support them in their fight to win these objectives," he said.[17]

It is not known whether Worthy knew that Malcolm X was about to leave the Nation of Islam at the time he interviewed Richardson, but the content of Worthy's article—and its publication two days after he and Richardson met—seemed more than coincidental. Ultimately, his piece functioned as a public notice that one of America's most highly respected civil rights activists was vouching for Malcolm's sincerity as he moved from the sidelines of the struggle—where he had long shouted about the problem of white supremacy—and joined its activist wing. The title of Worthy's article—"Mrs. Richardson Okeys Malcolm X"—punctuated this, and it implied that if readers agreed with Gloria Richardson on civil rights issues, they would likely agree with Malcolm X on such matters.

Malcolm X's first opportunity to work with Richardson came on the weekend following his break from the Nation of Islam. She and five dozen other activists filled the Eastern Light Masonic Lodge in Chester, Pennsylvania, on the afternoon of Saturday, 14 March to formally establish a new civil rights organization, and Malcolm had agreed to serve as a consultant. This new national organization—ACT—would lend aid to locally based community groups in the North that were fighting for better schools, better housing, and increased job opportunities for people of color.[18]

It was probably inevitable that an organization like ACT would be created. For many decades, radical black activists had been growing more and more dissatisfied with northern liberal politicians who were reluctant to push for progressive programs and reforms to improve black people's lives. Foremost among the issues were greater access to union jobs in the skilled trades, enforcement of antidiscrimination laws related to housing, and educational reforms to improve the increasingly poor public school systems. These activists were also highly critical of established civil rights organizations' "conservative" stances on these issues. A main target of their criticism was the NAACP, which was sometimes judged harshly by its own members as well. When W. E. B. Du Bois was editor of the NAACP's publication *Crisis* in the 1930s, he failed to convince his colleagues to decentralize the organization and adopt a radical strategy to achieve human rights. Ella Baker worked as a field secretary for the organization during the 1940s, and she found its leadership (which included Du Bois) to be egotistical and weak on organizing. While out in the field, Baker came across another barrier to organizing: local chapter members' elitism. Those people, she observed, were inclined to work for the liberation of the black masses as long as they met the criteria of middle-class respectability.[19]

Prior to the Cambridge movement, the most well-known conflict between the NAACP and a local movement occurred in the 1950s in Monroe, North Carolina. There, trouble arose when local NAACP leader Robert F. Williams began to take a more radical approach to racial problems. It started in the mid-1950s when he requested legal aid from the NAACP's national office in New York for two black boys (ages seven and nine) who had been charged with molesting a white girl they had allegedly kissed. Officials in New York declined to intervene in the case because they felt it was too closely related to the subject of interracial sex, a topic the NAACP preferred to avoid. Eventually, lawyers from outside the NAACP represented the boys, who were nevertheless convicted, and their ordeal became known as the "Kissing Case." Shortly after this tragedy, Williams became persona non grata within the NAACP because he was publicly advocating for black people to engage in armed self-defense.[20]

The activists who established ACT had their own laundry list of grievances against the NAACP. Richardson complained that the organization had tried to gain control of the Cambridge movement, and Stanley Branche alleged it had done the same in Chester, Pennsylvania. Other sore points centered on local NAACP chapters' failure to support school boycotts or, in some cases, their active opposition to them. ACT saw the NAACP's stance on boycotts as a telltale sign it would not support even more radical strategies to attack racial inequality, especially in housing and employment. ACT's founders wanted the movement to address those issues quickly, so they set out to assist local people who were prepared to work toward that goal.[21] As a group, ACT contained some of the nation's most radical thinkers and activists, and their collaboration accelerated the power shift within the black activist community, much as SNCC had done in the first half of the 1960s. In fact, ACT was essentially a northern equivalent of the southern-oriented SNCC. ACT's membership consisted of nine creative strategists—"firebrand militants," as *Jet* described them—who used a variety of tactics to achieve their goals. Each person specialized in community organizing, but some possessed additional expertise they lent to local organizers who sought ACT's assistance.[22]

Richardson provided training on leadership, negotiations, and economics. Others focused on housing, school boycotts, and job opportunities. Tackling the problem of housing was Jesse Gray, who, along with Richardson and Branche, had conceived of ACT in January 1964. Gray grew up in rural Louisiana in the 1920s and 1930s, and he left historically black Xavier University to join the merchant marines when World War II broke out. After the war he made his way to New York City, where he found work as a tailor. Gray headed a tenants' advocacy organization that pressured city officials to enforce housing laws and punish landlords who did not maintain their properties. In the fall and winter of 1963 Gray's group organized a rent strike in more than fifty Harlem apartment buildings; as a result, the City of New York placed two of the apartment buildings into receivership. Realizing that he had a major problem on his hands, Mayor Robert F. Wagner sent the New York state legislature and Governor Nelson Rockefeller some proposals that would allow the city to handle slum housing conditions more quickly and effectively. One of those proposals was to legalize rent strikes.[23]

Serving as ACT's chairman was Lawrence Landry, a Chicago native and Branche's brother-in-law. After earning degrees in sociology at the University of Chicago, Landry became a leader of the Chicago Area Friends of SNCC. Since the fall of 1963 he had been organizing and leading boycotts of

Chicago's public schools to end the racist treatment of black students. Also focusing on school boycotts was Julius Hobson, an Alabama-born economist employed by the federal government in Washington, DC. During the 1950s he had worked with the NAACP, and in the early 1960s he became the head of CORE's Washington's chapter. A *Washington Post* profile of Hobson stated that by the time he joined ACT, he had been involved in more than eighty civil rights demonstrations targeting racial discrimination in housing, education, and business. He had also helped organize the Freedom Rides in Maryland along US Route 40, as well as the March on Washington.[24]

Focusing on expanding job opportunities were the Reverend Milton Galamison, Herman Ferguson, and Nahaz Rogers. Armed with bachelor's and master's degrees in theology from Lincoln and Princeton Universities, respectively, Galamison moved from his hometown of Philadelphia to become the minister of Siloam Presbyterian Church in Brooklyn, New York. His long and successful track record in community outreach began in the mid-1950s, when he spent a semester in the French colony of Cameroon in West Africa as part of his church's outreach efforts there. In Brooklyn, Galamison over-saw his congregation's social services operations, which included a mental health clinic, remedial education, vocational career counseling, and a credit union. The church's secular components reflected Galamison's personal agenda to improve black people's lives through employment opportunities and better education. He helped organize the July 1963 protests at Manhattan and Brooklyn building projects where black and Latino workers had been denied the opportunity to work, and he organized a school boycott to protest New York City's segregated education system.[25] Ferguson was a schoolteacher from Queens who had been active in economic issues, including a selective buying campaign. Like Galamison, he pushed for increased skilled job opportunities for black and Latino workers. Rogers also had a background in education, but his main role was serving as an organizer for the Negro American Labor Council, whose mission was to increase the black unionized workforce and fight racial discrimination within labor unions.[26]

The Chester meeting kicked off at 1:00 p.m. when Landry told attendees that ACT's main purpose was to serve in a "coordinating and supporting" capacity for activists in cities throughout the country. "The sole qualification for membership in ACT," Landry added later, "is that one must act or utilize direct action to resolve civil rights disputes." It was a strategy that "more conservative organizations" were abandoning or even opposing. The day's presenters then updated the group about their local activities, such as selective buying campaigns and supporting candidates who were running for

ACT's founding meeting, Chester, Pennsylvania, 14 March 1964. Left to right: Lawrence Landry, Gloria Richardson, Dick Gregory, Malcolm X, and Stanley Branche. (Getty Images)

political office on the Freedom Now ticket. However, most of the meeting focused on the recent school boycotts in Chicago, New York, Cambridge, and Chester and how ACT could strategize to advance black liberation. The first person to speak was Dick Gregory, who, like Malcolm X, had agreed to serve as a consultant to the new organization. He said it was important for black people to become more efficient at their civil rights work, which would require them to get better at identifying their friends and their foes.[27]

When it was her turn to speak, Richardson presented an update about Cambridge's school boycott and CNAC's ongoing efforts to desegregate the school system, improve school buildings, and integrate black history into the curriculum. Landry talked about the Chicago school boycotts, which seemed to be threatening the power of the city's white political leaders, particularly Mayor Richard J. Daley, as well as the Chicago NAACP and Urban League. Galamison shared his frustration with the NAACP and CORE's national office for not supporting the school boycott in New York City scheduled for that coming Monday. Hobson told attendees about his plan for a 20 April boycott of Washington's public schools, accompanied by a week's worth of mass sit-ins and picketing throughout the city. His goal was to achieve an "equalizing" of the city's more and less affluent neighborhood schools. Rogers drew a line in the sand on the civil rights battlefield when he spoke of ACT's plan for the remainder of the year, which was to show people what was really at stake in the black freedom struggle by illustrating the stark contrast between ACT and moderate civil rights organizations. "Nineteen sixty-four is going to be the year of total involvement. We are not leaving any middle ground," he said. ACT's ability to achieve this goal would depend in large part on its members being unified in the fight for freedom and not letting their opponents foster divisions among them.[28]

The last presenter of the day was Malcolm X. Richardson had invited him to deliver the keynote speech, which was well received. "He did a very good job of doing . . . what was essentially his thing," she recalled. He delivered a rousing speech that focused on three main subjects: broadening the civil rights struggle, becoming unified in the freedom struggle, and defending black life. The portion of his speech that got the most ink in the press was his statement that black people have the right to defend themselves when attacked. At the conclusion of the meeting, Branche addressed the activists and told them there was a lot of work ahead of them, but they were up to the task. ACT's next meeting was scheduled for 18 April in Washington, DC, where the activists planned to help Hobson with his school boycott and mass demonstrations.[29]

ACT's inaugural meeting also gave Richardson and Malcolm a chance to deepen their ties. In between presenters' speeches, they discussed some pressing issues, one of which was the political education campaign Malcolm had proposed when he broke from the NOI. CNAC had organized voter registration drives and forums for voters to discuss the issues, and Richardson and her colleagues had informed voters how to use their political power more effectively. In Richardson's view, black voters could exert significant influence on the electoral process through the use of a bloc vote in the general election or by boycotting it altogether. She knew that either tactic might result in immediate short-term negative effects for black people, but she still believed that, in the long term, either strategy would lead to greater political leverage for black voters in subsequent elections.[30] Because of his outstanding oratory skills and high-profile status among black Americans, Richardson thought Malcolm X was the one person who could convince the black electorate to vote as a bloc or avoid the polls altogether. He agreed with Richardson's strategy and promised to deliver her message: if the political parties chose to ignore black America's social, economic, and political problems, they risked political chaos. She also asked Malcolm to include another warning in his speeches: if the Democratic and Republican Parties ignored black voters, black people might conclude that electoral politics had nothing to offer them, leaving them no choice but to resort to armed resistance. Richardson had seen this type of thinking take hold in Cambridge's black community, and she had addressed it in her speech at SNCC's benefit rally in New York City seven months earlier. A few black residents in Cambridge had warned her that if CNAC could not achieve positive results, they would have no choice but to use force. Richardson speculated that this same militant attitude probably existed in countless other black communities, so she asked Malcolm "to make it very clear that if it wasn't the ballots [then] it would be bullets," because "that was the only fallback position" black people had.[31]

Over the next three weeks, Malcolm X delivered three "ballot or bullet" speeches. The first was on 22 March at the Rockland Palace in Harlem, where he called for a massive voter registration drive in black communities and told black voters that they possessed the "power to determine who will sit in the White House and who will sit in the doghouse." Black voters could also use the electoral process to compel white politicians to protect all citizens from violence. If that failed, armed resistance was appropriate. "It's time for you and me to let the Government know it's ballots—or bullets." In case anyone misunderstood his reference to bullets, Malcolm provided a clear explanation: "I'm not talking anarchy or sedition. If they don't like what I'm saying, let the government do what it's supposed to. . . . If the government won't find out who bombed the church in Birmingham . . . then we'd better do something."[32]

Malcolm delivered his third "ballot or bullet" speech on 12 April at King Solomon Baptist Church in Detroit, where he and Richardson had first met. He said black people needed to be educated about the value of voting as a bloc to reward politicians who would fight for all citizens and to punish those who would perpetuate a race-based democratic system that privileged white people over black people. Malcolm warned that if America's leaders refused to treat black people as first-class citizens, a race war was a real possibility. "This is why I say it's the ballot or the bullet. It's liberty or it's death. It's freedom for everybody or freedom for nobody." In a rare display of hopefulness, Malcolm X talked about the choice America faced: "A revolution is bloody, but America is in a unique position. She's the only country in history, in the position actually to become involved in a bloodless revolution. . . . All she's got to do is give the black man in this country everything that's due him, everything."[33]

Richardson also spoke publicly about black electoral politics. Two days before Malcolm gave his first "ballot or bullet" speech, she traveled to Baltimore on a cold, wet evening to deliver a keynote address at the "Practicality of Politics" conference organized by the Maryland League of Women's Clubs. Held at Baltimore's War Memorial, the conference was a chance for Maryland's Democratic Party candidates (or their representatives) to seek black voters' support in that fall's congressional elections. The venue was an interesting location for the Cambridge leader to discuss politics because the War Memorial honored veterans of World War I who had answered President Woodrow Wilson's call to make the world "safe for democracy." The "lady general" of civil rights took a break from the racial battlefield to deliver a speech in which she implicitly argued that America itself was an unsafe place for democracy. She accused the Democratic and Republican Parties of taking black voters for granted and suggested they launch voter registration and education drives, which would force both parties to "buy [black people's] votes with deeds." Richardson also criticized white segregationists and black "Uncle Toms" who were undermining the civil rights movement and recommended that these people be targeted with economic boycotts, picketing, and demonstrations. She then reminded her audience of her philosophy about referenda on citizens' rights. At the time, there was a strong possibility that white Marylanders would use a statewide referendum to challenge a recently passed law that desegregated public accommodations, and Richardson advised that if this came to pass, black voters should boycott the referendum.[34]

In April, Richardson's travel schedule took her back to California and then concluded in the nation's capital. The trip out West was sponsored by the Los Angeles Non-Violent Action Committee (N-VAC), an organization that opposed California's pending referendum on a statewide open housing law. During her stay in Los Angeles, Richardson also met with a Mexican American group that shared its concerns about Chicanos' legal problems in Southern California.[35] She closed out the month at a Capital Press Club event in Washington that also featured Philadelphia's NAACP chapter president Cecil B. Moore. She repeated her assessment that black liberation was tied directly to increased economic opportunities and expressed her reservations about President Lyndon B. Johnson. During his tenure in Congress, Johnson had opposed fair employment practices legislation, and his recent refusal to support a stronger civil rights bill in Congress added to her concerns about the president. Additionally, given his legislative track record on civil rights, Richardson told her audience not to expect the president to do the right thing for black people.[36]

ACT's second meeting took place in Washington, DC, a couple of weeks after its founding. With the exception of Malcolm X (who was traveling in Africa), this gathering included most of the major participants at the Chester meeting. Their main task was to discuss how to facilitate cooperation among activists, which would lead to more effective campaigns for jobs, housing, and schools. Members pivoted to a discussion of the civil rights bill, which, contrary to the claims of the gradualist wing of the civil rights movement, did nothing to ameliorate black urban residents' lack of jobs, housing, and equal education. Lawrence Landry rejected the argument made by President Johnson and other national politicians that radical activists' protest tactics threatened the Senate's passage of the pending Civil Rights Act. "Negroes will be freed this year," Landry added, "because the Negroes in the ghettos will free themselves" with the assistance of ACT. Emphasizing his Chicago colleague's point was Nahaz Rogers, who reiterated a core tenet of the organization: "ACT will not function in a manner that is acceptable to white people. It will do things that are acceptable to Negroes."[37]

A recent addition to ACT was Congressman Adam Clayton Powell Jr., who had agreed to serve as a consultant. Richardson came up with the idea of inviting the Harlem lawmaker to establish a formal association with ACT after the two became friends in early February during his trip to Cambridge to investigate Dorchester County's poverty problem. Richardson liked Powell's combative style and found him "very charismatic. Very determined. Very Black oriented." While on the Eastern Shore, Powell publicly chastised local officials for refusing to request the much-needed food, and he used his political power and influence to get surplus food delivered to Dorchester County that winter. The ACT meeting allowed Powell to hammer the president and members of Congress who criticized black radicals' tactics. "I resent their paternalism and I resent them telling us what to do and what not to do. . . . In fact, I think [demonstrations] will help" get the bill passed, he said.[38]

A planned "stall-in" at the World's Fair in New York City the following week was exactly the type of unconventional protest ACT was likely to support. Organized by Brooklyn's CORE chapter, the stall-in was intended to cause a massive traffic jam on the highways leading to the fair, which ran through and along blighted black and Puerto Rican neighborhoods. This would give motorists an eye-opening view of the grinding poverty affecting their fellow citizens.[39] A massive police presence on the highways and the threat that CORE members would be arrested if the stall-in took place scared away all but a small number of protesters. Detractors called the stall-in a failure, but Jesse Gray argued that even the threat of a protest had significantly reduced the amount of traffic on the highways, which in turn resulted in fewer visitors passing through the exposition's turnstiles on opening day.[40] Just over a month later, ACT held its own "fair" in Harlem to keep the spotlight on northern urban poverty. ACT called its event the "Worst Fair," and it invited New York City's Mayor Robert Wagner, Governor Nelson Rockefeller, and President Johnson to attend. This time around, no one would be disrupting traffic, so the politicians could "drive freely through the ghetto" and stop at any one of the four apartment buildings designated as the fair's pavilions. At one location, the "United States Pavilion," visitors could see for themselves the stark reality of tenants who had "no landlord, no heat nor hot water for more than a year."[41]

ACT held a few more meetings over the next few months, and some of its members traveled outside their home base to lend support to other local struggles. For example, Jesse Gray spoke at a rally in Cambridge in late May, where he encouraged black tenants to withhold their rent.[42] Dick Gregory, Branche, and Richardson joined a Baltimore CORE contingent at the Social Security Administration building to protest the federal government's racist employment practices. Richardson tied this issue to CNAC's agenda when she noted, "Cambridge and Federal hiring are not separate issues but part of the same overall problem" of employment discrimination against black citizens. The next stop for ACT was Chicago, where members met on the last weekend of June. One point of business was a boycott of California's wine and produce industries as a response to a large monetary donation by a California realtor to defeat open housing legislation. Capping off the weekend meeting was a six-mile nighttime march by 200 people from the city's South Side to the US District Courthouse, where activists had been removed during a recent demonstration.[43]

From the planned stall-in at the World's Fair to the protest outside the Social Security Administration, ACT had shown its commitment to radicalizing the black liberation movement by lending support to local activists. This was the main factor that determined how people responded to Richardson and her colleagues. People concluded that ACT was either a threat to the movement or one of its saviors. However, there was one subject on which almost everyone agreed: ACT had expedited the power shift within the movement that had begun in 1960 with the creation of SNCC. By 1964, established civil rights leaders could no longer dictate the movement's goals and tactics because radicals like Richardson had chiseled their way into the public space and asserted their own vision of liberation. Supporting these radicals were countless local people who were tired of waiting for freedom. Black journalist Louis E. Lomax described this shift in an anecdote about a fictitious civil rights leader who arrived late to a civil rights parade, only to realize that the marchers had left him behind: "Please tell me which way the parade went; after all, I'm leading it." So noticeable was this shift that less than a month after ACT's founding, the *Pittsburgh Courier* ran a front-page article titled "Which Race Leader Has Most Power?" The piece profiled numerous prominent activists, including CORE's James Farmer and the NAACP's Roy Wilkins. However, activists from the movement's radical wing—Richardson, Malcolm X, Galamison, and Landry—dominated the article.[44]

Others noticed the change in leadership and expressed their opinion as to what it meant for the civil rights movement. *Boston Herald* columnist George Frazier concluded that Richardson's leadership in Cambridge was a tragedy that was likely to be repeated wherever the black masses believed that "compromise" was a dirty word. *Time* magazine observed that in Cambridge, as in other cities around the nation, "responsible Negro leadership . . . had suddenly given way before the thrust of militancy." The *Christian Science Monitor* wrote that national civil rights leaders had "default[ed]" their role as leaders because they had been unable to maintain a consensus among black Americans regarding the movement's goals, strategies, and tactics. This failure of leadership allowed "lone-wolf militants" to fill the leadership void. The three activists the paper cited as fitting this description all had ties to ACT: Richardson, Galamison, and Gregory.[45]

Criticisms popped up in the black press, too. *New York Amsterdam News* sportswriter Howie Evans praised the work of "freedom leaders" such as Martin Luther King Jr. and Gloria Richardson, yet he lamented the lack of unity among them and their organizations. Compounding this problem was the white media's "glamorizing [of] the methods of Jesse Gray, Malcolm X, and other such potential leaders, while giving lesser note to the Martin Luther Kings, James Farmers, etc." Evans believed the outcome was "mass confusion among the Negro populace across the country." The esteemed journalist James L. Hicks echoed Evans's argument. Hicks saw Cambridge's referendum vote as incontrovertible evidence that when black people supported local leaders, the civil rights movement was weakened because those same people failed to lend their full support to the more experienced and better qualified male leadership at the national level. Hicks noted that if an alien from outer space told a black American, "Take me to your leader," that alien should be introduced to one of the unofficial black leadership group known as the "Big Six," which Hicks described as black America's "high command." In Hicks's opinion, local activists should be asking these men for assistance and guidance in improving their communities, but something else was happening. "Too many self-appointed leaders . . . start too many small wars in the wrong place at the wrong time," Hicks wrote, and he indirectly criticized Richardson to make his point. "Our leaders start out to lead us on an assault on Gov. Wallace in Alabama and what happens—on the way down there some corporal persuades a third of our army to attack Cambridge, Maryland!"[46]

Other black journalists saw the power shift as a positive development and Gloria Richardson as one of the people responsible for it. She was "typical of new leaders emerging from 'the Negro Revolt' now sweeping the nation," wrote Chicago's *Daily Defender*, and the *Afro-American* called Richardson "a brave woman . . . standing up to a whole town, which does not know what to make of this kind of revolution made by the little people." The *Liberator*'s Dan Watts said Richardson and a number of other local leaders were in the vanguard of activists showing black Americans the way to freedom.[47]

The backgrounds of many established civil rights leaders and the process by which some of them rose to their positions were important factors that contributed to their loss of power. In his newspaper article "Struggle for Power Divides Community," black journalist Ofield Dukes wrote that white politicos had selected certain black men to be spokespersons of their race, which caused white people to view them as official leaders of the black community. Black people viewed this selection process as problematic because those "leaders" answered to their white sponsors instead of to black communities. The fact that many of those black men belonged to the middle class created more tension. "It is the lower class Negro stratum that experiences the brunt of the ill effects of racial discrimination and segregation," and if the middle-class "leadership is too slow in moving toward alleviation of these problems of bias, then the Negro on the street loses confidence in established and white-recognized Negro leadership." One Urban League official in Illinois predicted that this issue would cause a power vacuum that would be filled by radical activists who would try to quicken the pace of racial progress.[48]

Three events in the second half of 1964 showed how large the chasm was between ACT and the moderate wing of the movement. Believing that black protests would alienate moderate white voters and drive them to elect Republican Barry Goldwater as president, Martin Luther King Jr., Roy Wilkins, Whitney Young, and A. Philip Randolph took it upon themselves to call for a ban on demonstrations until after the presidential election. ACT responded sharply to this. Branche said that America had moved forward on race *because* of black people's demonstrations, not in spite of them, and it would be a critical strategic error not to use such an effective pressure tactic. The other two events came at the end of November when Wilkins and Farmer appeared on television news shows. While a guest on CBS's *Face the Nation*, Wilkins described FBI director J. Edgar Hoover as a "good public servant . . . with a long and distinguished career," which was why civil rights leaders had not asked President Johnson to replace him. Wilkins's comment was a slap in the face to the activists doing the heavy lifting in the South over the past three years, where they had routinely been attacked by white supremacists while Hoover's agents observed quietly from the sidelines. When Farmer appeared on ABC's *Issues and Answers*, he said CORE would not work with Black Nationalists or communists because "Negroes find it tough enough to be black without being both black and red." Farmer's position was essentially a surrender to the anticommunism hysteria known as the Red Scare, and it meant that CORE was restricting its ability to push the civil rights movement forward because it would have fewer allies in that struggle.[49] For the black people who were already impatient with the pace of change—especially the young ones—these events made ACT an attractive alternative to organizations like CORE and the NAACP.

ACT's rise came as a surprise to many white liberals, who believed the North was the promised land for black people. What these liberals did not understand was that systemic white racism in the North kept black people in social and economic ghettos. Separate surveys of New York City's black and white residents conducted in the summer of 1964 showed just how far apart the two groups were. Most black respondents held white people responsible for the systemic racism that kept black people on the lowest rung of the socioeconomic ladder—out of good jobs, in poor neighborhoods, and in lousy public schools where teachers did not care about students' success. The majority of white respondents did not support integrated schools if that meant transferring their children out of white neighborhood schools. Furthermore, they thought the black liberation struggle in New York had been "going too fast" and had "gone too far." Black and white respondents even disagreed on the former's use of nonviolent direct action protests. Most black people favored the tactic because they believed it worked, whereas most white people believed it "hurt the Negro cause."[50]

Anxiety about the direction of the civil rights movement could be found at the highest levels of the white community, and ACT's members and their associates were a main cause of that anxiety. Historian August Meier and a colleague made a similar (and contemporaneous) observation in the academic journal *New Politics.* They said that soon after ACT's formation, its leaders "frighten[ed] the white leadership to a greater awareness of the urgent need to improve the Negroes' condition of life." In addition to their position on protest tactics, ACT members' support for self-defense reinscribed the line of demarcation between the movement's radicals and moderates, and that subject was one of the most heavily discussed when people commented about ACT. One activist who had attended the organization's kickoff meeting claimed that NAACP officials in Philadelphia told the Chester Committee for Freedom Now (CCFN) "not to allow Malcolm X to come to" ACT's meeting, and if it did, the NAACP "could not work with" CCFN. Richardson claimed CNAC was also pressured to distance itself from Malcolm. The ILGWU was one of CNAC's financial contributors, but it threatened to pull its funding unless Richardson recanted her support for Malcolm's position on self-defense. She was unwilling to do so and told the union "to take the money."[51]

The ILGWU's response to Richardson's position illustrates a major belief among countless generations of white Americans about who has the right to use self-defense. As far back as America's colonial period, black people's use of the tactic had almost always been condemned by white people. NAACP official and attorney Clarence Mitchell Jr. addressed this issue in November 1963. While speaking at the Conference on Youth, Nonviolence, and Social Change at Howard University, he implied that self-defense is a right that white people reserved for themselves, as evidenced by their demand that black people, particularly men, "turn the other cheek" when attacked.[52]

Richardson knew that the right to defend oneself and one's property was a nonnegotiable right possessed by all Americans. The Eastern Shore's hunting culture contributed to Richardson's acceptance of firearms as a part of everyday life. Generations of St. Clair men had owned guns and hunted, and some St. Clair women occasionally joined them on these outings. Richardson never went hunting herself, but she did learn how to fire a rifle during an event sponsored by the women's auxiliary of Cambridge's black sportsmen's club.[53] No one within the Cambridge movement ever questioned black people's right to defend themselves, and to the residents of the Second Ward, self-defense was a form of collective resistance to white supremacy, just as mass demonstrations were. So if they rejected the use of self-defense, they would be severely restricting their ability to live to fight another day. In fact, on at least one occasion, Richardson's mother and her daughter Donna sat perched with rifles in second-floor windows guarding their Muir Street home. SNCC worker Mark Suckle wrote to another white student activist: "Last night, it was my turn to do phone duty at Gloria's. I sat all alone in an arm chair with a shot gun across my lap. The community is an armed camp."[54]

Richardson believed the black community's use of self-defense served as "a deterrent to further violence" because white terrorists realized they could lose their lives if they attacked the Second Ward. It also kept the Cambridge movement from being destroyed because it held the attackers "off a little," giving the activists time to adjust to changing dynamics on the ground. Ultimately, black residents' defense of their community drew the federal government into Cambridge's racial problems, and Richardson hinted that black people elsewhere could do the same. SNCC did not have a formal policy concerning self-defense, and members stood on both sides of the issue. Those who defended its use included Ella Baker, Ruby Doris Smith Robinson, Stokely Carmichael, and Fannie Lou Hamer. Importantly, they were not outliers within black America. In fact, Rosa Parks, W. E. B. Du Bois, and NAACP president Walter White also supported its use.[55]

Meier's *New Politics* article also discussed another subject that troubled moderates: a boycott of the polls. "At least one ACT leader is reported to have said that it would benefit the movement if such a boycott resulted in the election of a conservative like [Barry] Goldwater, because his intransigence in office would lead to a 'truly revolutionary situation.'" Richardson was probably the person who made that remark because she had been promoting an election boycott throughout the spring of 1964. One UPI reporter believed there was more than an outside chance of a black voter boycott that fall. If it materialized, it would be disastrous for the Democratic Party, but it would send a clear message to party leaders that black voters must be treated with respect because of their electoral power.[56]

Richardson's other tactical approach to electoral politics—a bloc vote—could also prove fatal to either the Democrats or the Republicans. Bloc voting has a long history in American democracy and has been used by various white ethnic and religious groups. If black voters used the tactic, Republicans and Democrats would have to vie for the black vote by making firm promises to improve the nation's social, economic, and political landscapes in the near future. According to Richardson, the Eastern Shore's Republican congressman Rogers Morton tried to dissuade her from advocating a bloc vote. Morton told her that Goldwater was a closet supporter of black people but could not say so publicly because he would lose the white conservative vote. As it turned out, the election results bore out Republicans' concerns about the black bloc vote. Only 6 percent of black voters cast their ballots for Goldwater, a massive drop from the 32 two percent Richard Nixon had received four years earlier.[57]

Complicating the political landscape for the two major parties, but espe-cially for northern Democrats, was the Freedom Now Party (FNP). Borrow-ing its name from the movement's call for immediate liberation, the FNP reflected the sense of political urgency felt by its creator, civil rights attorney Conrad J. Lynn, who had served as a defense attorney for the two black boys involved in North Carolina's "Kissing Case." Lynn organized the FNP because he believed the Republican Party had abandoned black citizens and he was concerned about the Democratic Party's right wing, which had been quite successful in undermining efforts by moderates and liberals to address racial inequality. Modeled after the African independence movements sweep-ing that continent, the FNP vowed to be a "self-relian[t]" political party to leverage black voters' strength and help them achieve their goal of liberation. Lynn rejected the popular claim that only through participation in the nation's two major political parties had black people made racial progress in recent years. Progress came, Lynn wrote, not from black voters' work within the bipartisan framework but from their application of pressure from the out-side. A black third party, he argued, could bring about more and quicker progress because it could give black voters the "'bargaining power'" they needed to gain political concessions from the Democrats and Republicans. Richardson supported Lynn and described the FNP as "a good tactic in terms of presenting issues." He even suggested Richardson and the Reverend Albert B. Cleage as candidates for an FNP presidential ticket, but Richardson had no interest in running for office. Instead, Lynn put all his energy into building the FNP at the local and state levels.[58]

Electoral politics continued to hold politicians' attention for the remain-der of 1964, especially because of what happened in Mississippi that summer. Since the end of Reconstruction, the state's Republican Party had been in mothballs, allowing the all-white Democratic Party to run Mississippi on its own terms. Rather than try to revitalize the dormant Republican Party, black citizens decided to enroll in the Democratic Party, but its white members prevented them from doing so. Black people responded to this disenfran-chisement by establishing the interracial Mississippi Freedom Democratic Party (MFDP), and during the summer of 1964 more than a thousand col-lege students from the North headed to the Magnolia State for "Freedom Summer," a massive voter education and registration campaign to help the MFDP create a viable challenge to the state's all-white delegation to the Democratic National Convention in Atlantic City.[59]

Richardson thought the MFDP was a "great" concept because it mobi-lized the black masses. In the process, it showed them how much real political power they had and how they could use that power to challenge the institutional racism of the state's political system. At the same time, it showed them that fighting for racial progress from within the system was a battle in its own right, and political leaders could change the rules of engagement to suit their own needs and desires. This became clear when the Democratic Party's credentials committee recognized Mississippi's all-white delegation as the party's official representative body. Many MFDP members and their supporters saw the national Democratic Party's decision as a betrayal of its own values and its purported commitment to being a truly interracial body.[60] The Democratic Party's move stunned the MFDP and its allies, but it did not shock Richardson. She had grown up in a political family and knew that compromise was an integral part of politics. Furthermore, her experiences with white politicians had proved to Richardson that most had no qualms about ignoring and denying black citizens' constitutional rights.

A case in point was President Johnson's push for a voting rights act in December 1964. He told Attorney General Nicholas Katzenbach: "I want you to write me the goddamndest, toughest voting rights act that you can devise."[61] Department of Justice lawyers drafted a bill that outlawed the practices and tactics that kept black citizens from voting, but the political reality was that the bill had to make it through Congress. So the lawyers revised it, creating a bill that Katzenbach believed was less likely to be filibustered by conservatives from both parties and would pass a constitutional challenge, should one arise. One way to prevent both from happening was to make the bill location specific rather than nationwide. Senator Everett Dirksen, a conservative Republican from Illinois, favored the bill's geographic limitations. "The idea," he said, "is to send the firewagon where the fire is." Richardson disagreed with his characterization of the disenfranchisement of black voters as a series of fires in just one part of the nation. To her, all of America was aflame, and the voting rights bill should cover the entire nation. "Blacks lived everywhere so why not [coverage] everywhere?" she asked rhetorically. Oddly, the bill did not apply to her home state of Maryland, where allegations of voter intimidation and voting "irregularities" were not uncommon.[62]

ACT's advocacy continued to push the boundaries of the civil rights movement, as well as changing its tenor. Jesse Gray called for community oversight of New York City's police force by "100 skilled black revolutionaries who are ready to die" to protect black communities from racially hostile, abusive, and corrupt police officers; this foreshadowed what the Black Panther Party for Self-Defense did in Oakland, California, in later years.[63] In June 1965 ACT leaders (with the exception of Richardson) formed the Organization for Black

Power (OBP), which served as ACT's political arm; its goal was to expand and deepen black people's political power in cities with large black populations. Lawrence Landry spoke about the opportunities and challenges facing these communities, which he implied constituted a nation within a nation. "Black people are in line to govern the cities just as the Irish and Poles once did. The problem is worse for us because of the suburban ring that has left the city a colony—controlled by absentee social workers, absentee police officials, absentee landlords." The OBP also addressed the newly established War on Poverty programs championed by President Johnson and written in large part by Congressman Adam Clayton Powell Jr. The OBP stressed the need for black citizens to be educated about these antipoverty programs, which it believed would maintain the racial and economic status quo.[64]

The creation of the OBP reinforced moderate civil rights leaders' belief that they were losing control over the movement's agenda, and to stop this trend, they felt they had to contain ACT's spreading influence. One of the most dramatic steps was taken by CORE's James Farmer, who expelled the organization's Brooklyn chapter because it did not cancel the stall-in at the World's Fair; two months later, Farmer expelled Julius Hobson. Government officials also seemed to be lining up against ACT. After Reverend Galamison resumed the school boycotts in New York City in the fall of 1964, he was arrested, tried, and convicted for encouraging students to stay home from school. Somewhat paradoxically, as black moderates' political standing within black America declined because of ACT and other black radical groups (such as the Revolutionary Action Movement and the Black Panther Party), their standing among white politicos rose because the latter saw black moderates as their best option when dealing with black communities' racial grievances.[65]

Ebony magazine's July 1964 issue included a lengthy and sympathetic profile of Gloria Richardson and her work in the civil rights movement. Many readers were impressed by her activism, and a few wrote her letters of appreciation, which the magazine published. One reader encouraged Richardson to keep up her activism because she "provides and exemplifies the type of leadership we need during this crucial period." What that reader did not know is that shortly after the July issue of *Ebony* hit the newsstands, Richardson made some important decisions that changed her relationship to the black liberation movement.[66] For one, she resigned from both CNAC and SNCC's executive committee. Then Richardson married Frank Dandridge, and she and her daughter Tamara moved to his home in New York City. These developments made regional and national news because of what they might mean for the

Cambridge movement and for the larger civil rights movement. A writer for Chicago's *Daily Defender* implied that Richardson's exit from the movement would diminish its vitality both in Cambridge and nationally.[67]

Other reports presented Richardson's decision to marry Dandridge as a reprioritizing of her life. She gave credence to that assumption when she said she was "'retiring from civil rights entirely and devoting [her] time to [her] family.'" What no one knew was that Richardson had always intended to be active in the Cambridge movement only for as long as she felt useful to it. She "wasn't in [the movement] for a career." Nor did she want to become an "icon" of the Cambridge movement, which would hinder black Cambridge from developing new leaders for the next phase of its struggle. Her concern was shared by SNCC's Jim Forman, who had warned of local movements falling victim to a "Messiah complex" or a type of groupthink in which "people would feel that only a particular individual could save them and [they] would not move on their own to fight racism and exploitation."[68]

Despite being one of ACT's founding members, Gloria Richardson stepped away from it as well. The last ACT event she attended was in Chicago in June 1964, a full year prior to her colleagues' creation of the OBP. Yet Richardson's move away from the activist wing of the black liberation movement did not mean she would be absent from the struggle. When Malcolm X created the Organization for Afro-American Unity (OAAU) in June 1964, Richardson accepted his invitation to join because it aligned with her humanist values. The OAAU would "unite Afro-Americans and their organizations around a non-religious and non-sectarian constructive program for Human Rights." Because Malcolm valued her views on race and politics, he sought Richardson's input when formulating the OAAU's founding charter.[69]

Richardson's membership in the OAAU was brief because Malcolm X was assassinated at the organization's meeting in Harlem's Audubon Ballroom on 21 February 1965. Tamara Richardson recalled her mother being "very sad" and "very distraught and angry" about Malcolm's murder. In hindsight, Gloria believed she had been warned about the assassination the previous spring, when members of the Nation of Islam had advised her to avoid appearing on the same stage as Malcolm. When she pressed them for details, they declined to elaborate, but after Malcolm's murder, Richardson realized what they had meant.[70]

A more obvious sign that Malcolm's life was in danger came a week before his assassination. In the early hours of 14 February, one or more terrorists threw multiple gasoline firebombs through the living room window of the East Elmhurst, Queens, home he shared with his wife and daughters. The entire family escaped without injury by fleeing through the backdoor. Malcolm had been in a legal dispute with the NOI, which owned the home and wanted Malcolm and his family to vacate the premises. A court had ordered the family to leave, but Malcolm had filed an appeal and was awaiting a decision when the home was bombed. Frank Dandridge visited Malcolm a couple of days after the bombing to let him know that Gloria was securing a place for his family to stay until they could find permanent housing. When Frank returned home, he told Gloria that Malcolm was "very tense" and had promised to call the couple after the OAAU meeting on 21 February.[71] That call would never come.

Richardson believed the US government was the force behind the "black people [who] pulled the trigger" and murdered her friend. "As long as he was in that Elijah Muhammad group, it was all right with [white people]," she said, but the government targeted Malcolm for neutralization when he expressed a willingness to work in coalition with people and groups despite their disagreements on tactics and strategies. Richardson was so affected by his death that she waited almost a year before listening to recordings of his speeches, which reminded her of Malcolm's brilliance.[72] His influence can be seen in her essay "Focus on Cambridge," which was published in the civil rights journal *Freedomways*. Drawn largely from her August 1963 SNCC fund-raiser speech, the essay is a more tightly argued text that contains a slightly more urgent call for racial progress. The alternative, Richardson warned, was a race war fought in part by black veterans who "America [had] trained . . . to kill and to be immune to death in order to win for an ideal— democracy." It was a line inspired by Malcolm's speech about "the field Negroes" who had served in the military and were willing to "bleed" for black people and take out their enemies.[73]

For her part, Richardson had a significant influence on Malcolm, especially with regard to his liberation agenda. For example, shortly after they became friends, Malcolm said he believed black youth had an important role in the freedom movement and that their perspectives were needed to interrogate issues and suggest solutions to problems. He had come to this conclusion in part because of his relationships with young radicals such as Revolutionary Action Movement member Max Stanford. Yet Richardson had been attesting publicly to the invaluable role of radical black youth in the movement since the early 1960s, observing that they would continue to be its visionaries. She undoubtedly said the same to Malcolm when they spoke privately.[74] Additionally, Richardson showed him how to build his Organization for Afro-American Unity from the ground up. Although Malcolm had extensive experience recruiting new members to the Nation of Islam, that type of work was very different from the community outreach and organizing that was the foundation of the black liberation movement's secular activist wing. With Richardson's aid, Malcolm learned the important elements of grassroots organizing that he needed to build his organization. Equally important was Richardson's help in easing Malcolm's transition from the politically insular and intellectually narrow NOI to the intellectually and politically vibrant radical black activist community. She challenged him to expand his mind-set about what tactics could work to push the struggle forward. Within six months of meeting Richardson, he had gone from believing in the NOI's dictum that black people should not engage in the political process to actively supporting voter registration drives and encouraging black people to leverage their electoral power through the use of a bloc vote.

After Malcolm X's death, Richardson never again established formal ties to a black rights group. She felt it was the younger generation's time to advance their own Black Power agenda, and she was pleased to see them doing so via newly established organizations such as the Revolutionary Action Movement and the Black Panther Party. Even CORE moved toward Black Power. By 1966, the moderate James Farmer was out as CORE's leader, replaced by the militant Floyd B. McKissick. Richardson's former ACT colleague Jesse Gray spoke at CORE's 1966 convention and received rousing applause when he told the audience the new phase of the black liberation movement would take place in the "back streets and alleys" of America's cities. He said for black people to achieve real Black Power, CORE and other like-minded organizations had to reach out to the black urban masses and harness their energy.[75]

Four weeks after CORE's convention, the NAACP held its own annual gathering. Speakers included Vice President Hubert Humphrey, who acknowledged that Black Power was on the ascent. Black moderates therefore needed to wage a battle for the hearts and minds of black youths, lest they turn to Black Power to solve their social, economic, and political problems. The NAACP had to convince young people of the value of integration as a goal, and it needed to persuade them that civil rights organizations were the most efficient channels for directing their energy. "The time has come," Humphrey declared, "to broaden the base of the civil rights movement—to reach out into the community and enlist vital new sources of energy and strength. . . . We must now reach out even further with the message: 'Brother, we need you for freedom.'"[76] In retrospect, the vice president's call was almost two years late.

Through her activism and leadership in both CNAC and ACT, Gloria Richardson fostered the kind of creative tension within the black liberation movement that helped Black Power percolate and develop in northern urban centers like New York, Newark, New Jersey, and Oakland, California, and she watched from the sidelines as that wave evolved. However, Richardson's break from the movement was short-lived because when protests resumed in Cambridge, she pivoted back to an activist stance.

10

"You Will Not Be Able to Stay Home, [Sister]"

A little more than 200 miles of earth separates Cambridge, Maryland, and New York City, but in the mid-1960s they were light-years apart. One was a small provincial town with a seasonal economy and light industry, and the other was a massive metropolis of finance and entertainment. Despite her move to New York, Gloria Richardson continued to feel connected to the Eastern Shore. She still had family there, and Cambridge would always be her home. If anything, her ties to that town increased when Donna and her husband moved back there and had their first child. Richardson also stayed plugged in to Cambridge's ongoing push for racial equality. That push was resisted by the white community, and racial tensions eventually boiled over in Cambridge in the summer of 1967. Richardson spent a lot of that summer in her family's old home on Muir Street, where she kept an eye on developments and helped the Second Ward recover after a massive fire leveled numerous blocks.

Also occurring during this time was a historic gathering in Newark, New Jersey, where black activists and community people from all over the country discussed the meaning of Black Power and how they could operationalize it. Richardson attended this event, and she found it interesting that the questions being asked were essentially the same ones young activists had answered during the student-led civil rights phase of the black freedom movement: What were their main goals, and who would lead the charge to achieve them? What tactics would they use, and how could they avoid being co-opted by competing interests? How could they maintain and expand their freedom movement in the face of continuing resistance from white America? Richardson's experiences during the civil rights movement had shown her that the answers could be found in SNCC's group-centered and member-driven model for social change. But Black Power advocates generally did not employ the SNCC model, and Richardson blamed that for their inability to devise and implement a truly radical agenda for black liberation.

New York

When Gloria Richardson moved to New York, most of its 7 million residents lived in racially segregated sections of the city. In contrast, Richardson, her daughter Tamara, and Frank Dandridge lived in a small apartment in the multiracial and multicultural enclave of Greenwich Village. His photojournalism career made for an exhilarating life, and it opened up an entertaining and intellectually stimulating world for the Cambridge transplants. Tamara accompanied Frank on photo shoots, and before the decade ended, the trio would head to West Hollywood for a few weeks while he shot stills on the set of Jules Dassin's movie *Uptight*, starring Ruby Dee and Julian Mayfield. Spattered in between brief meet and greets were dinners with prominent public figures and celebrities, including Sidney Poitier, Betty Friedan, Romare Bearden, and Wilt Chamberlain.[1]

Her exit from the movement also afforded Richardson the chance to return to a passion of hers—reading—and she devoured a wide variety of books purchased at Manhattan bookstores. The city's intellectual circle also opened up to Richardson. She came into contact with Dan Watts of the *Liberator*, autodidactic historian John Henrik Clarke, and playwright and poet LeRoi Jones (Amiri Baraka). The latter two belonged to the Harlem Writers Guild, a socially and politically oriented group that was influential in the black arts movement of the 1960s.[2] The New York intellectual to whom Richardson felt the strongest connection was James Baldwin. Dandridge was the author's personal photographer, and when he introduced Baldwin to Richardson, the two immediately hit it off. She had first developed an interest in his work when Paul Cowan inserted the title of Baldwin's book *The Fire Next Time* into the speeches she delivered in San Francisco and New York in 1963. Richardson found Baldwin "brilliant" and down to earth, and she appreciated that he "spoke truth to power," such as when he said the so-called Negro problem was actually a problem created by white people. Richardson also liked that he respected black youth's attempts to overthrow America's racial hierarchy. The two remained friends until Baldwin moved to France some years later.[3]

Despite her exit from the civil rights movement, Richardson stayed connected to SNCC, and when the organization opened an office in New York City near Union Square, she often went there to help out. Frank was supportive of Gloria's continued association with SNCC, but he did not want her "out in the streets" protesting. As the summer of 1967 arrived, it looked like that might be impossible to avoid.[4]

Back to Cambridge

Since leaving Cambridge in 1964, Richardson had been advising the Black Action Federation (BAF), CNAC's successor. Some former CNAC members, including Elaine Adams, established BAF because they felt that Cambridge's white power system was still impeding progress in all areas of black residents' lives. They were particularly angered by white people's decision to restrict black residents' access to the city pool. Racial tensions between black and white residents rose, and at one point, unidentified arsonists tossed Molotov cocktails at white-owned businesses in the Second Ward.[5] In addition to the pool issue, black residents' grievances included racial discrimination by law enforcement officers and in public- and private-sector employment. When a race relations aid to Maryland governor Spiro Agnew declined to meet with BAF about the black community's concerns and met instead with representatives of the local NAACP branch, BAF called a mass meeting for 8 July. Coincidentally, Richardson had been in Cambridge visiting family when BAF began its latest push against the town's political system. She decided to stick around while things were in flux, although white people feared she would only stoke racial tensions.[6]

BAF was not the only group holding a rally in Cambridge. On 15 July the white supremacist National States' Rights Party gathered to support George Wallace, who was considering another run for the presidency. The city's police chief worried that the event would lead to a racial confrontation, as it had the previous summer in Baltimore, when white attendees at a States' Rights Party rally had tried to enter a black neighborhood. Richardson told the press, "Everybody knows what will happen" if white people try that in Cambridge. BAF held a counterdemonstration to the Wallace rally, but there were no clashes. In response to black workers' demands for jobs, Governor Agnew sent a mobile job unit into the Second Ward for two weeks beginning in mid-July, where state employees provided career counseling and job referrals to more than eighty teenagers and young adults.[7] Richardson returned to New York City shortly thereafter, but she headed back to the Eastern Shore a few weeks later when the Second Ward caught fire.

Earlier in the summer, Elaine Adams had asked Richardson to arrange for SNCC's newly elected chairman H. "Rap" Brown to visit Cambridge and discuss Black Power ideology with BAF members. Brown and Richardson had known each other since 1963, when he had traveled to Cambridge to assist CNAC, and the two had recently reconnected when Richardson was volunteering at SNCC's New York City office.[8] Traveling from Newark,

New Jersey, where he had just attended the National Conference on Black Power, Brown arrived in Cambridge at approximately nine o'clock on the evening of Monday, 24 July. He climbed onto the roof of a parked car near the Pine Street Elementary School and began a forty-five-minute speech to 400 people by quoting Langston Hughes's poem "A Dream Deferred": "What happens to a dream deferred? Does it dry up like a raisin in the sun? Or does it explode?" Referring to the recent civil disturbances in Detroit and Newark, he said: "It's time for Cambridge to explode." Those explosions were not "riots," Brown argued, but an interconnected "rebellion" against the nation's racial status quo, and if Cambridge's white community did not accede to the black community's demands for change, they should "burn this town down."[9] After his speech, Brown stayed to speak with Adams. Later, he escorted one teenager back to her home while about two dozen other residents tagged along. Law enforcement officers viewed the group as an impromptu march headed toward the white section of the city, so they told the group to stop. With no warning, one of the officers fired his shotgun twice; one shot went over the heads of Brown and the others in the group, and the other shot hit the pavement in front of them. Brown received a superficial wound to his face when he was struck by pellets. He was treated at the local hospital and left Cambridge immediately thereafter.[10]

According to police reports, Brown had yelled out for black residents to "burn, loot, and shoot" law enforcement officers, but even if he said those things, no one heeded the call. Instead, the black residents rushed back to Pine Street, where they were confronted a short time later by a group of young white males who sped down the street in a car and either tossed lighted firecrackers or fired weapons at the residents. On a return trip down the same street, the vehicle's white occupants were greeted by gunfire from black residents. Elsewhere in the Second Ward, a white police officer was hit in the face, neck, and hand by a shotgun blast. This infuriated Police Chief Kinnamon, who wanted to "clear out" anyone lingering in the streets of the Second Ward. However, a state police commander and General Gelston (who had been dispatched to Cambridge ahead of Brown's arrival) convinced the chief that closing off the ward was the appropriate next step. General Gelston, who considered the situation stabilized, ordered his troops out of the city, while state and local police officers continued to patrol the ward. Around 1:00 a.m. someone set the Pine Street Elementary School on fire, but the fire department did not leave the station until forty-five minutes later, and when it arrived, the firefighters did not move in to extinguish the fire. Instead, they worked to prevent it from spreading to the city's business sector. The fire raged for another hour or so before any attempts were made to get it under control, but by that time, it had already spread to adjacent buildings. When the smoke cleared in the early hours of 25 July, more than two city blocks that had once contained homes and numerous black-owned businesses were nothing but rubble. Governor Agnew sent 700 National Guard troops into Cambridge, and Brown was being sought by law enforcement for inciting a riot. Contrary to popular belief, there was no riot that evening, and black residents never threatened firefighters or prevented them from entering the Second Ward.[11]

Upon hearing news of the fire, Richardson planned to travel to Cambridge so she could assess the situation herself. Her personal attorney and friend Jonathan W. Lubell offered to accompany her and handle some of the legal work for the black defendants who had been arrested. At the time, he was working at the Law Center for Constitutional Rights in Newark, New Jersey, and he enlisted the help of another lawyer at the center, William M. Kunstler, one of the nation's most prominent and powerful civil rights attorneys.[12] On 2 August, Richardson and the two lawyers arrived in Cambridge, and the next day they went to court to handle bail hearings for nine defendants (three juveniles and six adults). Richardson stayed in Cambridge to advise BAF, and she encouraged the organization to reframe the crisis as something other than a riot by a mob of angry black people. To that end, BAF sought a meeting with President Johnson's advisory commission on civil disorders to present BAF's version of events before and after the fire.[13]

Richardson returned to New York City in August but went back to Cambridge in late September to attend BAF's Black Power meeting. The gathering gave Second Ward residents the chance to discuss the still unresolved problems of unequal education, lack of jobs, and housing issues and to show their support for BAF's efforts to improve those issues. The meeting took place on Saturday, 30 September, at the home of Richardson's cousin Herbert St. Clair. Approximately 100 people assembled in his backyard to listen to half a dozen speakers who "preached Negro unity and black power." They also kept up the rhetorical assault on the white power structure in Cambridge and in the state of Maryland.[14]

Richardson criticized Governor Agnew for claiming that he was unaware of the black community's concerns, and she condemned his remark that seemed to blame black residents for the city's racial problems rather than address the reason for the recent conflicts. "Only white people hold the answer to whether there will be peace in the future," Richardson said, and if they refused to improve society, "the battle truly may be joined" in the coming year. It was a reference to the rise in militancy among America's white college students since 1965, especially those belonging to Students for a Democratic Society (SDS). The group had been organizing and demonstrating against the Vietnam War and the military draft, as well as protesting the nation's value system, which either justified exploitation or ignored it altogether. Richardson had anticipated that this group might crystallize within the nation's white community, but that could happen only if white people recognized something black people had always known: "The status quo is now intolerable."[15] Importantly, the issues and concerns raised by BAF and Richardson on that late September day had already been discussed and debated at the Black Power conference in Newark.

National Conference on Black Power

Approximately 1,000 black people from around the nation traveled to Newark, New Jersey, in the third week of July 1967 to attend the National Conference on Black Power. The four-day event commenced on Thursday, 20 July, and it was a truly diverse affair, with attendees representing a broad spectrum of social, economic, and political organizations, including SNCC, the Revolutionary Action Movement (RAM), the NAACP, the New England Grass Roots Organization (NEGRO), the National Council of Negro Women, the United Auto Workers, the Mississippi Freedom Democratic Party, and the A. Philip Randolph Institute. A variety of Black Nationalists attended the conference as well. There were territorial nationalists, who desired their own black nation; revolutionary nationalists, who advocated the use of electoral politics and, if necessary, armed struggle to end black people's social, economic, and political exploitation; and cultural nationalists, who looked to Africa's cultural history for elements that black Americans could use to repair and restructure their self and group identities.[16]

Largely a networking affair, the conference gave attendees the opportunity to share stories about their common problems and how to address them. With such disparate groups of people, disagreements arose regarding goals, strategies, and tactics. That, however, was viewed not as a stumbling block but as an opportunity to engage in fruitful dialogue. One participant said the event was like a "private family argument" where everyone could speak openly and candidly about how to move along the path of liberation. Much of the discussion was grounded in the tension between black people's desire to build stable economic and political power without being co-opted by the white power system. It was a conversation about how much they should retreat, if at all, to an all-black world and how much they should engage in the broader white world that controlled some of the day-to-day realities of black Americans. For example, should black people participate in Johnson's Great Society? If so, attendees argued for community control of local anti-poverty programs, but that raised the question of how local control might be accomplished. One point made throughout the conference was that the black middle class needed to realize that it was essentially no better off than its poor rural and urban counterparts. Skin color bound them all together, attendees argued, and when those in the middle class realized this, they could help form a united front and work for everyone's liberation.[17]

A few of the conference's better-known attendees were Floyd McKissick (CORE's new national director), James Farmer (CORE's former national director), the Reverend Jesse Jackson (SCLC), and H. Rap Brown. Dick Gregory also attended and addressed white people's interpretation of the term "Black Power" as an antiwhite movement that sought to invert the racial hierarchy so that black people oppressed white people. "White people panic at the sound of two simple words, Black Power . . . Why? Because when they hear us say Black Power, they think it is just like white power, and that means napalm, lynching, stealing (legally) and lying." Dozens of workshops filled the conference's schedule, including "The City and Black People," "Black Power through Black Politics," "Black Power and American Religion," and "New Roles for Black Youths." On Friday, conferees voted on numerous resolutions related to many of the workshops, such as whether to divide the United States into two countries (one for blacks and one for whites) and whether black people should boycott black churches that did not support the "black revolution." Some of the other resolutions were about opposing the Vietnam War and resisting the draft, establishing black institutions of higher learning to train "professional black revolutionaries," and establishing a body of operatives to "remove from critical positions all politicians serving to thwart" black people's obtainment of political power. No specifics were provided on how any of these resolutions, especially the last, might be carried out.[18]

Richardson had not been invited to the conference, a sign of how effectively she had receded into the background of the black liberation movement. Nevertheless, when she arrived on Saturday with Frank, who had been hired to cover the event, Richardson was welcomed with open arms, and she spoke on a couple of panels. She was impressed by the conferees' wide-ranging backgrounds and organizations, and such a dynamic mix of people gave her hope that a new phase of the movement could start. Still, she

Gloria Richardson, National Conference on Black Power, Newark, New Jersey, 22 July 1967. (Associated Press)

believed the future of Black Power depended on its ability to be flexible, adapting to local people's needs and conditions on the ground.[19]

One of those conditions, especially in northern urban locales, was the hopelessness of black people who had been suffering from systemic inequality in housing, education, and employment for decades. In fact, the Newark conference had come on the heels of a weeklong racial revolt in that city. Black Newark residents were already seething, and their anger boiled over when a black male taxicab driver was beaten by police officers after a traffic stop. It was the same volatile combination that had caused the racial revolt in Watts two years earlier. Allegations of police brutality, or the use of excessive force, had also touched off racial revolts in Harlem, Philadelphia, Jersey City, and Rochester, New York, in the summer of 1964. Richardson had predicted such events when she spoke with journalist William Worthy in March of that year, noting that the euphoria of the March on Washington had been followed by so few positive and tangible changes for black Americans. Fast-forward three years, and CORE's McKissick was now telling Black Power conferees the same thing. "No sane person could say we are not due for more violence," he said.[20]

Conference organizer Dr. Nathan Wright Jr. warned that if significant economic and political progress continued to elude black America, the nation might be engulfed in a race war by the early 1970s. Richardson had also spoken about this possibility in the summer of 1963 and again in her *Freedomways* essay from spring 1964.[21] The federal government shared this concern. In 1967 it established the National Advisory Commission on Civil Disorders (also known as the Kerner Commission) to learn why the revolts had occurred. The commission pointed to white America's role in alienating urban black people socially and economically: "What white Americans have never fully understood but what the Negro can never forget—is that white society is deeply implicated in the ghetto. White institutions created it, white institutions maintain it, and white society condones it." If white people did not dismantle their racially oppressive system, black people would continue to view them as a threat to their survival. In that type of climate, white reactionaries would arise, and so would militant black activists ready to agitate for freedom on their own terms.[22]

Richardson understood why some black people engaged in revolts. "I am not saying that violence is necessarily the answer," she said, "but I am not condemning the violence. It is a residue of frustration." She too felt this frustration, and even though her "own predilection is toward burning it down," she would not take that step. Nor would she support reprisals against white people who abused and murdered black people, because that would have violated her secular humanist principle that people should avoid harming one another. Yet revolts seemed to be "the only thing that America understands," and the nation's racial problems made revolts unavoidable. As such, she said, "there's no point in you standing up and talking about nonviolence" because that would not discourage the people who felt the need to revolt. Nevertheless, Richardson encouraged Cambridge's black residents—and, by extension, those in Newark and Detroit and other locales—to continue negotiating with white leaders and build another mass movement to fight politicians' foot-dragging on racial grievances.[23]

Black Power: An Assessment

As a distinct wave of the black liberation movement, Black Power emphasized a number of things. One was a black consciousness that reconceptualized what it meant to be black and American. Richardson believed that was "the best thing" to come out of Black Power, and it was exactly what she argued for when she addressed students at Howard University in November 1963.

She told them that, to be successful, the liberation struggle needed politically and socially conscious young people, and she appealed directly to the students' racial consciousness and their obligation to serve their race. "You must make up your minds that you are black. You must make up your minds that you will sacrifice." After the Black Power conference, she told a reporter that black consciousness needed to be developed early in black children's lives, and it had to be included in their formal education to serve as a bulwark against assaults on their psyches. Likewise, black adults would draw on this consciousness to develop a healthy group identity to serve as the basis of an economic and political program (broadly defined) leading to fruitful negotiations with white America.[24]

Black Power activists expected America to be desegregated in law and in fact, but they rejected integration as a goal. Instead, they advocated the creation of independent black organizations to carry on the freedom struggle at the grassroots level. "Black power may be the salvation, you know, if people are willing to work at it," Richardson said, and whoever led this new wave of the struggle would have "to be somebody that understands and articulates what these people feel." Implicit in Richardson's prognosis was the caveat that Black Power leaders would have to subordinate their egos and personal agendas to the greater good and organize local movements that addressed communities' needs.[25] Who would lead this new wave of activism, and what would their goals be? Those questions were quickly answered, and they affected how Black Power developed. Important in this regard was the ideological difference between cultural nationalists and revolutionary nationalists and their diverse liberation agendas. Revolutionary nationalists were focused on political organizing, and they were willing to work in coalitions, as the Black Panthers had done with white and Chicano radicals. Cultural nationalists tended to be racial separatists who focused on reclaiming African culture rather than political organizing, and they eschewed interracial coalitions.[26]

Richardson saw cultural nationalism as inherently flawed because it was based on the false premise that black culture was in need of repair. In fact, she believed it was strong and would not be diluted if black people entered America's social and economic systems in large numbers. She did not believe it was desirable for black people to assimilate into white America, but creating a separate world into which black people would withdraw was problematic as well. Richardson subscribed to W. E. B. Du Bois's concept that black American communities constituted "A Negro Nation within a Nation" and that black people should leverage their power to expand their opportunities in the white world rather than receding into racial isolation. If separatists truly accepted who they were, Richardson argued, they would not retire from the larger world but "would go into [white] society and stand on [their] own two feet." Her comments reiterated her long-standing belief that black and white people's destinies were intertwined, and the former should make the most of this reality by learning about their past and developing a healthy view of their black identity. Doing so would help them navigate American society, and Richardson even predicted that if white Americans ceased their widespread and systemic restriction of black people's social, economic, and political opportunities, all of America would benefit. These ideals of demonstrating a strong black identity and seizing opportunities were the basis of two James Brown songs from that era: "Say It Loud—I'm Black and I'm Proud" and "I Don't Want Nobody to Give Me Nothing (Open up the Door I'll Get It Myself)."[27]

Beliefs about leadership also revealed a rift among Black Power activists. Cultural nationalism had a strong patriarchal ethos that rejected women's leadership and promoted their supportive role to men. Maulana Karenga of the US Organization justified this sexist dictum by claiming that "male supremacy is based on three things: tradition, acceptance, and reason." The Black Panther Party argued that this was a counterrevolutionary position because it prevented women from fully utilizing their talents and energy on behalf of all black people.[28] Karenga's position was also based on a myth that was easily refuted by even a cursory review of black America's list of freedom fighters. That body had always contained women—including Gloria Richardson—a fact easily acknowledged by RAM founder Max Stanford and Black Panther communications secretary Kathleen Cleaver, who cited the Cambridge leader as one of her inspirations. To Cleaver, Richardson's activism was irrefutable evidence that a woman's place in the movement was wherever she felt it should be.[29]

To be fair, Karenga's belief about women was common in black America, where the subject of gender and leadership had been under discussion for some time, especially after the publication of "The Negro Family: The Case for National Action" in early 1965. Known as the Moynihan Report (because it was authored by Daniel Patrick Moynihan), this public policy piece advanced the idea that black men's psychic health had to be addressed for black America to move forward. Its author argued, "The Negro community has been forced into a matriarchal structure which, because it is so out of line with the rest of the American society, seriously retards the progress of the group as a whole, and imposes a crushing burden on the Negro male and, in consequence, on a great many Negro women as well." Many black Americans agreed with Moynihan's assertion, including Whitney Young and Dorothy

Height. Some grassroots women activists told *Ebony* that they would be willing to step back from the front lines of the struggle should more black men decide to step forward.[30]

Richardson was critical of the discourse that promoted black men's leadership simply to propel more men to the forefront of the struggle. It was, she said, "disrespectful of black men. . . . Because these men [were] quite capable of standing—in SNCC anyhow, standing on their own. . . . And so were the women and it wasn't to the degradation to either one of them." Women who did not accommodate men's desire to exert their masculinity paid a cost that ranged from being ignored to being rebuked publicly. Richardson claimed the latter happened to her when she participated in a radio discussion of Black Power. Appearing with her was Roy Innis of CORE, and according to Richardson, he called her a "castrator" during one of their exchanges. To Richardson, all the talk about promoting masculine leadership was evidence that too many people had been distracted from finding effective solutions to their collective problems.[31]

Black Power advocates' economic agenda also concerned Richardson. As early as the first Black Power conference in Newark, there had been a divide between activists who wanted a collective economic agenda and those who pushed capitalism as a solution to black America's problems. Newark conference organizer Dr. Nathan Wright Jr. subscribed to the capitalist approach, which was why white corporations were permitted to be among the event's sponsors. Corporations continued to support Black Power capitalism, and they were joined by white politicians such as President Richard M. Nixon, who believed Black Power capitalism was in alignment with free-market principles. Richardson, however, did not believe that Black Power capitalism would qualitatively alter the power dynamics between black and white communities, especially if white people were involved in it.[32]

Yet the bulk of Richardson's critique of Black Power concerned its political agenda, established in part by the book *Black Power: The Politics of Liberation in America* (1967). Its authors, Stokely Carmichael and political scientist Charles V. Hamilton, offered readers "a political framework and ideology" that black people could use to address their problems. Participation in the political system was a key element of that framework, and for that reason, Richardson found the book "conservative." She understood the value of electoral politics, and she believed it was an area Black Power groups would have to address, including sponsoring political education programs like those offered by CNAC. Black voters' increased political power at the local level would likely translate into some improvements in their lives, which was why in the 1960s Richardson supported George R. Kent, a self-described "responsible militant" who ran for the Second Ward's seat on Cambridge's City Council, and campaigned for Herman Badillo, who made an unsuccessful run to be the Democratic candidate for New York City mayor.[33]

Still, positive change at the state and federal levels would not be happening anytime soon. Those bodies were overwhelmingly filled with white legislators and executives who had to answer to majority-white constituencies that saw black people's progress as a zero-sum game in which white people were the losers. This was especially true in southern states dominated by white conservatives and racial reactionaries in the Democratic Party who would later jump to the Republican Party. Yet this mind-set was present all over the country, including in the Sun Belt. In California, Republicans under the leadership of Ronald Reagan were building a statewide political machine to further their conservative agenda. Richardson knew that negotiating and compromising are integral parts of a politician's job, and by immersing themselves in the white-controlled political system, black people were opening themselves up for frustration or even co-optation. She therefore believed that a more effective and politically safer option for black people was to apply massive pressure on the political system from outside of it.[34]

History has shown that for this type of program to work, many young activists are required to fill the ranks and do the daily work that is the basis of effective organizing. Despite Stokely Carmichael's claim in the spring of 1967 that recruitment of such people was about to take place on college campuses around the country, widespread and continuous recruitment never occurred. Richardson observed that Black Nationalists' failure to recruit large numbers of fresh troops undermined their ability to achieve the "substantial change" they sought.[35] She added that nationalists' focus on political theory, especially Marxism, and their creation of hierarchical groups bogged down their efforts to reach the masses. People at the local level appreciated Black Power groups' community outreach efforts, such as the Black Panthers' free breakfast program and medical clinics, but they also needed help addressing, in a systematic and comprehensive manner, the lack of jobs, poor housing, deficient education systems, and lack of health care. This would necessitate a large-scale volunteer corps to assist local people in solving their own problems. That social change model had worked well for SNCC just a few years earlier, but it was never adopted by the Black Nationalists, who, Richardson charged, ended up just "talking to each other."[36]

Black Power was challenged not only by these divisions between cultural and revolutionary nationalists but also by outside forces, particularly the federal government. The FBI's clandestine Counter Intelligence Program (COINTELPRO) spied on people deemed to be suspicious, dangerous, or a threat to national security. The FBI also placed agent provocateurs in Black Power organizations to foster animosity between members, as well as between members of different organizations. This strategy worked well for the government, and it was augmented by local police departments' raids and assaults on Black Power activists, some of whom died in those encounters.[37]

Black Power advocates did have some successes. In Newark, New Jersey, Amiri Baraka directed a vibrant social and political experiment. In other locations, women organized local movements focused on improving black people's opportunities to live long and fulfilling lives. For example, activists reinterpreted and expanded the Black Power agenda by focusing on housing and welfare rights, while black feminists established organizations that tirelessly fought sexism and violence against women, as well as increasing women's access to health care and family planning.[38] However, that type of activism never became an integral part of national Black Power organizations' agendas. Instead, Black Power became the antithesis of the Cambridge movement: proponents of Black Power advocated economic and political ideologies that, Richardson argued, could never radically alter black people's fundamental relationships to American political and economic institutions, and they established hierarchical leadership structures in their organizations. Both these decisions disappointed Richardson, who felt that Black Power activists could have easily avoided these traps if they had implemented the student movement framework from the early 1960s. It would be forty years before another youth movement would arise and challenge America's entrenched political and economic powers, and when that happened, Richardson hoped they would avoid the mistakes made by many Black Power advocates.[39]

11

Back to Work

The end of the 1960s was a turbulent time for the nation as well as for Gloria Richardson. She and Frank Dandridge divorced, and she had to rejoin the workforce. Finding a steady job was a significant challenge with numerous disappointments, but being a private person, Richardson kept her personal and professional problems largely to herself. Even many family members were unaware of the details of this chapter in her life, particularly about the divorce.

In time, Richardson adjusted to being single again, and she ultimately landed a series of jobs that allowed her to use her organizing and problem-solving skills to help people improve their lives, and she mentored others so that they could do the same. In many ways, her job experiences were extensions of the social justice work she had done during the civil rights movement, and they fulfilled her need to try to improve society. At the same time, Richardson stayed focused on racial politics and the struggles black people continued to face long after the movement ended. She has analyzed many of the major events of recent decades—the so-called war on terror, the state-sanctioned oppression of citizens, the collapse of the American economy, among others—as well as people's responses to them, including social change campaigns. Richardson has seen some of these campaigns evaporate due to people's divergent views about goals, strategies, tactics, and leadership. In spite of this, she still has hope that America will witness another full-fledged social change movement, because this is the only way to make meaningful progress. Richardson also believes that any new movement should be modeled on the student-led phase of the civil rights movement, which used creative tactics and strategies to change America for the better.

Hollywood had a tremendous effect on Gloria and Frank's marriage. In the summer of 1968, while working on the set of the film *Uptight*, Frank caught the movie bug and switched careers. The change offered Frank an artistic challenge and the chance to make significantly more money than he did taking photographs. His new career seemed promising almost from the start. He was awarded a two-year fellowship at the Center for Advanced Film Studies in Beverly Hills, and he directed an award-winning film.[1]

Frank did not consult Gloria about his career move. She understood his artistic ambition and his desire to make more money, but she did not understand why Frank's new life did not include her. When she learned that he was not just leaving New York but leaving her as well, Gloria was shaken to her core. "I don't think I quite believed it," she said, because she never suspected that anything was amiss in their relationship. Frank framed his decision to end their five-year marriage as a financial one, telling Gloria he would be a starving artist and would be unable to financially support her and Tamara for years to come. Whatever his reasons, Gloria felt rejected by the man she had once considered the love of her life. Their divorce was amicable enough, and Frank honored his generous promise to support her and Tamara for one year, giving Gloria plenty of time to find employment. A number of years after they split, Frank wrote Gloria a letter in which he apologized for leaving her and told her that "he still loved [her]," but they never reconciled.[2]

The stress of her divorce was compounded by her reentry into the job market. Feeling the need to talk to someone about her career concerns, Richardson sought the help of Josephine "Jo" Martin, a white psychiatrist with a practice in New York City. Martin was well known in the civil rights community because she had provided mental health services to activists in Mississippi in the mid-1960s as part of the Medical Committee for Human Rights, and she did the same for activists who made their way to New York. Richardson asked Martin to assess whether she would "fall apart" during high-stakes job interviews and whether she was capable of something she had not done since working for the federal government during World War II: taking orders from someone.[3] As it happened, Richardson was emotionally prepared to enter the workforce, and she did so not long after Frank left for California. In the spring of 1969 she started working as an administrative aide in the job training program of the world's largest advertising agency, J. Walter Thompson. This was just the first of half a dozen jobs Richardson obtained over the next ten years, and they all had one thing in common: a focus on improving the lives of people and their families.

The J. Walter Thompson program had been established in response to the civil unrest following Martin Luther King Jr.'s assassination in 1968, and it offered scholastic enrichment and professional mentoring and training to students and young people from some of New York City's black and Latino communities. Participants arrived at the firm's offices on New York's Upper

East Side in the morning to receive remedial education in language arts, history, and mathematics in an unstructured learning atmosphere, the goal being to prepare them to pass their General Educational Development (GED) exams. During the afternoon component, the students were paired with Thompson employees, who trained them in the basics of various occupations within the company, such as graphic design.[4] Richardson did some counseling, but mainly she developed and taught literature and history courses that were grounded in the students' racial and cultural backgrounds— in the process, raising students' consciousness about societal issues. One participant recalled that Richardson's course was "inspirational" because her lessons addressed the students' present needs, hopes, and desires, and she encouraged them to be agents of change in their own communities. Although white employees and managers did not seem to like her curriculum, Richardson judged the program a success, as indicated by the firm's hiring of a fair number of students who completed it. The company ended the program early the following year, possibly because, as Richardson speculated, it did not want to hire more black and Puerto Rican workers.[5]

Richardson's entry into the workforce occurred at a time when New York City's social institutions were fraying to a degree unseen in the city's modern history. For example, Columbia University students occupied campus buildings in April 1968 to protest the institution's association with defense industry companies that were profiting from the Vietnam War, as well as the university's plan to build a new gymnasium in a predominantly black neighborhood, despite the residents' objections. Richardson joined hundreds of others who responded to the students' plea to witness the university's efforts to retake control of the campus—a police action involving the use of excessive force against the students. The following year, Richardson answered another call from city residents—this time from Greenwich Village—where people were revolting against the New York City Police Department's harassment of patrons at a gay establishment, the Stonewall Inn. "It was horrible, the cops were just beating people from the bar," Richardson recalled, and the situation escalated to a revolt when residents confronted the police and fought with them. Importantly, the Stonewall revolt signaled the beginning of the modern gay liberation movement.[6]

Economic and political institutions were also coming apart at the seams. One of the main causes was the city's deindustrialization, a result of the growth of high-tech, automated industries that required fewer semiskilled and unskilled factory workers. By the end of the 1970s, New York City and the surrounding areas belonged to the Rust Belt, a composite of hundreds of northern and midwestern industrial centers that saw their well-paying industrial jobs transferred to the South and Southwest. Disappearing along with those jobs were the good salaries that permitted working-class adults to move into the middle class. New York City's public education system was also deteriorating, which meant that many children would be unprepared to enter this changing economy. Political fights erupted between competing interests—parents, teachers, the school board, and politicians—on how to correct that trend.[7]

As New York's tax base shrank, city politicians tried to exert greater control over municipal agencies' budgets, particularly by limiting municipal workers' salaries and benefits. Thousands of those city employees—teachers, sanitation workers, transit workers—responded by striking. The police department had to manage its own public relations crisis when officer Frank Serpico publicly disclosed the department's systemic corruption. On a personal level, residents commonly viewed New York as "a grungy, dangerous, bankrupt city without normal services most of the time," a place that many of them wanted to flee. Hollywood told the same narrative in films like *Midnight Cowboy* (1969), which depicted the city as a place where everyone was running a hustle, and *The French Connection* (1971), which was based on a true story about New York's heroin trade. Yet it was the vigilante payback movie *Death Wish* (1974) that portrayed New York in all its degradation, while simultaneously satisfying viewers' fantasies of eliminating the criminal population one perpetrator at a time.[8]

Despite the urban decay, Gloria Richardson did not consider leaving New York; she had made a life for herself there, and the city offered opportunities to find meaningful work. After J. Walter Thompson, Richardson landed a job as a program evaluation specialist at Neighborhood Board One, a community-based corporation responsible for developing and coordinating antipoverty programs under the umbrella of Harlem Youth Opportunities Unlimited and Associated Community Teams (HARYOU-ACT). She developed evaluation criteria, reviewed proposals, and supervised field staff. Ten months later, she took a job at New York's Community Training Institute as a cooperative resource developer. Established in 1967, the institute was a grassroots antipoverty agency that partnered with businesses and government agencies to train city residents to be more effective advocates for themselves and their communities. Richardson's main project was developing and implementing a food cooperative, which was essentially a buying club for the city's low-income residents.[9]

One day, Richardson ran into Charles Cobb Sr., who lived in her apartment building and was a minister in the United Church of Christ (UCC), a liberal and predominantly white Protestant denomination. He was working in the UCC's Commission for Racial Justice and offered Richardson a job as a program manager. She accepted because the job paid more and fit with her interest in civil rights advocacy. Richardson was soon traveling to North Carolina as part of the UCC's support for the Wilmington Ten, a group of black men and women on trial for firebombing a white-owned business in 1971. However, Cobb fired her about six months later when she refused to follow his directive to fire two employees because, in Richardson's opinion, they had not done anything to warrant termination.[10]

This marked the beginning of a difficult time because she was unemployed for about eighteen months. Richardson had plenty of interviews, but they failed to turn into job offers, perhaps because of her reputation for candor and her refusal to go along with a decision she felt was unfair. The fact that Richardson had, in her words, "bad-mouthed" plenty of civil rights workers over the years seemed to hurt her chances of getting a job. It was not uncommon for civil rights activists to experience adverse consequences because of their work; despite doing so much for their communities, many of these people lost their jobs because of the unwanted attention their presence brought to employers. One of the most glaring examples was Rosa Parks, the icon of the Montgomery bus boycott, who was fired from her job and could not obtain permanent employment for many years. Richardson was fortunate, in that she did not experience financial hardship; her family owned rental properties in Cambridge, which provided a steady income, but she did pay an emotional price.[11]

Richardson was eventually hired by the National Council of Negro Women (NCNW) as an assistant director in its New York office, a role that allowed her to return to the work she had found so rewarding during the movement. Her main responsibility was to use her organizational and leadership skills to develop "a black women's movement cutting across ideologies and groups—one that centers on issues at the state and local level."[12] As it happened, Richardson was not at the NCNW long enough to leave a footprint on its new initiative. She had a run-in with a high-ranking member of the organization and was let go for allegedly being an alcoholic. Richardson denied the charge and went on the offensive, lest the rumor gain traction and thwart any future attempts at finding work. She wrote a letter to the editors of *Ebony*, thanking them for a recent piece the magazine had published about her. She also mentioned that the NCNW leadership (which included Dorothy Height) had wrongly terminated her employment. "Although still somewhat bewildered," Richardson wrote, "I do very much regret that NCNW did and does not feel that I possess the leadership abilities their organization needs."[13] At this point, Richardson's old civil rights network kicked in and helped her out. When her former ACT colleague Jesse Gray learned of Richardson's situation, he contacted Fred Samuels, a city councilman and former chairman of HARYOU-ACT's board. Samuels pulled strings to get Richardson hired in HARYOU's main office as a program evaluator, and she eventually became director of the program evaluation department. She continued to work at HARYOU-ACT for a handful of years until the city government defunded the program due to a lack of public monies and politicians' declining commitment to antipoverty programs.[14]

In the end, Richardson got a civil service job with the City of New York, working in the Human Resources Administration's crisis intervention unit. One of her responsibilities was ensuring that monthly food distributions reached the city's needy families. Sometime later she took another civil service exam and earned a promotion to program officer in the city's Department for the Aging, whose mission was "to work for the empowerment, independence, dignity and quality of life of New York City's diverse older adults . . . through advocacy, education and the coordination and delivery of services." For many years, Richardson did similar work as a union delegate and mentored younger members, teaching them how to develop their leadership skills and use them to fight for better pay and benefits. Faye Moore, former president of Local 371, was mentored by Richardson, who showed her how to use her stubbornness to the union's advantage. By watching Richardson's consistent displays of toughness and integrity, Moore learned to be a better and more confident leader.[15]

At the time of her retirement in 2012, at the age of ninety, Richardson had spent years working on the department's contractual agreements with local not-for-profit organizations that provided a range of services to older residents, including transportation, legal services, and home delivery of meals. Most other Americans would have retired years (if not decades) earlier, but Richardson had a simple reason to keep working: "The jobs were interesting."[16] Yet there was another reason why she worked for so long: the jobs spoke to her secular humanism, which stresses the commonality of people's humanity and their right to justice and dignity. Her jobs allowed Richardson to work directly on those goals.

Since the 1960s, Richardson has stayed aware of the nation's justice and equality issues, and she continues to see evidence of systemic racism. Interestingly, she had not expected this to be the case back when she was leading the

Left to right: Jim Forman (former SNCC executive secretary), Gloria Richardson, and James Boardley (organizer of SAFE) at the homegoing service for SAFE's Johnnie Wilson in 1993. (Courtesy of James Boardley)

Cambridge movement. In 1964 she foresaw a promising future for black people, one in which they would see themselves as Americans first and black second. That would require white Americans to be much more fair and democratic, but Richardson was optimistic that this would happen. However, by the beginning of the twenty-first century, she had become pessimistic about the nation's ability to leap forward in terms of eliminating racism in housing, employment, education, the criminal justice system, and health care. She now considers herself a "native born Black" but not "an American" because, she said, "I don't have access to all those things white Americans have access to." She acknowledges that tremendous progress has been made in eliminating barriers to black people's freedom and equality, but a lot more progress would have to occur for her to consider herself an American.[17]

Richardson also continues to advocate for black liberation, and since the late 1980s she has seen a number of signs that another large-scale movement might be developing, but they have not lived up to their potential. The murder of black teenager Yusef Hawkins is a case in point. He and some of his black friends went to the Bensonhurst section of Brooklyn to inquire about buying a car, but when they got there, they were attacked by a mob of white youths who shot and killed Hawkins. It was the latest in a series of similar white-on-black attacks in the 1980s, and a cross section of New York's racial and ethnic communities organized marches to protest Hawkins's murder. Richardson hoped this would be the beginning of a new movement, but her hopes were dashed when some of the people involved in the demonstrations showed more interest in their own publicity than in building a grassroots movement. Specifically, she cited Baptist minister Alfred "Al" Sharpton Jr., whom she described as "a charlatan," as one of the main culprits, noting that his ego drove him to insert himself into the protests, which he was unprepared to aid. Richardson believes the nascent movement may have been purposely undermined by people from the inside, and once again she suspects Sharpton. This suspicion may have some credibility, considering he was an FBI informant at the time.[18]

After the al-Qaeda terrorists attacked the United States on 11 September 2001, Richardson immediately saw the need for a national protest movement targeting the US government when Congress passed the Patriot Act, which threatens people's liberties by, among other things, permitting government agencies to conduct extensive surveillance of citizens' electronic communications and digital footprints. She was surprised when there were no massive demonstrations against the Patriot Act, nor was there a sustained challenge to President George W. Bush after he commenced his war on Iraq.[19]

It appears that economic uncertainty and violence against black people might be the issues that spark a systematic challenge to state power, where the government's spying on US citizens and seemingly endless wars could not. The characteristics of that potential challenge are similar to local civil rights struggles of the 1960s. The first spark of activism came with the Occupy Wall Street movement, which sought to address economic inequality driven by corporate exploitation of consumers in the mortgage industry, retirement systems, and other areas of the economy. Protesters came from all racial groups and all walks of life, but especially young people facing massive student debt and a recession economy that would make it hard to repay those loans. Richardson saw these grassroots demonstrators' relatively long encampments in New York and other cities around the United States as evidence that they had "really plugged into what people were thinking" about the practice of rigging the economy for the wealthy at the expense of working people. The reason such a wide range of racial and ethnic groups shared the same opinion about the nation's super-rich, she added, was that corporate executives and others "went so far as to treat white folks like niggers.

And now white folks are beginning to realize that they've been screwed, too. And there's really no difference in the way that that one percent has treated anybody."[20]

A short time later, when the Black Lives Matter (BLM) movement began, Richardson thought it had the potential to develop into a sustainable grassroots movement. Initially organized to protest George Zimmerman's killing of unarmed teenager Trayvon Martin, the loosely based grassroots movement quickly expanded its scope of concerns to include police brutality and the general social and economic circumstances of black people in America. Started by three black women, BLM is a lot like the student-led phase of the civil rights movement; it is a black youth movement for and about black people's liberation.[21] While Occupy Wall Street has become a footnote to the mid-2010s, BLM activists have maintained a strong presence at the local level. This has allowed them to keep pressuring politicians to address the issues facing black people. However, the movement has had to confront challenges, such as its sustainability and expansion. These challenges were highlighted during a December 2014 protest in Washington, DC, organized by Al Sharpton's National Action Network (NAN). The event was focused on the recent killings of black people by law enforcement officers, in particular the killing of Michael Brown in Ferguson, Missouri. Since Brown's death, local activists had been building a movement to address a variety of issues, and some of those activists spoke publicly about their belief that Sharpton and NAN were co-opting the nascent Ferguson struggle for their own gain, although they denied that was their intent.[22]

The tension between Ferguson activists and NAN underscores a basic question about the black liberation movement: who will lead that movement? It was the same question the Cambridge activists had to answer in the early 1960s and the Black Power activists faced at the end of the decade. Today, Richardson believes the answer to this question remains the same: local people should be leading their own movements, identifying their own issues, and deciding how to resolve them. She hopes these young activists do not make the strategic mistake of thinking that someone with fame or fortune is a good candidate to lead the freedom struggle. For example, entertainers played important supportive roles in local and national organizations during the civil rights movement, and they continue to do so in the twenty-first century. However, the interpersonal styles that are strengths in hierarchical command-and-control business environments are not compatible with social movements that emphasize consultation among activists and the building of consensus on goals, strategies, and tactics.[23] In a *Village Voice* article on black leadership, Richardson discussed this issue and the general misconception about how leadership develops in social change movements. "Celebrities don't have time or energy—or the know-how. . . . Their egos carry them so far, and I don't know what kind of reality testing there is with that." For a movement to be viable and effective, its organizers must be efficient not only with social media and web-based information sharing but also with personal outreach in their neighborhoods. Richardson thinks celebrities and business-people, as well as religious leaders, either do not realize this fact or ignore it, and they are not prepared to do community-oriented grassroots work. The only logical choice for organizing a movement, in Richardson's opinion, is for activists to replicate the SNCC model because it encourages communities to identify their own leaders.[24]

Richardson's experiences with SNCC continue to influence her thinking about the elements of organizing. For one, she rejects the notion that today's youth activists need to be mentored by their elders on how to organize. She points out that it was the youth of America—high school and college students—who changed this nation more than five decades ago, and they did it by leading their elders, not the other way around. Richardson sees no reason why this would not hold true in the twenty-first century: "Young people today shouldn't be sitting around waiting for old folks to lead them into some new kind of millennium. Young people will have to do it themselves. They have to be willing to make their own way and their own mistakes. And they might as well do it while they're young, before they get into the part of their lives where they are raising families and cannot afford to take the risks. They should listen only to those older people who will support them, or who have some experience that may be useful but will not tell them what to do."[25]

To increase their chances of building a viable movement, activists must avoid becoming doctrinaire in their thinking about how to create just societies. "I don't think you should have any kind of ideology if you organize," Richardson said. "I think [ideologies] can lead you to destruction." Activists should feel free to use elements from various ideologies to help them achieve their goals, but no specific ideology—be it social, economic, or political—can solve all the problems faced by any group of people, and no ideology should be viewed as more than one part of the solution.[26] For example, voting on people's rights illustrates Richardson's point about the dangers of adhering to a political ideology that treats voting as the raison d'être of America's political system. A little more than a year after Cambridge's white voters used a referendum to defeat the charter amendment, white voters in the Midwest and on the West Coast used referenda to overturn open housing laws. In the late 1970s heterosexual people used referenda to repeal antidiscrimination laws that protected homosexual people, and since then, the former have used referenda and ballot initiatives to amend state constitutions to prevent same-sex partners from marrying. The US Supreme Court's 2015 ruling in favor of marriage equality (*Obergefell v. Hodges*) has settled that issue, but it will take some time before all forms of legal discrimination against lesbian, gay, and transgender people are outlawed. When equality-minded citizens are faced with the prospect of voting on any group's rights, Richardson thinks they should boycott the polls.[27]

Furthermore, Richardson argues that voting in general elections is commonly an ineffective tactic to achieve fundamental social change because it relies on the consent of the nation's political leaders. Voting can bring about changes, but they tend to be incremental ones that occur through a gradual process, and only when people's electoral power has not been diluted by legal means such as voter identification laws and gerrymandering. Consequently, the electorate needs to avoid voting for the sake of voting and consider using the strategy of election boycotts at all levels of government when there is no meaningful choice with regard to candidates or no belief that the election will be free and fair. If nothing else, an election boycott can prevent people from legitimizing a political system that often ignores their concerns and sometimes works against their rights and interests.[28]

Richardson believes people should petition and lobby their government officials and should vote in elections when doing so might produce the desired outcome, but these civic actions commonly do not bring about the type or degree of change that most social justice–minded people want, and not as quickly as they want it. When people realize that they cannot expect the political system to take the lead in moving the nation forward, they may reach the same conclusion Richardson did during the civil rights movement: working from outside the political system is the most effective way of bringing about change. Whether the issue is world peace, police brutality, gun violence, or globalization's impact on workers' rights and the environment, Richardson recommends the same action: "If everything else doesn't work then I think you should make it uncomfortable for them to exist. . . . You have to be in their faces 'til it gets uncomfortable" for politicians and corporate leaders to keep opposing activists' demands.[29]

The struggle for freedom and justice is an eternal one, and social activism is a difficult undertaking because so much of it is done from the margins of society, which means there is little public encouragement and support.

Compounding this situation are social, economic, and political mechanisms that discourage people's participation in transformative movements. Social ostracism, loss of one's job or livelihood, and governmental harassment are just a few of the deterrents for people who want to change the world. Even so, Richardson believes that people—especially young people—must work with like-minded individuals to push forward the freedom movements in their communities. Politicians and other powerful people will fight them "every step of the way," she said, but when people "[stick] together they [can] achieve some things."[30]

Organizing a community does not require large numbers of people. Many of the local struggles against white supremacy during the 1960s began with only a dozen or so people, and many of them grew into larger movements. Of course, this took time, and in the case of the Cambridge movement, it took approximately eighteen months. Thus, twenty-first-century activists should remember that change does not happen overnight, and they will experience highs and lows. Still, they should be fortified by the knowledge that the United States has experienced fundamental social and political changes since the 1950s, and those achievements were possible because of the work by grassroots activists who were committed to freeing themselves and the nation as a whole.[31]

Conclusion

When Gloria Richardson was asked how she would like to be remembered, she replied: "I guess I would like for them to say I was true to my belief in black people as a race." Her answer reveals a deep commitment to the struggle for black liberation, grounded in an understanding that since colonial times, millions of black people have been forced to sacrifice life and limb in the building and enriching of this nation. Because of this, white America should dismantle its racial hierarchy. Richardson believes so strongly in black people's entitlement to real and meaningful freedom that she never thought twice about risking her life during the civil rights movement. Still, she knew that bravery alone would not be enough to bring about societal change, so she used her leadership abilities and sociological training to further the cause of human rights, and in doing so, she carried on her family's tradition of race service. Richardson's activist work was so important to her that, when asked if she could live at any time in American history, when that would be, she chose the mid-1960s because "there was a lot of ferment and ideas and struggles to finish freeing black people in the progression from slavery . . . a lot of ground was covered at that time."[1]

The civil rights movement also served as the vehicle by which Richardson reached self-actualization. Donna Richardson recalled her mother's life being so restricted by racism that "she was looking for something to stimulate her," and the Cambridge movement was what got Gloria Richardson going each day. The movement itself, Donna added, "kind of infused life into our house," and it had a noticeable effect on her mother. "I could see a change in her" as she became "passionate" about the movement and had something to "focus" her energy on. Gloria Richardson's relationship to the movement was essentially the same as that of fellow SNCC member Casey Hayden: "[The movement] was everything: home and family, food and work, love and a reason to live."[2]

Not surprisingly, if given the chance to do it all over again, Richardson would not do anything differently. Her confidence comes from a mixture of things. For one, Richardson's parents and her extended family groomed her for race service, and perhaps more important, they encouraged her to be her own person and to stand up for herself. That socialization was reinforced at Howard University by professors who challenged Richardson to use her critical thinking and her education to advance her race. Her understanding that "nobody has all the answers" was developed during her years at Howard and validated during the Cambridge movement, when she and her fellow grassroots activists engaged in rigorous dialogue and debate to identify their own needs and problems and find creative solutions. If readers of this biography gain anything from Richardson's story, she hopes it is the lesson that when people with a shared goal join together, they can "fight city hall" and win, and that can lead to a radically transformed society. In addition, she wants people to remember that voting is not a panacea for black people's problems; rather, it is "one egg in a basket" of tactics that can be used to bring about some changes.[3]

After living in relative obscurity since the mid-1960s, over the last ten years, Richardson has been receiving recognition for her human rights activism. She has been awarded honorary doctorates and numerous public service awards and citations. A Maryland bar association and a Cambridge street have been named after her, and she is depicted in a mural at the entrance to Cambridge; she is also included in materials promoting Maryland history. Over the last handful of years, Richardson once again entered the nation's consciousness when commemorations of the March on Washington's fiftieth anniversary highlighted her experiences at the original event in 1963. This biography continues her reintroduction to the public and reveals the all-important philosophical underpinnings of her activism.[4]

From a scholarship standpoint, Richardson's story both expands and challenges narratives about the civil rights and Black Power waves of the black liberation movement. It broadens our view of political leadership and intellectualism beyond the male-centric scholarly interpretations of 1960s black protest. Richardson's personality traits were critical to her success as a leader of the Cambridge movement and ACT. She stayed true to her belief that black people's rights were nonnegotiable and she showed herself to be strong-willed, unassuming, polite, and open to other people's ideas and input. Just as important was her refusal to leverage her political and social power for personal gain. This amalgam of traits and ethics fostered a respectful environment in which Cambridge's ground troops, so to speak, entered the battle for freedom each day knowing that Richardson was as committed to them as they were to her. The histories of the Cambridge movement and

Gloria Richardson and former Black Panther Paul Coates at the Reginald F. Lewis Museum of Maryland African American History and Culture, Baltimore, 3 October 2006. (Courtesy of Joseph R. Fitzgerald)

Gloria Richardson's leadership of it will require scholars to expand their understanding of where Black Power began and who played a role in its creation. Using the findings from the community survey Richardson designed, the Cambridge Nonviolent Action Committee implemented a social justice campaign that focused on access to jobs, decent housing, and health care—an agenda Black Power advocates would soon adopt throughout the nation. As such, Cambridge was the soil where Richardson planted a seed of Black Power, and she nurtured it through strong leadership and a radical vision that understood the nexus between race and class oppression. She then stimulated Black Power's growth when she cofounded ACT, which spread the Cambridge movement's successes to northern cities. Adding to Richardson's significance as a progenitor of Black Power was her unconditional support of black people's right to use the tactic of armed self-defense and the high value she placed on black American culture.

Because this biography foregrounds Richardson's social, economic, and political philosophies and why she acted on them, it also challenges a commonly held but nevertheless false view that black women are primarily doers rather than thinkers. The foundation of her philosophies was secular humanism, a belief system that affirms all human life and promotes a nonhierarchical social system based on fairness and equity. Specific examples of Richardson's philosophies can be found in her civil rights goals and the strategies and tactics she used to achieve them, such as creative chaos carried out through obfuscation, silence, economic boycotts, threats of demonstrations, and a boycott of the polls. Richardson was instrumental in bringing Cambridge's white power structure to heel and forcing it to implement tangible programs to improve black people's lives. For this, and for her role in helping to expand the black liberation movement beyond the issues of open accommodations and voting rights, Richardson has earned a place in the pantheon of radical black freedom fighters and intellectuals, a body that includes such notable figures as David Walker, Harriet Tubman, Ida B. Wells-Barnett, and W. E. B. Du Bois.

Although she is not optimistic about America's ability to honestly confront its history of systemic racism, Richardson has seen black people's lives improve since the 1960s, and she is hopeful that progress can continue. In the early 1960s she described Cambridge as a microcosm of race in America, and it continues to be that. To Richardson's surprise and satisfaction, the city has moved forward socially and politically since the tumultuous years of the 1960s. The election and reelections of Mayor Victoria Jackson-Stanley are evidence of that progress. Her initial win in 2008 marked two firsts for Cambridge: she was the first black person and the first woman elected mayor of the city. A couple of black residents have established a new community organization, Eastern Shore Network for Change, whose "mission is to raise awareness of issues in Dorchester County and to creatively work with the community to inform, educate, and foster change which leads to social and economic empowerment." In the summer of 2017 the group held "Reflections on Pine," a series of events highlighting the importance of the Cambridge movement, as well the need for residents citywide to come together to work on racial healing and improving the quality of life for all.[5]

Despite these important developments, Richardson is concerned with the direction the Cambridge government has taken recently, particularly the decision to allow the privatization of the public housing units built in the 1960s as a direct result of protests by CNAC. That push for privatization,

Richardson argues, is a step backward in guaranteeing residents access to affordable housing. Such developments reinforce her belief that the political system operates in ways that undermine and disempower people, and it needs to be held accountable and corrected.[6] That was one reason she accepted an invitation to speak in 2015 at the Law for Black Lives conference at Columbia University, sponsored by the Center for Constitutional Rights. The event offered people the opportunity to improve their understanding of the nation's legal system, its negative impacts on people of color, and how people committed to racial justice can organize and work to improve the criminal justice system. Richardson found the event "amazing" because the dozens of panels and workshops reflected the creative thinking about organizing that had been key to SNCC's success (some of the workshops were "Rapid Response to Uprisings: Building Jail Support & Legal Observing," "Encrypt by Any Means Necessary," "Building Movement-Based Local Policy Campaigns," and "Economics of Police Violence: Police Unions, Private Prisons, Municipal Fees").[7]

As she often does when she speaks at such events, Richardson talked about the Cambridge movement and how black youths were the catalyst for change in that city. Nowadays, another generation of young black people is pushing the freedom movement forward, and these activists, many of whom are active in Black Lives Matter, have already learned that they are not alone in their struggle. There is an array of like-minded groups from all walks of life—Dream Defenders, #SayHerName, Black Youth Project 100, United for a Fair Economy, and the religiously oriented Moral Mondays movement in North Carolina—willing to join them in the fight, and together they can move the nation closer to being a bastion of freedom and equality for all. Richardson is confident that if these people continue to organize locally, pick their own leaders, and stay independent of political and corporate interests, they have a good chance of achieving their goals.

She also predicts an increased sense of urgency as these activists confront the realities of Donald Trump's presidency. Speaking at Harlem's Schomburg Center for Research in Black Culture a few weeks after the 2016 presidential election, Richardson recalled living through the 1930s and witnessing western Europeans' embrace of fascism. She pointed out the parallel between what happened there and white America's embrace of Trump—a person who spouted propaganda that scapegoated ethnic and religious minorities as the source of America's problems, proposed the creation of a Muslim registry, and nominated people with direct ties to white supremacists to fill top administration positions. This rightward political realignment was enabled by tens of millions of white American voters who, Richardson argued, either ignored or did not believe the clear indications of Trump's authoritarian tendencies. She attributed their decision to support Trump to their belief in "American exceptionalism," which is the idea that the United States is qualitatively different from all other nation-states and thus would never allow an autocratic politician to be president. Later, she implied that those same Americans may end up playing the role of "the good [G]ermans" who provide "cover" to the Trump administration if it starts to move down the road of authoritarianism.[8] Richardson believes people can fight this right-wing political movement by using SNCC's successful community organizing model, but they must ensure that their agendas are nonideological and nonsectarian if they want to attract people from all parts of the social, economic, and political spectrums. Furthermore, they can manage their expectations about progress and keep up their morale by accepting that they will make some mistakes, but they will learn from those mistakes and grow stronger because of them.

Some years ago, Richardson spoke at a black history event that took place a few days before her ninety-second birthday. Near the end of the program, she said the pace of social change in America needed to "hurry up."[9] Some people in the audience thought she was being sarcastic, so they laughed at her comment, but Richardson did not mean it as a joke. Since the 1920s, she has wanted only what is reasonable and right for black people: freedom now. Only a freedom that encompasses the totality of black life will suffice for Richardson, and although she does not expect to see this type of freedom in her own lifetime, she hopes her great-grandson experiences it—sooner rather than later. Gloria Richardson knows that even if this freedom is achieved, people will have to work in creative ways to ensure that opponents of black liberation are unable to chip away at it. Her story is a case study of how that work can be accomplished.

Acknowledgments

There is an extensive list of people who provided me aid, comfort, and support as I created this biography of Gloria Richardson. While I can't cite the entire list here, I give recognition and thanks to those people who had a special role or influence in this book's creation.

Scholars who have been important to my intellectual and scholarly development and whose influences can be seen in this book are Noam Chomsky, Patricia Hill Collins, Kimberlé Crenshaw, John Dittmer, W. E. B. Du Bois, Joe R. Feagin, Paula Giddings, Regina Gramer, bell hooks, Joy James, Chana Kai Lee, David Levering Lewis, Kay Mills, Charles M. Payne, Rick Perlstein, Sonja Peterson-Lewis, Mark Poster, Barbara Ransby, Patricia Schechter, Timothy B. Tyson, Deborah Gray White, Hayden White, Robert "Bob" Young, and Howard Zinn.

Two individuals—Zelbert Moore and Joyce A. Joyce—have been the most influential since I began college after serving in the US Air Force. Dr. Moore was my mentor in the black studies baccalaureate program at the State University of New York at New Paltz. It was in his interdisciplinary course Afro-Brazilian History that I learned to aspire to the highest academic and intellectual standards of my undergraduate years. That course prepared me for the rigors of graduate school and for my own career as a professor. Dr. Moore also convinced me to abandon my plan to rejoin the air force, arguing that I could do more for society by becoming a historian than by becoming a military officer. I think he may have been right. Dr. Joyce, an English professor, mentored me at Temple University while I was a doctoral student in African American studies. She introduced me to critical race theory and taught me to be a stronger and more effective writer; it would be impossible to overstate the importance of each to my intellectual development and scholarship production. Additionally, she challenged me to become a better person and to produce scholarship that people could use to improve their society. Dr. Joyce demonstrated exemplary academic standards, intellectual rigor, and honesty. She was also passionate about my academic, professional, and personal development. To Dr. Joyce and Dr. Moore I give thanks from

231

the bottom of my heart, and I promise to do for my students what both of them did for me: listen, advise, challenge, and intervene when necessary.

Numerous people helped me gain access to the sources I used for this biography. Ja A. Jahannes provided me with access to a copy of his 1988 interview with Gloria Richardson, which is a vein of gold I mined early in my research. It contains an incredible amount of information on her life leading up to and during the civil rights movement. Jahannes also provided access to Gloria Richardson herself. He contacted her and vouched for me when she didn't respond to my letters seeking her cooperation on this biography. He convinced Ms. Richardson to agree to the intrusive process that is biographical research, and for that I am forever grateful. He passed away in 2015, so I will never know his thoughts on the completed project, but I hope he would have found it a valuable addition to black history. I also want to acknowledge the invaluable data I collected from more than thirty interviewees. These people shared special stories and insights about Ms. Richardson that allowed me to add a personal texture to her story, and this biography is qualitatively better because of what they shared with me. I thank them all.

Library directors and research librarians provided me with access to valuable sources, as well as their assistance and time. Foremost among them are Anne Schwelm and Adam Altman of Cabrini University. Thanks also to Aslaku Berhanu of Temple University's Charles L. Blockson Afro-American Collection and Dr. Clifford Muse, Joellen ElBashir, Ishmael Childs, and Amber Junipher at Howard University's Moorland Spingarn Research Center. Additionally, Susan Pevar of Lincoln University collected and sent me the records of Richardson's maternal relatives who attended that school, and Selicia Gregory Allen of Virginia Union University's library system did the same for Richardson's paternal family who attended that institution. Jennifer A. Neumyer, special collections and outreach librarian at the Frederick Douglass Library of the University of Maryland Eastern Shore, provided information on H. Maynadier St. Clair's relationship to Morgan State University. I am also grateful to Cynthia P. Lewis, director of archives at the Martin Luther King Center, and staff member Elaine Hall for giving me access to the papers of the Southern Christian Leadership Conference and Student Nonviolent Coordinating Committee. Frances S. Pollard and Janice Keesling of the Virginia Historical Society were very helpful in my research of southern Virginia history.

Thanks to Clarence Logan and Andrew Moursund, who shared their clippings files with me. A special thank you to three research assistants: Emilie Sunnergren, Nathan Kuehnl, and Le Datta Grimes. Emilie obtained copies of two important editorials located at the Boston Public Library, and Nathan researched Detroit, Michigan, newspapers for stories about Ms. Richardson's visit to that city in the fall of 1963. Le Datta spent hours in the archives of the University of Kentucky, where she reviewed Congressman Rogers Morton's papers. All this assistance allowed me to spend my time more judiciously on other tasks, and it saved me a small fortune in travel costs. Before I submitted the manuscript to the University Press of Kentucky, Brent Reif proofread it, and his countless hours of work helped shorten the publication timeline. This favor is one for which I will be eternally grateful. I owe a special debt of gratitude to two Cabrini University officials: Dr. Jeff Gingerich, provost and vice president for academic affairs, and president Dr. Donald Taylor. Since I began working at Cabrini, they have been enthusiastic about my scholarship on Ms. Richardson, and they generously provided funds to purchase user licenses for many of the photographs that appear in this book. I appreciate all their support.

Literally dozens of people replied to my emails and phone calls concerning this biography. Personal documents such as photos and letters, and public documents such as deeds and wills are vital to every historian who sets out to tell a person's story. I was fortunate and am very thankful that a large number of people had some type of source they shared with me or facilitated my acquisition of by pointing me in the right direction. This was the case with my research on Richardson's family. Denise Oliver-Velez and Scott Wright gathered census data, which played a key role in telling the stories of Richardson's families in Maryland and Virginia. My ability to write about her paternal family in Virginia was greatly enhanced by the assistance of Scott Wright. A professional genealogist, Scott saved me a lot of time and resources when he researched various aspects of Richardson's family before I traveled to Virginia. I was constantly impressed by his creative thinking as we tracked down data. I also enjoyed our mealtime conversations during which we brainstormed about where to look for other pieces of data (actually, Scott did most of the brainstorming). Christina Batipps and Keesha Patterson helped me locate sources on Richardson's maternal family. Christina, a cousin of Richardson's, supplied me with, among other items, Richardson's family tree and leads on various related documents. Keesha walked me through the process of navigating Maryland's state archives in Annapolis. Her family's Washington residence also served as my base of operations during a two-day research trip to Howard University.

My research trip to Virginia and the King Center archives in Atlanta, Georgia, was financed by a gift from my mother, Thérèse Fitzgerald. This was the second of two gifts from my mother that helped prepare me to be a historian. The first was her admonishment that I shouldn't believe everything I see, hear, and read. I also credit my mother with being a catalyst for my interest in black history. Her view of the world is framed by her Christian liberation theology, and because of that, she taught me to believe in a god that wants people to live in just and equitable societies. This is why I felt drawn to black studies, a problem-driven and solution-oriented discipline, and specifically to the history of the civil rights movement.

There are other people who deserve to be acknowledged, specifically, my colleagues in Cabrini University's Department of History and Political Science. They are highly professional and ethical people, as well as outstanding professors and scholars who have set a high standard for me to meet. I hope I am earning my place among them. I extend a special "thank you" to my dear friend and department chair Darryl Mace. We met in graduate school at Temple University and immediately became friends, and since then our friendship has deepened and strengthened. He has looked out for me in many ways over the years, and his unceasing kindness and generosity, as well as his intellect and professional astuteness, aided me in my long journey to publish this book. I've told Darryl he reminds me a lot of the two best leaders I had in the air force—Master Sergeant Bonaparte P. Moore and Colonel Herschel Kaufman—because like them, he leads by example. Additionally, Darryl read various iterations of this biography and provided a valuable analysis of its strengths and weaknesses, especially the latter. This biography is stronger because of his review.

Since my graduate school years, Peter B. Levy (York College, Pennsylvania) has been the biggest champion of my work on Gloria Richardson. I owe him endless favors because he wrote the definitive story of the Cambridge movement, which I used to identify many of the primary and secondary sources I included in my own work. Furthermore, he read two earlier versions of the manuscript and gave me substantive feedback on each chapter. Peter is an academician and a mentor who is a credit to our profession. I stand on his shoulders. Dr. Cynthia Griggs Fleming, coeditor of the series Civil Rights and the Struggle for Black Equality in the Twentieth Century, has been supportive of my work since I reached out to her in 2006 to inquire about her own biographical subject, Ruby Doris Smith Robinson. I also appreciate Dr. Fleming's detailed reading of the manuscript and her important suggestions for improving key parts of it. Jeanne Theoharis read an earlier version of this book and made insightful recommendations on how it could be fortified. Her review, along with those by two anonymous readers, resulted in a final version that is tighter and more effectively argued. All these reviews reaffirm the lesson of the Akan proverb: "One head alone does not go into council."

Throughout the fifteen years I worked on this project, many family members and friends showed heartfelt interest in my work on Ms. Richardson, and I want them to know how much I appreciate all the times they indulged me and let me talk about her (especially my in-laws). Tya Young, one of Ms. Richardson's granddaughters, has been one of the biggest cheerleaders of this book, and she kept my spirits up when I was in the last phases of completing her grandmother's life story. My wife, Kathy Corlew, supported me tirelessly throughout these years. She never complained about competing with Gloria Richardson for my time and attention, although she did have her limits. Once, as we headed off for vacation, she insisted, "No GR after we land." Kathy also provided me with the love and encouragement I needed to push through the tougher times of my corporate and academic careers. My sister Elenita Fitzgerald (the smartest person I've ever known) also helped me through those tough times. I wouldn't have been able to complete this biography or successfully navigate my careers without Elenita's and Kathy's love and support and excellent advice.

Finally, I must thank Gloria Richardson. She is a wonderful person who shared so much of herself over the years as I worked on her story. She provided me with access to her family and friends as well as her personal papers. Most important, Ms. Richardson shared her voice through our many interviews and countless emails. It was through these exchanges that I learned many intimate details of her life and how she views the world. I am grateful I got to know the lady who seemed so far beyond my reach back in 2002. I learned that she has a good sense of humor and an excellent memory about the civil rights movement, and she was evenhanded when speaking about people. I even got to see her dreaded "side-eye" on a couple of occasions when I had asked a question to which she thought I should already know the answer. Ms. Richardson didn't agree with every one of my interpretations or assessments of her history and activism, but she always respected my right to have them. Every biographer should be as lucky as I was to work with such a generous and understanding subject. I hope she finds this book worthy of her years of time and attention.

Notes

Abbreviations

Afro-Am   *Afro-American* (Baltimore)
DB   *Daily Banner* (Cambridge, MD)
GR   Gloria Richardson
JRF   Joseph R. Fitzgerald
NYT   *New York Times*
WP   *Washington Post*

Introduction

1. The texts on Richardson include a full-length local study of the Cambridge movement and an unpublished master's thesis. See Annette K. Brock, "Gloria Richardson and the Cambridge Movement," in *Women in the Civil Rights Movement: Trailblazers and Torchbearers, 1941–1965*, ed. Vicki L. Crawford, Jacqueline Anne Rouse, and Barbara Woods (Bloomington: Indiana University Press, 1990), 121–44; Anita K. Foeman, "Gloria Richardson: Breaking the Mold," *Journal of Black Studies* 26 (May 1996): 604–15; Paula Giddings, *When and Where I Enter: The Impact of Black Women on Race and Sex in America* (New York: Quill, 1984), 290–92; Sharon Harley, "Chronicle of a Death Foretold," in *Sisters in the Struggle: African-American Women in the Civil Rights–Black Power Movement*, ed. Bettye Collier-Thomas and V. P. Franklin (New York: NYU Press, 2001), 174–96; Peter B. Levy, *Civil War on Race Street: The Civil Rights Struggle in Cambridge, Maryland* (Gainesville: University Press of Florida, 2003); Sandra Y. Millner, "Recasting Civil Rights Leadership: Gloria Richardson and the Cambridge Movement," *Journal of Black Studies* 26 (July 1996): 668–87; Lynne Olson, *Freedom's Daughters: The Unsung Heroines of the Civil Rights Movement from 1830 to 1970* (New York: Scribner, 2001), 278–83; Belinda Robnett, *How Long? How Long? African American Women in the Struggle for Civil Rights* (New York: Oxford University Press, 1997), 161–65; Edward Trever, "Gloria Richardson and the Cambridge Civil Rights Movement, 1962–1964" (master's thesis, Morgan State University, 1994); Jenny Walker, "The 'Gun-Toting' Gloria Richardson: Black Violence in Cambridge, Maryland," in *Gender in the Civil Rights Movement*, ed. Peter J. Ling and Sharon Monteith (New York: Garland, 1999), 169–86. Harley and Millner discuss the Cambridge movement's influence on the development of Black Power.

2. Katherine Mellen Charron, *Freedom's Teacher: The Life of Septima Clark* (Chapel Hill: University of North Carolina Press, 2009); Barbara Ransby, *Ella Baker and the Black Freedom Movement: A Radical Democratic Vision* (Chapel Hill: University of North Carolina Press, 2003); Joanne Grant, *Ella Baker: Freedom Bound* (New York: Wiley, 1998); Chana Kai Lee, *For Freedom's Sake: The Life of Fannie Lou Hamer* (Urbana: University of Illinois Press, 1999); Kay Mills, *This Little Light of Mine: The Life of Fannie Lou Hamer* (New York: Plume, 1993); Jeanne Theoharis, *The Rebellious Life of Mrs. Rosa Parks* (Boston: Beacon Press, 2013); Cynthia Griggs Fleming, *Soon We Will Not Cry: The Liberation of Ruby Doris Smith Robinson* (Lanham, MD: Rowman & Littlefield, 1998). There are many dozens of similar stories yet to be told. Importantly, edited books about black women activists tell some of these stories and cover some of the issues they confronted. See Crawford, Rouse, and Woods, *Women in the Civil Rights Movement;* Ling and Monteith, *Gender in the Civil Rights Movement;* Collier-Thomas and Franklin, *Sisters in the Struggle;* Dayo F. Gore, Jeanne Theoharis, and Komozi Woodard, eds., *Want to Start a Revolution? Radical Women in the Black Freedom Struggle* (New York: NYU Press, 2009).

3. The concept of the long movement was first developed by Jacquelyn Dowd Hall in her essay "The Long Civil Rights Movement and the Political Uses of the Past," *Journal of American History* 91, no. 4 (March 2005): 1233–63. Valuable discussions of this concept, including its limitations, can be found in Sundiata Keita Cha-Jua and Clarence Lang, "The 'Long Movement' as Vampire: Temporal and Spatial Fallacies in Recent Black Freedom Studies," *Journal of African American History* 92, no. 2 (Spring 2007): 265–88; Hasan Kwame Jeffries, *Bloody Lowndes: Civil Rights and Black Power in Alabama's Black Belt* (New York: NYU Press, 2010), 257–58, n. 15.

See "Universal Declaration of Human Rights," United Nations, 10 December 1948, accessed 2 August 2017, http://www.ohchr.org/EN/UDHR/Documents/UDHR_Translations/eng.pdf. Article 22 of the declaration implies the right to open accommodations. Jeffries posits the concept of "'freedom rights'" as an all-encompassing category of rights for which black people have been fighting since the nineteenth century. I find his concept interesting, although I prefer the term "human rights" because it captures more fully the essence of the BLM. See Jeffries, *Bloody Lowndes*, 4.

4. It is too early to tell if the Black Lives Matter movement is its own distinct wave or a continuation of the Black Power wave.

5. For a discussion of the idea of the "beloved community," see Clayborne Carson, *In Struggle: SNCC and the Black Awakening of the 1960s* (Cambridge, MA: Harvard University Press, 1995), 21, 23–24. Also see Mills, *This Little Light of Mine*, 19–21. The phrase "moral evil of racism" comes from an oral history of a human rights activist speaking about Hamer, quoted in Charles M. Payne, *I've Got the Light of Freedom: The Organizing Tradition and the Mississippi Freedom Struggle* (Berkeley: University of California Press, 1995), 242. Also see Lee, *For Freedom's Sake*, 63, 121–22, and 152. The Mississippi Freedom Labor Union was an organization of black field hands, domestic servants, and farm equipment operators who worked to end their exploitation by their employers, whereas the Freedom Farm was an attempt to create "economic self-sufficiency" for black people in rural Mississippi.

Ella Baker was one activist whose engagement with religion influenced her activism. She initially embraced the Baptist missionary ideals of her mother and used them while working in organizations such as the Young Negroes' Cooperative League when she moved to New York City. By her early thirties, however, Baker "was no longer a devoutly religious person"; instead, she had developed a radical humanist orientation as she worked on behalf of black America. See Ransby, *Ella Baker*, 64–81.

6. Clark, Baker, and Parks worked extensively in local movements and in various organizations' advocacy campaigns, whereas Hamer and Richardson led local movements.

7. Charron, *Freedom's Teacher*, 119; Payne, *I've Got the Light of Freedom*, 276; Françoise N. Hamlin, *Crossroads at Clarksdale: The Black Freedom Struggle in the Mississippi Delta after World War II* (Chapel Hill: University of North Carolina Press, 2012), 43–44.

8. Robnett, *How Long?* 13, 17, 19. Sharon Harley was the first to point out that Robnett's bridge leader concept does not fully apply to Richardson. See Harley, "Chronicle of a Death Foretold," 176–77.

9. I was unable to determine through Charron's biography of Clark whether she supported the right of armed self-defense. Scholars have been chronicling women's radicalism more and more, to the benefit of civil rights and Black Power histories. For an excellent discussion of gender, leadership, and the normalcy of black radical women's activism, see the introduction to Gore, Theoharis, and Woodard, *Want to Start a Revolution?* 7–10. The book itself expands our understanding of these women and the locations where they applied their radical views of black liberation.

10. Some book-length treatments of the civil rights movement outside the South are Martha Biondi, *To Stand and Fight: The Struggle for Civil Rights in Postwar New York City* (Cambridge, MA: Harvard University Press, 2003); Matthew J. Countryman, *Up South: Civil Rights and Black Power in Philadelphia* (Philadelphia: University of Pennsylvania Press, 2007); and Patrick T. Jones, *The Selma of the North: Civil Rights Insurgency in Milwaukee* (Cambridge, MA: Harvard University Press, 2009). Edited works on the topic include Jeanne Theoharis and Komozi Woodard, eds., *Freedom North: Black Freedom Struggles Outside of the South, 1940–1980* (New York: Palgrave Macmillan, 2003); Jeanne Theoharis and Komozi Woodard, eds., *Groundwork: Local Black Freedom Movements in America* (New York: NYU Press, 2005).

1. Foundations

1. Roland C. McConnell, ed., *Three Hundred and Fifty Years: A Chronology of the Afro-Am in Maryland, 1634–1984* (Annapolis: Maryland Commission on Afro-Am History and Culture for the Maryland State Department of Economic and Community Development, 1985), 1; Levy, *Civil War on Race Street*, 12; Ross M. Kimmel, "Free Black People in Seventeenth Century Maryland," *Maryland Historical Magazine* 71, no. 1 (1976): 21, 22–24.

2. Kay Kajiyyah McElvey, "Early Black Dorchester, 1776–1870: A History of the Struggle of African-Americans in Dorchester County, Maryland, to Be Free to Make Their Own Choices" (dissertation, University of Maryland, College Park, 1991), 49, 42, 51, 53, 320–21, 378. The actual number of black people in Dorchester in 1704 totaled 199, out of a population of 2,312. Maryland had the largest number of free

black people of any state in the nation. See McConnell, *Three Hundred and Fifty Years*, 2, 4, 5; Levy, *Civil War on Race Street*, 12–13.

3. 1850 US Census, District 1, Dorchester, MD, ser. M432, roll 291, p. 388B; 1860 US Census, Cambridge, Dorchester, MD, ser. M653, roll 473, p. 353; 1870 US Census, Cambridge, Dorchester, MD, ser. M593, roll 585, p. 352A; 1880 US Census, Cambridge, Dorchester, MD, roll 508, p. 135A, Enumeration District 26. For Cyrus St. Clair's tax records, see Internal Revenue Assessment Lists for Maryland, 1862–1866, National Archives Microfilm Publication Series M771, Records of the Internal Revenue Service, Record Group 58, National Archives, Washington, DC, retrieved from Ancestry.com. For apprenticeships of black people, see Helena Sorrell Hicks, "The Black Apprentice in Maryland Court Records from 1661 to 1865" (dissertation, University of Maryland, 1988), 108–9; McConnell, *Three Hundred and Fifty Years*, 9. For the St. Clair family's literacy and schooling, see the censuses of 1850, 1860, 1870, and 1880. H. Maynadier St. Clair's obituary states that he "attended local schools" in Dorchester and Morgan College. See "Ex-Councilman Buried in Md.," *Afro-Am*, 23 April 1949, 2. I have been unable to confirm H. M. St. Clair's attendance at Morgan College. For Morgan State's history as a teaching school, see "Brief History of Morgan State University," Morgan University, accessed 22 September 2011, http://www.morgan.edu /About_MSU/University_History.html. For black people's literacy rates and education in Cambridge, see McElvey, "Early Black Dorchester," 365, 209, 80, 367–68; Levy, *Civil War on Race Street*, 14, 16.

4. McConnell, *Three Hundred and Fifty Years*, 6; McElvey, "Early Black Dorchester," 257, 279–80, 281, 367–68, 387, 389; John Hope Franklin and Alfred Moss, *From Slavery to Freedom: A History of African Americans*, 7th ed. (New York: McGraw-Hill, 1994), 186–87; McElvey, "Early Black Dorchester," 394–95.

5. "Cambridge News," *Afro-Am*, 3 August 1898, 1; *Afro-Am*, 6 August 1898, 1; *Afro-Am*, 13 August 1898; "Correspondence," *Afro-Am*, 10 June 1899, 1; Eleanor S. Bruchey, "The Industrialization of Maryland: 1860–1914," in *Maryland: A History, 1632–1974*, ed. Richard Walsh and William Lloyd Fox (Baltimore: Maryland Historical Society, 1974), 396–498; Robert J. Brugger, *Maryland: A Middle Temperament, 1634–1980* (Baltimore: Johns Hopkins University Press, 1988), 321; C. Christopher Brown, "One Step Closer to Democracy: African American Voting in Late Nineteenth-Century Cambridge," *Maryland Historical Magazine* 95, no. 4 (2000): 429, 430; C. Christopher Brown, "Chapter Twelve: Cambridge at Early 20th Century" (unpublished manuscript), 1–2, 3, 4 (copy in author's possession); Levy, *Civil War on Race Street*, 18.

6. Brown, "Chapter Twelve," 2, 3, 4, 6–7, 9, 12, 13, 14.

7. The Merry Band (also known as the Merry Cornet Band and the Merry Band of Cambridge) was one of the Second Ward's social institutions; Richardson's uncle Cyrus belonged to the band before moving to New York City to work as a jazz musician. See "Frederick Douglass," *Sun*, 25 September 1877, 4. Also see GR, email to JRF, 24 October 2009; "Cambridge News," *Afro-Am*, 19 November 1898, 2; "Cambridge," *Afro-Am*, 6 May 1899, 1; "Pythians in Council," *Afro-Am*, 27 July 1907, 1; "Waugh Church Cambridge Raises Large Sum of Money," *Afro-Am*, 15 November 1918, 4; "Draft Boys Feted," *Afro-Am*, 27 October 1917, 5; "Carl Diton Plays at Cambridge," *Afro-Am*, 30 December 1911, 1. For information on Cyrus St. Clair, see "Mrs. Ida

Bennett," *Afro-Am*, 12 December 1936, 23; Scott Yanow, *Classic Jazz* (San Francisco: Backbeat Books, 2001), 203; obituary, "Cyrus St. Clair," *DB*, 23 March 1954, 5. For more information on excursions and celebrity visits, see "Local Items," *Afro-Am*, 17 September 1898, 1; advertisements, *Afro-Am*, 30 August 1913, 6 September 1913, 27 June 1914; "Cambridge," *Afro-Am*, 28 February 1919, A6; "Cambridge, Md.," *Afro-Am*, 26 May 1928, 14; "Masonic Grand Lodge," *Afro-Am*, 13 July 1929, 10; "What Lodges Are Doing," *Afro-Am*, 5 December 1931, 18; "Afro Visitors," *Afro-Am*, 12 November 1932, 1; "Gadabouting," *Afro-Am*, 13 May 1933, 18; "Salisbury," *Afro-Am*, 3 August 1935, 15. Occasionally, the visiting entertainers stayed at the St. Clair home. See GR, interview with JRF, 20 June 2007; GR, email to JRF, 16 October 2009.

  8. "153 Converts," *Afro-Am*, 4 February 1899, 1; "Cambridge," *Afro-Am*, 4 June 1898, 1; "Cambridge," *Afro-Am*, 6 May 1899, 1; " "Pastors to Start Religious Campaign," *Afro-Am*, 23 December 1911, 6; "W. H. M. S. Meets," *Afro-Am*, 9 August 1918, 1; "Cambridge, Maryland," *Afro-Am*, 29 December 1928, 7; "Notes from Our Correspondents," *Afro-Am*, 19 February 1916, 6; "Cambridge," *Afro-Am*, 28 February 1919, A6; "Cambridge," *Afro-Am*, 26 January 1935, 15; GR, interview with JRF, 14 September 2002.

  9. "The State of Maryland: Closing of Colored Schools in Dorchester," *Sun*, supplement, 1 March 1888; "Correspondence," *Afro-Am*, 20 May 1899, 1; "Leonidas C. James Heads Teachers," *Afro-Am*, 6 December 1924, 2; "Princess Anne Is Branded a Fire Trap, by Nice," *Afro-Am*, 9 March 1935, 14; *Princess Anne Academy Catalogue, 1935–1936* (Princess Anne, MD, 1935), 7, Special Collections Department, Frederick Douglass Library, University of Maryland Eastern Shore. I thank Jennifer A. Neumyer, special collections and outreach librarian, for providing a copy of this document. Also see 1900 US Census, Cambridge, Dorchester, MD, ser. T623, roll 621, p. 26B, Enumeration District 36; Dorchester County Commercial Directory, Cambridge 1908–1909, transcribed by Frank Collins, CollinsFactor.com, accessed 20 September 2011, http://www.collinsfactor.com/directories/1908dorchester/1908cambridge -a-c.htm; "Our People at Cambridge, Md., Prosperous—No Race Friction," *Afro-Am*, 1 May 1909, 6; GR, interviews with JRF, 14 September 2002, 2 August 2003; Brown, "Chapter Twelve," 23–25, 26.

  10. The Eastern Star was a gender-integrated fraternal society dedicated to fostering morality and charitable acts among its members. See GR, interview with JRF, 14 September 2002; "About the Order of the Eastern Star," General Grand Chapter of the Eastern Star, accessed 20 September 2011, http://www.easternstar.org/about _oes.html; "Mrs. Washington Elected President," *Afro-Am*, 3 August 1912, 1; Deborah Gray White, *Too Heavy a Load: Black Women in Defense of Themselves, 1894–1994* (New York: W. W. Norton, 1999), 54. The Knights of Pythias was founded near the end of the Civil War with a goal of fostering interregional understanding between northern and southern men. By the time Richardson's grandfather joined the order, it had lodges around the nation, although they were usually racially segregated in the southern states, including Maryland. H. M. St. Clair's obituary states that he also belonged to the Odd Fellows and the Elks; see "Ex-Councilman Buried in Md.," *Afro-Am*, 23 April 1949, 2. "What Lodges Are Doing, Masons Honor T. H. Kiah, Deputy Master," *Afro-Am*, 2 April 1932, 16; "History of the Knights of Pythias," The Pythians: The Order of the Knights of Pythias, accessed 12 August 2011,

http://www.pythias.org/about/pythstory.html; "Pythians Banquet Prominent Visitor," *Afro-Am*, 23 January 1909, 5; "Pythians Hold Annual Session," *Afro-Am*, 24 August 1915, 1; "Pythians Elect Supreme Delegate," *Afro-Am*, 25 July 1925, A9; "Heads Pythians," *Afro-Am*, 30 July 1927, 4.

11. "Watty Elected 24th Term to Head Pythians," *Afro-Am*, 1 August 1931, 3.

12. Brown, "One Step Closer to Democracy," 428, 430–432, 433, 434; Brown, "Chapter Twelve," 33–37; "Town Elections at Cambridge," *Sun*, supplement, 21 June 1888; "Cambridge," *Afro-Am*, 11 June 1898, 1; "Cambridge Gleanings," *Afro-Am*, 25 June 1898, 1; "Our People at Cambridge, Md., Prosperous—No Race Friction," *Afro-Am*, 1 May 1909, 6; "Town Council Proceedings," *DB*, 18 May 1922, 2; "Town Council Proceedings," *DB*, 25 March 1931, 5; "St. Clair Re-elected," *Afro-Am*, 19 July 1918, 1; "St. Clair Re-elected to Council after 24 Years," *Chicago Defender* (national ed.), 26 July 1930, 3.

13. C. Fraser Smith, *Here Lies Jim Crow: Civil Rights in Maryland* (Baltimore: Johns Hopkins University Press, 2008), 60; "Cambridge," *Afro-Am*, 8 October 1920, 11; "1st Dist., Convention for State G.O.P.," *Afro-Am*, 4 October 1930, 5; "Roosevelt Getting Some Raw Deals," *Afro-Am*, 15 June 1912, 1; "Maryland Names Negro Delegates," *Atlanta Daily World*, 5 June 1932, B1; George L. Hart, *Official Report of the Proceedings of the Twentieth Republican National Convention, Held in Chicago, Illinois, June 14, 15 and 16, 1932* (New York: Tenny Press, 1932), 60.

14. "Defense Council Gets to Work," *Afro-Am*, 29 September 1917, 1; "Interracial Committee Appointed in Maryland," *Chicago Defender*, 20 September 1924, 3; "Gov. Ritchie Gets Interracial Report," *Afro-Am*, 21 January 1927, 20; "Inter-racial Commission on Segregation," *Afro-Am*, 1 February 1924, 9.

15. "Republican 'Special,'" *Sun*, 12 June 1896, 8; "On to St. Louis," *Sun*, 13 June 1896, 10; "No Rooms for Negroes: St. Louis Hotels Still Bar out the Colored Man," *Chicago Daily Tribune*, 11 June 1896, 3; GR, interview with JRF, 14 September 2002.

16. "Colored Republicans," *Sun*, 8 March 1897, 7.

17. "Remarkable Resolutions Adopted by Lincoln League of America," *Chicago Defender*, 28 June 1919, 10; "Lincoln League Stirs South," *Chicago Defender*, 28 June 1919, 1, 10; "Group of City Negroes Received by Harding," *Sun*, 14 April 1921, 22.

18. Oscar Handlin and Mary Handlin, "Origins of Southern Labor System," *William and Mary Quarterly* 7, no. 2 (1950): 216; Philip D. Curtin, *The Atlantic Slave Trade: A Census* (Madison: University of Wisconsin Press, 1969), 156–57; Philip D. Morgan and Michael L. Nicholls, "Slaves in Piedmont Virginia, 1720–1790," *William and Mary Quarterly* 46, no. 2 (1989): 215, 216, 217; Ervin L. Jordan Jr., *Black Confederates and Afro-Yankees in Civil War Virginia* (Charlottesville: University of Virginia Press, 1995), 10–11, 18–19; Brenda E. Stevenson, *Life in Black and White: Family and Community in the Slave South* (New York: Oxford University Press, 1997), 166–69, 175.

19. Richardson's great-grandfather was born to a woman enslaved by Charles H. and Elizabeth C. Fowlkes, a white couple living in Lunenburg County. Sometime in the 1840s Elizabeth Fowlkes moved to Mecklenburg County, where she died before 1850. A friend of hers, James Hayes Sr., executed her estate and disposed of her property, including the five people she had enslaved. One of them was a man by the name

of "Jim." In 1853 Hayes sold Jim for $900 to his brother, George L. Hayes. Four years later, George Hayes recorded the birth of a child to two of the people he enslaved. The birth record does not list the child's first name, but the child's parents' first names are recorded as "Jim" and "Mary Ann." See Scott Wright, "Hayes Family Research Summary," 26 August 2009, 1–4 (copy in author's possession). Wright is a professional genealogist residing in Virginia's Southside region.

For evidence of the Fowlkeses living in Lunenburg County, see the deed of sale between them and Kenner Craller of Nottoway County, Nottoway County Deed Book 4, p. 515, Nottoway County Court House, Nottoway County, VA. For the role of James Hayes (sometimes spelled "Hayse") as executor of Mrs. Fowlkes's estate and the number of black people he enslaved, see Mecklenburg County Will Book 17, p. 81, Mecklenburg County Courthouse, Boydton, VA; 1850 US Census, Slave Schedules, Mecklenburg, Virginia, ser. M432, roll 1009, from Ancestry.com, Provo, UT. For James's and George's familial relationship, see 1850 US Census, Mecklenburg County, Virginia, regiment 22, ser. M432, roll 960. For the sale of "Jim," see Mecklenburg County, Virginia, Chancery Cases 1860–076, Library of Virginia, Richmond. For the recording of the birth of a black child named James W. Hayes in 1857, see Leslie Anderson Morales and Beverly Pierce, eds., *Virginia Slave Births Index, 1853–1865*, vol. 3, *H–L* (Westminster, MD: Heritage Books, 2007), 126, Alexandria Library (Victoria, VA), Local History/Special Collections. For data on the black people George L. Hayes enslaved in 1850, see 1850 US Census, Slave Schedules, Mecklenburg, Virginia, ser. M432, roll 1009; 1900 US Census, Flat Creek, Mecklenburg, Virginia, ser. T623, roll 1718, p. 8B, Enumeration District 54. Wright believes that the documentary record "certainly points" to a woman enslaved by Charles and Elizabeth Fowlkes giving birth to James Hayes. However, he writes that "there's no clear, irrefutable evidence to prove it." See Scott Wright, email to JRF, 11 December 2010. I believe the evidence is sufficient to conclude that James Hayes's mother was enslaved by the Fowlkes family.

20. Henry J. McGuinn and Tinsley Lee Spraggins, "Negro in Politics in Virginia," *Journal of Negro Education* 26, no. 3 (1957): 378, 379; Susan L. Bracey, *Life by the Roaring Roanoke: A History of Mecklenburg County, Virginia* (Mecklenburg, VA: Mecklenburg County Bicentennial Commission, 1977), 246, 247, 255.

21. Steven Hahn, *A Nation under Our Feet: Black Political Struggles in the Rural South from Slavery to the Great Migration* (Cambridge, MA: Belknap, 2003), chap. 8; Charles E. Wynes, *Race Relations in Virginia, 1870–1902* (Charlottesville: University of Virginia Press, 1961), 9–10, 18–20, 29, 51–52, 59; James T. Moore, "Black Militancy in Readjuster Virginia, 1879–1883," *Journal of Southern History* 41, no. 2 (1975): 167, 168, 172, 173; George C. Scurlock et al., "Additional Information and Corrections in Reconstruction Records," *Journal of Negro History* 5, no. 2 (1920): 242–43; Andrew Buni, *The Negro in Virginia Politics, 1902–1965* (Charlottesville: University Press of Virginia, 1967), 50–53, 60; A. A. Taylor, "The Negro an Efficient Laborer," *Journal of Negro History* 11, no. 2 (1926): 364, 369; Stewart E. Tolnay, *The Bottom Rung: African American Family Life on Southern Farms* (Urbana: University of Illinois Press, 1999), 9, 12; C. Vann Woodward, *Origins of the New South, 1877–1913* (Baton Rouge: Louisiana State University Press, 1951), 178.

22. Personal Property Tax Records, Mecklenburg County, 1870, reel 637, Library of Virginia, Richmond; Wright, "Hayes Family Research Summary," 5; 1880 US

Census, Flat Creek, Mecklenburg, Virginia, roll 1378, p. 42, Enumeration District 147. Jim Hayes was now going by the name James Hayes. Scott Wright believes the son listed as "Washington" was James Washington (Gloria Richardson's grandfather), with his age inflated a couple of years. Mecklenburg Register of Marriages Book 1, p. 350, l. 84, Mecklenburg County Courthouse, Boydton, VA. Wright cites the Mecklenburg Register of Marriages (p. 331, l. 33) as the source of the wedding registration. See Wright, "Hayes Family Research Summary," 6; 1900 US Census, Flat Creek, Mecklenburg, Virginia, ser. T623, roll 1718, p. 8B, Enumeration District 54; 1910 US Census, Virginia, Buckhorn, Mecklenburg, Virginia, ser. T624, roll 1635, p. 5A, Enumeration District 0054.

23. Personal Property Tax Records, Mecklenburg County, 1893, reel 1871, Library of Virginia, Richmond. For information on the 1890 census, see http://www.archives.gov/genealogy/census/1890/1890.html. For James W. Hayes's occupation as a farmer, see the 1900 and 1910 censuses. For James Hayes's connection to George L. Hayes's daughter Emma F. Hayes Edmonson, see "Gayle v. Hayes' admr. et al.," Mecklenburg County, Virginia, Chancery Cases 1884–029, Library of Virginia, Richmond. For James W. Hayes's land purchase from J. W. and Emma Edmonson, see "J. W. Edmonson, et al. to J. W. Hayes," Mecklenburg Deed Book 54, p. 412. For a description and map of the land, see Mecklenburg Deed Book 43, p. 84; Personal Property Tax Records, Mecklenburg County, 1916, reels 4345–46, Library of Virginia, Richmond. Also see Wright, "Hayes Family Research Summary," 9; *A Handbook of Virginia*, 7th ed. (Richmond: Department of Agriculture and Immigration of the State of Virginia, 1919), 161–62. Virginia Hayes Shields and her husband, Calvin K. Shields Sr., provided the information about the crops raised by the Hayes family; telephone interview with JRF, 10 February 2005.

24. Wynes, *Race Relations in Virginia*, 69, 71, 72n17, 76–78; W. E. B. Du Bois, "The Negroes of Farmville, Virginia: A Social Study," in *W. E. B. Du Bois: A Reader by William Edward Burghardt Du Bois*, ed. David L. Lewis (New York: Henry Holt, 1995), 231. Also see "Wholesale Lynching in Virginia," WP, 25 December 1890, 6; June Dailey, "Deference and Violence in the Postbellum Urban South: Manners and Massacres in Danville, Virginia," *Journal of Southern History* 63, no. 3 (1997): 553–90. For the deed, see Mecklenburg Deed Book 55, pp. 521–22. The date of the land transfer was 8 January 1898. The church still stands today on the same land.

25. James D. Watkinson, "William Washington Browne and the True Reformers of Richmond, Virginia," *Virginia Magazine of History and Biography* 97 (1989): 376–77, 382, 383, 386, 394, 395; William Patrick Burrell and D. E. Johnson Sr., *Twenty-Five Years History of the Grand Fountain of the United Order of True Reformers: 1881–1905* (Richmond, VA: Grand Fountain, United Order of True Reformers, 1909), 149, 158, 168, 267, 294, 462. For the deed record, see Mecklenburg Deed Book 70, pp. 190–91; "Local Sites Highlight Education Heritage," *Mecklenburg (VA) Sun*, 17 February 2010, B1.

26. Bracey, *Life by the Roaring Roanoke*, 248–51; 1900 US Census, Flat Creek, Mecklenburg, Virginia, ser. T623, roll 1718, p. 8B, Enumeration District 54; *Hartshorn Memorial College Catalog, 1920–1921* (Richmond: Virginia Union University and Hartshorn Memorial College, 1921), 25 (available in Virginia Union University archives; copy in author's possession). For James Mathew's schooling, see "Dr. James

Mathew Hayes Claimed by Death in N. News," *New Journal and Guide* (Norfolk, VA), 23 August 1930, 12.

Boydton Academic and Bible Institute was located in Boydton, approximately ten miles southwest of Union Level. Established in 1878, the institute offered primary education to children and trained young women and men to be teachers or ministers. The institute eventually offered children a secondary education and boarding services. See Historical Marker Database, accessed 13 July 2010, http://www.hmdb.org/marker.asp?MarkerID=30917&Print=1.

27. James Mathew Hayes, draft registration cards for World War I, National Archives Microfilm Publication M1509, roll 035, Virginia, Mecklenburg County A–V, Philadelphia; *Southern Workman* 66, no. 11 (November 1937): 359. Documentation of John E. Hayes's presence at Virginia Union University (VUU) is from correspondence and archival materials. According to Marilyn A. Brooks, an associate registrar at VUU, the university does not have students' transcripts from the time of John Hayes's attendance. Marilyn A. Brooks, email to JRF, 4 March 2010. Also see *Virginia Union University Catalog, 1910–1911* (Richmond, VA: Williams Printing Company, 1911), 55 (available in Virginia Union University archives; copy in author's possession); Selicia Gregory Allen (archivist and special collections librarian at VUU's L. Douglas Wilder Library), email to JRF, 3 March 2010. While he was in Richmond, John worked as a waiter. See 1910 US Census, Virginia, Buckhorn, Mecklenburg, Virginia, ser. T624, roll 1635, p. 5A, Enumeration District 0054. For James's, John's, and Lawrence's graduation from Howard University, see *Howard University: Alumni Today, 2010* (Brewster, NY: Harris Connect, 2010), 140, 141, 154.

28. For the Great Migration, see Isabel Wilkerson, *The Warmth of Other Suns: The Epic Story of America's Great Migration* (New York: Random House, 2010).

29. John Edward Hayes, Howard University transcript for the years 1913–1917 (copy in author's possession). For the racial and ethnic demographics of the capital, see Francine Curro Cary, ed., *Washington Odyssey: A Multicultural History of the Nation's Capital* (Washington, DC: Smithsonian Books, 2003), chaps. 7–10; James Borchert, *Alley Life in Washington: Family, Community, Religion, and Folklife in the City, 1850–1970* (Urbana: University of Illinois Press, 1980), 2–6, 166–74; Constance McLaughlin Green, *The Secret City: A History of Race Relations in the Nation's Capital* (Princeton, NJ: Princeton University Press, 1967), 124, 155–60, 164, 165–66, 178.

30. Audrey Elisa Kerr, *The Paper Bag Principle: Class, Colorism, and Rumor and the Case of Black Washington, D.C.* (Knoxville: University of Tennessee Press, 2006), 40–41, 54; Willard B. Gatewood, *Aristocrats of Color: The Black Elite, 1880–1920* (Bloomington: Indiana University Press, 1990), 16. For a detailed analysis of Washington, see chapter 2.

31. "Brief History of Howard University," Howard University, accessed 29 August 2011, http://www.howard.edu/explore/history.htm; John Edward Hayes, Howard University transcript for the years 1913–1917; GR, interview with JRF, 20 June 2007; GR, email to JRF, 23 October 2009; World War I Selective Service System Draft Registration Cards, 1917–1918, Washington County, District of Columbia, Draft Board 8, M1509, roll 1556843, National Archives and Records Administration, Washington, DC. The draft card lists John's address as 408 T Street NW. It also lists him as an employee of the Long Island Railroad system, a division of

Pennsylvania Railroad. For John Hayes's graduation date from Howard, see *Howard University: Alumni Today, 2010*, 141; GR, personal conversation with JRF, 1 December 2016.

32. Gatewood, *Aristocrats of Color*, 39. For John E. Hayes's membership in Alpha Phi Alpha, see "Druggist Buried in Cambridge," *Afro-Am*, 17 December 1946, 3. For the Fowler sisters' graduation from Howard's Pharmacy School in 1916, see "From a Woman in Business," *Afro-Am*, 26 August 1916, 6. Mable St. Clair began attending Baltimore's Colored High School in 1912; see "Mid-Winter Promotions," *Afro-Am*, 3 February 1912, 8. The Fowler sisters graduated from Baltimore's Colored High School in 1913; see "These Will Graduate," *Sun*, 12 June 1913, 5; 1910 US Census, Ward 18, Baltimore (Independent City), Maryland, ser. T624, roll 559, p. 9A. Dr. Fowler was a founder of Baltimore's black Mutual Benefit Society and its black hospital, Provident Hospital; he belonged to the Knights of Pythias. The Fowlers lived at 1065 West Lexington Street. For more on Charles Fowler, see "Pythians Elect Supreme Delegate," *Afro-Am*, 25 July 1925, A9; "Board of Provident Votes to Merge," *Afro-Am*, 12 October 1923, A8; advertisement, *Afro-Am*, 27 October 1928, 39; "Gadabouting," *Afro-Am*, 13 May 1933, 18. Mable's parents sent her to Baltimore because they wanted her to receive training as a classical pianist (something that was unavailable in Cambridge), and Baltimore's public school system, though racially segregated, offered a more rigorous education than Cambridge's. See GR, interview with JRF, 28 March 2005; GR, emails to JRF, 30 October 2004, 16 October 2009, 14 November 2011.

33. Mable completed her primary education at Public School 116. "Public Schools Closed—Many Promotions," *Afro-Am*, 1 July 1911, 4; "Mid-Winter Promotions," *Afro-Am*, 3 February 1912, 8; "These Will Graduate," *Sun*, 12 June 1913, 5; "62 Get Diplomas: Colored High School Commencement Held at the Lyric," *Sun*, 19 June 1915, 3; "Cambridge Happenings," *Afro-Am*, 7 July 1917, 2; "Advertisement: The Cheyney Training School for Teachers," *Crisis*, June 1917, 56; *Lincoln University Catalogue, 1922–1923* (Hampton, VA: Hampton Institute Press, 1923), 66, accessed 24 August 2010, http://www.lincoln.edu/library/specialcollections/catalogueissues/1923.pdf; "Boston U. Grad," *Afro-Am*, 9 July 1927, 5; "Cambridge, Md.," *Afro-Am*, 23 June 1928, 16; GR, interview with JRF, 14 September 2002.

34. GR, interview with JRF, 2 August 2003; "Cambridge," *Afro-Am*, 28 February 1919, A6; "Cambridge," *Afro-Am*, 1 March 1918, 4; "Cambridge," *Afro-Am*, 8 October 1920, 11.

35. GR, emails to JRF, 26 September 2011, 29 November 2011; 1930 US Census, Baltimore (Independent City), Maryland, roll 860, p. 12A, Enumeration District 258; "Professional News: In Memoriam: Hayes," *Journal of the National Medical Association* 39, no. 5 (September 1947): 220. I am unaware of any military service records that can confirm that Richardson's father was an army medic during World War I. This is because most of the documents concerning soldiers who were discharged from the army during and after World War I were destroyed by a major fire at the National Archives in St. Louis, Missouri, in 1973. See "The 1973 Fire, National Personnel Records Center," National Archives, accessed 17 November 2011, http://www.archives.gov/st-louis/military-personnel/fire-1973.html.

See 1920 US Census, Baltimore Ward 19, Baltimore (Independent City), Maryland, ser. T625, roll 666, p. 4B, Enumeration District 333; City Directories of the

United States, segment IV, 1902–1935, Baltimore, MD, Micro CD 47, year 1920, roll micro 1242, p. 1028, Maryland Historical Society, Baltimore. The directory lists John's address as "613 N Gilmor," but this is likely an error because James M. Hayes's home address and other entries for Hayes list 513. For John Hayes's pharmacy's location at 1059 Lexington Street, see "St. Clair–Hayes," *Afro-Am*, 24 June 1921, 10; advertisement, *Afro-Am*, 11 March 1921, 7.

36. Eleanor S. Bruchey, "The Development of Baltimore Business, 1880–1914," *Maryland Historical Society Magazine* 64, no. 1 (1969): 18–19, 21, 31; Jo Ann E. Argersinger, *Toward a New Deal in Baltimore: People and Government in the Great Depression* (Chapel Hill: University of North Carolina Press, 1988), 2.

37. Argersinger, *Toward a New Deal in Baltimore*, 2, 3, 4; "Help Wanted: Male," *Sun*, 30 October 1902, 3; "Advertisement: Brager Department Store," *Sun*, 18 March 1905, 5.

38. Argersinger, *Toward a New Deal in Baltimore*, 3, 4; Karen Olson, "Old West Baltimore: Segregation, African-American Culture, and the Struggle for Equality," in *The Baltimore Book: New Views of Local History*, ed. Elizabeth Fee, Linda Shopes, and Linda Zeidman (Philadelphia: Temple University Press, 1991), 57, 59; "Mayor Signs West Measure," *Sun*, 8 April 1911, 9; Bruchey, "Industrialization of Maryland: 1860–1914," 396–497; Harold McDougall, *Black Baltimore: A New Theory of Community* (Philadelphia: Temple University Press, 1993), 41; Argersinger, *Toward a New Deal in Baltimore*, 4; Susanne E. Green, "Black Republicans on the Baltimore City Council, 1890–1931," *Maryland Historical Magazine* 74 (September 1979): 203, 204–7, 211, 213, 214, 219.

39. "Cambridge," *Afro-Am*, 5 September 1919, 6; "Dr. Jackson Kicked Out," *Afro-Am*, 16 October 1920, 1; "Monster Mass Meeting," *Afro-Am*, 11 November 1921, 14; "Large Crowds at Health Meetings," *Afro-Am*, 7 April 1922, 6; "Bar Association Elects Officers," *Afro-Am*, 7 March 1925, 10; "Notes from Baltimore," *Chicago Defender*, 18 August 1928, A11; "Reception to Doctors' Wives Season's Most Brilliant Affair," *Afro-Am*, 25 August 1928, 10; "St. Clair–Hayes," *Afro-Am*, 24 June 1921, 10; "Councilman St. Clair's Daughter Married," *Afro-Am*, 1 July 1921, 10; "In the Society Whirl," *Afro-Am*, 1 July 1921, 10. The address of the home was 910 Stricker Street; see City Directories of the United States, segment IV, 1902–1935, Baltimore, MD, Micro CD 49, year 1922, roll micro 1244, p. 915; 1930 US Census, Baltimore (Independent City), Maryland, roll 860, p. 12A, Enumeration District 258. For John's pharmacy, see City Directories of the United States; "New Incorporations," *Afro-Am*, 12 August 1921, 6; display ads, *Sun*, 18 July 1922, 12, and 21 September 1923, 7; advertisement, *Afro-Am*, 7 March 1924, 10. For Provident Hospital and Hayes's work there, see Robert L. Jackson and Emerson C. Walden, "A History of Provident Hospital, Baltimore, Maryland," *Journal of the National Medical Association* 59, no. 3 (May 1967): 157–59, 161, 164; "Maryland News," *Chicago Defender*, 9 July 1932, 12; Jessica I. Elfenbein, *The Making of a Modern City: Philanthropy, Civic Culture, and the Baltimore YMCA* (Gainesville: University Press of Florida, 2001), 58–60, 63–64, 67, 70–71. The Y's address was 1619 Druid Hill Avenue. For more information on the Druid Hill district and Baltimore's cultural scene, see Gatewood, *Aristocrats of Color*, 77; McDougall, *Black Baltimore*, 42; Stuart L. Goosman, *Group Harmony: The Black Urban Roots of Rhythm & Blues* (Philadelphia: University of

Pennsylvania Press, 2005), 3–5; GR, interviews with JRF, 14 September 2002, 28 March 2005; GR, emails to JRF, 30 June 2010, 4 November 2011.

40. "Royal Offers Attractive Bills," *Afro-Am*, 23 January 1926, 6; "Dance Halls," *Afro-Am*, 9 October 1926, 7; "In Dance Halls," *Afro-Am*, 15 September 1928, 12; "Dance Halls," *Afro-Am*, 22 December 1928, 16; "Go to the New Albert Monday Night," *Afro-Am*, 19 October 1929, A9; Olson, "Old West Baltimore," 65; "Society," *Afro-Am*, 20 April 1923, 7; "Bar Association Elects Officers," *Afro-Am*, 7 March 1925, 10; "Society," *Afro-Am*, 20 February 1926, 14; "The Novelty Club," *Afro-Am*, 27 February 1926, 18; "Fashionable Events Feature Week's Social Activities," *Afro-Am*, 7 May 1927, 13; "Society," *Afro-Am*, 11 February 1928, 15; "Pat to Pansy: Martha Harmon Entertains Friends," *Afro-Am*, 11 August 1928, 17; "Notes from Baltimore," *Chicago Defender*, 18 August 1928, A11; "Reception to Doctors' Wives Season's Most Brilliant Affair," *Afro-Am*, 25 August 1928, 10; "Pat to Pansy," *Afro-Am*, 8 September 1928, 14; "Clara Robinson's Birthday Party," *Afro-Am*, 24 November 1928, 17; "Pat to Pansy: Xaveria Gordon's Lovely Party," *Afro-Am*, 26 January 1929, 13; "Pat to Pansy," *Afro-Am*, 16 February 1929, 15; "Pat to Pansy," *Afro-Am*, 2 March 1929, 15; "Pat to Pansy," *Afro-Am*, 16 March 1929, 13; "Pat to Pansy," *Afro-Am*, 23 March 1929, 15; "Pat to Pansy," *Afro-Am*, 24 August 1929, 17; "At Home with Parents," *Afro-Am*, 31 August 1929, 17; "Mrs. Edward Fisher's Party," *Afro-Am*, 26 October 1929, A17; "Pat to Pansy," *Afro-Am*, 1 February 1930, A12; "Pat to Pansy," *Afro-Am*, 15 February 1930, 13; "Pat to Pansy," *Afro-Am*, 1 March 1930, 13; "Pat to Pansy," *Afro-Am*, 7 June 1930, 18; "Happy Pals' Industrial Club of Y.W.C.A. Gives Pretty Party," *Afro-Am*, 21 June 1930, A5; "Druggist Buried in Cambridge," *Afro-Am*, 17 December 1946, 3.

2. Get Up, Stand Up

1. "State Accorded Distinction Again," *DB*, 6 May 1922, 1, 2.

2. "Weather," *NYT*, 7 May 1922, 30; Gloria St. Clair Hayes Richardson's birth certificate, recorded on 15 May 1922, copy in author's possession; "Physicians [Doubt?] Afro's Camel Story," *Afro-Am*, 25 August 1922, 14; GR, interviews with JRF, 14 September 2002, 2 August 2003.

3. GR, interviews with JRF, 14 September 2002, 2 August 2003, 30 October 2004, 28 March 2005, 19 June 2005; GR, emails to JRF, 24 February 2010, 30 September 2011, 3 November 2011; "Asst. Supervisors Named for Schools," *Afro-Am*, 10 April 1926, 10; "22 of 35 Baltimore Public Schools Have Never Been Christened," *Afro-Am*, 17 January 1931, 16; "19 Schools Have Been Named," *Afro-Am*, 19 March 1932, 20 (school 119 was named for the *Afro-American*'s John H. Murphy Sr.); "Baltimore's Juvenile Society Is Entertained at Edgewater," *Afro-Am*, 20 July 1929, 13; "Pat to Pansy," *Afro-Am*, 20 July 1929, 17; "Randolph Waters, Junior's Tenth Birthday Party," *Afro-Am*, 14 December 1929, A17; "Elaborate Birthday Party Tendered Little Doris Buckner," *Afro-Am*, 29 March 1930, A13; "Junior Social Notes," *Afro-Am*, 24 September 1932, 19.

4. GR, interview with JRF, 30 October 2004; GR, emails to JRF, 19 June 2005, 23 October 2009, 16 June 2010, 30 June 2010, 1 November 2011, 6 March 2012;

"Pat to Pansy," *Afro-Am*, 3 August 1929, 17; "Pat to Pansy," *Afro-Am*, 23 August 1930, 19.

5. James W. Hayes died in 1925. See Wright, "Hayes Family Research Summary," 10. Also see Mecklenburg County Deed Book 94, p. 415, Mecklenburg County Courthouse, Boydton, VA. Bettie Hayes died on December 26, 1926. See Bureau of Vital Statistics, Death Certificate*s* (post-1912), 1926, December (Carroll–York) and delayed volumes, V:897–902, certificates 28287–30967, accession 36390, reel 155, Library of Virginia, Richmond. At one point, Helen Salene lived with Richardson's family in Baltimore. Truly Hayes and his family lived in Hampton, Virginia, where he worked as a carpentry instructor at Hampton Institute. See GR, interview with JRF, 14 September 2002; GR, emails to JRF, 18 October 2010, 6 September 2011, 5 December 2011. For Truly Hayes's work at Hampton Institute, see *Southern Workman* 66, no. 11 (November 1937): 359.

For Richardson's family's travels, see "Cambridge," *Afro-Am*, 2 December 1921, 7; "Society," *Afro-Am*, 20 July 1923, 6; "Society," *Afro-Am*, 21 September 1923, A6; "Cambridge, MD," *Afro-Am*, 18 July 1925, A15; "Balto. Society Folk Recall All Socials," *Afro-Am*, 27 August 1927, 13; "Personals," *Afro-Am*, 3 September 1927, 11; "Cambridge, MD," *Afro-Am*, 10 September 1927, 6; "Baltimore, Md.," *New York Amsterdam News*, 16 November 1927, 18; "At Home with Parents," *Afro-Am*, 31 August 1929, 17; "Pat to Pansy," *Afro-Am*, 2 August 1930, A12; GR, interviews with JRF, 30 October 2004, 17 July 2010.

One family visit in the late 1920s stands out to Richardson, and it shows how well connected her family was. Her uncles Frederick and Herbert St. Clair and her cousin Carroll St. Clair were enjoying an evening of alcohol-induced revelry on Stricker Street (even though it was during Prohibition). Their partying was so loud that someone called the police, and when they arrived, Richardson's father dropped the name "Tom Smith." Richardson recalled that it was "like a magic name" because once the police heard it, they left without issuing a summons or making an arrest. For almost eight decades Richardson thought Smith must have been a judge her father knew, but recently she learned he was actually Thomas R. Smith, a black kingpin in Baltimore's illegal gambling world and a power broker in its political scene, a man who could make or break police officers' careers. See GR, interviews with JRF, 25 July 2008, 17 July 2010; Smith, *Here Lies Jim Crow*, 107, 114, 117–19. This event may have occurred in 1928, when Herbert was a recent Lincoln University graduate and Carroll was an intern at Provident Hospital. See "Pat to Pansy," *Afro-Am*, 19 October 1929, A17; Jackson and Walden, "History of Provident Hospital," 161.

6. GR, interviews with JRF, 2 August 2003, 30 October 2004, 25 July 2008, 17 July 2010; GR, email to JRF, 1 November 2011; "Cambridge, MD," *Afro-Am*, 10 January 1925, 11.

7. GR, interviews with JRF, 20 June 2007, 25 July 2008; GR, email to JRF, 16 October 2009; "Raymond Pace Alexander, Biographical Sketch," University of Pennsylvania Archives and Records Center, accessed 18 December 2011, http://www.archives.upenn.edu/faids/upt/upt50/alexander_rpa.html. Sadie Alexander was the first black American woman to earn a doctorate, as well as the first black woman to graduate from the University of Pennsylvania's law school. See "Sadie Tanner Mossell Alexander, Biographical Sketch," University of Pennsylvania Archives and Records

Center, accessed 18 December 2011, http://www.archives.upenn.edu/faids/upt/upt50/alexander_stma.html; David A. Canton, *Raymond Pace Alexander: A New Negro Lawyer Fights for Civil Rights in Philadelphia* (Jackson: University Press of Mississippi, 2010), 35–36. See also "History of Highland Beach," Town of Highland Beach, MD, accessed 13 December 2011, http://highlandbeachmd.org/; Gatewood, *Aristocrats of Color*, 77.

Richardson went to Camp Atwater, which is located just outside of East Brookfield, Massachusetts. The *Afro-American* described Atwater as the "best known in the country, and best equipped," and it was the camp of choice for parents from New York, Baltimore, and Washington, DC, who wanted their children to experience the great outdoors. Because she was frightened by the numerous snakes around the camp, Richardson attended for only one or two summers. "No Dresses for a Month," *Afro-Am*, 12 September 1931, 20; "How They Do It at Camp Atwater," *Afro-Am*, 20 August 1932, 20; "116 Girls at Camp Atwater," *Afro-Am*, 20 August 1932, 8; GR, interview with JRF, 19 June 2005; GR, emails to JRF, 1 June 2010, 16 June 2010, 3 November 2011.

8. Gatewood, *Aristocrats of Color*, 248; GR, interviews with JRF, 2 August 2003, 20 June 2007; GR, emails to JRF, 16 June 2010, 6 June 2012; Gloria Richardson, "The Energy of the People Passing through Me," in *Hands on the Freedom Plow: Personal Accounts by Women in SNCC*, ed. Faith S. Holsaert et al. (Champaign: University of Illinois, 2010), 274.

9. GR, interview with Ja A. Jahannes, 8 April 1988; GR, interviews with JRF, 14 September 2002, 2 August 2003, 19 June 2005, 20 June 2007; "Cambridge Free Library to Open Next Week," *DB*, 9 May 1922, 2.

10. Argersinger, *Toward a New Deal in Baltimore*, 1, 8. There is no listing for James M. Hayes in the 1929 and 1930 directories. See City Directories of the United States, segment IV, 1902–1935, Baltimore, MD, Maryland Historical Society. For James M. Hayes and his family's migration to Newport News, Virginia, and their presence in that city in 1930, see 1930 US Census. Newport News, Newport News (Independent City), Virginia, roll 2469, p. 13A, Enumeration District 13. Younger brother Lawrence was also living with James and his family in Newport News. For Cambridge's lack of a black pharmacist, see Mary Annetta St. Clair Wesley, interview with JRF, 28 October 2004; GR, interviews with JRF, 2 August 2003, 30 October 2004. Wesley, a cousin of Richardson's, grew up in Cambridge.

11. Levy, *Civil War on Race Street*, 21; David Henry, *Up Pine Street: A Pictorial History of the African American Community of Cambridge, Maryland 1884–1951*, vol. 1 (Woodstock, MD: David Henry, 2003); "Cambridge Opens New Playground," *Afro-Am*, 30 August 1930, A13; "Pat to Pansy," *Afro-Am*, 7 February 1931, 19; "Pat to Pansy," *Afro-Am*, 14 March 1931, 8.

12. GR, email to JRF, 9 March 2012. Richardson said her family read the *Baltimore News-Post* and *Baltimore Sun* more often than the *Banner*. See "Record Crabbing Season Expected," *DB*, 23 March 1931, 1; "Chesapeake Bridge Is Recommended," *DB*, 11 March 1931, 1; American Legion advertisement, *DB*, 12 March 1931, 3.

13. GR, interview with JRF, 17 July 2010; "Maryland State," *Chicago Defender* (national ed.), 16 January 1932, 17; "Pat to Pansy," *Afro-Am*, 6 February 1932, 22. Mable Hayes was a sponsor of Cambridge's Sophisticates Club.

14. Richardson's grandfather also used initials when signing his name. GR, interviews with JRF, 14 September 2002, 30 October 2004, 19 June 2005, 17 July 2010; GR, email to JRF, 2 November 2009.

15. GR, interviews with JRF, 14 September 2002, 2 August 2003, 17 July 2010; H. M. St. Clair quoted in Richardson, "Energy of the People Passing through Me," 280.

16. GR, interview with Ja A. Jahannes; GR, emails to JRF, 20 December 2011, 9 March 2012; GR, interviews with JRF, 14 September 2002, 2 August 2003, 30 October 2004; Richardson, "Energy of the People Passing through Me," 273–74.

17. Richardson does not recall ever being required to read an etiquette book, which were popular among her family's socioeconomic group. GR, interviews with JRF, 14 September 2002, 2 August 2003, 30 October 2004; GR, email to JRF, 16 June 2010. See Gatewood, *Aristocrats of Color*, 183.

18. GR, interview with JRF, 30 October 2004; GR, radio interview with Dick Gordon, 16 January 2009; Richardson, "Energy of the People Passing through Me," 274. Also see Gloria Richardson, book proposal, 9. Richardson wrote a cover letter for this proposal, dated 7 November 1967, in which she states that the manuscript proposal was "done last spring." I understand this to mean that she completed it in the spring of 1967. Also see GR, interview with Ja A. Jahannes; GR, interview with JRF, 14 September 2002.

19. GR, interviews with JRF, 14 September 2002, 30 October 2004. For two sources that discuss functional segregation without actually using the term, see Askia Muhammad, "The Benefits of Brown . . . but at What Cost?" BET.com, 18 May 2004, accessed 24 February 2005, http:/msnbc.msn.com/id/5006732/print/1/displaymode/1098/; "Veterinary Medicine: The Most Racially Segregated Field in Graduate Education Today," *Journal of Blacks in Higher Education* 42 (online ed.), accessed 24 February 2005, http:/www.jbhe.com/news_views/42_veterinary_schools.html.

20. GR, interview with JRF, 30 October 2004.

21. Jennifer Ritterhouse, *Growing up Jim Crow: How Black and White Children Learned Race* (Chapel Hill: University of North Carolina Press, 2006), 44, 82–83; Smith, *Here Lies Jim Crow*, 98, 104.

22. Ritterhouse, *Growing up Jim Crow*, 44, 82–83; Smith, *Here Lies Jim Crow*, 157–58. The store that sent clothes to the St. Clairs was Richardson's Style Shop (no relation). Richardson also wrote that after World War II, many of Cambridge's white store owners jettisoned their rule against black people trying on clothes. GR, interview with JRF, 25 July 2008; GR, emails to JRF, 30 September 2011, 7 November 2011.

23. Ritterhouse, *Growing up Jim Crow*, 190–93; GR, interview with JRF, 14 September 2002.

24. "Church as Usual for Godfearing Sho' Lynchers," *Afro-Am*, 12 December 1931, 1; "Eye Witness to Lynching Tells How Mob Acted," *Afro-Am*, 12 December 1931, 1, 2; "Doctor Deserts Home after Seeing Mob," *Afro-Am*, 12 December 1931, 1, 2; "Cambridge, MD," *Afro-Am*, 8 October 1927, 16; GR, interview with JRF, 14 September 2002; GR, email to JRF, 19 May 2010.

25. "Attacker Slain and Burned in Maryland," *WP*, 19 October 1933, 1; Clarence Mitchell, "Mob Members Knew Prey Was Feeble-Minded," *Afro-Am*, 28 October 1933, 3; GR, interview with JRF, 17 August 2002.

26. Henry J. McGuinn, "Equal Protection of the Law and Fair Trials in Maryland," *Journal of Negro History* 24, no. 2 (April 1939): 159; GR, interview with JRF, 14 September 2002. I was unable to identify the ex-convict or the event Richardson recalled.

27. "Five States' Guests at Cambridge Ball," *Afro-Am*, 27 February 1932, 19; "Fiancée at Bier of Cambridge Attorney," *Afro-Am*, 8 October 1932, 15; "Cambridge Lawyer Dies at Hospital," *DB*, 28 September 1932, 5; "Colored Lawyer Buried Yesterday," *DB*, 3 October 1932, 5; GR, interviews with JRF, 14 September 2002, 12 April 2012.

28. GR, interviews with JRF, 14 September 2002, 2 August 2003, 17 July 2010, 22 February 2012; Robert Ford (parish administrator at St. James Episcopal Church), email to JRF, 30 September 2009. Ford wrote: "On page 40, in the 1934 *Yearbook and Church Directory of St. James' First African Episcopal Church*, the Communicant Membership list shows a Dr. J. E. Hayes and a Mrs. Mabel Hayes as members who now live in Cambridge Maryland." For information on St. James and Mable's work there, see Gatewood, *Aristocrats of Color*, 74–75; "Maryland: Cambridge, MD," *Afro-Am*, 9 January 1926, 16; "Churches Open Bible Vacation Schools," *Afro-Am*, 5 July 1930, A12; "St. James Junior Choir to Appear in Recital," *Afro-Am*, 29 November 1930, 20.

29. Richardson does not recall attending Sunday school at St. James Church in Baltimore. See GR, interviews with JRF, 14 September 2002, 2 August 2003, 17 July 2010.

30. GR, interviews with JRF, 14 September 2002, 17 July 2010. For black humanism, see Anthony B. Pinn, *African American Humanist Principles: Living and Thinking Like the Children of Nimrod* (New York: Palgrave Macmillan, 2004), 13–22, 27–28; Norm R. Allen, ed., *African-American Humanism: An Anthology* (Buffalo, NY: Prometheus Books, 1991), pt. 2, chaps. 7–12.

31. GR, interviews with JRF, 14 September 2002, 20 March 2004, 24 July 2004, 28 March 2005, 17 July 2010. According to Richardson, her uncle Herbert was a biology and chemistry teacher at the high school.

32. GR, interviews with JRF, 14 September 2002, 30 October 2004; GR, email to JRF, 30 September 2011. John Hayes used corporal punishment on Gloria only once. His preferred method of discipline was to talk with his daughter and explain why she was wrong to disobey her parents. "I would go through hell to keep from having one of those lectures," she said.

33. "School Named for Him," *Afro-Am*, 10 December 1932, 22. Interestingly, Richardson does not recall ever hearing about Booker T. Washington or Black Nationalist Marcus Garvey. She first learned of Garvey after moving to New York City in the mid-1960s. GR, interviews with JRF, 14 September 2002, 2 August 2003, 24 July 2004, 31 August 2004, 28 March 2005, 17 July 2012. Richardson's transcript from Howard University (copy in author's possession) contains a section that lists some of the courses she took in high school, including a half-credit course in "Negro History." Also see GR, interview with Ja A. Jahannes.

34. Richardson graduated with an "Academic Course" diploma. The other course of education at Frederick D. St. Clair High School was "General Course." See "County Schools to Graduate 225," *DB*, 21 May 1938, 1; GR, interviews with JRF,

14 September 2002, 2 August 2003, 30 October 2004, 17 July 2010; GR, emails to JRF, 2 November 2009, 1 and 3 November 2011, 23 August 2012.

35. GR, interviews with JRF, 14 September 2002, 2 August 2003, 30 October 2004; GR, email to JRF, 2 November 2009.

3. Capital Gains

1. GR, interviews with JRF, 14 September 2002, 2 August 2003, 30 October 2004, 19 June 2005; Richardson, "Energy of the People Passing through Me," 276.

2. GR, interviews with JRF, 2 August 2003, 24 July 2004, 17 July 2010.

3. GR, interviews with JRF, 14 September 2002, 2 August 2003, 30 October 2004, 17 July 2010.

4. James D. Anderson, *The Education of Blacks in the South, 1860–1935* (Chapel Hill: University of North Carolina Press, 1988), 244; Clifford L. Muse Jr., "Howard University and the Federal Government during the Presidential Administrations of Herbert Hoover and Franklin Delano Roosevelt, 1928–1945," *Journal of Negro History* 76, no. 1 (Winter–Autumn 1991): 1–2, 4, 5–8, 11; Howard University advertisement, *Crisis*, August 1938, 252; David Levering Lewis, *W. E. B. Du Bois: The Fight for Equality and the American Century, 1919–1963* (New York: Henry Holt, 2000), 138, 450.

5. Marybeth Gasman et al., "Unearthing Promise and Potential: Our Nation's Historically Black Colleges and Universities," in *Association for the Study of Higher Education Report 35, no. 5* (Somerset, NJ: John Wiley & Sons, 2010), 5–9; Anderson, *Education of Blacks in the South*, chap. 2.

6. E. Franklin Frazier, "A Note on Negro Education," *Opportunity*, March 1924, 75–77; Carter G. Woodson, *The Mis-education of the Negro* (Trenton, NJ: Africa World Press, 1990), 52; W. E. B. Du Bois, "The Negro College," *Crisis* 41 (August 1933): 175–77; Lewis, *W. E. B. Du Bois, 1919–1963*, 134, 139–45; George Streator, "Negro College Radicals," *Crisis* 41 (February 1934): 47; Langston Hughes, "Cowards from the Colleges," *Crisis* 41 (August 1934): 226–28. Also see W. Edward Farrison, "Negro Scholarship," *Crisis* 41 (February 1934): 33–34.

7. For Richardson's coursework by semester, see Gloria Richardson, Howard University transcript (copy in author's possession). For the names of most of her freshman year's professors, see *Howard University Bulletin: Annual Catalogue 1938–1939*, vol. 18, 30 April 1939, 14, 124, 145, 147, Moorland-Spingarn Research Center, Howard University. See also GR, interview with JRF, 19 June 2005; Jonathan Scott Holloway, *Confronting the Veil: Abram Harris Jr., E. Franklin Frazier, and Ralph Bunche, 1919–1941* (Chapel Hill: University of North Carolina Press, 2001), 158; Brian Urquhart, *Ralph Bunche: An American Life* (New York: W. W. Norton, 1993), 56–57; press release, Lincoln University, Office of Marketing, accessed 9 March 2010, http://www.lincoln.edu/marketing/pr/news0429043.html; Ahmad Rahman, *The Regime Change of Kwame Nkrumah: Epic Heroism in Africa and the Diaspora* (Basingstoke, UK: Palgrave Macmillan, 2007), 179, 221n3. Nkrumah had become friends with Bunche in the late-1930s, when the former was finishing his last year at Lincoln University and began visiting the Howard campus.

8. GR, interviews with JRF, 2 August 2003, 19 June 2005. Richardson took three courses with Logan. See Richardson's transcript; *Howard University Bulletin: Annual Catalogue 1939–1940*, vol. 19, 15 May 1940, 18, 133; *Howard University Bulletin: Annual Catalogue 1940–1941*, vol. 20, 15 May 1941, 18, 141; *Howard University Bulletin: Annual Catalogue 1941–1942*, vol. 21, 15 May 1942, 17, 160; "'Bad Negro with a Ph.D.,'" *Chicago Defender* (national ed.), 10 July 1943, 20; Kenneth Robert Janken, *Rayford W. Logan and the Dilemma of the African-American Intellectual* (Amherst: University of Massachusetts, 1993), 111, 115, 146–47, 206, 211; Holloway, *Confronting the Veil*, 126.

9. Richardson's transcript; *Howard University Bulletin: Annual Catalogue 1940–1941*, 151; GR, interview with JRF, 17 July 2010; Alain L. Locke, *The New Negro, an Interpretation* (New York: Albert & Charles Boni, 1925); Leonard Harris and Charles Molesworth, *Alain L. Locke: The Biography of a Philosopher* (Chicago: University of Chicago Press, 2008), 139; "Refused to Serve Colored Men," *WP*, 31 August 1901, 3; "A Literary Tribute to Sterling A. Brown," Howard University Libraries, accessed 22 October 2012, http://www.howard.edu/library/reference /guides/SterlingBrown.htm; Sterling A. Brown, "The American Race Problem as Reflected in American Literature," *Journal of Negro Education* 8, no. 3 (July 1939): 275–90; Sterling A. Brown, "Folk Literature," in *The Negro Caravan*, ed. Sterling A. Brown, Arthur P. Davis, and Ulysses Lee (New York: Dryden Press, 1941), sec. 4; Joyce A. A. Camper, "Sterling Brown: Maker of Community in Academia," *African American Review* 31, no. 3 (1997): 437–41.

10. Richardson's transcript; GR, interviews with JRF, 2 August 2003, 24 July 2004, 19 June 2005; *Howard University Bulletin: Annual Catalogue 1939–1940*, 129; *Howard University Bulletin: Annual Catalogue 1941–1942*, 154; *Howard University Bulletin: Annual Catalogue 1940–1941*, 137; *Howard University Bulletin: Annual Catalogue 1941–1942*, 155; Camper, "Sterling Brown," 437–41; Fahamisha Patricia Brown, "And I Owe It All to Sterling Brown: The Theory and Practice of Black Literary Studies," *African American Review* 31, no. 3 (1997): 449–53; Claude McKay, "If We Must Die," in *Let Nobody Turn Us Around: Voices of Resistance, Reform, and Renewal*, ed. Manning Marable and Leith Mullings (New York: Rowman & Littlefield, 2000), 246.

11. GR, interviews with JRF, 14 September 2002, 24 July 2004, 17 July 2010; "80 Given State Scholarships," *Afro-Am*, 12 August 1939, 24; Richardson's transcript; *Howard University Bulletin: Annual Catalogue 1939–1940*, 158.

12. Holloway, *Confronting the Veil*, 137, 152; "E. Franklin Frazier, 1894–1962: Sociologist, Educator, Author, Scholar—A Bio-Bibliography," Howard University, accessed 24 October 2012, http://www.howard.edu/library/social_work_library /Franklin_Frazier.htm; E. Franklin Frazier, "The Pathology of Race Prejudice," *Forum*, June 1927, 856–61; E. Franklin Frazier, *The Negro Family in Chicago* (Chicago: University of Chicago Press, 1932).

13. Holloway, *Confronting the Veil*, 126; GR, interviews with JRF, 2 August 2003, 17 July 2010; GR, interview with Ja A. Jahannes.

14. GR, interview with Ja A. Jahannes; Arthur P. Davis, "E. Franklin Frazier (1894–1962): A Profile," *Journal of Negro Education* 31, no. 4 (Autumn 1962): 433; Richardson's transcript; *Howard University Bulletin: Annual Catalogue 1940–1941*,

168; *Howard University Bulletin: Annual Catalogue 1941–1942*, 110; GR, interviews with JRF, 2 August 2003, 24 July 2004. Richardson said that during her graduate course with Frazier, she helped him with his research on black storefront churches. See GR, interview with Ja A. Jahannes.

15. *Daily Banner*, 9, 12, 15 July 1937; "General Strike Called in Ohio City by C. I. O., Violence in Cambridge," *Sun*, 24 June 1937, 1, 2; "Whites Join Protest which Frees Worker," *Afro-Am*, 3 July 1937, 16; "Home Union Pact Signed by Phillips," *Sun*, 24 July 1937, 4; "Cambridge Union Files Papers Here," *Sun*, 28 July 1937, 4; "Phillips Packing Company Pays Colored Group Million a Year," *Afro-Am*, 28 August 1937, 2; Levy, *Civil War on Race Street*, 22; GR, interview with JRF, 14 September 2002; GR, email to JRF, 29 October 2012.

16. GR, interviews with JRF, 2 August 2003, 17 July 2010. In our July 2010 interview, Richardson implied that she disagreed with the advocates of communism who moved away from the "idealistic" goals of the economic philosophy and used "authoritarian" methods to further communism. For communism and humanism, see Pinn, *African American Humanist Principles*, 28.

17. Reynolds was from Chester, Pennsylvania. She and Richardson were friends before they attended Howard. Upshaw was from East Chicago, Indiana, and Joyner was from North Carolina. See "Chester," *Afro-Am*, 30 March 1935, 18; "Otto McClarrin's Seaboard Merry-Go-Round," *Afro-Am*, 20 July 1940, 12; "Vacationing," *Chicago Defender*, 6 June 1942, 10; GR, interview with JRF, 17 July 2010; Margaret Willis Reynolds, telephone interview with JRF, 16 April 2005. In 1940 Richardson attended Omega fraternity's Mardi Gras dance with Raymond Savory Jr. See "Otto McClarrin's Seaboard Merry-Go-Round," *Afro-Am*, 16 March 1940, 15; GR, interviews with JRF, 14 September 2002, 2 August 2003, 31 August 2004; Edward Brooke, telephone interviews with JRF, 9 August 2007, 23 February 2010.

18. GR, interviews with JRF, 14 September 2002, 31 August 2004, 17 July 2010, 5 December 2011.

19. GR, interviews with JRF, 14 September 2002, 17 July 2010, 5 December 2011. Richardson dated men of all shades of blackness—from light to dark. For Carter's life and careers, see "W. Beverly Carter, the Reluctant Hero," *WP*, 13 May 1975, B13, B15; "Diplomat, Newsman W. Beverly Carter Jr., 61, Dies," *WP*, 10 May 1982, B4; "Beverly Carter, U.S. Diplomat Dead at 61," *Afro-Am*, 15 May 1982, 1; "William Beverly Carter (1921–1982)," Office of the Historian, Bureau of Public Affairs, United States Department of State, accessed 4 November 2012, http://history.state .gov/departmenthistory/people/carter-william-beverly. For Carter's statement that Mable Hayes thought he was "too dark," see Joyce Ladner, email to JRF, 2 November 2012. Carter made the comment to Ladner when she was in Addis Ababa, Ethiopia, in 1973 to attend a conference.

20. GR, interviews with JRF, 14 September 2002, 2 August 2003, 24 July 2004, 30 October 2004, 20 June 2007, 17 July 2010. Bethune had been in Cambridge to deliver a talk at the city's armory. See "Noted Negro Educator to Speak at Cambridge Armory," *DB*, 25 November 1939, 6. For the families' networking, see "Cambridge," *Afro-Am*, 22 October 1938, 22; Kerr, *Paper Bag Principle*, 49.

21. GR, interviews with JRF, 2 August 2003, 24 July 2004, 17 July 2010; Gatewood, *Aristocrats of Color*, 154, chap. 2; Samuel Barrett, "A Plea for Unity," *Colored*

American Magazine 7 (1904): 49, accessed 15 June 2010, http://hdl.handle.net /2027/ucl.b3793664. Another source that chronicles black Washington's color problems is Kerr, *Paper Bag Principle*, 40–41, 54.

22. GR, interviews with JRF, 14 September 2002, 2 August 2003, 24 July 2004, 28 March 2005, 17 July 2010. For another woman's story about colorism in Howard's sororities, see Kerr, *Paper Bag Principle*, 95, 96. For AKA pledging and admission, see "Gala 'George Washington Ball' Given for AKA Aspirants," *Hilltop*, 2 8 February 1939, 4; "AKA Probates Roam Campus," *Hilltop*, 13 April 1939, 6; "Sorority News," *Hilltop*, 20 November 1940, 3; "Alpha Kappa Alpha Briefs," *Hilltop*, 19 December 1941, 9. Richardson is featured in the AKA's group photo in the 1942 edition of Howard University's yearbook, the *Bison*, Moorland-Spingarn Research Center Library.

23. Green, *Secret City*, 243. For segregation in general in DC, see Edward Brooke's and Walter Washington's interviews with the National Visionary Leadership Project, accessed 24 November 2012, http://www.visionaryproject.org/brookeedward/ and http://www.visionaryproject.org/washingtonwalter/. For desegregation of DC's institutions as well as civil rights protests against companies, see Green, *Secret City*, 217–19, 227, 231, 233, 241, 243. The grocery store chains were A & P and Sanitary (later renamed Safeway).

24. "Negro Protest," *WP*, 25 July 1938, X6; "Job Fight in D.C. Won by Picketing," *Chicago Defender* (national ed.), 25 March 1939, 5; "NNA Cites Job Gains from Year of Picketing," *Afro-Am*, 1 July 1939, 28; "Alliance Claims Victory in New Store Opening," *Afro-Am*, 23 September 1939, 24; Walter Washington, interview with the National Visionary Leadership Project; Edward Brooke, interviews with JRF; Edward Brooke, *Bridging the Divide: My Life* (New Brunswick, NJ: Rutgers University Press, 2007), 16.

25. GR, interviews with JRF, 14 September 2002, 2 August 2003, 17 July 2010; Edward Brooke, interviews with JRF; "'Radical' Integrationist," *NYT*, 13 July 1963, 6.

26. GR, interview with Ja A. Jahannes; GR, interview with JRF, 17 July 2010; "Challenges Segregation at Washington Terminal," *Afro-Am*, 18 April 1942, 10. According to Richardson, the glove incident probably occurred at Woodard & Lothrop department store.

27. GR, interview with Ja A. Jahannes. Also see GR, interview with JRF, 17 July 2010; GR, email to JRF, 19 December 2012; Patricia J. Williams, "Spirit-murdering the Messenger: The Discourse of Finger-pointing as the Law's Response to Racism," in *Critical Race Feminism*, ed. Adrien Katherine Wing (New York: NYU Press, 1997), 234.

28. GR, interview with John Britton, 11 October 1967; GR, interviews with JRF, 14 September 2002, 2 August 2003, 20 June 2007, 17 July 2010; GR, email to JRF, 20 November 2012; Margaret Willis Reynolds, interview with JRF; "All Silent Anent Picket of Howard Dean," *Chicago Defender* (national ed.), 31 May 1941, 4; "H.U. Women Strike; Dean Called Hitler," *Afro-Am*, 31 May 1941, 23.

29. GR, interviews with JRF, 2 August 2003, 17 July 2010; "Overheard in the Capital," *Afro-Am*, 21 March 1942, 16.

30. Clifford L. Muse Jr., "The Howard University Players," Howard University, February 2001, accessed 16 December 2009, http://www.huarchivesnet.howard

.edu/howarcorSketch1.htm; "Howard Players Present Drama," *Hilltop*, 21 April 1941, 1; "Howard Players Booked May 9," *WP*, 4 May 1941, L9; program for *Kind Lady* by Edward Chodorov, directed by Ella H. Weaver, Howard Players, 9 May 1941, Moorland-Spingarn Research Center Archives, box Dept. of Theatrical Arts: Howard Players, folder Howard Players Programs, 1939, 1941. For Richardson's directorial work in *The Male Animal*, see the *Bison* (Howard University's yearbook), 1942, Moorland-Spingarn Research Center Library; *Howard University Bulletin: Annual Catalogue 1941–1942*, 153; GR, interview with Ja A. Jahannes; GR, interviews with JRF, 24 July 2004, 17 July 2010.

31. GR, interviews with JRF, 14 September 2002, 2 August 2003, 19 June 2005, 20 June 2007, 17 July 2010. For Richardson's Spanish 2 course (taught by Ben Frederick Caruthers) and her failing grade, see Richardson's transcript; *Howard University Bulletin: Annual Catalogue 1941–1942*, 181.

32. "Howard Marks Anniversary with Festival," *WP*, 16 May 1942, 23.

4. Dreams Deferred

1. GR, interview with JRF, 24 July 2004.

2. "Vacationing," *Chicago Defender*, 6 June 1942, 10; GR, interview with JRF, 20 June 2007.

3. "College Youth Hopeful in War," *NYT*, 22 March 1942, D6; "Overheard in the Capital," *Afro-Am*, 28 March 1942, 17; GR, interviews with JRF, 24 July 2004, 17 July 2010; GR, email to JRF, 21 March 2011.

4. "Mrs. Hobby Named Director of WAAC," *NYT*, 16 May 1942, 15; "Qualifications for WAAC Chiefs Listed," *WP*, 18 May 1942, 15; "Women Here Rush for Army Service," *NYT*, 19 May 1942, 16; "WAAC Rolls Not Yet Opened, but Recruits Flock in Here," *WP*, 22 May 1942, 14; "40 Women to Be Sent to WAAC," *Afro-Am*, 23 May 1942, 1, 2; James G. Thompson, "Should I Sacrifice to Live 'Half-American'?" *Pittsburgh Courier*, 31 January 1942, 3; GR, interviews with JRF, 2 August 2003, 20 March 2004.

5. GR, interviews with JRF, 2 August 2003, 20 March 2004; GR, emails to JRF, 7 August 2013, 15 August 2013.

6. GR, interviews with JRF, 2 August 2003, 24 July 2004; GR, email to JRF, 16 October 2009; GR, interview with Robert Penn Warren, 2 March 1964. For Roy Ellis's work as a civil servant, see "Capital Spotlight," *Afro-Am*, 4 July 1942, 4; "USES Post May Go to Woman," *Afro-Am*, 27 April 1946, 12.

7. Her last work site was the Office of Price Administration. GR, interview with JRF, 17 July 2010.

8. "Old and New Meet Beside Choptank in Pleasant and Bustling Cambridge," *Sun*, 23 December 1945, A1.

9. "H. M. St. Clair Died This Morning," *DB*, 12 April 1949, 1; Richardson, book proposal, 9; GR, interviews with JRF, 14 September 2002, 19 June 2005.

10. GR, interviews with JRF, 14 September 2002, 2 August 2003, 24 July 2004, 19 June 2005, 17 July 2010.

11. GR, interview with Ja A. Jahannes.

12. GR, interviews with JRF, 2 August 2003, 24 July 2004, 17 July 2010.
13. "Sun Calendar," *Sun*, 25 February 1945, 41; marriage certificate of Gloria St. Clair Hayes and Harry Donald Richardson, accession MSA SC 5458-104-4375, Maryland State Archives, Annapolis (copy in author's possession); GR, interview with Ja A. Jahannes; GR, interviews with JRF, 17 July 2010, 24 July 2004. Fannie St. Clair died on 6 April 1945 (copy of death certificate in author's possession).
14. GR, email to JRF, 30 June 2010; GR, interview with JRF, 17 July 2010; Jackson and Walden, "History of Provident Hospital," 159. About six weeks before Donna was born, Gloria went to Baltimore to live with family friends Ethel and Amos Blake until she gave birth. Berkley Butler was Richardson's doctor in Baltimore; he was a friend of her parents and her cousin Carroll St. Clair.
15. GR, interview with JRF, 17 July 2010; GR, email to JRF, 30 September 2011; Donna Richardson, telephone interview with JRF, 31 January 2008; Tamara Richardson, telephone interview with JRF, 13 June 2009; Charlayne Hunter Gault, "Heirs to a Legacy of Struggle: Charlayne Hunter Integrates the University of Georgia," in *Sisters in the Struggle: African-American Women in the Civil Rights–Black Power Movement*, ed. Bettye Collier-Thomas and V. P. Franklin (New York: NYU Press, 2001), 76.
16. "Cop Jailed in Killing of Fellow Officer, Wounding of Physician," *Afro-Am*, 22 March 1947, 1, 2; "Officer Who Killed Fellow Policeman Given Ten Years," *Afro-Am*, 31 May 1947, 13; "If You Ask Me," *Afro-Am*, 10 August 1957, 12; Donna Richardson, interview with JRF; Tamara Richardson, interview with JRF; GR, interviews with JRF, 30 October 2004, 20 June 2007; Barbara Elizabeth Wesley Lassiter, interview with JRF, 28 October 2004; Jacqueline Fassett, telephone interview with JRF, 3 May 2012. Incidentally, Jackie Fassett told me that Richardson was the only person in the Second Ward with whom she had a deep connection, and it was based in large part on a desire to fight the city's racial caste system. The Fassetts moved from Cambridge to Baltimore in the summer of 1957, but Dr. Fassett kept his office in Cambridge for some time afterward. See "If You Ask Me," *Afro-Am*, 10 August 1957, 12.
17. John Edward Hayes's death certificate, Maryland State Archives, Annapolis; "Druggist Buried in Cambridge," *Afro-Am*, 17 December 1946, 3; "Colored Lawyer Buried Yesterday," *DB*, 3 October 1932, 5; "All Units Held Integrated at Cambridge Hospital," *WP*, 16 July 1965, A8; GR, interview with JRF, 14 September 2002.
18. "Prominent Doctor Passes Away," *DB*, 2 April 1948, 5; "H. M. St. Clair Hurt in Auto Crash," *DB*, 11 April 1949, 1; "H. M. St. Clair Died This Morning," *DB*, 12 April 1949, 1. St. Clair's death certificate (copy in author's possession) states that he died from an "intracranial injury" resulting from a fractured skull. The accident occurred near Millington, Maryland. Gloria's daughter Donna was also in the car. Cambridge City Council meeting minutes, 13 April 1949, Book 1943–1949, p. 354, Cambridge City Hall, Cambridge, MD; "Ex-Councilman Buried in Md.," *Afro-Am*, 23 April 1949, 2; GR, interviews with JRF, 2 August 2003, 30 October 2004, 12 April 2012; Donna Richardson, interview with JRF.
19. Advertisement, *Afro-Am*, 27 September 1947, 11; "Round about the Town: Mossell-Gaines Nuptials," *Afro-Am*, 1 December 1917, 3; "One Man's Family Tree," *Afro-Am*, 7 February 1953, 22L; GR, interview with Ja A. Jahannes; GR, interviews with JRF, 25 July 2008, 17 July 2010, 12 April 2012; GR, emails to JRF, 19 December

2012, 7 August 2013. One of the pharmacists was Aaron Mossell, a brother of Sadie T. Alexander; the other was a "Dr. Swain."

20. GR, interviews with JRF, 19 June 2005, 17 July 2010; Donna Richardson, interview with JRF; Tamara Richardson, interview with JRF. Richardson thought Tamara's story about her mother throwing a glass was probably true.

21. For the Richardsons' divorce decree, see Dorchester County Circuit Court (Maryland) (Equity Papers), 1958–1959, OR/08/14/030, box 181, case number list 8871–8932, MSA T2318–127, Maryland State Archives, Annapolis. The divorce papers do not contain allegations of infidelity against either party. Also see Tamara Richardson, interview with JRF; GR, interview with Ja A. Jahannes.

22. Jacqueline Fassett, interview with JRF.

23. Established in the mid-1870s by Alexander Crummell, a black Episcopal priest, St. Luke's congregation always included prominent members of the city's black community. Richardson's friend Edward Brooke and his family were parishioners, as were Roy and Ida Ellis. Richardson joined St. Luke's not because she subscribed to its theology but because getting confirmed was "fashionable," and belonging to the parish offered her networking opportunities. The latter was particularly important to Richardson because she planned to live in Washington after college and believed that belonging to St. Luke's would increase her job prospects. See Kerr, *Paper Bag Principle*, 105; "The Private Life of Edward Brooke," *Reading (PA) Eagle*, 16 July 1975, 28; Virginia Brown-Nolan (St. Luke's rector), telephone interview with JRF, 25 February 2010; GR, interview with JRF, 17 July 2010.

24. Richardson had Donna baptized only because it was what Fannie St. Clair wanted. See GR, email to JRF, 16 June 2010; Gloria and Harry Richardson's marriage certificate; Book of Marriages for 1945" and "1922–1969 Baptisms, Confirmations and Burials of Great Choptank Parish," Christ Episcopal Church, Cambridge, MD. Information about the Richardsons' marriage and church attendance and Donna's baptism came from Robin Abbott (parish administrator at Christ Episcopal Church), emails to JRF, 1 and 2 March 2010.

25. GR, interview with Ja A. Jahannes; GR, interview with JRF, 17 July 2010; GR, email to JRF, 9 May 2012; Donna Richardson, interview with JRF; Tamara Richardson, interview with JRF; Jacqueline Fassett, interview with JRF.

26. "If You Ask Me: Cambridge—A Friendly City," *Afro-Am*, 21 August 1954, 26; "Chesapeake Span Opened to Traffic," *NYT*, 31 July 1952, 25; "Cambridge Fire Hits Legion Hall," *Sun*, 19 February 1955, 24; "Giving the Professional Touch," *Sun*, 8 March 1960, 12.

27. "Bill Ending Segregation Due State Senate Vote Today," *Sun*, 24 March 1955, 36, 22; "Rights," *Afro-Am*, 2 April 1955, 14; "Jim Crow: U.S. Appeals Court Ends State, City Beach Segregation," *Afro-Am*, 26 March 1955, 14.

28. The only time Richardson noticed white people staring at them was when Banton was mistaken for a famous opera singer. GR, interview with JRF, 17 July 2010. The quote about "feeling perfectly normal and human" is from "Negro Lauds Life in 'Free' Canada," *Montreal Gazette*, 18 July 1963, 2; all others are from Richardson, "Energy of the People Passing through Me," 275. At the time of their trip, Banton was a nationally recognized leader in the field of social work; she was employed as superintendent of the Kruse School, a reformatory for black girls just outside of

Wilmington, Delaware. Her maiden name was Nicholson, and she graduated from Baltimore's Colored High School in 1922. In the late 1920s Banton's father lived on Stricker Street, just up the block from Richardson and her family. See "124 Get Diplomas from Colored High," *Sun*, 24 June 1922, 5; "Would Not Put Y'uth Back in School," *Afro-Am*, 10 September 1927, 11; "Ex-Baltimore Divorcee Weds Philly Hotelman," *Afro-Am*, 16 March 1929, 5; "They Attend National Social Work Meeting," *Afro-Am*, 6 June 1936, 6; "Mrs. Banton to Represent U.S. at Conference in India," *Afro-Am*, 22 November 1952, 11; "28 Get Degrees at Del. State," *Afro-Am*, 12 June 1943, 15; Carol Hoffecker and Annette Woolard, "Black Women in Delaware's History," in *A History of African Americans of Delaware and Maryland's Eastern Shore*, ed. Carole Marks, University of Delaware, 1997, accessed 29 August 2010, http://www.udel.edu/BlackHistory/blackwomen.html.

29. GR, interviews with JRF, 17 July 2010, 1 April 2011; Jacqueline Fassett, interview with JRF; Donna Richardson, interview with JRF; Tamara Richardson, interview with JRF.

30. George C. Grant, "Desegregation in Maryland since the Supreme Court Decision," *Journal of Negro Education* 24, no. 3 (Summer 1955): 279.

31. "Dorchester Post Is Given to Negro," *Sun*, 21 June 1956, 9; "Desegregation Delay Sought in Dorchester," *WP*, 1 July 1955, 45; "Dorchester to Admit Negroes to White 12th Grade Classes," *WP*, 11 August 1956, 18; "Few Classes to Be Mixed in New Term," *Sun*, 18 August 1956, 28; "School Anti-segregation Edict Hit at Dorchester Meeting," *Sun*, 31 August 1956, 26; "Maryland School Integration— Ranges from Compulsory to Voluntary Systems," *Sun*, 5 May 1957, A3; "Maryland Shows Integration Gain," *NYT*, 31 August, 1958, 36.

32. "Integrated Statistics," *Sun*, 12 January 1958, 12; Jacqueline Fassett, interview with JRF.

33. Cambridge City Council meeting minutes, 26 June 1950, 20 June 1955, 26 March 1956, Book 1950–1956, pp. 441, 366, 434; 22 July 1957, Book 1957–1964, p. 529. For Richardson's membership in the Second Ward Recreational League, see the organization's "Financial Report for 1956," Cambridge City Council documents, folder 1957, Miscellaneous, Cambridge City Hall, Cambridge, MD. For Richardson's statement about the SWRL, see GR, interview with JRF, 12 April 2012. For the Ed/Rec program, see GR, emails to JRF, 7 November 2011, 10 April 2012; GR, interview with JRF, 12 April 2012; Jacqueline Fassett, interview with JRF. For the City Council meeting of 12 May 1958, see Book 1957–1964, p. 573. There are no subsequent entries in the City Council's minutes indicating that city officials made any effort to fund or otherwise support the Ed/Rec program.

34. GR, emails to JRF, 19 December 2012, 3 September 2015; GR, interview with Robert Penn Warren.

35. GR, interview with Ja A. Jahannes; "Cambridge Copes with Disaster," *Afro-Am*, 12 February 1952, 3.

36. For an excellent text on women's postwar activism, see Joanne Meyerowitz, ed., *Not June Cleaver: Women and Gender in Postwar America, 1945–1960* (Philadelphia: Temple University Press, 1994).

37. GR, interview with Ja A. Jahannes. For Downs's run for office, see Levy, *Civil War on Race Street*, 28.

5. Shock Therapy, Round One

1. "Race Bars Lowered in Crisfield," *DB*, 30 December 1961, 1. For African diplomats' encounters at Maryland restaurants, see "End of Racial 'Incidents' Is Demanded: Tawes Deplores Insults to African Envoys in Restaurants," *Sun*, 12 July 1961, 38; "Rebuffs to African Diplomats Defended by Cafes on Rte. 40," *WP*, 17 September 1961, A24; "U.S. Making Headway in Bid to End Maryland Segregation," *NYT*, 8 October 1961, 56. Black Americans commonly obtained only take-out service at these establishments.

2. "Into Midstream," *DB*, 30 December 1961, 10.

3. Rebecca de Schweinitz's *If We Could Change the World: Young People and America's Long Struggle for Racial Equality* (Chapel Hill: University of North Carolina Press, 2009) is an outstanding work on black youths' role in the modern black liberation movement. Additionally, there are numerous excellent studies of local civil rights movements, particularly from Mississippi. See Emilye Crosby, *A Little Taste of Freedom: The Black Freedom Struggle in Claiborne County, Mississippi* (Chapel Hill: University of North Carolina Press, 2005); John Dittmer, *Local People: The Struggle for Civil Rights in Mississippi* (Chicago: University of Illinois Press, 1995); Payne, *I've Got the Light of Freedom*.

4. Bill Hansen, email to JRF, 9 June 2013; "Students to Test Restaurants," *DB*, 13 January 1962, 1.

5. For the definitive work on Till's murder and its role in the civil rights movement, see Darryl C. Mace, *In Remembrance of Emmett Till: Regional Stories and Media Responses to the Black Freedom Struggle* (Lexington: University Press of Kentucky, 2014).

6. Tom Kahn and August Meier, "Recent Trends in the Civil Rights Movement," *New Politics* 3 (Spring 1964): 34–53 (reprint; copy in author's possession); Howard Zinn, *SNCC: The New Abolitionists* (Cambridge, MA: South End Press, 2002), 7; Carson, *In Struggle*. 3, 20–21.

7. Bill Hansen, email to JRF, 9 June 2013; "Students to Test Restaurants," *DB*, 13 January 1962, 1; Levy, *Civil War on Race Street*, 36–44. For Robinson's activism, see Charles E. Cobb Jr., *On the Road to Freedom: A Guided Tour of the Civil Rights Trail* (Chapel Hill, NC: Algonquin Books, 2008), 56–57.

8. "20 Freedom Riders Due in Magistrate's Court," *DB*, 15 January 1962, 1, 2; Richardson, book proposal, 14.

9. "20 Freedom Riders Due in Magistrate's Court," *DB*, 15 January 1962, 1, 2.

10. "Freedom Ride Will Be Held," *DB*, 19 January 1962, 1; "Children Are Used as Pickets," *DB*, 25 January 1962, 1; "Reaction Split over Sit-ins in Cambridge," *WP*, 23 January 1962, A8. Mace's Lane High School replaced Frederick Douglass St. Clair High School, which had burned down.

11. "NAACP Asks Assurances of Adequate Protection," *DB*, 18 January 1962, 1; "A Community of Law, Order," *DB*, 18 January 1962, 10; "Freedom Ride Will Be Held," *DB*, 19 January 1962, 1.

12. "Jarman Questions Sincerity of Integrationists' U.S. Plea," *Sun*, 29 January 1962, 30, 22; "Officials Decline Comment on Integrationist Telegram," *DB*, 29 January 1962, 1; "Md. Freedom Rider Lands 'Smack in the Middle of H--1,'" *Afro-Am*, 27 January 1962, 1, 10; "Pickets Are Picketed in Cambridge," *DB*, 29 January 1962, 1.

13. "Two Views," *DB*, 17 January 1962; "Reaction Split over Sit-ins in Cambridge," *WP*, 23 January 1962, A8; John W. Ringold, letter to the editor, *DB*, 25 January 1962; "Children Are Used as Pickets," *DB*, 25 January 1962, 1; Levy, *Civil War on Race Street*, 43.

14. "Two Views," *DB*, 17 January 1962; "Reaction Split over Sit-ins in Cambridge," *WP*, 23 January 1962, A8.

15. "Outside Pressure," *DB*, 5 January 1962, 10; "Students to Test Restaurants," *DB*, 13 January 1962, 1; "Children Are Used as Pickets," *DB*, 25 January 1962, 1; "The Third Strike," *DB*, 26 January 1962; "One Fact Stands Out," *DB*, 7 February 1962, 6; William Henry Chafe, *Civilities and Civil Rights: Greensboro, North Carolina, and the Black Struggle for Equality* (New York: Oxford University Press, 1980), 7, 249.

16. "A Point of Contact," *DB*, 30 January 1962, 6; "Undercover Leaders," *DB*, 31 January 1962; "One Fact Stands Out," *DB*, 7 February 1962, 6.

17. Jacqueline Fassett, interview with JRF; "Clergyman Calls Freedom Riders 'Children Sent to Do a Man's Job,'" *DB*, 15 January 1962, 1; "Two Views," *DB*, 17 January 1962; "Extremists Direct Hate Campaign at Educator," *DB*, 29 January 1962, 1, 2; "No Violence Wanted," *Afro-Am*, 3 February 1962, 4.

18. "Two Views," *DB*, 17 January 1962; Levy, *Civil War on Race Street*, 28.

19. GR, interview with Robert Penn Warren; Levy, *Civil War on Race Street*, 29; GR, interview with JRF, 17 August 2002.

20. GR, interview with John Britton; Richardson, book proposal, 14.

21. Ibid.; Richardson, "Energy of the People Passing through Me," 277–78; Levy, *Civil War on Race Street*, 46–47; GR, email to JRF, 9 January 2013.

22. "City Commission Reports on Equal Opportunities Work," *DB*, 17 January 1962, 1; "Job Opportunities for Negroes Open, Says EOC," *DB*, 15 May 1962, 1.

23. GR, interview with Robert Penn Warren; Peter S. Szabo, "An Interview with Gloria Richardson Dandridge," *Maryland Historical Magazine* 89, no. 3 (1994): 349; Richardson, "Energy of the People Passing through Me," 277–78.

24. GR, interviews with JRF, 17 August 2002, 17 July 2010; Richardson, "Energy of the People Passing through Me," 278; "'Radical' Integrationist," *NYT*, 13 July 1963, 6; Bill Hansen, email to JRF, 9 June 2013.

25. Richardson, book proposal, 16; Szabo, "Interview with Gloria Richardson Dandridge," 349, 350.

26. Student Nonviolent Coordinating Committee, "Founding Statement," 15–17 April 1960, Civil Rights Movement Veterans.org, accessed 6 July 2017, http://www.crmvet.org/docs/sncc1.htm; Pinn, *African American Humanist Principles*, 30; GR, interview with JRF, 17 August 2002; Richardson, "Energy of the People Passing through Me," 289; Levy, *Civil War on Race Street*, 52.

27. "Selective Buying Is Called 'Ill-Advised,'" *DB*, 13 July 1962, 1; Richardson, book proposal, 16; Bill Hansen, email to JRF, 9 June 2013; Levy, *Civil War on Race Street*, 52.

28. Richardson, "Energy of the People Passing through Me," 278–79. Ella Baker was the only other person dressed like Richardson and her cousin. For the spring 1962 conference, see Carson, *In Struggle*, 66–67.

29. GR, interview with JRF, 30 October 2004; Ransby, *Ella Baker*, 80–81.

30. Fleming, *Soon We Will Not Cry*, 96; GR, interview with JRF, 30 October 2004; Dorie Ladner, telephone interview with JRF, 19 May 2009; Joyce Ladner, telephone interview with JRF, 30 March 2005.

31. Ibid.; Richardson, "Energy of the People Passing through Me," 279.

32. Richardson, "Energy of the People Passing through Me," 278–80.

33. "The Negro Ward of Cambridge, Maryland: A Study in Social Change," September 1963, Cambridge Nonviolent Action Committee (CNAC) Papers, State Historical Society of Wisconsin, Madison (copy in author's possession). Swarthmore College professors processed the survey data and reported it to CNAC. See GR, interview with JRF, 17 August 2002.

34. "Over the Fence," *DB*, 12 July 1962, 4; "Freedom Riders Turn Attention to New Activities on Eastern Shore," *Afro-Am*, 23 June 1962, 28; "Wildcat Pickets," *DB*, 16 May 1962, 14.

35. Tamara Richardson, interview with JRF; Donna Richardson, interview with JRF; Donna Richardson, email to JRF, 16 August 2013; "First Students File for Cambridge School Transfers," *Afro-Am*, 7 August 1962, newspaper clipping, folder "Civil Rights," Cambridge Library Vertical File. Also see "Integration Comes to Two Schools," *DB*, 4 September 1962, 1; "3 Girls Return to Negro School," *Sun*, 18 September 1962, 40, 26; "Three Colored Students Withdraw from C.H.S., Lonesomeness Cited," *DB*, 18 September 1962, 1.

36. GR, email to JRF, 22 August 2013; GR, interview with Robert Penn Warren; "Dorchester's Vote," *DB*, 8 November 1962, 14.

37. Enez Grubb, interview with Sandy Harney, 27 August 1997 (copy in author's possession); GR, interview with John Britton; GR, interviews with JRF, 17 August 2002, 30 May 2013; Levy, *Civil War on Race Street*, 51–52.

38. Rev. T. M. Murray to Rev. Martin Luther King, 28 June 1962, and D. McDonald to Rev. T. M. Murray, 11 July 1962, both letters in subgroup A, series II, subseries 1, box 45, folder 32, Martin Luther King Jr. Papers, King Center, Atlanta; GR, interview with JRF, 17 August 2002. Richardson claimed that King wanted a $3,000 retainer to speak in Cambridge, which CNAC could not afford. I have been unable to corroborate this claim.

39. "Public Housing Meeting," *DB*, 21 March 1962, 10; Levy, *Civil War on Race Street*, 55.

40. "Commissioners Get Letter on Housing," *DB*, 15 August 1962, 1 (emphasis added). The county commissioners' minutes for August 1962 do not mention the letter from Waugh Methodist Episcopal Church; nor is it included with the minutes. See Dorchester County Commissioners' Minutes, box 12/9/1958 to 11/20/1962, Dorchester County Office Building, Cambridge, MD. Officially at least, Richardson was a member of the Waugh congregation, but she did not recall knowing about the letter. See GR, interview with JRF, 12 April 2012. For details about the public housing proposal, why it was needed, and why the commissioners rejected it, see "Up to the County," *DB*, 9 February 1962, 10; "A Historic No," *DB*, 15 February 1962, 10.

41. "Chronic Unemployment Ignited Cambridge Strife," *WP*, 21 July 1963, B10; Levy, *Civil War on Race Street*, 25–27.

42. Murray quoted in "Selective Buying Is Called 'Ill-Advised,'" *DB*, 13 July 1962, 1; "Anti-Bias Drive Pushed," *Sun*, 14 July 1962, 17; "Boycott Stores in Maryland,"

Daily Defender, 21 August 1962, 5; "Cambridge, Md., Boycott," *Pittsburgh Courier*, 25 August 1962, 24; "With Progress, Responsibility," *DB*, 29 August 1962, 10.

43. "Chronic Unemployment Ignited Cambridge Strife," *WP*, 21 July 1963, B10; Levy, *Civil War on Race Street*, 55.

44. "Cambridge Port Project Is Called Community's Top Story of 1962," *DB*, 31 December 1962, 1–2; "Unfinished Business," *DB*, 31 December 1962, 3; "Albany Girl Would Give up Her Life for Freedom," *DB*, 4 August 1962, 6.

6. Shock Therapy, Round Two

1. Richardson, "Energy of the People Passing through Me," 278–80.

2. "Delegation Asks Sheriff to Give Some Thought to Hiring Negro Jail Employees," *DB*, 4 January 1963, 1.

3. "Tax Men Close 4 Selro Plants," *Sun*, 8 January 1963, 38; "Closed Firm May Reopen," *Sun*, 10 January 1963, 15; "100 Jobs Due at New Plant in Cambridge," *Sun*, 4 April 1963, 45; Richardson, "Energy of the People Passing through Me," 289–90; GR, email to JRF, 27 June 2012.

4. Herbert Hill, "Black Workers, Organized Labor, and Title VII of the 1964 Civil Rights Act: Legislative History and Litigation Record," in *Race in America: The Struggle for Equality*, ed. Herbert Hill and James E. Jones Jr. (Madison: University of Wisconsin Press, 1993), 298–300. For a general history of the ILGWU (although it does not include much analysis of race), see Gus Tyler, *Look for the Union Label: A History of the International Ladies Garment Workers Union* (Armonk, NY: M. E. Sharpe, 1995). My thanks to Nathan Godfried, PhD, for his insights into the ILGWU and his suggestions on race and labor history, particularly Herbert Hill's works.

5. Cambridge City Council meeting minutes, 25 March 1963, Book 1957–1964, p. 957, Cambridge City Hall, Cambridge, MD; Cambridge Nonviolent Action Committee, "Requests," n.d., Clarence Logan clippings file (copy in author's possession); "Civil Rights Group Asks Council for More Action," *DB*, 26 March 1963, 1.

6. "Race Bars' End Sought," *WP*, 27 March 1963, B6; Cambridge City Council meeting minutes, 25 March 1963, Book 1957–1964, p. 957.

7. "Maryland Group Moves to Desegregate Theatre" *Daily Defender*, 27 March 1963, 16; "17 Arrested in Protests in Cambridge," *Sun*, 31 March 1963, 48, 36; "17 Students Jailed in Cambridge Protest," *Afro-Am*, 6 April 1963, 14.

8. Ibid.

9. For an excellent discussion of movement culture and why it was important to create, see David S. Cecelski, *Along Freedom Road: Hyde County, North Carolina, and the Fate of Black Schools in the South* (Chapel Hill: University of North Carolina Press, 1994), 89. For the military aspect of the Cambridge movement, see Levy, *Civil War on Race Street*, 76. The high school student was Malone LeCompte. Richardson said he also "used his ham radio during the night watches for" the Second Ward. See GR, email to JRF, 18 June 2014.

10. "Freedom Riders Are Fined in Circuit Court," *DB*, 4 May 1962, 1; GR, interview with JRF, 17 August 2002; Faith Holsaert, "Resistance U," in *Hands on the*

Freedom Plow: Personal Accounts by Women in SNCC, ed. Faith Holsaert et al. (Urbana: University of Illinois Press, 2010), 183–84.

11. "Delaware's Negroes Win College Rights," *NYT*, 10 August 1950, 25; "Cancel Bias at Delaware University," *Chicago Defender* (national ed.), 19 August 1950, 12; "Univ. of Delaware Doors Open to All," *Afro-Am*, 2 September 1950, 9.

12. "Freedom Riders Are Fined in Circuit Court," *DB*, 4 May 1962, 1; Ruth Van D. Todd, "Background of Tension: A Stalemate in Race Relations," *Sun*, 22 April 1963, 12.

13. GR, interviews with JRF, 17 August 2002, 30 May 2013; GR, email to JRF, 8 April 2011; "54 Are Found Disorderly in Cambridge," *Sun*, 8 May 1963, B40, 31; "Penny Fines Suspended," *DB*, 8 May 1963, 1, 4.

14. For more on the politics of respectability, see Marisa Chappell, Jenny Hutchinson, and Brian Ward, "'Dress Modestly, Neatly . . . as if You Were Going to Church': Respectability, Class and Gender in the Montgomery Bus Boycott and the Early Civil Rights Movement," in *Gender in the Civil Rights Movement*, ed. Peter J. Ling and Sharon Monteith (New York: Garland, 1999), 69–100.

15. GR, interview with Ja A. Jahannes; GR, interview with JRF, 17 August 2002. Ella Baker also rejected the politics of respectability and the idea that a town "drunk" should not be involved in the movement. See Ransby, *Ella Baker*, 226–27, 259.

16. "Judge Henry Hospitalized," *WP*, 4 June 1963, B1; "Judge Henry Well," *WP*, 3 August 1963, C10; "Judge Henry Resigns," *Sun*, 1 April 1964, 44; "Judge Henry Dies on Shore," *Sun*, 6 April 1973, A13; Levy, *Civil War on Race Street*, 78.

17. "Sit-ins May Become Daily Occurrence Here," *DB*, 14 May 1963, 1; "62 Jailed Tuesday in Protests," *DB*, 15 May 1963, 1; "40 Negroes Arrested in Cambridge," *Sun*, 15 May 1963, 54, 36; Richardson, "Energy of the People Passing through Me," 283–84; GR, interview with Dick Gordon; Enez Grubb, interview with Sandy Harney.

18. GR, interview with Robert Penn Warren; Szabo, "Interview with Gloria Richardson Dandridge," 352; GR, interviews with JRF, 31 August 2004, 20 June 2007; Richardson, "Energy of the People Passing through Me," 283–84; William Hall, telephone interview with JRF, 22 February 2004; "Cambridge Youth Hit in Protest," *Afro-Am*, 27 April 1963, 14.

19. "Racial Demonstrations Called Off Indefinitely," *DB*, 18 May 1963, 1; "Tension Mounts in Cambridge," *Afro-Am*, 25 May 1963, 13.

20. Levy, *Civil War on Race Street*, 79; "White Leaders to Draft Cambridge Peace Offer," *WP*, 17 May 1963, C2; "Cambridge Group Defends City's Racial Situation," *Sun*, 23 May 1963, 40. The name of Henry's group is mentioned in "Cambridge Still Tension-Ridden," *WP*, 13 June 1963, A8. The CIU replaced the ineffectual Equal Opportunities Commission, created in 1961.

21. "NAACP Praises Judge," *DB*, 25 May 1963, 1; "Tension Mounts in Cambridge," *Afro-Am*, 25 May 1963, 13; "Picketing to Resume Today," *DB*, 27 May 1963, 1; "Student Pickets Arrested for Disorder, Race Negotiations Are Threatened," *DB*, 28 May 1963, 1.

22. "Pickets at Prayer Are Arrested in Cambridge," *DB*, 31 May 1963, 1.

23. "Mob of 2,000 Hangs Negro in Maryland," *NYT*, 19 October 1933; "Four in Maryland Held as Lynchers Freed by Court," *NYT*, 30 November 1933; "No Protests in Cambridge Yesterday," *DB*, 1 June 1963, 1; "Negro Girl Released from Jail," *DB*, 4 June 1963, 1; "Names in the News," *Afro-Am*, 8 June 1963, 2.

24. Levy, *Civil War on Race Street*, 80–81; "Racial Violence Hits Cambridge Last Night," *DB*, 11 June 1963, 1.

25. "Mood Is One of Bitterness," *Afro-Am*, 22 June 1963, 1, 14; "3 Fires Set in Cambridge," *Sun*, 13 June 1963, 54.

26. Ibid.; "Negro Moderate Is Target, CORE to Send in More Demonstrators," *DB*, 13 June 1963, 1; Richardson quoted in "3 Fires Set in Cambridge," *Sun*, 13 June 1963, 54. Also see "Negroes Parade in Cambridge, Md.," *NYT*, 13 June 1963, 17; "Cambridge Still Tension-Ridden," *WP*, 13 June 1963, A8.

27. "Negro Moderate Is Target," *DB*, 13 June 1963, 1; "3 Fires Set in Cambridge," *Sun*, 13 June 1963, 54; "Negroes Parade in Cambridge, Md.," *NYT*, 13 June 1963, 17.

28. "Negro Moderate Is Target," *DB*, 13 June 1963, 1; "Cambridge Still Tension-Ridden," *WP*, 13 June 1963, A8; "12 Cambridge Pickets Are Released on Bond," *WP*, 14 June 1963, A4.

29. "Negro Moderate Is Target," *DB*, 13 June 1963, 1; "White Mob Forms in Cambridge," *Sun*, 14 June 1963, 44; "Mob Rule Feared in Cambridge," *Baltimore News-Post* (evening ed.), 14 June 1963, 1.

30. "Riot Averted as Whites March in Cambridge, Md.," *NYT*, 14 June 1963, 14; Jhan Robbins and June Robbins, "Why Didn't They Hit Back?" *Redbook*, July 1963, CORE reprint, n.d., Civil Rights Movement Veterans (CRMVET), accessed 1 July 2012, http://www.crmvet.org/info/core_nv_redbook.pdf; "Gloria Richardson: Lady General of Civil Rights," *Ebony*, July 1964, 24; Stokely Carmichael and Ekwueme Michael Thelwell, *Ready for Revolution: The Life and Struggles of Stokely Carmichael (Kwame Ture)* (New York: Scribner, 2005), 340; Richardson, "Energy of the People Passing through Me," 285; Donna Richardson, interview with JRF.

31. "City Council Asks Martial Law Here," *DB*, 14 June 1963, 1; "500 National Guard Troops on Duty in City," *DB*, 15 June 1963, 1; "Cambridge, Md., Put under Martial Law to Bar Race Strife," *NYT*, 15 June 1963, 1, 9; "Talks with Negroes Halted by Leaders in Cambridge, Md.," *NYT*, 17 June 1963, 1, 13; "Negro Leaders Unhappy as Bid for Cambridge Ordinance Fails," *Sun*, 2 July 1963, 40. Peter Levy states that Grubb left CNAC because she was "emotionally exhausted." See Levy, *Civil War on Race Street*, 116.

32. GR, interview with John Britton; GR, interview with Ja A. Jahannes; GR, interview with JRF, 17 August 2002.

33. GR, interview with JRF, 17 August 2002; Susan Gal, "Between Speech and Silence: The Problems of Research on Language and Gender," in *Gender at the Crossroads of Knowledge: Feminist Anthropology in the Postmodern Era*, ed. Micaela di Leonardo (Berkeley: University of California Press, 1991), 175–76; "Talks with Negroes Halted by Leaders in Cambridge, Md.," *NYT*, 17 June 1963.

34. GR, interview with JRF, 17 August 2002.

35. Ibid.; Richardson, "Energy of the People Passing through Me," 284–85; GR, email to JRF, 11 September 2015; "Cambridge Showdown Is Averted between Negro Pickets, Troops," *WP*, 19 June 1963, A1.

36. "Threat by NAACP Leader Irks City, 500 Troops Stay," *DB*, 17 June 1963, 1; "Pickets at Prayer Are Arrested in Cambridge," *DB*, 31 May 1963.

37. "CNAC Refuses to Declare Moratorium on Protests," *DB*, 5 June 1963, 1; "Talks with Negroes Halted by Leaders in Cambridge, Md.," *NYT*, 17 June 1963, 1,

13; "Cambridge Plans an Equality Law," *NYT*, 20 June 1963, 19; "Cambridge," *Sun*, 21 June 1963, 40; "Third Meeting Held at Justice Dept. on Cambridge Crisis," *WP*, 22 June 1963, B2.

38. "Call Off Cambridge Marches," *Chicago Tribune*, 19 June 1963, 5; "Cambridge Showdown Is Averted between Negro Pickets, Troops," *WP*, 19 June 1963, A1; "Negroes Bar Cambridge March after Parleys in Washington" *NYT*, 19 June 1963, 23; "Cambridge Plans an Equality Law," *NYT*, 20 June 1963, 19; "Mood Is One of Bitterness," *Afro-Am*, 22 June 1963, 14; Carson, *In Struggle*, 21–22, 33, 67.

39. "Cambridge Plans an Equality Law," *NYT*, 20 June 1963, 19.

40. Robinson quoted in "Racial Talks Lag in Cambridge, Md.," *NYT*, 22 June 1963, 10. Other articles also reported this alleged agreement; see "Negotiations to End Cambridge's Racial Troubles Called Off," *Sun*, 22 June 1963, 28; "Third Meeting Held at Justice Dept. on Cambridge Crisis," *WP*, 22 June 1963, B2; "Negroes in Cambridge Reject a City Referendum," *NYT*, 23 June 1963, 59.

41. "CNAC Refuses to Declare Moratorium on Protests," *DB*, 5 June 1963, 1; "The Local Response," *DB*, 5 June 1963, 10.

42. Ibid.; "Picketing to Resume in Cambridge," *DB*, 6 June 1963, 1; "Mood Is One of Bitterness," *Afro-Am*, 22 June 1963, 14; "Threat by NAACP Leader Irks City, 500 Troops Stay," *DB*, 17 June 1963, 1; "Cambridge, Md., Gets New Threat," *NYT*, 18 June 1963, 23.

43. For examples of black communities that rejected moderate leaders, see Carson, *In Struggle*.

44. Szabo, "Interview with Gloria Richardson Dandridge," 356; GR, interview with JRF, 14 April 2005; GR, emails to JRF, 16 December 2011, 9 January 2013, 19 February 2013; Richardson, "Energy of the People Passing through Me," 278. Maceo Hubbard was the first person to offer Richardson the jobs training directorship (through her mother Mable); ultimately, Morgan State professor Melvin H. Humphrey was hired. See "At Least 150 to Be Involved," *Afro-Am*, 17 September 1963, 19, 20, Clarence Logan clippings file. At the time, Welcome was a rising star in Maryland's Democratic Party and the first black woman elected to the House of Delegates (1962). She was also the first black woman elected to the Maryland senate, making her the first black woman elected to that office in American history. "Maryland Women's Hall of Fame: Verda Welcome," Maryland State Archives, 2001, accessed 7 June 2012, http://www.msa.md.gov/msa/educ/exhibits/womenshall/html/welcome.html.

45. GR, interview with JRF, 22 January 2013; GR, email to JRF, 19 February 2013. Richardson stated that Clarence Logan conveyed the Kennedy administration's threat to her, but Logan claimed he did not know about Richardson's story and did not recall passing along any message. Clarence Logan, email to JRF, 18 February 2013.

46. "Deadlock Continues, No Protests Hinted," *DB*, 25 June 1963, 1; "Cambridge Talks Resume," *NYT*, 28 June 1963, 12; "Mrs. Richardson," *Afro-Am*, 27 July 1963, 13.

47. Cambridge City Council meeting minutes, 1 July 1963, Book 1957–1964, p. 983; "Change in City Charter Is Approved by Council," *DB*, 2 July 1963, 1; "Negro Leaders Unhappy as Bid for Cambridge Ordinance Fails," *Sun*, 2 July 1963, 40;

"Cambridge Council Adopts Amendment to Charter on Public Accommodations," *WP*, 2 July 1963, B1.

48. "Negro Leaders Unhappy as Bid for Cambridge Ordinance Fails," *Sun*, 2 July 1963, 40; "Gloria Says Rights Boycott Will Continue in Cambridge," *Pittsburgh Courier*, 13 July 1963, 19.

49. "Martial Law to End," *NYT*, 3 July 1963, 10; "Guardsmen Ordered to Leave," *DB*, 8 July 1963, 1; "2 Rallies Staged in Cambridge, Md.," *NYT*, 9 July 1963, 18.

50. "Racial Protests Resumed in City," *DB*, 9 July 1963, 1; "Justice Dept. Negro to Attempt to Mediate Cambridge Race Issue," *WP*, 10 July 1963, A7; "4 Held for Sit-in in Cambridge, Md.," *NYT*, 11 July 1963, 18; "Troops Ordered on Alert after Cambridge Clash," *WP*, 12 July 1963, A1, A8; *Lincoln University Catalogue, 1922–1923*, 66, accessed 24 August 2010, http://www.lincoln.edu/library/specialcollections/catalogueissues/1923.pdf. Upon earning his law degree from Harvard University in 1927, Hubbard was hired by Raymond Pace Alexander's Philadelphia law firm. Canton, *Raymond Pace Alexander*, 35–36. Also see GR, interviews with JRF, 17 August 2002, 2 August 2003, 17 July 2010; GR, email to JRF, 26 September 2013.

51. "Troops Ordered on Alert after Cambridge Clash," *WP*, 12 July 1963, A1, A8; "Five White Men Shot in Race Riots, Nat. Guard Troops Returning," *DB*, 12 July 1963, 1, 5; "Five Whites Shot in Cambridge, Md.; Guard in Control," *NYT*, 12 July 1963, 1.

52. Ibid.; "Blazing Guns Mark Freedom Fight: Embattled Defenders Fire from Rooftops," *Afro-Am*, 20 July 1963, 1, 2; "Indefinite Peace Now in Cambridge," *Afro-Am*, 13 July 1963, 14; "End of Truce Due in Cambridge, Md.," *NYT*, 15 July 1963, 20.

53. "We Urge an Injunction," *DB*, 13 July 1963, 1; "White Reporter Is Excluded from Negro Rally," *DB*, 28 June 1963; "Cambridge's Business Dips in Racial Squeeze," *Evening Sun*, 26 June 1963, C20, C18, Clarence Logan clippings file; "Gloria Says Rights Boycott Will Continue in Cambridge," *Pittsburgh Courier*, 13 July 1963, 19.

54. "Cambridge Rule Eased by Troops," *WP*, 17 July 1963, A1, A4; Richardson, "Energy of the People Passing through Me," 280–81.

55. "Transcript of the President's News Conference on Foreign and Domestic Matters," *NYT*, 18 July 1963; "Cambridge Is Hopeful," *NYT*, 19 July 1963, 7; "Cambridge, Md. Leader Views Kennedy Criticism," *Atlanta Daily World*, 20 July 1963, 1; "Mrs. Richardson," *Afro-Am*, 27 July 1963, 13.

56. "Cambridge Is Hopeful," *NYT*, 19 July 1963, 7; "Tear Gas Is Used in Cambridge, Md.," *NYT*, 21 July 1963, 1, 44; "Maryland," *Afro-Am*, 27 July 1963, 2.

57. "Maryland," *Afro-Am*, 27 July 1963, 2.

58. "Gloria Richardson in D.C. Sun., July 21," *Afro-Am*, 20 July 1963, 14; "In Cambridge: General Stops Prayer Meetings," *Beaver County (PA) Times*, 22 July 1963, 1.

59. GR, interview with JRF, 17 August 2002; "Robert Kennedy Meets Key Cambridge Figures," *WP*, 23 July 1963, A1.

60. John Lewis, *Walking with the Wind: A Memoir of the Movement* (New York: Simon & Schuster, 1998), 212.

61. *DB*, 24 July 1963, 1. Wright quoted in Smith, *Here Lies Jim Crow*, 204–5, and on the radio show *Midday with Dan Rodricks*, WYPR.com, "The 50th Anniversary of the Cambridge Riots," 13 June 2013; GR, email to JRF, 17 November 2013; "Why Do Women Always Have to Smile?" Slate.com, 18 June 2013, accessed 23 June 2013, http://www.slate.com/articles/double_x/doublex/2013/06/bitchy_resting _face_and_female_niceness_why_do_women_have_to_smile_more.html. For more information on smiling and other facial expressions and how they are perceived, see Marianne LaFrance, *Why Smile: The Science behind Facial Expressions* (New York: W. W. Norton, 2013).

62. GR, interview with JRF, 17 August 2002.

63. "Robert Kennedy Meets Key Cambridge Figures," *WP*, 23 July 1963, A1; GR, interviews with JRF, 17 August 2002, 24 July 2004, 25 July 2008; GR, email to JRF, 16 October 2009; Wendell E. Pritchett, *Robert Clifton Weaver and the American City: The Life and Times of an Urban Reformer* (Chicago: University of Chicago Press, 2008), 10, 11. A week before Weaver talked with Richardson, Cambridge's Housing Authority had also tied CNAC's demonstrations (albeit indirectly) to the Housing Authority's decision to delay the start of the federal housing project. See "Malkus Accepts N.A.A.C.P. Attack," *Sun*, 22 July 1963, 30. Weaver has the distinction of being the first black person in US history to be appointed to a cabinet-level position—Secretary of Housing and Urban Development; he was nominated for the job by President Kennedy's successor, Lyndon B. Johnson.

64. GR, interview with JRF, 5 December 2011.

65. GR, interview with John Britton; GR, interview with JRF, 17 August 2002; GR, interview with Dick Gordon.

66. For the content of the agreement, see *Civil Rights during the Kennedy Administration, 1961–63*, pt. 2, *The Papers of Burke Marshall, Assistant Attorney General for Civil Rights*, microfilm ed. (Frederick, MD: University Publications of America, 1986), reel 26; "The Text of the Cambridge, Md., Accord," *NYT*, 24 July 1963, 16; "Gloria Richardson," *Newsweek*, 5 August 1963.

67. GR, interview with JRF, 17 August 2002.

68. "Racial Agreement for Cambridge 'Delights' Tawes," *Sun*, 24 July 1963, 1; "Victory for Cambridge," *DB*, 24 July 1963, 1; "Good Judgment, Faith, Confidence," *DB*, 25 July 1963, 10; "Pact Calms Cambridge, Md., Mood," *Christian Science Monitor*, 25 July 1963, 11.

69. "Pact Calms Cambridge, Md., Mood," *Christian Science Monitor*, 25 July 1963, 11. For the concessions made in Birmingham and Jackson, see "Birmingham Pact Sets Timetable for Integration," *NYT*, 11 May 1963, 1, 8; "The Birmingham Story," *NYT*, 26 May 1963, 58; "Birmingham Is Orderly under Truce," *WP*, 30 June 1963, A12; "Reach Mississippi Race Accord," *Chicago Tribune*, 19 June 1963, 4.

70. "Cambridge Leaders Defy Martial Law," *Atlanta Daily World*, 16 July 1963, 1; "Gloria, the Leader," *Daily Defender*, 17 July 1963, 12; "Qualified Lawyers," *Amsterdam News*, 31 August 1963, 47.

71. "Chronic Unemployment Ignited Cambridge Strife," *WP*, 21 July 1963, B10.

72. Rachel Brown, "A Summer in Cambridge," *Horn Book Magazine* 40, no. 3 (June 1964): 315–19; "The Negro Ward of Cambridge, Maryland," September

1963, Cambridge Nonviolent Action Committee Papers, State Historical Society of Wisconsin, Madison.

7. A Nonnegotiable Right

1. "JFK Mobilizes Womanpower in Fight for Civil Rights," *WP*, 11 July 1963, B1. Kennedy had held similar meetings with religious leaders, businesspeople, labor leaders, and governors. Also see Diane Nash, telephone interview with JRF, 29 April 2010.

2. "The Women Meet with President," *New York Amsterdam News*, 20 July 1963, 1, 2; "Patricia Harris Co-chairman of Powerful Rights Lobby," *Jet*, 25 July 1963, 8–9. Secretary of State Dean Rusk and Secretary of Defense Robert McNamara were also at the meeting. Richardson stated that she "refused to shake [President Kennedy's] hand. You know, everybody's running around shakin' his hand." See GR, interview with JRF, 17 August 2002; GR, email to JRF, 24 April 2014. Also see Diane Nash, email to JRF, 10 May 2010.

3. Diane Nash, email to JRF, 10 May 2010; GR, interviews with JRF, 17 August 2002, 20 March 2004; "Racial Protests Resumed in City," *DB*, 10 July 1963, 1; "Women Have Mixed Feeling on President's Plea for Support," *Afro-Am*, 20 July 1963, 8.

4. GR, interviews with JRF, 25 July 2008, 4 March 2009; Rachel (Brown) Cowan, email to JRF, 25 July 2008. The California trip included two firsts for Richardson: flying in an airplane and traveling with a white person. She felt comfortable traveling with Cowan and found flying exciting. Cowan's father, Louis G. Cowan, created and produced the television game show *The $64,000 Question*.

5. GR, interview with JRF, 4 March 2009; "Big Meeting for Negro Rights Here," *San Francisco Chronicle*, 30 July 1963, 1, 11. Thanks to Sonthonax "Sonny" Vernard for obtaining a copy of this article. Richardson disputes the *San Francisco Chronicle*'s claim that she wanted to achieve desegregation by working from within the political system rather than through street demonstrations. See GR, interview with JRF, 17 July 2010. Also see "Cambridge Has Quiet Weekend," *DB*, 29 July 1963, 1; "Cambridge Leader at West Coast Mass Rally," *Daily Defender*, 1 August 1963, 4.

6. GR, interview with JRF, 20 June 2007; Geoffrey Cowan, email to Rachel (Brown) Cowan, 25 July 2008 (copy in author's possession); Geoffrey Cowan, email to JRF, 24 August 2013.

7. "Cambridge Leader at SNCC Rally Friday," *New York Amsterdam News*, 17 August 1963, 5; "Gloria Richardson Explains Cambridge, Maryland to N.Y.," *New York Amsterdam News*, 24 August 1963, 18; photograph, "Center of Attraction," *New York Amsterdam News*, 24 August 1963, 18.

8. Gloria Richardson, "Cambridge, Maryland, 'City of Progress' for Rich," *New America*, 31 August 1963, 4, Bobst Tamiment Archives vertical file, New York University. The piece inaccurately states that 16 August 1963 was the date of Richardson's speech; the correct date is 23 August 1963. I am indebted to Thomas F. Jackson, PhD, for providing a copy of the speech.

9. Ibid.

10. Ibid.

11. "Cambridge Race Vote Set Oct. 1," *Sun*, 20 August 1963, 36, 22.

12. Carson, *In Struggle*, 91–93, 94; GR, interview with Dick Gordon; Mary King, *Freedom Song: A Personal Story of the 1960s Civil Rights Movement* (New York: William Morrow, 1987), 183.

13. Avon Rollins Sr., "August 28th 1963—The March on Washington," Civil Rights Movement Veterans (CRMVET), 14 June 2008, accessed 17 July 2011, http://www.crmvet.org/info/mowrolin.htm; GR, email to JRF, 21 August 2013; Courtland Cox, email to JRF, 22 August 2013.

14. Richardson, "Energy of the People Passing through Me," 287; "The Defender Marched," *Daily Defender*, 3 September 1963, 12, 13 "Ticker: Among Those Marching," *Jet*, 12 September 1963, 12–13; GR, interview with Robert Penn Warren. For the political aspects of SNCC members' clothing choices in general and at the March on Washington specifically, see Tanisha C. Ford, *Liberated Threads: Black Women, Style, and the Global Politics of Soul* (Chapel Hill: University of North Carolina Press, 2015), chap. 3.

15. Carson, *In Struggle*, 91–92; Agnes E. Meyer, letter to the editor, *NYT*, 2 July 1963, 28.

16. Bruce Smith, emails to JRF, 9 and 10 November 2011; "Gregory and Flagg Take Office Oath," *Afro-Am*, 10 November 1962, 13; GR, interviews with JRF, 17 August 2002, 19 June 2005; GR, emails to JRF, 3 November 2011, 21 August 2013; Richardson, "Energy of the People Passing through Me," 288.

17. Richardson, "Energy of the People Passing through Me," 283; GR, email to JRF, 23 August 2013; Rollins, "August 28th 1963—The March on Washington"; "200,000 Jam Mall in Mammoth Rally in Solemn, Orderly Plea for Equality," *WP*, 29 August 1963, A1, A12; "200 Countians to Participate in Rights March," *DB*, 27 August 1963, 1; "City and State Contingents Swell Throng on D.C. March," *Sun*, 29 August 1963, 1, 12; Donna Richardson, email to JRF, 22 August 2013.

18. Diane Nash did not attend either because she and her husband, James Bevel, were in Birmingham getting some rest. Diane Nash, interview with JRF; Diane Nash, email to JRF, 1 September 2013. For Richardson's attendance and the two streams of marchers, see GR, email to JRF, 21 August 2013; "Strong Women Were Pillars behind Civil Rights Movement," *USA Today*, 19 August 2013, accessed 22 August 2013, http://www.usatoday.com/story/news/nation/2013/08/19/march-on-washington-women/2648011/; "Ten Things to Know about the March on Washington," Teaching Tolerance, 28 August 2012, accessed 22 August 2013, http://www.tolerance.org/blog/ten-things-know-about-march-washington; Joyce Ladner, email to JRF, 22 August 2013; "The March Begins," 28 August 1963, Open Vault, WGBH Media Library and Archives, accessed 22 August 2013, http://openvault.wgbh.org/catalog/march-592217-the-march-begins. Bates's speech in its entirety was 143 words.

19. "Capital Is Occupied by a Gentle Army," *NYT*, 29 August 1963, 1, 17; David Levering Lewis, *King: A Biography* (Urbana: University of Illinois Press, 1978), 225; GR, email to JRF, 21 August 2013.

20. GR, interview with JRF, 17 August 2002; Richardson, "Energy of the People Passing through Me," 288; "The Defender Marched," *Daily Defender*, 3 September

1963, 12, 13; "Standing on 'the Shoulders of Bob Ming,'" *Washington Times*, 7 December 2008, accessed 3 August 2010, http://www.washingtontimes.com /news/2008/dec/7/standing-on-the-shoulders-of-bob-ming/print/.

21. GR, interview with JRF, 17 August 2002; GR, interview with Dick Gordon; Richardson, "Energy of the People Passing through Me," 288; Wallace H. Terry, "Washington March Cast Church in New Civil Rights Role," *WP*, 31 August 1963, A13. O'Boyle was operating as a proxy of the Kennedy administration.

22. "Restrained Militancy Marks Rally Speeches," *WP*, 29 August 1963, A14.

23. "Racial Agreement for Cambridge 'Delights' Tawes: Opposition," *Sun*, 24 July 1963, 1; "Don't Sign It," *DB*, 5 August 1963.

24. "Don't Sign It," *DB*, 5 August 1963; "Compromise or Chaos," *DB*, 8 August 1963, 14; "State Accorded Distinction Again," *DB*, 6 May 1922, 2; "Petition Containing over 1,600 Signers Is Filed," *DB*, 9 August 1963, 1; "After the Truce," *Afro-Am*, 10 August 1963, 15; "Cambridge Race Vote Set Oct. 1," *Sun*, 20 August 1963, 36, 22.

25. For the Wisconsin and New York referendum votes, see Eric Foner, *Free Soil, Free Labor, Free Men: The Ideology of the Republican Party before the Civil War* (New York: Oxford University Press, 1995), 287, 285. For the Kansas and Ohio referenda of 1867, see Clayborne Carson, Emma J. Lapsansky-Werner, and Gary B. Nash, *African American Lives: The Struggle for Freedom*, vol. 2 (New York: Pearson Longman, 2005), 273. For men's use of referenda concerning women's suffrage, see "Suffrage Wins in New York; Mad with Joy," *Chicago Daily Tribune*, 7 November 1917, 1; "Obstacles in Path of Nation-Wide Suffrage," *NYT*, 27 January 1918, 1, 4. For the St. Louis housing referendum, see "The Right to Occupy One's Property," *NYT*, 22 April 1916, 10. For Little Rock's segregation referendum, see "Faubus Urges Vote against Integration," *WP*, 19 September 1958, A15; "Faubus Disputes View of Lawyers," *NYT*, 22 September 1958, 22; "Little Rock Backs Faubus," *Chicago Daily Tribune*, 28 September 1958, 1. For Maryland's and California's referendum challenges to desegregation enforcement and open housing laws, see "Petitions Block a Maryland Law to Combat Bias," *NYT*, 2 June 1963, 1, 70; "California Split on 'Fair' Housing," *NYT*, 4 April 1963, 25; "Vote in Berkeley," *Christian Science Monitor*, 6 April 1963, 11.

26. "Petition Is Ready in Cambridge," *Sun*, 8 August 1963, 44, 31; "Three More Petitions Are Filed," *DB*, 10 August 1963, 1.

27. "Negroes to Support Referendum," *DB*, 13 August 1963, 1; "Cambridge Race Vote Set Oct. 1," *Sun*, 20 August 1963, 36, 22.

28. GR, interview with JRF, 3 December 2003; "Cambridge Cost State $160,000," *Afro-Am*, 10 August 1963, 13; "Leader Says 'Miracle' Needed in Cambridge," *Afro-Am*, 24 August 1963, 13; "Citizens Are Encouraged to Vote," *DB*, 26 August 1963, 1; "Cambridge Leaders Back Vote," *Afro-Am*, 27 August 1963, 22. The election director for Dorchester County's Board of Elections, Karin B. Kuntz, could not find any documents related to Richardson's voting history in Cambridge. See Karin B. Kuntz, email to JRF, 24 July 2012.

29. "Supporters and Foes of Amendment Stage Meetings," *DB*, 24 September 1963, 1; "2 Factions Clash in Cambridge, Md.," *NYT*, 29 September 1963, 78; "Integration Leader Quits in Cambridge," *Sun*, 25 September 1963, 48, 28; "Cambridge Leader Decides Not to Quit," *NYT*, 26 September 1963, 29.

30. "Cambridge Pact Off; 'Bad Faith' Charged by Negro Leadership," *Sun*, 23 June 1963, 46; "Cambridge Cost State $160,000," *Afro-Am*, 10 August 1963, 13; GR, interview with JRF, 17 August 2002; Richardson, "Energy of the People Passing through Me," 283; GR, email to JRF, 17 October 2013. Robinson did not respond to my query about whether he had done what Richardson claimed. See Reggie Robinson, emails to JRF, 4 and 5 March 2010; JRF, emails to Reggie Robinson, 2, 4, 5, and 15 March 2010.

31. "Gov. Wallace Defends Self, Raps 'Outside' Intervention," *Sun*, 14 September 1963, 28, 17. The show aired on WJZ-TV, the local ABC affiliate. Malkus had made the same allegations before. See "Malkus Accepts N.A.A.C.P. Attack," *Sun*, 22 July 1963, 30; "Mayor Charges that Mrs. Richardson Hopes to Defeat Amendment and Get Back in the News," *DB*, 28 September 1963, 1; "Cambridge Warned to Support Race Law," *WP*, 30 September 1963, A1, A6. Newspaper columnist George Frazier was the first to compare Richardson to the French freedom fighter. See George Frazier, "Be Like a Buddhist," *Boston Herald*, 25 July 1963, 12.

32. Margaret Willis Reynolds, interview with JRF; Edward Brooke, interview with JRF; Jacqueline Fassett, interview with JRF; Barbara Wesley Lassiter, interview with JRF; Donna Richardson, interview with JRF; GR, interview with JRF, 5 December 2011.

33. Audre Lorde, "The Uses of Anger: Women Responding to Racism," in *Sister Outsider: Essays and Speeches* (Freedom, CA: Crossing Press, 1984), 127. Two biographers have written about how their subjects' anger was a catalyst for their activism. See Chana Kai Lee, "Anger, Memory, and Personal Power: Fannie Lou Hamer and Civil Rights Leadership," in *Sisters in the Struggle: African-American Women in the Civil Rights–Black Power Movement*, ed. Bettye Collier-Thomas and V. P. Franklin (New York: NYU Press, 2001), 139–70; Patricia A. Schechter, *Ida B. Wells-Barnett & American Reform, 1880–1930* (Chapel Hill: University of North Carolina Press, 2001), 13–14.

34. GR, interview with JRF, 17 August 2002; Richardson, "Energy of the People Passing through Me," 274.

35. GR, interview with John Britton; GR, interviews with JRF, 17 August 2002, 30 May 2013; "Leaders Ask for Heavy Vote," *Afro-Am*, 28 September 1963, 1, 2.

36. "Council Receives 11 Protests," *DB*, 24 September 1963, 1; "Don't-Vote Rally Small," *Sun*, 27 September 1963, 30; "CNAC Is Refused Permission to Use Church to Hold Meeting Last Night," *DB*, 27 September 1963, 1; "Split Widens in Negro Ranks at Cambridge: Cites a New Start," *WP*, 27 September 1963, A5; "Leaders Ask for Heavy Vote," *Afro-Am*, 28 September 1963, 1, 2; "2 Factions Clash in Cambridge, Md.," *NYT*, 29 September 1963, 78.

37. "Don't-Vote Rally Small," *Sun*, 27 September 1963, 30; "CNAC Is Refused Permission to Use Church to Hold Meeting Last Night," *DB*, 27 September 1963, 1.

38. "Heavy Vote Expected in Tuesday's Referendum," *DB*, 30 September 1963, 1; "Voting over New Crisis; Cambridge," *Afro-Am*, 12 October 1963, 14.

39. Richardson, "Energy of the People Passing through Me," 282; "Vote Nears in Cambridge, Md.," *NYT*, 22 September 1963, 72.

40. "Cambridge Votes Today on Charter," *Sun*, 1 October 1963, 38, 25; "Negroes to Support Referendum," *DB*, 13 August 1963, 1.

41. Schechter, *Ida B. Wells-Barnett*, 172–73, 186, 217, 242; Lee, *For Freedom's Sake*, 30, 42, 67; "Vote Nears in Cambridge, Md.," *NYT*, 22 September 1963, 72; Levy, *Civil War on Race Street*, 98; Herbert Spencer, *Social Statics: Or, the Conditions Essential to Human Happiness Specified* (London: John Chapman, 1851), 211–12.

42. "Cambridge Votes Today on Charter," *Sun*, 1 October 1963, 38, 25; "Integration Leader Quits in Cambridge," *Sun*, 25 September 1963, 48, 28; "Negroes Ask Vote Boycott," *Sun*, 26 September 1963, 12; "Md. Negroes Shun Polls in Vote on Integration of Public Places," *Chicago Daily Defender* (daily ed.), 2 October 1963, 4. For Birmingham's racial strife, see "Birmingham Is Orderly under Truce," *WP*, 30 June 1963, A12; "Birmingham," *NYT*, 22 September 1963, 169.

43. "A Test of Leadership," *DB*, 30 September 1963, 10.

44. "Chance in Cambridge," *Sun*, 9 August 1963, 12.

45. Pine Street Elementary School was the Second Ward's polling station. "Registration, Voting Places," *DB*, 28 September 1963, 1; "Cambridge Public Accommodations Amendment Loses by 274 Votes," *DB*, 2 October 1963, 1; "Voting over New Crisis; Cambridge," *Afro-Am*, 12 October 1963, 14.

46. George Frazier, "Mrs. Richardson: True Segregationist," *Boston Herald*, 19 June 1963, 12; George Frazier, "Be Like a Buddhist," *Boston Herald*, 25 July 1963, 12. See *DB*, 21 June 1963, for a reprint of Frazier's June column. For another take on Frazier and his view on race, see Charles Fountain, *Another Man's Poison: The Life and Writings of Columnist George Frazier* (Chester, CT: Globe Pequot Press, 1984). I thank Steve Kodesch for his assistance in locating a copy of Fountain's book.

47. "Tragic Decision," *Evening Sun*, 2 October 1963, Clarence Logan clippings file; "Cambridge, Md.—A Study in Pathos," *Christian Science Monitor*, 7 October 1963, 16 (emphasis added); "Civil Rights: A Zealot's Stand," *Time*, 11 October 1963, accessed 20 June 2011, http://www.time.com/time/magazine/article /0,9171,873084,00.html.

48. William S. White, "Era of Negro Extremism?" *Victoria (TX) Advocate*, 8 October 1963, 4. Another white journalist who criticized Richardson in his syndicated column was Robert G. Spivack, "Mrs. Gloria Richardson of Cambridge Md., Is a Most Courageous Woman," *Michigan Chronicle*, 16 November 1963, D4.

49. "Misleadership in Cambridge," *Pittsburgh Courier*, 12 October 1963, 10; "Issues: Good and Bad," *Los Angeles Sentinel*, 17 October 1963, A6.

50. "Cambridge Vote," *Sun*, 5 October 1963, 10. For King's role on Baltimore's Human Relations Commission, see "King Denies Harassment of Police at Demonstration," *Sun*, 21 March 1964, 34, 22. King wrote his letter as a private citizen.

51. The author(s) of Federalist Paper No. 51 wrote: "It is of great importance in a republic not only to guard the society against the oppression of its rulers, but to guard one part of the society against the injustice of the other part. Different interests necessarily exist in different classes of citizens. If a majority be united by a common interest, the rights of the minority will be insecure." "The Federalist Papers: No. 51," *The Avalon Project: Documents in Law, History and Diplomacy*, Lillian Goldman Law Library, Yale Law School, 2008, accessed 19 October 2017, http://avalon.law .yale.edu/18th_century/fed51.asp. For Morse's statements, see "Morse Lauds Boycott of Cambridge Poll," *Worker*, 8 October 1963, 7, Andrew Moursund's Cambridge movement clippings file (copy in author's possession); "Sen. Morse Says

Boycott Was Right," *DB*, 3 October 1963, 1. A US Supreme Court case from 1943 buttressed Richardson's and Senator Morse's argument that the referendum was illegitimate. See *West Virginia State Board of Education v. Barnette*, 319 U.S. 624 (1943), Cornell University Law School, accessed 14 August 2014, http://www.law.cornell.edu/supremecourt/text/319/624.

52. "Mrs. Richardson's Revolt," *Liberator*, November 1963, 2. Watts was also the chairman of the Liberation Committee for Africa. See "400 Picket U.N. in Salute to Castro and Lumumba," *NYT*, 19 February 1961, 1, 18.

53. "Voting over New Crisis; Cambridge," *Afro-Am*, 12 October 1963, 14; "Racial Problem Threatens Life of Town in Maryland," *Spokesman-Review* (Spokane, WA), 3 October 1963, 33.

54. "Cambridge Leaders Back Vote," *Afro-Am*, 27 August 1963, 22; "White and Negro Leaders to Meet Monday to Discuss Racial Crisis," *DB*, 3 October 1963, 1; "Cambridge Coals Rekindled," *Christian Science Monitor*, 3 October 1963, 18; "Cambridge Citizens to Continue Bias Fight," *Daily Defender*, 3 October 1963, 4; "Voting over New Crisis; Cambridge," *Afro-Am*, 12 October 1963, 14.

55. "Bi-racial Committee to Meet," *DB*, 22 October 1963, 1; "Cambrid[g]e's New Peace Group Meets," *WP*, 23 October 1963, B8.

56. Ibid.; "Cambridge Story: Gloria Sees Trouble," *Afro-Am*, 26 October 1963, 13.

57. Cambridge Nonviolent Action Committee, "Cambridge, Maryland: Background Information," n.d., 2–3 (copy in author's possession). The press release "was specifically drafted for wide distribution," Richardson recalled, and copies were printed and mailed to local and national media outlets as well as various federal agencies. GR, email to JRF, 21 January 2014.

58. "Shore Trial Is Assailed," *Sun*, 8 November 1963, 11; "Man Acquitted of Assault on Negro Girl," *WP*, 8 November 1963, A3. For an outstanding book on blacks' response to whites' sexualized terrorism and the America's criminal justice system's failure to punish the offenders, see Danielle L. McGuire, *At the Dark End of the Street: Black Women, Rape, and Resistance—A New History of the Civil Rights Movement from Rosa Parks to the Rise of Black Power* (New York: Vintage, 2010).

59. Ibid.

60. "Protests Called off at Cambridge, Md., in Mourning Period," *NYT*, 30 November 1963, 8; "Delay Mass Protests in Cambridge," *New York Amsterdam News*, 7 December 1963, 43; "Reduce Troops in Cambridge: Negroes Threaten to March," *Daily Defender*, 17 December 1963, 28; GR, email to JRF, 25 November 2013.

61. GR, interview with Robert Penn Warren.

62. Ibid.; Bruce Bartlett, *Wrong on Race: The Democratic Party's Buried Past* (New York: Palgrave Macmillan, 2009), 157.

63. "Human Relations Committee Notes Progress in Reducing Racial Tension," *DB*, 18 December 1963, 1; "1963 Headlines Show Community Had Strength to Ride Out Crises," *DB*, 31 December 1963, 1.

64. "Racial Story Is Dominated by Woman Leader," *DB*, 31 December 1963, 3.

65. "The Year as Seen by a Camera," *Afro-Am*, 4 January 1964, 12; "Defender's 1963 Honor Roll, 10 Named," *Chicago Defender*, 11–17 January 1964, 1, 3.

8. Creative Chaos

1. "Workers Spend XMas in Jail," *Student Voice*, 30 December 1963, 1, 3; "Mrs. Richardson to Protest Bias," *Sun*, 30 December 1963, S20; "Dick Gregory Leads March on Restaurants," *Atlanta Daily World*, 1 January 1964, 1, 4; "Agreement Reached over Restaurants," *Atlanta Daily World*, 4 January 1964, 1; "Gregory, SNCC Get Action in Ga. Restaurant Blitz," *Jet*, 16 January 1964, 5.

2. SNCC's three-day conference over the Thanksgiving weekend in 1963 was the organization's first significant pivot toward economic issues. At that conference, titled "For Food and Jobs," participants talked about how to combat racial discrimination in hiring and how, in the words of John Lewis, they could create "an America where no man is hungry, none jobless." See "Force U.S. to Act, Rights Unit Told," *NYT*, 30 November 1963, 8; "U.S. Takes Part in Rights Parley," *NYT*, 1 December 1963, 50; Lewis quoted in "Negro Leaders Give Their Views: Prospects for '64 in the Civil Rights Struggle," *Negro Digest*, January 1964, 9, 12–13. For CNAC's economic agenda, see CNAC, "Cambridge, Maryland: Background Information," 1.

3. "350 Students Hear Dick Gregory at SNCC Meet," *Afro-Am*, 27 April 1963, 18; "Atlanta Sit-in Planned by Cambridge Group," *WP*, 30 December 1963, A6. For information on Robert Moses and SNCC's executive committee meeting in December 1963, see Carson, *In Struggle*, 26, 51, 104–5; Ransby, *Ella Baker*, 314–15; John Lewis, "A Trend toward Aggressive Nonviolent Action," in *Black Protest Thought in the Twentieth Century*, 2nd ed., ed. August Meier, Elliott M. Rudwick, and Francis L. Broderick (Indianapolis: Bobbs-Merrill, 1971), 352–60; "SNCC Gathering Hears New Directions for Movement," *Harvard Crimson*, 22 April 1964, accessed 27 April 2011, http://www.thecrimson.com/article/1964/4/22/sncc-gathering-hears-new-directions-for/?print=1.

4. "Cambridge Protests," *Afro-Am*, 4 January 1964, 14; Anthony Sagona, telephone interview with JRF, 24 March 2004. Another Brooklyn CORE member who remarked about the area's poverty was Arnie Goldwag; see Arnie Goldwag, telephone interview with JRF, 3 February 2004. "A Journey into 'Outskirts of Hope,'" *WP*, 19 January 1964, E1, E5.

5. Maryland Advisory Committee to the United States Commission on Civil Rights, *Report on Maryland: Employment*, February 1964, 19–21; "Shore Retraining Program Sought by Rights Leader," *Sun*, 27 June 1963; "Morton to Back Retraining on Shore if Need Is Shown, *Afro-Am*, 29 June 1963; "U.S. to Aid Shore Job Training," *Baltimore News-Post*, 16 September 1963, 1; "At Least 150 to Be Involved," *Afro-Am*, 17 September 1963, 20, 19; "New Training Plan Meant to Aid Shore," *Sun*, 17 September 1963, 40, 27, all in Clarence Logan clippings file.

6. "Cambridge Is Warned by Negroes," *WP*, 29 January 1964, A5; "Rights Group Urges Strong Anti-Bias Bill," *Sun*, 31 January 1964, 40, 24; "Cambridge Racial Ills Aired at Hill Hearing," *WP*, 31 January 1964, A8; "Parley Fails to End Crisis in Cambridge," *NYT*, 31 January 1964, 11; CNAC, "Cambridge, Maryland: Background Information," 1, 2; CNAC, "Demands," n.d. (copy in author's possession; emphasis in original). The allegation against members of the Industrial Development Commission is found in this document.

10

7. Curricula uniformity and standardized textbooks were two elements of CNAC's plan to improve children's education. See "Cambridge Boycott Hit: Schools Head to Fail Pupils and May Charge Parents," *Sun*, 8 February 1964, 5; "Cut Classes Pupils Asked," *Sun*, 11 February 1964, 10; "Cuts Both Ways," *Sun*, 12 February 1964, 16; "Effect of School Boycott Stirs Debate in Cambridge: Mrs. Richardson's Figures Disputed by City," *WP*, 12 February 1964, C1, C5.

The *Sun*'s editors came out against the school boycott, too. They argued it was the same illegitimate tactic proposed by white segregationist parents in Maryland's Talbot County in 1957. What the editors failed to realize was that the white parents in Talbot County had tried to prevent integration and equal access to a quality education, whereas the black parents in Dorchester County were trying to achieve those things for their children.

8. "Use of Surplus Food Gets Cambridge Study," *WP*, 20 February 1964, C17; "Maryland Guardsmen Hold 15 in Protest for Jobs at Cambridge," *NYT*, 26 February 1964, 24; "Troops Smash Negro Protest in Cambridge," *Chicago Tribune*, 26 February 1964, 2; "Cambridge Negroes Resume Protests," *Student Voice*, 3 March 1964, 2; GR, email to JRF, 3 October 2014.

9. "Use of Surplus Food Gets Cambridge Study," *WP*, 20 February 1964, C17.

10. "U.S. Food Program Erupts in Maryland," *Christian Science Monitor*, 7 March 1964, 3.

11. "300 Students Protest in Shore Town," *Sun*, 24 February 1964, 32, 23. For black students' fear of being assaulted by whites at night, see Don Lundy, telephone interview with JRF, 16 September 2004. Boardley organized SAFE, and Wilson joined it when he transferred to Maryland State College from Bowie State College. See James Boardley, telephone interview with JRF, 25 June 2014; GR, email to JRF, 3 October 2014.

12. "20 Arrested in Clash of Paraders, Police at Princess Anne," *WP*, 27 February 1964, A1, A4; "28 Arrested as 300 March on the Shore," *Sun*, 27 February 1964, 46, 33; "Police Use Dogs, Hoses, to Rout Shore Students," *Afro-Am*, 29 February 1964, 1–2.

13. "28 Arrested as 300 March on the Shore," *Sun*, 27 February 1964, 46, 33; "Police Use Dogs, Hoses, to Rout Shore Students," *Afro-Am*, 29 February 1964, 1–2; GR, interview with JRF, 26 June 2008; GR, emails to JRF, 17 and 23 March 2014, 3 October 2014. The man bent over the car was Clarence Cromwell, a cousin of Cambridge resident Dwight Cromwell. Jim Nichols was the person who retrieved Richardson from the men's dorm and drove her back to Cambridge. James Boardley, interview with JRF.

14. GR, interview with JRF, 26 June 2008; John Kady, telephone interview with JRF, 10 December 2005. Kady was UPI's Baltimore bureau manager from October 1963 until January 1965. "28 Arrested as 300 March on the Shore," *Sun*, 27 February 1964, 46, 33; Mitchell quoted in "Police Use Dogs, Hoses, to Rout Shore Students," *Afro-Am*, 29 February 1964, 1–2; "Shore Town Protests Are Called Off," *Sun*, 29 February 1964, 30, 18; "In Maryland, Dogs, Fire Hoses Quell Protests," *Student Voice*, 3 March 1964, 1, 4. During this time, white supremacists also burned a cross near the college campus.

15. Jonathan Beirne Streff, "Reading Race: The Roots of the Chester, Pennsylvania, Race Riot of 1917" (master's thesis, Temple University, 1999), 54–59; Richard E. Harris, *Politics and Prejudice: A History of Chester (Pa) Negroes* (Apache Junction, AZ: Relmo Publishers, 1991), 115–18.

16. Richardson's charges obtained from Vanessa Suter, telephone message to JRF, 30 June 2004. Suter is the officer in charge of the Chester, Pennsylvania, police force's arrest records. See also "107 Arrested at Chester, Pa., in 5th Day of School Protest," *NYT*, 3 April 1964, 23; "107 Arrested in Rights March," *WP*, 3 April 1964, B10; "Rights Heads End Protest in Chester," *Sun*, 5 April 1964, 3; "Chester Leaders Hit NAACP Official's Act," *Daily Defender*, 8 April 1964, 10. Richardson's FBI file contains additional details about the arrests and the amounts of the fine and bond that are not included in the newspaper articles. See Federal Bureau of Investigation File No. 100-442421 (Gloria R. Dandridge), copy in author's possession. Broadmeadows prison was located in Thornton, Pennsylvania.

Two months after their arrests, the demonstrators were indicted by a Delaware County grand jury, and a June trial date was set. Because of various legal decisions and delays, the trial never occurred. Seven years later, a Pennsylvania judge dismissed all charges against Richardson and the other arrestees. "Pennsylvania Indicts Gloria Richardson," *Sun*, 6 June 1964, 20; "Chester Cases Voided Seven Years Later," *Crisis* 78, no. 3 (April–May 1971): 100.

17. The two prospective students were Vivian Malone and James Hood. "Wallace: Zero for Kennedy," *Christian Science Monitor*, 5 November 1963, 12; "Gov. Wallace Files to Run in Maryland's Primary," *WP*, 10 March 1964, A1.

18. "A Day to Watch," *DB*, 4 May 1964, 4; John Kady, interview with JRF. Steve Broening was the other reporter.

19. "Uninvited Guest," *Time*, 22 May 1964, accessed 9 August 2007, http://www.time.com/time/printout/0,8816,871094,00.html; "'Hate' Groups Back Wallace Bid," *NYT*, 14 May 1964, 27. Gerald L. K. Smith was one of the more infamous white supremacists who supported Wallace.

20. "Wallace to Speak from City Tonight," *DB*, 11 May 1964, 1; "Wallace at RFC Arena," *DB*, 12 May 1964, 1; "Cambridge Baby Dies in Troopers' Tear Gas Mist," *Jet*, 28 May 1964, 8–9; James "Peter" Hinde, "Report on Carmelite Involvement at Cambridge, MD . . . May 11, '64," n.d., copy in author's possession. Hinde was among eight Catholics from Whitefriars Hall in Washington, DC, who drove to Cambridge to support CNAC's anti-Wallace rally. James "Peter" Hinde, email to JRF, 5 January 2014. Also see GR, interview with Peter Goldman, 18 May 1969. Richardson said the speaker from the Nation of Islam was named Lonnie X, while Hinde said his name was Ronnie 3X. I believe the man was Lonnie 3X Cross. See "Dr. Lonnie 3-X Is No Malcolm X," *Afro-Am*, 25 April 1964, 14; Clifton E. Marsh, *The Lost-Found Nation of Islam in America* (Lanham, MD: Scarecrow Press, 2000), 54.

21. Carmichael and Thelwell, *Ready for Revolution*, 96, 248; Cleveland Sellers, *The River of No Return* (New York: William Morrow, 1973), 20–21, 57, 67–68. The type of greeting Wallace would receive from black residents was set the night before he arrived. On the evening of Sunday, 10 May, four dozen young people from the Second Ward paraded through their neighborhoods singing songs, setting off firecrackers, and throwing rocks. Richardson was out in the streets trying to convince the youths not to

escalate their protests because that could lead to a confrontation with National Guards-men. See "Cambridge Negroes Protest on Wallace," *NYT*, 11 May 1964, 25.

For Wallace's speech and CNAC's response, see "Wallace to Speak from City Tonight," *DB*, 11 May 1964, 1; "Cambridge Negroes Protest on Wallace," *NYT*, 11 May 1964, 25; John Kady, interview with JRF; Richardson, "Energy of the People Passing through Me," 286–87; GR, interview with JRF, 17 July 2010; GR, email to JRF, 31 December 2013. Richardson first encountered the term "creative chaos" when she read a document produced by the Institute for Policy Studies in Washing-ton, DC, where she served as a consultant in the spring of 1964.

22. John H. Britton, "Woman behind Cambridge Racial Revolt: Female Dynamo Had City at Point of Explosion before Truce," *Jet*, 8 August 1963, 17; Sellers, *River of No Return*, 71; GR, interview with JRF, 2 August 2003.

23. This was the second confrontation of the night between marchers and the National Guard. See "Wallace at RFC Arena," *DB*, 12 May 1964, 1, 2; "Racial Hot-bed, Cambridge, Md.," *Daily Defender*, 13 May 1964, 1, 3; John T. Kady, "Many Clash in Cambridge Protest Involving Death," *Atlanta Daily World*, 16 May 1964, 4; "Uninvited Guest," *Time*, 22 May 1964; "MD Guardsmen Use Gas," *Afro-Am*, 23 May 1964, 1, 2; "Cambridge Baby Dies in Troopers' Tear Gas Mist," *Jet*, 28 May 1964, 8–9; GR, interview with JRF, 20 March 2004; Richardson, "Energy of the People Passing through Me," 286–87; GR, email to JRF, 25 February 2013.

24. "Cambridge Freedom Fighters Tell Boycott, Rent Strike, Vote Plans," *Afro-Am*, 23 May 1964, 15; "MD Guardsmen Use Gas," *Afro-Am*, 23 May 1964, 1, 2. A trial never took place.

25. "Negroes Hold New Protest in Cambridge," *Sun*, 13 May 1964, 48, 30; "MD Guardsmen Use Gas," *Afro-Am*, 23 May 1964, 1, 2; "Troops Again Use Tear Gas to Quell Demonstrations," *DB*, 15 May 1964, 1; "4 Guardsmen Are Injured in Cambridge," *Sun*, 26 May 1964, 42, 28.

26. Brian Ward, *Just My Soul Responding: Rhythm and Blues, Black Consciousness and Race Relations* (Berkeley: University of California Press, 1998), 314; Dick Greg-ory, telephone interview with JRF, 21 July 2008; Richardson, "Energy of the People Passing through Me," 285.

27. "Guard Considers Negro Comedy Show Tonight," *DB*, 27 May 1964, 1; "Ban Imposed on Meetings in Cambridge," *Sun*, 27 May 1964, 54, 36; "ACT Invites LBJ to 'Worst Fair,'" *Daily Defender*, 27 May 1964, 3; "Integrationists Demand Closing Down of White Entertainment Facilities," *DB*, 28 May 1964, 1; "Racial Panel to Be Fixed by Governor," *Sun*, 29 May 1964, 44, 26; "Guard's Chief Permits Gregory Show," *Chicago Tribune*, 29 May 1964, 8; "Tension in Cambridge Lessened by Gregory: Withdrew Order," *WP*, 1 June 1964, A6; "Negroes Threat 'to Close Town' Backs Gregory," *Jet*, 11 June 1964, 7; Dick Gregory, *Up from Nigger* (New York: Stein & Day, 1976), 49; GR, emails to JRF, 3 May 2012, 13 May 2013.

28. "Integrationists Demand Closing Down of White Entertainment Facilities," *DB*, 28 May 1964, 1; "Racial Panel to Be Fixed by Governor," *Sun*, 29 May 1964, 44, 26.

29. "Racial Talk Is Held Here," *Sun*, 13 June 1964, 11.

30. The Miles Committee was originally called the Governor's Committee on Cambridge. "Racial Panel to Be Fixed by Governor," *Sun*, 29 May 1964, 44, 26;

"Racial Talk Is Held Here," *Sun*, 13 June 1964, 11; "Racial Arbiter Hopeful," *WP*, 28 June 1964, A6; "Clarence Miles, GBC Founder, Dies at 80," *Sun*, 9 October 1977, B1; "Whites in Cambridge, Md., 'Beginning to See Light': Economics Recognized as Heart of Problem," *Pittsburgh Courier* (national ed.), 27 June 1964, 9.

31. "Racial Talk Is Held Here," *Sun*, 13 June 1964, 11; "Shore Racial Report Given: Following Is Text of Study by Miles Committee," *Sun*, 6 July 1964, 23.

32. GR, interview with Robert Penn Warren; "Cambridge Negroes to Get Park Jobs," *WP*, 3 June 1964, A8; "Guard Ordered out of City: Troops to Leave Here Saturday," *DB*, 8 July 1964, 1. Morgan State's Melvin Humphries was a part of this jobs training program. See "Professor Brings Ray of Light to Cambridge," *WP*, 4 June 1964, C7.

33. "Guard Ordered out of City: Troops to Leave Here Saturday," *DB*, 8 July 1964, 1; "Negro Elected to Head Cambridge, Md., Council," *NYT*, 21 July 1964, 20; "Maryland City Gives High Post to Negro Leader," *Christian Science Monitor*, 22 July 1964, 5; Levy, *Civil War on Race Street*, 110.

34. "In New Directions," *DB*, 16 July 1964, 13.

35. For a history of the passage of the Civil Rights Act of 1964, including President Johnson's personal and political journey leading up to his signing of the act, see Todd Purdum, *An Idea Whose Time Has Come: Two Presidents, Two Parties, and the Battle for the Civil Rights Act of 1964* (New York: Henry Holt, 2014). For the black press's reaction to the Civil Rights Act's passage, see "A Giant First Step," *Afro-Am*, 27 June 1964, 1, 2; "Hail the New Law," *New York Amsterdam News*, 4 July 1964, 1.

36. "CNAC Is Not Expecting to Test New Law," *DB*, 2 July 1964, 1; "Negroes Test Law in City," *DB*, 6 July 1964, 1; "Negroes Fail in Test of Rights Law at Two Cambridge Places," *DB*, 7 July 1964, 1; Levy, *Civil War on Race Street*, 115, 117–18.

37. "Up Front . . . Down South, What's in a Word," *Pittsburgh Courier*, 4 January 1964, 11; Novella Baldwin, letter to the editor, *DB*, 14 July 1964; GR, interview with JRF, 17 August 2002; James Baldwin, *The Fire Next Time* (New York: Vintage International, 1993), 94.

38. "Personally and Socially: Civil Rights Fighter to Wed," *New York Amsterdam News*, 27 June 1964, 22; "Rights Leader Praises Council President Choice," *DB*, 23 July 1964, 1; "The Chips Are Down," *New York Amsterdam News*, 25 July 1964, 19; "Washington Dateline," *Pittsburgh Courier*, 1 August 1964, 18. Richardson's mother did not abide by the news blackout on her daughter's marriage to Dandridge; she discussed it with a reporter from *Jet*. See "Cambridge Seeks Leader to Replace Mrs. Richardson," *Jet*, 18 June 1964, 9.

39. GR, email to JRF, 20 February 2014.

40. "Cambridge Seeks Leader to Replace Mrs. Richardson," *Jet*, 18 June 1964, 9; "Choptank Waterfront Urged as State Park," *WP*, 19 June 1964, B5 (emphasis added). For Richardson's trip to Washington, see "Whites in Cambridge, Md., 'Beginning to See Light': Economics Recognized as Heart of Problem," *Pittsburgh Courier* (national ed.), 27 June 1964, 9. For the change in leadership of the Cambridge movement, see "Guard Ordered out of City: Troops to Leave Here Saturday," *DB*, 8 July 1964, 1; "Student Group Takes over Rights Drive in Cambridge," *Sun*, 1 September 1964, 10.

41. "One-Man Force Keeping Guard up in Cambridge," *Sun*, 22 August 1964, 17.

42. "Gloria Richardson Weds, Quits Civil Rights Work," *WP*, 1 September 1964, A4; Carmichael and Thelwell, *Ready for Revolution*, 340; Murray Kempton, "Gloria, Gloria," *New Republic*, 16 November 1963, 15.

43. "A Cauldron of Hate," *Time*, 19 July 1963, accessed 9 August 2007, http://www.time.com/time/magazine/article/0,9171,896863,00.html; "Uninvited Guest," *Time*, 22 May 1964, accessed 9 August 2007, http://www.time.com/time/printout/0,8816,871094,00.html; "'Radical' Integrationist," *NYT*, 13 July 1963, 6. Interestingly, authors Clara Fraser and Richard S. Fraser interpreted Richardson's quote as evidence that she "lacked confidence in herself as a leader." See the Frasers' *Crisis and Leadership* (Seattle, WA: Red Letter Press, 2000), 177, n. 36.

44. George Frazier, "Be Like a Buddhist," *Boston Herald*, 25 July 1963, 12; Regine Pernoud and Narue-Veronique Clin, *Joan of Arc: Her Story*, trans. Jeremy Duquesnay Adams (New York: St. Martin's Press, 1998), 89, 90, 111, 116, 120, 135, 164, 285, 293.

45. GR, interview with JRF, 17 August 2002; Richardson, "Energy of the People Passing through Me," 290. Whitehurst, who was always referred to as "Mrs. John L. Whitehurst," was also a member of the University of Maryland Board of Regents. See "Shore Racial Report Given," *Sun*, 6 July 1964, 23; "Mrs. Whitehurst's Funeral Is Scheduled for Tuesday," *Sun*, 27 February 1971, A13.

46. Glenda Elizabeth Gilmore, *Gender and Jim Crow: Women and the Politics of White Supremacy in North Carolina, 1896–1920* (Chapel Hill: University of North Carolina Press, 1996), 42–43. For texts that discuss gender construction and social attitudes about appropriate gender roles in society after World War II and during the civil rights movement, see Giddings, *When and Where I Enter*, chap. 14; Meyerowitz, *Not June Cleaver;* Peter J. Ling and Sharon Monteith, eds., *Gender and the Civil Rights Movement* (New Brunswick, NJ: Rutgers University Press, 2004); Steve Estes, *I Am a Man! Race, Manhood, and the Civil Rights Movement* (Chapel Hill: University of North Carolina Press, 2005).

47. GR, interview with John Britton.

48. Kempton, "Gloria, Gloria," 16; Richardson, "Energy of the People Passing through Me," 290.

49. Robbins and Robbins, "Why Didn't They Hit Back?"; "'I'm Hurt,'" *Afro-Am*, 2 November 1963, 1, 2; "What Ever Happened to . . . Gloria Richardson: Civil Rights Leader Now Works with NCNW," *Ebony*, February 1974, 138.

Although Richardson could not recall the name of the doctor, he was among a group of researchers studying why crime rates declined in black communities where there was an active civil rights struggle. Cambridge was one of the communities the researchers studied and wrote about in their report. See GR, interview with JRF, 4 March 2009; GR, email to JRF, 26 April 2012; "Nonviolence/Violence," *Howard Magazine*, January 1966, 5–8; "Researchers Claim Rights Drive Provides an Alternative to Crime," *Charleston (SC) News and Courier*, 13 February 1966, 9-B.

50. "Freedom, H of K Parade Theme," *Daily Defender*, 22 June 1964, 5; "If You Ask Me," *Afro-Am*, 4 June 1963, 3; "Negro Elks Convene Today in Frederick," *WP*, 22 June 1963, B6; "Elks Honor Race Leader," *Sun*, 20 June 1963, 38; "City's

Compromise Plan Is Rejected by Integrationists," *DB*, 24 June 1963, 1; "Rights Leaders Given Award," *Sun*, 7 March 1964, 11. Richard Allen founded the AME Church in Philadelphia in the late eighteenth century. It was the nation's first independent black Protestant denomination.

51. Lee, *For Freedom's Sake*, 43, 44; "1963—Year of Racial Crises in Maryland," *DB*, 26 December 1963, 10.

52. Lemuel Chester, interview with JRF, 8 January 2007; Larry Chester, interview with JRF, 8 January 2007; Dwight Cromwell, interview with Sandy Harney, 27 August 1997; *Women of Triumph II*, executive producer Everett L. Marshburn (Baltimore: Maryland Public Television, 1998), videocassette.

53. William Hall, interview with JRF. Hall was a member of Howard University's Nonviolent Action Group. Other activists attested to Richardson's positive character, intelligence, leadership, and commitment to the civil rights movement. See Arnie Goldwag, interview JRF; Don Lundy, interview with JRF; Cleveland Sellers, telephone interview with JRF, 24 February 2004.

54. Cleveland Sellers, interview with JRF; Joyce Ladner, interview with JRF; John H. Britton, telephone interview with JRF, 8 July 2005. Journalist John Kady also commented favorably about Richardson's intellect; see John Kady, interview with JRF.

55. Suckle went on to join SNCC's staff in Atlanta. See Mark Suckle, interview with JRF, 26 December 2013; "Gloria Richardson: Lady General of Civil Rights," *Ebony*, July 1964, 23.

56. Ibid.; "'Radical' Integrationist," *NYT*, 13 July 1963, 6; "Cambridge: Status Quo Stand," *Afro-Am*, 20 July 1963, 1, 31; "Gov. Tawes, Vacationists, and, 'Go It, Gloria!'" *Afro-Am*, 3 August 1963, 5; Britton, "Woman behind Cambridge Racial Revolt," 14–20; "Gloria Richardson Explains Cambridge, Maryland to N.Y.," *New York Amsterdam News*, 24 August 1963, 18; Kempton, "Gloria, Gloria," 16; "Mrs. Richardson Okeys Malcolm X," *Afro-Am*, 10 March 1964, 16; "Milestones," *Time*, 11 September 1964, accessed 31 March 2008, http://www.time.com/time/printout/0,8816,830688,00.html.

57. John H. Britton, interview with JRF; John Kady, interview with JRF.

58. Gregory, *Up from Nigger*, 46; Dick Gregory, interview with JRF.

59. Paul Robeson, *Here I Stand* (Boston: Beacon Press, 1958), 105; C. T. Vivian, telephone interview with JRF, 23 March 2011. Vivian was one of the Nashville residents who continued the Freedom Rides in Alabama in 1961.

60. "Mrs. Richardson to Speak," *Sun*, 22 May 1964, 12; Szabo, "Interview with Gloria Richardson Dandridge," 354.

61. Ransby, *Ella Baker*, 364–65; Belinda Robnett, "Women in the Student Non-Violent Coordinating Committee: Ideology, Organizational Structure, and Leadership," in *Gender and the Civil Rights Movement*, ed. Peter J. Ling and Sharon Monteith (New Brunswick, NJ: Rutgers University Press, 2004), 131. For SNCC's culture of creativity and personal development, see Ransby, *Ella Baker*, 364. Reagon quoted in Robnett, "Women in the Student Non-Violent Coordinating Committee," 136.

62. Fleming, *Soon We Will Not Cry*, 96–97; Casey Hayden and Mary King, "Sex and Caste: A Kind of Memo from Casey Hayden and Mary King to a Number of

Other Women in the Peace and Freedom Movements," 1965, accessed 18 February 2014, http://uic.edu/orgs/cwluherstory/CWLUArchive/memo.html. Other members of SNCC have written about their experiences with sexism. See Cynthia Washington, "We Started from Different Ends of the Spectrum," *Southern Exposure* 9, no. 4 (Winter 1977): 14, and various essays in Faith S. Holsaert et al., eds., *Hands on the Freedom Plow: Personal Accounts by Women in SNCC* (Urbana: University of Illinois Press, 2010). For Beal's work in SNCC and her essay "Double Jeopardy," see Student Nonviolent Coordinating Committee, Stanford University, n.d., accessed 18 February 2014, http://www.stanford.edu/~ccarson/articles/black_women_3.htm; Frances Beal, "Double Jeopardy: To Be Black and Female," in *The Black Woman: An Anthology*, ed. Toni Cade Bambara (New York: Mentor, 1970), 90–100.

63. Stokely Carmichael and Cleveland Sellers were two of the activists who were headed to Mississippi. See Carmichael and Thelwell, *Ready for Revolution*, chap. 16; Sellers, *River of No Return*, 77; Cathy Wilkerson, "'It Was All Men Talking:' Cathy Wilkerson on 1960s Campus Organizing," in *History Matters: The U.S. Survey Course on the Web*, George Mason University, accessed 21 July 2017, http://historymatters .gmu.edu/d/6913.html. Wilkerson joined Students for a Democratic Society as well as the Weather Underground.

64. GR, interview with Gil Noble, quoted in Brock, "Gloria Richardson and the Cambridge Movement," 123–24 (emphasis in original). Richardson had made the same point back in February 1964 in her speech to the Women's International League for Peace and Freedom. See "Grind Them Down," *Afro-Am*, 15 February 1964, 14. Also see Joyce Ladner, interview with JRF; Cleveland Sellers, interview with JRF.

65. GR, interview with JRF, 17 August 2002; Richardson, "Energy of the People Passing through Me," 282. For Kennedy's attention to poverty issues, see "Kennedy Pledges Attack on Slums," *NYT*, 7 October 1964, 37; "Kennedy Seeking 2 Posts in Senate," *NYT*, 20 December 1964, 4; "Promises of Aid Given by Kennedy," *NYT*, 20 January 1966, 25; "Senate Probes Farm Wage: $1.20 Minimum Sought," *Christian Science Monitor*, 29 March 1966, 5; "Kennedy Condemns Backlash," *WP*, 24 October 1966, A1, A9; "Kennedy: 2 Years after His Election," *NYT*, 14 November 1966, 1, 44; "From the RFK Memorial Poverty Tour: Fields Ripe with Injustice," Robert F. Kennedy Memorial Center for Human Rights, accessed 23 February 2014, http://rfkcenter.org/from-the-rfk-memorial-poverty-tour-fields-ripe-with-injustice. John Lewis also thought the Cambridge movement raised Kennedy's consciousness about poverty and discrimination. During a break during negotiations of the "Treaty of Cambridge" in July 1963, Robert Kennedy pulled Lewis aside and told him: "John, the people, the young people of SNCC, have educated me. You have changed me. Now I understand." Lewis, *Walking with the Wind*, 212–13.

66. Kwame Ture (Stokely Carmichael) interview in Bud Schultz and Ruth Schultz, eds., *The Price of Dissent: Testimonies to Political Repression in America* (Berkeley: University of California Press, 2001), 212; C. T. Vivian, interview with JRF; GR, emails to JRF, 21 and 22 January 2014. At the time, Reddick was a professor at Coppin State College near Baltimore. See "Press Distorts 'True Image' of African Life, Professor Says," *Afro-Am*, 11 November 1961, 9; "Lawrence Reddick, 85, Historian and Writer," *NYT*, 16 August 1995, D20; "Reddick, Lawrence Dunbar (1910–1995)," in *Martin Luther King, Jr., Research & Education Institute: King*

Encyclopedia, n.d., accessed 13 February 2014, http://mlk-kpp01.stanford.edu /kingweb/about_king/encyclopedia/reddick_lawrence.html.

For King's statement about the SCLC's economic goal, see "Negro Leader Speaks, Strives for Political Power In 1964," *Lodi (CA) News-Sentinel*, 21 January 1964, 2. King made this point again in "Negro Leaders Give Their Views: Prospects for '64 in the Civil Rights Struggle," *Negro Digest*, January 1964, 8, 13–14. The NAACP's Roy Wilkins contributed a mini-essay to the same issue of *Negro Digest* (8, 10–11), and he too highlighted jobs as an important element of the movement's agenda for 1964.

67. Relman Morin, "Civil Rights '64 . . . Fight or Freedom," *Windsor (Canada) Star*, 26 February 1964, 13, accessed 27 April 2011, http://news.google.com /newspapers?id=7jI_AAAAIBAJ&sjid=S1EMAAAAIBAJ&pg=5878,3448505&dq= boycott+election+1964+negroes&hl=en.

68. Peter Guralnick, *Dream Boogie: The Triumph of Sam Cooke* (New York: Little, Brown, 2005), 552. Cooke performed on the evening of Friday, 7 February 1964.

9. Vanguard

1. "Schedule 'Ride to Freedom,'" *Michigan Chronicle*, 2 November 1963, A3; "Rights Groups Stage Rival Parleys Here," *Detroit News*, 10 November 1963, 4B; "Detroit Slates 'Black Summit' for Northern Leaders," *Jet*, 14 November 1963, 4.

2. "'Ride to Freedom' Rally Set in Detroit," *WP*, 7 November 1963, A6; "Rights Groups Stage Rival Parleys Here," *Detroit News*, 10 November 1963, 4B; "'Ride to Freedom' Is Held," *News-Palladium* (Benton Harbor, MI), 11 November 1963, 2, accessed 5 June 2014, http://www.newspapers.com/newspage/21626284/; "Adam Powell Calls for Detroit Unity," *Michigan Chronicle*, 16 November 1963, A3; "Zagging with Ziggy," *Michigan Chronicle*, 23 November 1963, D5; "Talk Is of a Revolution—Complete with Mixed Blood," *Jet*, 28 November 1963, 14–19; GR, interview with JRF, 30 October 2004; GR, emails to JRF, 4 and 6 June 2014.

3. "Talk Is of a Revolution—Complete with Mixed Blood," *Jet*, 28 November 1963, 14–19; Grace Lee Boggs, "Living for Change: Part III; Malcolm's Speech in Detroit Marks Turning Point," *Michigan Citizen*, 25 April 1998, B1; GR, interview with JRF, 30 October 2004.

4. "Rights Rivals Map Separate Rallies," *Detroit Free Press*, 9 November 1963; GR, interview with Peter Goldman; GR, interview with JRF, 30 October 2004. For the United Auto Workers' racism problem, see David M. Lewis-Colman, *Race against Liberalism: Black Workers and the UAW in Detroit* (Urbana: University of Illinois Press, 2008). For other examples of labor's racism, see Bruce Nelson, *Divided We Stand: American Workers and the Struggle for Black Equality* (Princeton, NJ: Princeton University Press, 2002).

5. GR, interview with Ja A. Jahannes; GR, interview with Peter Goldman; GR, interview with JRF, 30 October 2004; GR, email to JRF, 4 June 2014.

6. "'Freedom Now' Heads Answer GOAL Call," *Michigan Chronicle*, 9 November 1963, A1, A4; "Mixup Cuts Rights Rally Attendance," *Detroit Free Press*, 10 November 1963, 8A; "Rights Groups Stage Rival Parleys Here," *Detroit News*, 10 November 1963,

4B; "Powell Seeks Negro Unity," *Detroit News*, 11 November 1963, 1A, 24A; "Malcolm X Blasts 'Big Six,'" *Michigan Chronicle*, 16 November 1963, A1, A4; "Talk Is of a Revolution—Complete with Mixed Blood," *Jet*, 28 November 1963, 14–19; GR, interview with Peter Goldman; GR, interview with JRF, 17 July 2010. The NGLC workshops were held in the Master Hall of Mr. Kelley's Recreation Center located on Chene Street in Detroit, and they began at 8:00 a.m. on Saturday, 9 November.

7. "Malcolm X Blasts 'Big Six,'" *Michigan Chronicle*, 16 November 1963, A1, A4; "Talk Is of a Revolution—Complete with Mixed Blood," *Jet*, 28 November 1963, 14–19; Albert B. Cleage Jr., *Black Christian Nationalism: New Directions for the Black Church* (New York: William Morrow, 1971), xvii, xviii–xix. Boggs, "Living for Change: Part III," B1; Angela D. Dillard, *Faith in the City: Preaching Radical Social Change in Detroit* (Ann Arbor: University of Michigan Press, 2007), 357.

8. "Malcolm X Blasts 'Big Six,'" *Michigan Chronicle*, 16 November 1963, A1, A4; Malcolm X, "Message to Grassroots," 10 November 1963, TeachingAmerican-History.org, accessed 10 May 2014, http://teachingamericanhistory.org/library/document/message-to-grassroots/.

9. Malcolm X, "Message to Grassroots."

10. "Talk Is of a Revolution—Complete with Mixed Blood," *Jet*, 28 November 1963, 15; GR, interview with Peter Goldman; GR, interview with JRF, 30 October 2004.

11. "Rights Groups Stage Rival Parleys Here," *Detroit News*, 10 November 1963, 4B; Elmwood Casino advertisement, *Detroit News*, 11 November 1963, 12A; "Pearl Bailey Gives Hand to Joe Louis," *Detroit News*, 12 November 1963, 11D; Redd Foxx advertisement, *Detroit News*, 13 November 1963, 2C. Bennett was a physician to professional boxers, which was how Richardson met Louis. See "Billy Rowe's Note-book," *Oakland (CA) Post*, 30 October 1968, 24; "Dr. Robert C. Bennett, Physician to Boxers," *Afro-Am*, 15 February 1975, 6; GR, interview with JRF, 17 July 2010; GR, emails to JRF, 4, 5, 12, and 18 June, 17 and 24 July 2014. Vivian attended the Northern Negro Leadership Conference but did not recall meeting Richardson in Detroit; see C. T. Vivian, interview with JRF. Richardson claimed that during her visit with Louis he proposed marriage, but she declined his offer; GR, dinner conversation with JRF, 8 April 2015.

12. "Local Postmen Attend D.C. Political Workshop," *New York Amsterdam News*, 15 February 1964, 28; GR, interview with JRF, 4 March 2009; "League for Peace Maintains Triple Goals," *WP*, 11 December 1949, S12; "Enlist Youth Army for a Moral War," *WP*, 21 June 1960, B7; "Peace League Prexy Lauds Freedom Riders," *Afro-Am*, 8 July 1961, 8; "WILPF Delegates to Convene for Legislative Seminar," *WP*, 3 February 1963, F12; "Peace Protest," *Sun*, 16 May 1963, 24; "Grind Them Down," *Afro-Am*, 15 February 1964, 14. Richardson said she stayed informed about Africa's independence movements and supported them, but they did not influence her activism or racial consciousness. GR, interview with JRF, 30 October 2004.

13. Levy, *Civil War on Race Street*, 128–29; "At Abyssinian" *New York Amster-dam News*, 7 March 1964, 31; "Asks New Trial for Bill Worthy," *Afro-Am*, 22 September 1962, 1, 2; George Breitman, ed., *Malcolm X Speaks: Selected Speeches and Statements* (New York: Grove Press, 1990), 3; "William Worthy, a Reporter Drawn to Forbidden Datelines, Dies at 92," *NYT*, 17 May 2014, accessed 24 May 2014,

http://www.nytimes.com/2014/05/18/us/william-worthy-a-reporter-drawn-to
-forbidden-datelines-dies-at-92.html.

14. "Mrs. Richardson Okeys Malcolm X," *Afro-Am*, 10 March 1964, 16, accessed
17 April 2011, http://news.google.com/newspapers?id=1mY8AAAAIBAJ&sjid=D
CoMAAAAIBAJ&pg=1694%2C6977757; GR, interview with Robert Penn Warren;
Malcolm X, postcard to GR, 20 February 1964 (copy in author's possession); *Chicago
Daily Defender*, 6 February 1964, 5; "Malcolm X's Role Dividing Muslims," *NYT*,
26 February 1964, 39.

15. GR, interview with Peter Goldman; Richardson, "Energy of the People Passing through Me," 293; GR, email to JRF, 23 September 2012; "Harlem History:
Twenty Two West ('22 West')," *Harlem World Magazine*, 25 September 2011,
accessed 24 September 2012, http://harlemworldmag.com/2011/09/25/harlem
-history-twenty-two-west-22-west/.

16. Malcolm X's problems with Muhammad began when he learned the NOI
leader was a philanderer. "Malcolm X Scores U.S. and Kennedy,'" *NYT*, 2 December
1963, 21; "Malcolm X Silenced for Remarks on Assassination of Kennedy," *NYT*,
5 December 1963, 22; GR, interview with Peter Goldman; "Suit by Elijah Muhammad's Heirs Opens the Muslim Nation's Books," *NYT*, 15 February 1982, D6.
Grace Lee Boggs interpreted the closing of Malcolm's speech the same way Richardson did. See Boggs, "Living for Change: Part III," B1.

17. "Malcolm X Plans a New Negro Group," *Chicago Tribune*, 9 March 1964, 3;
"Malcolm X Splits with Muhammad," *NYT*, 9 March 1964, 1, 42; William W. Sales
Jr., *From Civil Rights to Black Liberation: Malcolm X and the Organization of Afro-
America Unity* (Boston: South End Press, 1994), 71.
Malcolm led a relatively conventional private life in terms of gender roles, but his
public association with Richardson and his admiration for African and black American
women showed that he was progressive on gender issues with respect to black libera-
tion struggles. See "400 Picket U.N. in Salute to Castro and Lumumba," *NYT*,
19 February 1961, 1, 18; David Gallen, *Malcolm X: As They Knew Him* (New York:
Carroll & Graf, 1992), 31–32.

18. For details of ACT's founding meeting, see "Minutes: National Temporary
Freedom Day Committee Meeting," Chester, PA, 14 March 1964, 1–4 (copy in
author's possession); GR, interview with Peter Goldman; Richardson, "Energy of the
People Passing through Me," 293; GR, email to JRF, 25 March 2014.

19. For urban liberalism, see Theoharis and Woodard, *Freedom North*; Biondi, *To
Stand and Fight*. For the NAACP, see Lewis, *W. E. B. Du Bois: 1919–1963*, 294–95,
300; Ransby, *Ella Baker*, 105, 109, 120–22.

20. Timothy B. Tyson, *Radio Free Dixie: Robert F. Williams and the Roots of
Black Power* (Chapel Hill: University of North Carolina Press, 1999), 108–10,
149–65.

21. GR, interview with Peter Goldman; Richardson, "Energy of the People
Passing through Me," 293.

22. "Minutes: National Temporary Freedom Day Committee Meeting," 1–4;
"'Rights' Unit Offers Aid: Function Described," *Christian Science Monitor*, 4 May
1964, 4; "Announce Formation of New Super-Militant Group," *Jet*, 7 May 1964, 7;
GR, interview with Peter Goldman; GR, interview with JRF, 4 March 2009.

23. "Volunteers Check Harlem Tenements," *NYT*, 20 August 1961, 75; "Harlem Slum Fighter: Jesse Gray," *NYT*, 31 December 1963, 32; "Slum Tenants Take Rats to Court and Win," *Chicago Tribune*, 31 December 1963, A5; "City Acts to Take over 2 Harlem Slum Buildings," *NYT*, 11 February 1964, 30; "'Rights' Unit Offers Aid," *Christian Science Monitor*, 4 May 1964, 4; "Jesse Gray, 64, Leader of Harlem Rent Strikes," *NYT*, 5 April 1988, D25.

24. "Lawrence A. Landry, 61, Dies; Civil Rights Activist," *WP*, 8 June 1997, B6; "Lawrence A. Landry, Civil Rights Activist," *Chicago Tribune*, 8 June 1997, accessed 24 March 2014, http://articles.chicagotribune.com/1997-06-08/news/9706080295_1 _mr-landry-militant-negroes. The dates of the Chicago school boycotts were 22 October 1963 and 23 February 1964. See "Landry Bares Traffic Tieup Plans Here: Token Movement Linked to N.Y. 'Stall-in,'" *Chicago Tribune*, 20 April 1964, 4. Landry was married to Branche's sister, Dolorea.

For information on Hobson, see "'Riders' Pick Those Slated for Arrest," *Sun*, 8 November 1961, 44, 40; "CORE Keeps Marching in Merit Hiring Drive," *Afro-Am*, 17 March 1962, 8; "25 Negroes Stage Sit-in at Restaurant," *WP*, 18 June 1962, B2; "New CORE Post for J. W. Hobson," *Afro-Am*, 21 July 1962, 13; "Hobson: A Militant," *WP*, 20 June 1967, A4.

25. "Galamison Gets Mission to Africa," *Afro-Am*, 18 June 1955, 9; "200 Racial Pickets Seized at Building Projects Here," *NYT*, 23 July 1963, 1, 18; "Calm Rights Leader: Milton Arthur Galamison," *NYT*, 17 December 1963, 43; "Galamison Quotes Odds of 50–50 for a Third Boycott before June," *NYT*, 23 March 1964, 18.

26. For information on Ferguson, see "Pickets Chain Themselves to Cranes," *NYT*, 6 September 1963, 1; "Businessmen Give Negroes Training," *NYT*, 15 November 1963, 23. For information on Rogers, see "Negro Labor Council Names Executive Unit," *Sun*, 31 May 1960, 11; "The Negro Labor Council," *NYT*, 6 June 1960, 28; "Panelists to Discuss Graduates' Future," *Chicago Daily Tribune*, 8 April 1962, NW8. Some of the other attendees at ACT's founding were Johnnie Wilson (representing SAFE at Maryland State College in Princess Anne), New York City's Reverend Carl McCall, Philadelphia's Louis Smith, Chester's Richardson James, and a "Mrs. Flood" from Wilmington, Delaware. See "Minutes: National Temporary Freedom Day Committee Meeting," 1–4.

27. "Minutes: National Temporary Freedom Day Committee Meeting," 1–3; "Dick Gregory Defends Negro School Boycotts," *WP*, 15 March 1964, A4; "ACT Meets in Washington to Outline Plans," *Chicago Defender*, 18 April 1964, 1; "'Rights' Unit Offers Aid," *Christian Science Monitor*, 4 May 1964, 4. For black people's economic boycott of Princess Anne businesses, see "Boycott Squeezes Hard on Princess Anne Shops," *WP*, 1 March 1964, B1.

28. "D.C. School Boycott Set," *Sun*, 9 March 1964, 9; "11 Negro Leaders Hit School Boycott Plan," *WP*, 11 March 1964, C1; "Minutes: National Temporary Freedom Day Committee Meeting," 1–3; "Use of School Boycott as a Weapon Splits Negro Leaders," *WP*, 17 March 1964, C1; "Galamison Quotes Odds of 50–50 for a Third Boycott before June," *NYT*, 23 March 1964, 18; Richard D. Kahlenberg, *Tough Liberal: Albert Shanker and the Battles over Schools, Unions, Race, and Democracy* (New York: Columbia University Press, 2009), 57–58. Walter E. Fauntroy was the SCLC official in Washington.

29. "Minutes: National Temporary Freedom Day Committee Meeting," 4; "Negroes Mapping School Boycotts in 3 Cities Feb. 25," *NYT*, 6 February 1964, 1; "Negro Rifle Clubs Urged, Malcolm X Ridicules Dependence on the Law," *Sun*, 16 March 1964, 8; Malcolm X, interview with A. B. Spellman, 19 March 1964, *Monthly Review* 16, no. 1 (May 1964), accessed 5 March 2009, http://www.monthlyreview .org/564mx.htm; GR, interview with Peter Goldman.

30. GR, interview with Peter Goldman; GR, interview with JRF, 30 October 2004.

31. Richardson told various interviewers how she asked Malcolm X to speak about a black bloc vote and an election boycott, as well as black Americans relying on bullets if their political power had not increased appreciably by the end of 1964. See GR, interview with Peter Goldman; GR, interview with Ja A. Jahannes; Szabo, "Interview with Gloria Richardson Dandridge," 356; GR, interviews with JRF, 21 January 2004, 30 October 2004, 17 July 2010. Also see Richardson, "Energy of the People Passing through Me," 291, 293.

32. "1,000 in Harlem Cheer Malcolm X: 'Ballots or Bullets' Program Urged by Black Muslim," *NYT*, 23 March 1964, 18; "Malcolm X Planning Rally to Choose 'Bullets or Ballots,'" *Sun*, 23 March 1964, 7; "Malcolm X Tells Negroes to Use Ballots and Bullets," *Chicago Tribune*, 23 March 1964, 22; "3,000 Cheer Malcolm X at Opening Rally in Harlem," *Militant*, 30 March 1964, 1; Peter Goldman, *The Death and Life of Malcolm X* (Champaign: University of Illinois Press, 1979), 150. The second "ballot or bullet" speech was on Friday, 3 April 1964 at the Cory Methodist Church in Cleveland, Ohio. See Breitman, *Malcolm X Speaks*, chap. 3.

33. Malcolm X, "The Ballot or the Bullet," 12 April 1964, accessed 5 March 2013, http://americanradioworks.publicradio.org/features/blackspeech/mx.html. The threat was made in Chicago in April 1964. Chicago's grassroots civil rights activists (which included ACT's Lawrence Landry) created a political space where citizens found room to challenge the Democratic Party's political machine. See "Negroes Launch Chicago 'Revolt,'" *Christian Science Monitor*, 11 April 1964, 7; "Negro Boycott of Democrats Is Threatened," *Chicago Tribune*, 14 April 1964, 2.

34. "Rights Heads Are Jubilant," *Sun*, 15 March 1964, 36, 14; "Pop Conference to Hear Gloria," *Afro-Am*, 21 March 1964, 1, 2; "Weather," *WP*, 20 March 1964, B16; "Mrs. Richardson Hits 'Uncle Toms,'" *Sun*, 21 March 1964, 23.

35. The N-VAC rally was held at the People's Independent Church. See "Gloria Richardson; Rights Leader, Here," *Los Angeles Sentinel*, 2 April 1964, A5; flyer, Los Angeles N-VAC, April 1964 (copy in author's possession). I thank Bruce Hartford for providing a copy of the flyer. Also see GR, interview with JRF, 4 March 2009. Richardson stayed with Leo Branton Jr., the highly respected Los Angeles civil rights lawyer. In 1972 Branton would successfully defend Angela Davis in her trial for the kidnapping and murder of a California state judge two years earlier. Branton recalled meeting Richardson on more than one occasion during the 1960s (including once in Danville, Virginia), but he did not recall meeting her in California. Leo Branton Jr., telephone interview with JRF, 3 September 2009. For more on Branton, see "Leo Branton Jr., Activists' Lawyer, Dies at 91," *NYT*, 27 April 2013, accessed 9 August 2014, http://www.nytimes.com/2013/04/28/us/leo-branton-jr-who -defended-angela-davis-dies-at-91.html?_r=0. Incidentally, Richardson claimed she

never traveled to Danville, Virginia, to lend assistance to the movement there. GR, interview with JRF, 4 March 2009; GR, email to JRF, 3 September 2009.

36. "Capital Spotlight," *Afro-Am*, 25 April 1964, 4; "Today's Events," *WP*, 28 April 1964, B26; "Cloture Eyed as Dixie Refuses to O.K. Rights Vote," *Sun*, 30 April 1964, 1, 10; "Be Registered to Vote, Congressman Tells Protesters" *Jet*, 14 May 1964, 15–16; Michael R. Gardner, *Harry Truman and Civil Rights: Moral Courage and Political Risks* (Carbondale: Southern Illinois University Press, 2003), 82.

37. "ACT Meets in Washington to Outline Plans," *Chicago Defender*, 18 April 1964, 1; "Rights Men Move to Coordinate" *New York Amsterdam News*, 18 April 1964, 7; "Militant Negroes Form New Group," *NYT*, 19 April 1964, 44; "Landry Bares Traffic Tieup Plans Here," *Chicago Tribune*, 20 April 1964, 4; "Powell Backing 'Stall-in' at World's Fair," *Daily Defender*, 20 April 1964, 3; "Announce Formation of New Super-Militant Group," *Jet*, 7 May 1964, 7. The meeting was held at the city's Masonic Temple.

38. "Stand up and Fight," *Daily Defender*, 6 February 1964, 1; *Salisbury (MD) Times*, 7 February 1964, 1, accessed 16 April 2014, http://www.newspapers.com /newspage/27686884/; "Powell Backing 'Stall-in' at World's Fair," *Daily Defender*, 20 April 1964, 3; GR, interview with Ja A. Jahannes; GR, interviews with JRF, 20 June 2007, 17 July 2010; GR, email to JRF, 25 March 2014.

39. "Powell Backing 'Stall-in' at World's Fair," *Daily Defender*, 20 April 1964, 3; Brian Purnell, "'Drive Awhile for Freedom': Brooklyn CORE's 1964 Stall-in and Public Discourses on Protest Violence," in *Groundwork: Local Black Freedom Movements in America*, ed. Jeanne Theoharis and Komozi Woodard (New York: NYU Press, 2005), 49.

40. The odds had always been against the stall-in being more than a highly publicized threat. Galamison made this point the day after the demonstration when he noted that most black car owners would not risk having their vehicles impounded, not to mention getting arrested and fined for their actions. See "Stall-in Leaders Erred on Backing," *NYT*, 23 April 1964, 1, 29.

41. Jesse Gray said the place should be declared a "disaster area" by state and federal officials, and they should include it in an urban renewal project. See "Ban Imposed on Meetings in Cambridge," *Sun*, 27 May 1964, 54, 36; "ACT Invites LBJ to 'Worst Fair,'" *Daily Defender*, 27 May 1964, 3.

42. "Negroes Plan a Rent Strike in Cambridge," *WP*, 22 May 1964, F10; "Race March Called Off," *Sun*, 22 May 1964, 19; "Unite with Whites, Leaders Urge; Guard Unit Mixed," *Jet*, 4 June 1964, 8–9. ACT held a meeting at Harlem's Mount Morris Park Presbyterian Church on 23 May. Approximately fifty people attended the event, including Dick Gregory and Lawrence Landry. See "Militant Rights Movement Holds Parley in Harlem," *NYT*, 24 May 1964, 3.

43. "100 Picket U.S. Agency over Hiring," *WP*, 29 May 1964, D6; "Protest Held at Woodlawn," *Sun*, 29 May 1964, 26; "Social Security Warned," *Afro-Am*, 6 June 1964, 1, 10. Richardson did not participate in the march. ACT also planned to shadow and picket Pennsylvania governor William W. Scranton, who was scheduled to visit Chicago and meet with Illinois delegates to the upcoming Republican National Convention. See "ACT Meets Here, Will Boycott Calif. Goods," *Daily Defender*, 29 June 1964, 3; "Scranton Faces Rights Protest," *Chicago Tribune*, 29 June 1964, 1, 8;

"Chicago Rights Group Pickets U.S. Building," *WP*, 30 June 1964, A6; GR, email to JRF, 9 July 2014.

44. Louis E. Lomax, *The Negro Revolt* (New York: Harper & Row, 1962), xiv; "Which Race Leader Has Most Power?" *Pittsburgh Courier* (national ed.), 11 April 1964, 1, 4, clipping in "Civil Rights" folder, Cambridge Library Vertical File.

45. George Frazier, "Be Like a Buddhist," *Boston Herald*, 25 July 1963, 12; George Frazier, "Mrs. Richardson: True Segregationist," *Boston Herald*, 19 June 1963, 12; "A Cauldron of Hate," *Time*, 19 July 1963, accessed 9 August 2007, http://www.time .com/time/magazine/article/0,9171,896863,00.html; "The Racial Chasm—II," *Christian Science Monitor*, 24 June 1964, 14.

46. Howie Evans, "A Negro Plan," *New York Amsterdam News*, 10 October 1964, 18; James Hicks, "Another Angle: Follow the Leader," *New York Amsterdam News*, 12 October 1963, 11, 54. Also critical of Richardson and other radical leaders was *Los Angeles Sentinel* writer P. L. Prattis. See "Issues: Good and Bad," *Los Angeles Sentinel*, 17 October 1963, A6.

47. "Revolt Leader," *Daily Defender*, 15 July 1963, 1; "Go It, Gloria!" *Afro-Am*, 3 August 1963, 5; Dan Watts, "Mrs. Richardson's Revolt," *Liberator*, November 1963, 2.

48. Ofield Dukes, "Struggle for Power Divides Community," *Michigan Chronicle*, 16 November 1963, A5. ACT's Julius Hobson also believed this was the case. Established leaders had to avoid militancy if they wanted to keep receiving donations from supporters. Exacerbating this problem was leaders' concern about maintaining their "image." According to Hobson, this concern was rooted in leaders' middle-class aspirations, which caused them to be "most concerned with maintaining their positions" instead of fighting for black liberation. See "ACT Meets Here, Will Boycott Calif. Goods," *Daily Defender*, 29 June 1964, 3. The Urban League officer was Harold Baron. See "Has Non-Violence Philosophy Failed?" *Michigan Chronicle*, 16 November 1963, A3.

49. "Key Negro Groups Call on Members to Curb Protests," *NYT*, 30 July 1964, 1, 12; "Negro Leaders Split Again," *Chicago Defender* (national ed.), 1 August 1964, 1, 2; Wilkins and Farmer quoted in "Wilkins Calls Hoover 'Good Public Servant,'" *WP*, 23 November 1964, A8.

50. "Civil Rights Battle Lines Hardening in the North," *NYT*, 22 March 1964, E4; "Negroes' View of Plight Examined in Survey Here," *NYT*, 27 July 1964, 1, 19; "Poll Shows Whites in City Resent Civil Rights Drive," *NYT*, 21 September 1964, 1, 26.

51. Kahn and Meier, "Recent Trends in the Civil Rights Movement," 34–53 (reprint; copy in author's possession, pp. 5–6). Richard James was the CCFN member who made this claim about the NAACP. See "Minutes: National Temporary Freedom Day Committee Meeting," 2. For Richardson's claim about the ILGWU, see GR, interview with Ja A. Jahannes.

52. "Dr. King, Others Forecast Violence in Rights Struggle" *Jet*, 21 November 1963, 6–7; Joy James, *Shadow Boxing* (New York: St. Martin's Press, 1999), 53. At the turn of the twentieth century, black self-defense and constitutional rights were discussed publicly. See "Bad Nigger with a Winchester," *WP*, 7 August 1901, 4; "Bad for the Negroes," *WP*, 8 August 1901, 3; "Negro's Right to Self-Defense," *WP*, 12 August 1901, 4.

53. Richardson's cousin Herbert St. Clair Jr. collected guns, and her mother Mable was one of the women who went hunting. The club was called the Cedar Meadow Rod and Gun Club. GR, interview with JRF, 20 June 2007.

54. For Mable and Donna's guard duty, see Richardson, "Energy of the People Passing through Me," 291–92; Suckle quoted in Wesley Hogan, "How Democracy Travels: SNCC, Swarthmore Students, and the Growth of the Student Movement in the North, 1961–1964," *Pennsylvania Magazine of History and Biography* 126, no. 3 (July 2002): 448. Another black community that used armed self-defense resided in Danville, Virginia. See King, *Freedom Song*, 91.

55. "Mrs. Richardson Okeys Malcolm X," *Afro-Am*, 10 March 1964, 16. Also see Szabo, "Interview with Gloria Richardson Dandridge," 358; Theoharis, *Rebellious Life of Mrs. Rosa Parks*, 212–13; Walter Francis White, *A Man Called White: The Autobiography of Walter White* (Athens: University of Georgia Press, 1995), 70; David Levering Lewis, *W. E. B. Du Bois: Biography of a Race, 1868–1919* (New York: Henry Holt, 1993), 335; Ransby, *Ella Baker*, 193, 211–12, 323; Fleming, *Soon We Will Not Cry*, 88; Carson, *In Struggle*, 164; Lee, *For Freedom's Sake*, 74. For recent and comprehensive scholarship on black people's use of armed self-defense, see Akinyele Omowale Umoja, *We Will Shoot Back: Armed Resistance in the Mississippi Freedom Movement* (New York: NYU Press, 2013); Nicholas Johnson, *Negroes and the Gun: The Black Tradition of Arms* (Amherst, NY: Prometheus Books, 2014); Charles E. Cobb Jr., *This Nonviolent Stuff'll Get You Killed: How Guns Made the Civil Rights Movement Possible* (New York: Basic Books, 2014).

56. Kahn and Meier, "Recent Trends in the Civil Rights Movement," 34–53 (reprint p. 6); "Pop Conference to Hear Gloria," *Afro-Am*, 21 March 1964, 1, 2; "Weather," *WP*, 20 March 1964, B16; "Mrs. Richardson Hits 'Uncle Toms,'" *Sun*, 21 March 1964, 23; "Cambridge Freedom Fighters Tell Boycott, Rent Strike, Vote Plans," *Afro-Am*, 23 May 1964, 15; "Demos Could Lose Negro Vote at Polls," *Bonham (TX) Daily Favorite*, 10 June 1963, 4.

57. "How Big Is the Bloc Vote?" *NYT Sunday Magazine*, 25 October 1964, 32, 124, 126; GR, interview with JRF, 17 July 2010; "Negro Organizations Have Little to Offer," *Oregon Bulletin*, 9 July 1964, 4; "G.O.P. Seeks Clues to Party Future in Study of Vote," *NYT*, 8 November 1964, 1, 75; "Why Won't the GOP Compete for African American Votes?" *WP*, 8 October 2010, A19. A review of Rogers C. B. Morton's papers (housed at the University of Kentucky, Lexington) did not reveal any evidence corroborating Richardson's claim that he spoke with her. See Le Datta Grimes, email and research findings to JRF, 25 January 2015. Incidentally, Paul Robeson argued for black voters' use of the bloc vote; see *Here I Stand*, 107.

58. "An All-Negro Party for '64 Is Formed," *NYT*, 24 August 1963, 1, 9; Conrad J. Lynn, "Letters to the Times: No Racism in Negro Party," *NYT*, 26 October 1963, 26; "National Slate Considered by Freedom Now Party," *NYT*, 15 January 1964, 38; "Conrad J. Lynn, a Veteran Civil-Rights Lawyer, Is Dead at 87," *NYT*, 18 November 1995, 12; GR, interview with JRF, 4 March 2009. Richardson thought Lynn considered Cleage for president and her vice president. GR, email to JRF, 24 April 2014.

59. "Mississippi Freedom Party Bids for Democratic Convention Role," *NYT*, 21 July 1964, 19.

60. GR, interview with JRF, 30 October 2004. For an in-depth story of the MFDP's challenge to Mississippi's all-white Democratic Party, see Dittmer, *Local People*, chap. 12.

61. Johnson quoted in Gary May, *Bending toward Justice: The Voting Rights Act and the Transformation of American Democracy* (New York: Basic Books, 2013), 47–48.

62. The Voting Rights Act did not address the larger problem of gerrymandering. In places like Cambridge, white politicos used de facto gerrymandering by creating racially based ward systems. Dirksen quoted in "Katzenbach, Dirksen Draft Broader Voting Rights Bill," *Sun*, 2 April 1965, 4. See also "Vote Bill Draft Attacks Poll Tax in Local Balloting," *NYT*, 6 April 1965, 18; "9 Senate Liberals Alter the Voting Bill," *NYT*, 9 April 1965, 6. For Richardson's thoughts about the Voting Rights Act, see GR, interview with JRF, 30 October 2004; GR, email to JRF, 15 December 2011. For stories about voting irregularities and intimidation in Maryland, see "Man Accused in Election Probe in 4th," *Sun*, 16 March 1955, 38; "Voting Turnout Varies Widely," *Sun*, 5 November 1958, 48; "Maryland Voters Choose Johnson," *NYT*, 4 November 1964, 3.

Interestingly, according to Richardson, Maceo Hubbard told her that he and other DOJ attorneys had originally written a more strongly worded bill that would have covered the entire nation. Richardson's claim is not corroborated by Gary May, author of *Bending toward Justice*, or Ari Berman, author of *Give Us the Ballot: The Modern Struggle for Voting Rights in America* (New York: Picador, 2015). See GR, email to JRF, 15 December 2011; GR, email to SNCC listserv, 24 January 2014; May, *Bending toward Justice*, 47–48, 50–51, 59, 69–70; Gary May, email to JRF, 23 October 2014; Ari Berman, email to JRF, 23 October 2014; Howard A. Glickstein, email to JRF, 30 October 2014.

63. "'Guerrilla War' Urged in Harlem: Rent Strike Chief Calls for '100 Revolutionaries,'" *NYT*, 20 July 1964, 16. Gray claimed he was beaten by New York City police on 18 July 1964.

64. "New Negro Group Moves against Poverty Project," *WP*, 6 July 1965, A6; "Black Power Group Goal High Politics," *WP*, 9 July 1965, A2; "Rights Group Asks Boycott of Anti-Poverty," *Afro-Am*, 17 July 1965, 14.

The concept of a nation within a nation was posited in 1934 by W. E. B. Du Bois, "A Negro Nation within a Nation," in *Ripples of Hope: Great American Civil Rights Speeches*, ed. Josh Gottheimer (New York: Basic Civitas Books, 2003), 170–73. For Powell's role in drafting War on Poverty legislation, see "Be Registered to Vote, Congressman Tells Protesters," *Jet*, 14 May 1964, 14–16. Richardson disagreed with the OBP's position on antipoverty programs; she believed they would benefit black people. See "Cambridge Rights Leader Marries," *NYT*, 1 September 1964, 20. It should be noted that shortly after the OBP's founding, Jesse Gray publicly opposed the Vietnam War. See "The Programs: Mr. Gray Out," *NYT*, 28 August 1965, 20.

65. "Militant Negroes Form New Group," *NYT*, 19 April 1964, 44; "Hobson Expelled by National Core," *WP*, 21 June 1964, A6. Hobson was undeterred by his expulsion; within a couple of weeks he was already planning to continue to focus on economic issues, as well as initiate a political education program for the city's black residents. See "ACT Chapter Here Planned by Hobson," *WP*, 7 July 1964, A6. For

information on Galamison, see "Galamison Quotes Odds of 50–50 for a Third Boycott before June," *NYT*, 23 March 1964, 18; "Galamison Planning Prolonged Boycott of 31 Junior Highs," *NYT*, 14 November 1964, 16; "Galamison Seized in School Boycott," *NYT*, 21 January 1965, 1, 22; "Galamison Held in Boycott Rally," *NYT*, 12 February 1965, 60; William L. Van Deburg, *New Day in Babylon* (Chicago: University of Chicago Press, 1992), 306; Herbert Haines, *Black Radicalism and the Civil Rights Mainstream* (Knoxville: University of Tennessee Press, 1988).

66. "Gloria Richardson: Lady General of Civil Rights," *Ebony*, July 1964, 23–26, 28, 30–31; "Letters to the Editor: Gloria Richardson," *Ebony*, September 1964, 13. Another *Ebony* reader, Henry J. Fisher, was an active-duty sailor who told the editor that he admired Richardson's stance during Cambridge movement. Richardson noted that CNAC received numerous positive letters from black military personnel stationed in Europe and Vietnam. GR, interview with JRF, 30 October 2004.

67. Marriage certificate for Gloria Richardson and Frank Dandridge, 25 August 1964 (copy in author's possession). Also see "Cambridge Rights Leader Marries," *NYT*, 1 September 1964; "Confetti," *Daily Defender*, 9 September 1964, 11; GR, interview with JRF, 24 July 2004.

68. "Gloria Richardson Weds, Quits Civil Rights Work," *WP*, 1 September 1964, A4; GR, interview with JRF, 24 July 2004. Also see "Cambridge Rights Leader Marries," *NYT*, 1 September 1964, 20; "Mrs. Richardson Reveals Wedding," *Daily Defender*, 1 September 1964, 8; "Gloria Richardson Weds Photographer," *New York Amsterdam News*, 5 September 1964, 1; "Milestones," *Time*, 11 September 1964, accessed 31 March 2008, http://www.time.com/time/printout/0,8816,830688,00.html; "Cambridge Leader Quits Rights Role for Marriage," *Jet*, 17 September 1964, 23; GR, interview with JRF, 19 June 2005; Jim Forman, *The Making of Black Revolutionaries* (Seattle, WA: Open Hand Publishing, 1985), 255. Richardson said that Bob Moses made her aware of the importance of not becoming an icon. For Moses's thoughts on this subject, see Carson, *In Struggle*, 139.

69. "Black Power Group Goal High Politics," *WP*, 9 July 1965, A2; Szabo, "Interview with Gloria Richardson Dandridge," 356. The OAAU was modeled after the Organization of African Unity, a transnational political body created to build unity among newly independent African nations. See Organization of African-American Unity (OAAU) membership drive letter, 24 June 1964, "Organization of African-American Unity (OAAU)" FBI file, reel 1, secs. 1–6, copy in African-American Department, Enoch Pratt Free Library, Baltimore, MD.

Richardson was not at the OAAU's inaugural meeting in June because she was in Chicago at the ACT meeting. She attended only a couple of OAAU meetings and did not recall contributing to the OAAU's charter. GR, interviews with JRF, 25 July 2008, 4 March 2009; Bruce Perry, *Malcolm: The Life of a Man Who Changed America* (Barrytown, NY: Station Hill, 1991), 294–95.

70. Tamara Richardson, interview with JRF; GR, interview with Peter Goldman; "Malcolm X Killer Freed after 44 years," CNN.com, 28 April 2010, accessed 1 December 2014, http://www.cnn.com/2010/CRIME/04/26/malcolmx.killer/.

Richardson identified one of the NOI members as a photographer for *Muhammad Speaks*, but she could not recall his name. However, she said he is the man holding a camera and standing two people to her right in the photograph attached to the story "Non Violence in Cambridge," *Afro-Am*, 27 July 1963, A5. GR, interview with JRF, 2 June 2011.

71. "Malcolm X Flees Firebomb Attack," *NYT*, 15 February 1965, 1, 21. Malcolm lost his appeal, and four days later he vacated the premises. See "Malcolm X Averts Writ by Moving Out," *NYT*, 19 February 1965, 31; GR, interview with Peter Goldman; GR, interview with JRF, 25 July 2008. Richardson secured the parsonage of St. John's Methodist Church in Newark, New Jersey, as temporary housing for Malcolm and his family. Her stepfather, the Reverend Theodore Boothe, was its minister. See "Rev. Hazzard Named to Phila. Church," *Afro-Am*, 30 July 1960, 5.

72. GR, interview with Peter Goldman. Also see GR, interview with JRF, 17 July 2010.

73. Malcolm X, "Message to Grassroots"; Gloria Richardson, "Focus on Cambridge," *Freedomways* 4, no. 1 (1964): 33–34. The article can also be found in "Civil Rights" folder, Cambridge Library Vertical File.

74. "Malcolm X to Organize Gun Clubs," *Afro-Am*, 21 March 1964, 1, 2.

75. "CORE Will Insist on 'Black Power': Delegates Also Oppose War in Vietnam— Offer Aid to Draft Resisters," *NYT*, 5 July 1966, 1, 22.

76. "V. P. Humphrey Speaks," *Afro-Am*, 6 August 1966, A5.

10. "You Will Not Be Able to Stay Home, [Sister]"

The title of this chapter is adapted from the song "The Revolution Will Not Be Televised," by Gil Scott-Heron, on the album *Small Talk at 125th and Lenox*, Flying Dutchman/RCA Records, 1970.

1. Nathan Glazer and Daniel P. Moynihan, *Beyond the Melting Pot: The Negroes, Puerto Ricans, Jews, Italians, and Irish of New York City* (Cambridge, MA: MIT Press, 1970), 24; Thomas Piri, *Down These Mean Streets* (New York: Knopf, 1967), 24–25; *Chicago Daily Defender*, 20 May 1968, 14. Their Hollywood trip occurred in the summer of 1968, and they stayed at the Sunset Marquis Hotel. GR, interviews with JRF, 4 March 2009, 12 April 2012; GR, email to JRF, 19 January 2015; Tamara Richardson, interview with JRF.

2. Alexis De Veaux, *Warrior Poet: A Biography of Audre Lorde* (New York: W. W. Norton, 2004), 38–39; GR, interviews with JRF, 14 September 2002, 20 June 2007, 4 March 2009, 28 June 2015; GR, emails to JRF, 19 January 2015, 13 March 2015.

3. GR, interview with Robert Penn Warren; GR, interviews with JRF, 19 June 2005, 20 June 2007. For Dandridge as Baldwin's photographer, see James Campbell, *Talking at the Gates: A Life of James Baldwin* (Berkeley: University of California Press, 1991), 190. Richardson's *Freedomways* article also includes a reference to Baldwin's book. Also see Herb Boyd, *Baldwin's Harlem: A Biography of James Baldwin* (New York: Atria Books, 2008), 2–4; Lynn Orilla Scott, "Challenging the American Conscience, Re-imagining American Identity: James Baldwin and the Civil Rights Movement," in *A Historical Guide to James Baldwin*, ed. Douglas Field (New York: Oxford University Press, 2009), 142; David Adams Leeming, *James Baldwin: A Biography* (New York: Knopf, 1994), 233.

4. "Personally and Socially," *New York Amsterdam News*, 11 December 1965, 18; GR, interview with JRF, 17 July 2010; GR, email to JRF, 13 March 2015.

5. GR, interview with John Britton; GR, interviews with JRF, 24 July 2004, 4 March 2009; Levy, *Civil War on Race Street*, 137; "Community Center in Cambridge, Md., Opened to Negroes," *NYT*, 6 March 1967, 24; "Pool Stirs Tension in Maryland Town," *NYT*, 30 June 1967, 15. The fight over the pool had been going on for more than a year. See "Gloria in Cambridge for Protest," *Afro-Am*, 6 July 1965, 6.

6. "Pool Stirs Tension in Maryland Town," *NYT*, 30 June 1967, 15; "Agnew Seeks Racial Peace in Cambridge," *Sun*, 8 July 1967, B18; Donna Richardson, email to JRF, 3 April 2015; GR, emails to JRF, 5 and 6 April 2015; GR, dinner conversation with JRF, 8 April 2015.

7. "Burch to Attend Racist Rally, Set to Get Injunction," *Sun*, 14 July 1967, C6; "Mobile Job Unit Places Thirteen in Cambridge," *Sun*, 20 July 1967, C6; Levy, *Civil War on Race Street*, 138. The *Sun* stated that Richardson stayed in Cambridge until 19 July, but Richardson claimed she never stayed that long in Cambridge (almost a month, by newspaper accounts) after she moved to New York. GR, dinner conversation with JRF, 8 April 2015.

8. Szabo, "Interview with Gloria Richardson Dandridge," 358; GR, interview with JRF, 4 March 2009; GR, comment at "Conversations in Black Freedom Studies: The Biography of Global Black Power Politics," Schomburg Center for Research in Black Culture, Harlem, NY, 1 May 2014. For information on Brown, see Carson, *In Struggle*, 251–52.

9. "S.N.C.C. Chief Shot in Cambridge, Md.," *NYT*, 25 July 1967, 1, 20. Peter Levy has written the definitive story of the events in Cambridge on 24–25 July 1967. See Levy, *Civil War on Race Street*, 139–43.

10. Ibid.

11. Ibid. The police officer who was shot was Russell E. Wroten. Russell Wroten, telephone interview with JRF, 2 August 2009.

12. Lubell was Frank Dandridge's attorney, and Richardson met him through her husband. GR, interviews with JRF, 21 January 2004, 4 March 2009. For information on Lubell, see "Bar Head Asks Harvard to Fire Lubell Brothers," *Christian Science Monitor*, 7 April 1953, 7; "Harvard Won't Dismiss 2," *NYT*, 9 April 1953, 16; "2 Mum on Red Queries; Teacher Asks Drafting," *Sun*, 28 April 1953, 7; "Deferred Twins Upheld," *NYT*, 29 April 1953, 16: "Harvard Law Review Tries Making Amends for Blackballing Lubell," *Christian Science Monitor*, 16 March 1978, 7; Jonathan Lubell, telephone interview with JRF, 17 September 2009. For information on Kunstler, see "Mississippi Seats under Challenge," *NYT*, 5 December 1964, 19; "William Kunstler, 76, Dies; Lawyer for Social Outcasts," *NYT*, 5 September 1995, A1, B6; "William Kunstler, Guerrilla in the Theater of Justice," *WP*, 6 September 1995, C1, C3; "May It Displease the Court: Quotations of a Radical Lawyer," *NYT*, 10 September 1995, E7; GR, email to JRF, 12 May 2015. For the remainder of the 1960s, Kunstler would serve as legal counsel for both black radicals (including H. Rap Brown) and white ones.

13. "Guard Takes Its Force out of Cambridge," *Sun*, 2 August 1967, C22, C6; "Bail Is Set in Cambridge," *Sun*, 4 August 1967, C7; "4 Seized in Cambridge Fires," *Sun*, 6 August 1967, D20; GR, interview with JRF, 4 March 2009; GR, email to JRF,

12 May 2015. Richardson said he three traveled to Cambridge on a chartered plane, paid for by Lubell and Kunstler. GR, email to JRF, 12 May 2015; "U.S. Loan Aid Is Requested by Cambridge," *Sun*, 8 August 1967, C22, C7. Also see "Cambridge Militants Ask Riot Panel's Ear," *Sun*, 8 August 1967, 7.

14. "Board to Ask Cambridge to Keep Cool," *Sun*, 29 September 1967, C24, C12; "Cambridge Meeting Calm; Police Outnumber Militants," *WP*, 1 October 1967, C4; "March Halted in Cambridge," *Sun*, 1 October 1967, 26, 16; Levy, *Civil War on Race Street*, 162.

15. Ibid.; "Church Padlocked; 'B.P.' Rally Moved," *Afro-Am*, 7 October 1967, 1, 2; Richardson, "Focus on Cambridge," 34. For the white student movement of the mid-1960s, see Todd Gitlin, *The Sixties: Years of Hope, Days of Rage* (New York: Bantam, 1993), 168, 169, 182–88, chap. 8.

16. "The 'Power' Shows Its Strength," *WP*, 30 July 1967, B1, B5. For the list of the organizations, see Cedric Johnson, *Revolutionaries to Race Leaders: Black Power and the Making of African American Politics* (Minneapolis: University of Minnesota Press, 2007), 61. For the distinctions among nationalists, see Van Deburg, *New Day in Babylon*, chap. 4.

17. "'Black Power' Parley in Newark, *Christian Science Monitor*, 25 July 1967, 3; "The 'Power' Shows Its Strength," *WP*, 30 July 1967, B1, B5.

18. Ibid.

19. GR, interview with John Britton; GR, interview with JRF, 17 July 2010.

20. "Teen-aged Parade Protests Killing," *NYT*, 18 July 1964; "Riots Viewed against History of Clashes Almost as Old as U.S.," *NYT*, 11 September 1964; "40 Years on, Newark Re-examines Painful Riot Past," National Public Radio, 14 July 2007, accessed 11 April 2015, http://www.npr.org/templates/story/story.php?storyId=11966375; "Jersey City Negroes Riot after Arrest of 2," *Chicago Tribune*, 3 August 1964, 3; "Rochester Police Battle Race Riot," *NYT*, 25 July 1964, 1, 9; "Negro Youths Battle Police in Rochester," *Christian Science Monitor*, 27 July 27, 1964, 12; "Call National Guard in Rochester Rioting," *Chicago Tribune*, 27 July 27, 1964, 1, 2. For Richardson's prediction of racial revolts, see "Mrs. Richardson Okeys Malcolm X," *Afro-Am*, 10 March 1964, 16. McKissick quoted in "Reporters Attacked at Newark," *WP*, 23 July 1967, A1, A15.

21. "The 'Power' Shows Its Strength," *WP*, 30 July 1967, B1, B5; Richardson, "Focus on Cambridge," 34. For her 1963 warning about the possibility of a race war, see Gloria Richardson, "Cambridge, Maryland, 'City of Progress' for Rich," *New America*, 31 August 1963, 4. Richardson also warned of the possibility of a race war when she was interviewed by Robert Penn Warren.

22. Report of the National Advisory Commission on Civil Disorders, Summary of Report, 1968, 1, Milton S. Eisenhower Foundation, accessed 2 September 2010, http://www.eisenhowerfoundation.org/docs/kerner.pdf. For an analysis of the urban upheavals of 1967, see Louis C. Goldberg, "Ghetto Riots and Others: The Faces of Civil Disorder in 1967," *Journal of Peace Research* 5, no. 2 (1968): 116–32. For an analysis of factors that contributed to black people's decisions to use nonviolent direct action and civil unrest to achieve liberation, see Donald Von Eschen, Jerome Kirk, and Maurice Pinard, "The Disintegration of the Negro Non-Violent Movement," *Journal of Peace Research* 6, no. 3 (1969): 215–34.

23. GR, interview with Robert Penn Warren; GR, interview with John Britton; "A Look Back at Cambridge," *Washington Evening Star*, 4 August 1967, A2, Howardiana Biographical Files, folder "Gloria Richardson Dandridge," Moorland-Spingarn Research Center's Library Division Reading Room. In her interview with Britton, Richardson shared her reasons for not joining a revolt: "This is not to say that I would personally go out and burn anything because in the first place I don't know how. And in the second place I have a family. I don't want to end up in jail for the rest of my life."

24. The Conference on Youth, Nonviolence, and Social Change was held on 5–6 November 1963. See "Dr. King Is Featured Speaker in Rights Confab at Howard U.," *Daily Defender*, 29 October 1963, A5; "Howard U. Conference," *Negro Digest*, March 1964, 78–91; "Dr. King, Others Forecast Violence in Rights Struggle," *Jet*, 21 November 1963, 6–7; A Look Back at Cambridge," A2; GR, interview with John Britton; GR, interview with JRF, 20 March 2004.

25. "Civil Rights Movement Facing Revolution within a Revolution," *NYT*, 21 July 1968, 1, 44; GR, interview with John Britton. Richardson said her understanding of Black Power was the one commonly found at the local level by the black people who supported it and who were its intended beneficiaries. GR, interview with JRF, 20 March 2004.

26. For Black Panther coalitions, see Bobby Seale, *Seize the Time* (Baltimore: Black Classic Press, 1991), 207–11; Amy Sonnie and James Tracy, *Hillbilly Nationalists, Urban Race Rebels, and Black Power: Community Organizing in Radical Times* (New York: Melville House, 2011), chap. 2.

27. GR, interview with Robert Penn Warren. See Du Bois, "Negro Nation within a Nation," 170–73. For her thoughts on the nation-within-a-nation concept, see Richardson, book proposal, 1967. Richardson also discussed the different meanings of "integration." Depending on who used it and in what context, it could mean blacks' assimilation into white America or blacks' opportunities to enter social, economic, and political spaces as first-class citizens. GR, interview with Peter Goldman. Brown released "Say It Loud—I'm Black and I'm Proud" in 1968 on the King Records label. "I Don't Want Nobody to Give Me Nothing (Open up the Door I'll Get It Myself)" is on the album titled *Sex Machine* (King Records, 1970).

28. Clyde Halisi and James Mtume, eds., *The Quotable Karenga* (Los Angeles: US Organization, 1967), 21. For more of Karenga's sexist beliefs, see the section titled "House System," 20–21. US was a pronoun, not an abbreviation or acronym. Bobby Seale, "Bobby Seale Explains Panther Politics," *Guardian*, 21 February 1970, 10; Huey P. Newton, "A Letter from Huey P. Newton to the Revolutionary Brothers and Sisters about the Women's Liberation and Gay Liberation Movements," *Black Panther*, 21 August 1970, 5.

29. Max Stanford (aka Muhammad Ahmad), telephone interview with JRF, 24 February 2010; Kathleen Neal Cleaver, "Racism, Civil Rights, and Feminism," in *Critical Race Feminism*, ed. Adrien Katherine Wing (New York: NYU Press, 1997), 36–37; "The Panthers, II: How They Began; How They Grew," *People's World*, 13 July 1968, 1, 9; "Why They Joined the Panthers: 'Didn't Want to Lose Manhood,'" *Daily World*, 19 July 1968, 5. *People's World* and *Daily World* were newspapers of the Communist Party USA (copies in author's possession).

30. "The Negro Family: The Case for National Action," 29, 34, US Department of Labor, Office of Policy Planning and Research, March 1965, accessed 20 May 2015, http://web.stanford.edu/~mrosenfe/Moynihan%27s%20The%20Negro%20 Family.pdf. The report also mischaracterized the black family as matriarchal, when in fact it was matrifocal. For a good summary of the critical analysis of the Moynihan Report, see Giddings, *When and Where I Enter*, 325–30. Also see Phyl Garland, "Builders of a New South," *Ebony*, August 1966, 37.

31. GR, interview with JRF, 17 August 2002; Giddings, *When and Where I Enter*, 316–17; Elaine Brown, *A Taste of Power: A Black Woman's Story* (New York: Anchor Books, 1993), 357; "WBAI: Debate, 'Black Power,'" *NYT*, 20 August 1966, 23; Szabo, "Interview with Gloria Richardson Dandridge," 354. Innis's reputation as a "vigorous advocate of male leadership" for CORE adds credibility to Richardson's allegation. See August Meier and Elliott M. Rudwick, *CORE: A Study in the Civil Rights Movement, 1942–1968* (New York: Oxford University Press, 1973), 292. Innis did not reply to my numerous communiqués seeking his response to Richardson's claim. Incidentally, according to Richardson, Giddings's book incorrectly states on page 317 that it was a group of CORE men in Cambridge who called her a "castrator." GR, interview with JRF, 3 December 2003.

32. Johnson, *Revolutionaries to Race Leaders*, 62, 64–66, 233 n. 16; Vincent Harding et al., *We Changed the World: African Americans, 1945–1970* (New York: Oxford University Press, 1997), 164; GR, interview with John Britton; GR, interview with JRF, 17 July 2010. Black cultural and intellectual critic Harold Cruse slammed the black capitalism approach as a step backward: "Black Power is nothing but the economic and political philosophy of Booker T. Washington given a 1960's militant shot in the arm and brought up to date." Harold Cruse, *Rebellion Or Revolution?* (Minneapolis: University of Minnesota Press, 2009), 201.

Two additional texts on Black Power and business are Laura Warren Hill and Julia Rabig, eds., *The Business of Black Power: Community Development, Capitalism, and Corporate Responsibility in Postwar America* (Rochester, NY: University of Rochester Press, 2012), and Karen Ferguson, *Top Down: The Ford Foundation, Black Power, and the Reinvention of Racial Liberalism* (Philadelphia: University of Pennsylvania Press, 2013).

33. Stokely Carmichael and Charles V. Hamilton, *Black Power: The Politics of Liberation in America* (New York: Random House, 1967), n.p. (preceding the preface). Carmichael and Hamilton reiterated their book's agenda when they talked with the press and made public appearances. See "Stokely Here; Joins in 'Cool Summer' Call: But He Tells WSO a Tale that Happens to Be False," *Chicago Daily Defender*, 15 May 1967, 1, 3, 4; "Black Power—Rhetoric to Reality: A Profile of Charles V. Hamilton," *Crimson* (Harvard University's student paper), 20 March 1968, accessed 15 May 2015, http://www.thecrimson.com/article/1968/3/20/black-power-rhetoric-to-reality/?page=single; GR, interview with John Britton; GR, interviews with JRF, 20 March 2004, 30 October 2004, 20 June 2007; GR, email to JRF, 15 May 2015; "Cambridge City Council Race Comes to a Close," *Sun*, 8 July 1969, C8. For an analysis of how Carmichael and Hamilton's book was received, see Peniel E. Joseph, *Waiting 'til the Midnight Hour: A Narrative History of Black Power in America* (New York: Henry Holt, 2006), 200–201.

34. For more on white voters' electoral power, see Lisa McGirr, *Suburban Warriors: The Origins of the New American Right* (Princeton, NJ: Princeton University Press, 2001); Mark Brilliant, *The Color of America Has Changed: How Racial Diversity Shaped Civil Rights Reform in California, 1941–1978* (New York: Oxford University Press, 2012). GR, interview with John Britton; GR, interviews with JRF, 20 March 2004, 30 October 2004, 20 June 2007; GR, email to JRF, 15 May 2015. Incidentally, Peniel Joseph has a qualitatively different assessment of Black Power activists' increased participation and investment in the political system. He notes that it (and other things) "reflected the maturity of Black Power radicalism after its eclipse of the civil rights old guard and its newfound domination of community activism and politics." Joseph, *Waiting 'til the Midnight Hour*, 277.

35. "Stokely Here; Joins in 'Cool Summer' Call: But He Tells WSO a Tale that Happens to Be False," *Chicago Daily Defender*, 15 May 1967, 1, 3, 4; GR, interview with JRF, 20 March 2004. Cedric Johnson has a similar take on Black Power conferences. He writes that they "were organized around an inherently ambiguous notion of black unity politics that elided issue-specific organizing. Whereas conference success was determined by the diversity and volume of attendance, few of the organizers possessed the labor power or financial resources to maintain concerted action among the geographically dispersed participants beyond the weekend mobilization." Johnson, *Revolutionaries to Race Leaders*, 62, 64–66.

36. "The Black Panthers: Negro Militants Use Free Food, Medical Aid to Promote Revolution," *Wall Street Journal*, 29 August 1969, 1, 12; Robnett, "Women in the Student Non-Violent Coordinating Committee," 158; GR, interviews with JRF, 20 March 2004, 30 October 2004.

For more histories of Black Power organizations, see Jeffrey O. G. Ogbar, *Black Power: Radical Politics and African American Identity* (Baltimore: Johns Hopkins University Press, 2004); Charles E. Jones, ed., *The Black Panther Party [Reconsidered]*, (Baltimore: Black Classic Press, 2005); Kathleen Cleaver and George Katsiaficas, eds., *Liberation, Imagination, and the Black Panther Party: A New Look at the Panthers and Their Legacy* (New York: Routledge/Taylor & Francis, 2001).

37. "The Black Panthers: Negro Militants Use Free Food, Medical Aid to Promote Revolution," *Wall Street Journal*, 29 August 1969, 1, 12; William Worthy, "Militants Being Killed, Jailed or Forced to Run," *Afro-Am*, 8 March 1969, 1, 6; Ward Churchill and Jim Vander Wall, *The COINTELPRO Papers: Documents from the FBI's Secret Wars against Dissent in the United States* (Boston: South End Press, 1990); Joseph, *Waiting 'til the Midnight Hour*, 242; Ogbar, *Black Power*, 199.

Richardson was one of the activists the FBI spied on, and it compiled a dossier about her; see Federal Bureau of Investigation File No. 100-442421 (Gloria R. Dandridge). Interestingly, she claimed that NAACP member Stanley Branche was an FBI informant who spied on her and the Cambridge movement. GR, interviews with JRF, 17 August 2002, 4 March 2009; GR, emails to JRF, 10 and 11 October 2013, 22 December 2013.

38. Komozi Woodard, "It's Nation Time in NewArk: Amiri Baraka and the Black Power Experiments in Newark, New Jersey," in *Freedom North: Black Freedom Struggles Outside the South, 1940–1980*, ed. Jeanne Theoharis and Komozi Woodard (New York: Palgrave Macmillan, 2003), 287–311; Komozi Woodard, "Message from the Grassroots: The Black Power Experiment in Newark, New Jersey," in *Groundwork: Local*

Black Freedom Movements in America, ed. Jeanne Theoharis and Komozi Woodard (New York: NYU Press, 2005), 77–96; Premilla Nadasen, *Welfare Warriors: The Welfare Rights Movement in the United States* (New York: Routledge, 2004); Premilla Nadasen, *Rethinking the Welfare Rights Movement* (New York: Routledge, 2012); Rhonda Y. Williams, *The Politics of Public Housing: Black Women's Struggles against Urban Inequality* (New York: Oxford University Press, 2005); Rhonda Y. Williams, *Concrete Demands: The Search for Black Power in the 20th Century* (New York: Routledge, 2014); Kimberly Springer, *Living for the Revolution: Black Feminist Organizations, 1968–1980* (Durham, NC: Duke University Press, 2005).

39. GR, interviews with JRF, 17 July 2010, 12 April 2012.

11. Back to Work

1. The Center for Advanced Film Studies was sponsored by the American Film Institute. See "Young Filmmakers Find Study Haven," *NYT*, 30 September 1969, 40; "$30,000 Grants for Film Study Are Awarded to 2 Young Men," *NYT*, 7 October 1970, 41; "Student Film Festival: When You're out of Schlitz . . . ," *Columbia Daily Spectator* (Columbia University newspaper), 15 October 1970, 4–5; GR, interview with Ja A. Jahannes; GR, interview with JRF, 7 July 2010.

2. One of Richardson's résumés from the early 1970s (copy in author's possession) lists the couple's separation as occurring in 1969. For the details of her divorce and her feelings about it, see GR, interviews with JRF, 19 June 2005, 4 March 2009, 17 July 2010, 28 June 2015; GR, email to JRF, 7 July 2015. Also see GR, interview with Ja A. Jahannes; Dorie Ladner, interview with JRF.

3. GR, interviews with JRF, 17 July 2010, 28 June 2015; GR, email to JRF, 4 August 2015. See "Josephine Martin, Healer of Rights Workers, Dies at 84," *NYT*, 23 July 2000, accessed 7 July 2015, http://www.nytimes.com/2000/07/23/us/josephine-martin-healer-of-rights-workers-dies-at-84.html; John Dittmer, *The Good Doctors: The Medical Committee for Human Rights and the Struggle for Social Justice in Health Care* (New York: Bloomsbury, 2009), 128.

4. Lois Wiley is a former SNCC worker who connected Richardson with the person who set up J. Walter Thompson's program. See Richardson's résumé; GR, interviews with JRF, 24 July 2004, 25 July 2008; GR, email to JRF, 12 July 2015; Purcell Jeter, telephone interview with JRF, 27 June 2008; "Advertising: A Big Year for the Biggest Agency," *NYT*, 14 September 1969, F16; Laurie Goldstein (human resources administrator at J. Walter Thompson), email to JRF, 16 February 2005.

5. Richardson witnessed Christian employees of J. Walter Thompson speak openly and negatively about Jewish people, and some employees smoked marijuana in their offices. Interestingly, those behaviors were included in episodes of the television show *Mad Men*, a drama about New York's advertising industry in the 1960s. See GR, interviews with JRF, 24 July 2004, 26 June 2008, 25 July 2008; Purcell Jeter, interview with JRF.

6. "Columbia's Radicals of 1968 Hold a Bittersweet Reunion," *NYT*, 28 April 2008, accessed 21 July 2015, http://www.nytimes.com/2008/04/28/nyregion/28columbia.html?scp=1&sq=columbia+1968&st=nyt&_r=0; "Homo Nest Raided,

Queen Bees Are Stinging Mad," *New York Daily News*, 6 July 1969, reprinted by Public Broadcasting Service, *American Experience*, accessed 21 July 2015, http://www.pbs.org/wgbh/americanexperience/features/primary-resources/stonewall-queen-bees/; GR, email to JRF, 7 July 2015.

7. Diane Ravitch, *The Great School Wars: New York City, 1805–1973* (New York: Basic Books, 1974), chaps. 23–33.

8. "Portrait of an Honest Cop," *New York Magazine*, 3 May 1971; Vincent Cannato, *The Ungovernable City: John Lindsay and His Struggle to Save New York* (New York: Basic Books, 2001); Edmund White, *City Boy: My Life in New York during the 1960s and '70s* (New York: Bloomsbury USA, 2009), 1, 210–11.

9. There were twenty-six such neighborhood boards. See Richardson's résumé; GR, interview with JRF, 28 June 2015. For information on HARYOU-ACT, see "Youth Program in Harlem Aided; $480,000 in Federal Money to Help Fight Delinquency," *NYT*, 14 August 1962, 23; "'Power Struggle' in Harlem Scored,'" *NYT*, 17 June 1964, 50; "HARYOU-ACT Sets $118 Million Budget," *NYT*, 25 June 1964, 19; "Poverty Boards: Money Is the Key," *NYT*, 4 March 1968, 24. For an insider's story of the early years of HARYOU-ACT, see Cyril deGrasse Tyson, *Power and Politics in Central Harlem, 1862–1964: The HARYOU Experience* (New York: Jay Street Publishers, 2004). For a background on the Community Training Institute, see "Leaders Bridge Community Business 'Gap,'" *Chicago Daily Defender*, 30 May 1970, 32. Also see Richardson's résumé; GR, interviews with JRF, 24 July 2004, 17 July 2010.

10. GR, interviews with JRF, 24 July 2004, 25 July 2008, 28 June 2015. For the Wilmington Ten, see "The Case against the Wilmington Ten," *NYT Magazine*, 3 December 1978, 60, 62, 64, 66, 70, 74, 76, 79; "When Justice Grinds Slow," *NYT*, 2 January 2013, accessed 15 July 2015, http://www.nytimes.com/2013/01/03/opinion/slow-justice-for-the-wilmington-10.html; "UCC Celebrates Pardons of Wilmington Ten 40 Years after Wrongful Conviction," United Church of Christ, 2 January 2013, accessed 15 July 2015, http://www.ucc.org/ucc-celebrates-pardons-of. Cobb was the father of SNCC member Charles Cobb Jr. See "Charles Earl Cobb, 82, Minister and Advocate for Civil Rights," *NYT*, 4 January 1999, accessed 15 July 2015, http://www.nytimes.com/1999/01/04/nyregion/charles-earl-cobb-82-minister-and-advocate-for-civil-rights.html.

11. GR, interview with JRF, 17 July 2010; Theoharis, *Rebellious Life of Mrs. Rosa Parks*, chap. 5.

12. "What Ever Happened to . . . Gloria Richardson: Civil Rights Leader Now Works with NCNW," *Ebony*, February 1974, 138; GR, interviews with JRF, 25 July 2008, 17 July 2010, 28 June 2015; Joyce Ladner, interview with JRF.

13. GR, letter to the editor, *Ebony*, May 1974, 18; GR, interviews with JRF, 24 July 2004, 25 July 2008, 28 June 2015. I contacted the NCNW on numerous occasions and shared Richardson's version of why she was fired, but my attempts to obtain a formal response from the NCNW concerning Richardson's claim were unsuccessful.

14. GR, email to JRF, 25 March 2010; GR, interviews with JRF, 17 July 2010, 28 June 2015. For information on Samuels, see "Sutton Says Harlem Is Prisoner of Few Who Are Criminals," *NYT*, 11 November 1972, 27; "N.Y. Officials Form Anti-crime Unit," *Afro-Am*, 16 December 1972, 6; "Optimism Comes to Harlem: 10 Years after

Riots, the Future Is Discussed," *WP*, 21 July 1974, A1, A4. For HARYOU-ACT's defunding, see "Changes in the City's Antipoverty Program," *NYT*, 2 March 1979, B12; "For City Antipoverty Effort, a New Era," *NYT*, 8 December 1979, 25, 27.

15. GR, interview with JRF, 28 June 2015; Faye Moore, telephone interview with JRF, 26 January 2004. Other union members praised Richardson's contributions to the union and to the residents of New York City. See Charlene Mitchell, telephone interview with JRF, 17 February 2004; Charles Ensley, telephone interview with JRF, 21 December 2004. Ensley was also a president of Local 371. For his and Moore's time as president, see "NYC Union President Faye Moore Ousted in Surprise Vote," *City & State NY*, 3 May 2011, accessed 19 July 2015, http://archives.cityandstateny.com /nyc-union-president-faye-moore-ousted-in-surprise-vote/; "About the DFTA," New York City Department for the Aging, accessed 19 July 2015, http://www.nyc.gov /html/dfta/html/about/about.shtml.

16. GR, interviews with JRF, 24 July 2004, 28 June 2015; GR, email to JRF, 28 December 2015.

17. GR, interview with Robert Penn Warren; GR, interviews with JRF, 20 June 2007, 17 July 2010; GR, interview with Dick Gordon. For evidence of continued racial discrimination, see "Affordable Housing, Racial Isolation," *NYT*, 29 June 2015, accessed 23 July 2015, http://www.nytimes.com/2015/06/29/opinion/affordable -housing-racial-isolation.html; "BofA Fined $2.2M in Racial Discrimination Case," *USA Today*, 23 September 2013, accessed 23 July 2015, http://www.usatoday .com/story/money/business/2013/09/23/bank-of-america-racial-discrimination /2857835/; John Kucsera and Gary Orfiel, "New York State's Extreme School Segregation: Inequality, Inaction and a Damaged Future," Civil Rights Project (UCLA Law School), March 2014, accessed 23 July 2015, http://civilrightsproject.ucla.edu /research/k-12-education/integration-and-diversity/ny-norflet-report-placeholder /Kucsera-New-York-Extreme-Segregation-2014.pdf; Michelle Alexander, *The New Jim Crow: Mass Incarceration in the Age of Colorblindness* (New York: New Press, 2012); "The Science of Research on Racial/Ethnic Discrimination and Health," *American Journal of Public Health* 102, no. 5 (May 2012).

18. GR, interviews with JRF, 20 March 2004, 30 October 2004. For New York City's civil rights struggles from the mid-1940s through the mid-1960s, see Biondi, *To Stand and Fight*; Brian Purnell, *Fighting Jim Crow in the County of Kings: The Congress of Racial Equality in Brooklyn* (Lexington: University Press of Kentucky, 2013). For information on Hawkins's murder, see "Bishop Questions Protest Marches in Racial Slaying," *NYT*, 30 August 1989, accessed 23 July 2015, http://www.nytimes. com/1989/08/30/nyregion/bishop-questions-protest-marches-in-racial-slaying. html; John Desantis, *For the Color of His Skin: The Murder of Yusuf Hawkins and the Trial of Bensonhurst* (New York: St. Martin's Press, 1991). For Sharpton's work as an informant, see "Protest Figure Reported to Be a U.S. Informant," *NYT*, 21 January 1988, accessed 23 July 2015, http://www.nytimes.com/1988/01/21/nyregion /protest-figure-reported-to-be-a-us-informant.html; "Al Sharpton Admits He Was an FBI Mob Informant, Says He Was Threatened," *Newsday*, 8 April 2014, accessed 23 July 2015, http://www.newsday.com/news/new-york/al-sharpton-admits-he -was-an-fbi-mob-informant-says-he-was-threatened-1.7642245. Two years before Hawkins's murder, Sharpton was involved in the kidnapping and rape hoax perpe-

trated by Tawana Brawley, a fifteen-year-old black girl from upstate New York. See Robert D. McFadden et al., *Outrage: The Story behind the Tawana Brawley Hoax* (New York: Bantam, 1990).

19. GR, interviews with JRF, 19 June 2005, 26 June 2008; GR, email to JRF, 7 January 2014; "Threats and Responses: News Analysis," *NYT*, 17 February 2003, accessed 24 July 2015, http://www.nytimes.com/2003/02/17/world/threats -and-responses-news-analysis-a-new-power-in-the-streets.html; "Viewpoint: Why Was the Biggest Protest in World History Ignored?" Time.com, 15 February 2013, accessed 24 July 2015, http://world.time.com/2013/02/15/viewpoint-why-was -the-biggest-protest-in-world-history-ignored/; "Behold the Hatred, Resentment, and Mockery Aimed at Anti–Iraq War Protesters," *Atlantic*, 21 March 2013, accessed 24 July 2015, http://www.theatlantic.com/politics/archive/2013/03/behold-the -hatred-resentment-and-mockery-aimed-at-anti-iraq-war-protesters/274230/; "Surveillance under the USA PATRIOT Act," American Civil Liberties Union, accessed 24 July 2015, https://www.aclu.org/surveillance-under-usa-patriot-act.

20. GR, interview with JRF, 5 December 2011; "Thousands Gather Near Foley Square as Occupy Wall Street Protests Swell," *Star Ledger* (NJ), 17 November 2011, accessed 12 December 2011, http://www.nj.com/news/index.ssf/2011/11/thous ands_gather_near_foley_sq.html; Todd Gitlin, *Occupying Wall Street: The Inside Story of an Action that Changed America* (Chicago: Haymarket Books, 2012).

21. See http://blacklivesmatter.com/about/. Black Lives Matter and Occupy Wall Street are part of a general trend, beginning in the early 2010s, of young people organizing and protesting against college tuition hikes, cuts to family planning services, police brutality, and mass incarceration. See "From the Deep South to the Midwest, a Generation Demands Justice," *Nation*, 23 July 2013, accessed 9 June 2015, http://www.thenation.com/blog/175353/deep-south-midwest-generation -demands-justice.

22. "Thousands Join Al Sharpton in 'Justice for All' March in D.C.," *WP*, 13 December 2014, accessed 26 July 2015, http://www.washingtonpost.com/nat ional/health-science/sharpton-to-lead-justice-for-all-march-in-dc/2014/12/13/36 ce8a68–824f-11e4–9f38–95a187e4c1f7_story.html; "The Fierce Urgency of Now: Why Young Protesters Bum-Rushed the Mic," TheRoot.com, 14 December 2014, accessed 26 July 2015, http://www.theroot.com/articles/culture/2014/12/the _fierce_urgency_of_now_why_young_protesters_bum_rushed_the_mic.html; GR, emails to JRF, 10 September 2014, 22 October 2014, 13 December 2014.

23. GR, interview with JRF, 2 August 2003. For the phenomenon of confusing fame with social activism leadership, see Jonathan L., "Tales from a Black Filled Childhood: Who Will Lead My Black Generation . . . No One?" Black Youth Project, 26 April 2013, accessed 28 April 2013, http://www.blackyouthproject.com/2013/04/tales-from-a -black-filled-childhood-who-will-lead-my-black-generation-no-one/#more-32306; Jenée Desmond-Harris, "What Young Activists Could Teach Jay Z," TheRoot.com, 26 July 2013, accessed 9 June 2015, http://www.theroot.com/articles/culture/2013/07 /jay_zs_response_to_belafonte_criticism_what_young_activists_could_teach_him.html.

24. Thulani Davis, "It's Time to Call for New Black Leadership, We Need You," *Village Voice*, 18–24 February 2004, 32–34, 37, http://www.villagevoice.com/news /we-need-you-6408334.

25. Richardson, "Energy of the People Passing through Me," 295. Political scientist Sekou Franklin's research on the activism of black youth supports Richardson's viewpoint that people from the ministerial and political realms subscribe to a leadership philosophy that is not compatible with group-centered and member-driven grassroots organizing. "Indeed," he writes, "many young activists have no problem working in intergenerational movement infrastructures as long as seasoned or older activists respect their voice and autonomy." Franklin quoted in "To Sustain Black Lives Matter Movement, Younger and Older Activists Need to Learn from Each Other," *Atlanta Black Star*, 29 January 2015, accessed 26 July 2015, https://atlantablackstar.com/2015/01/29/black-lives-matter-youth-militancy-civil-resistance-part/. For scholarly works on black youths' activism since the civil rights movement, see Sekou M. Franklin, *After the Rebellion: Black Youth, Social Movement Activism, and the Post–Civil Rights Generation* (New York: NYU Press, 2014); Cathy J. Cohen, *Democracy Remixed: Black Youth and the Future of American Politics* (New York: Oxford University Press, 2010).

26. GR, interviews with JRF, 3 December 2003, 20 March 2004, 30 October 2004. For excellent discussions of how ideology can be antithetical to liberation movements, see Susan Griffin, "The Way of All Ideology," *Signs: Journal of Women in Culture and Society 7*, no. 3 (1982): 641–60; bell hooks, *Feminist Theory from Margin to Center* (Boston: South End Press, 1984), 160–63.

27. GR, interview with JRF, 17 July 2010. For open housing challenges, see "Fair-Housing Flop?" *Wall Street Journal*, 1 February 1965, 1, 14; "Fair-Housing Law Fought in States," *NYT*, 23 February 1964, R1, R6; "U.S. Protection Asked in Vote Drive," *Afro-Am*, 22 February 1964, 1, 2; "Fair Housing Law Loses in Seattle," *NYT*, 12 March 1964, 23; "Akron Voters Repeal Fair Housing Law," *Chicago Tribune*, 5 November 1964, 4. For anti–gay rights referenda of the 1970s, see "Miami Area Voters Repeal Homosexual Rights Law," *Sun*, 8 June 1977, A1; "Law on Homosexuals Repealed in St. Paul," *NYT*, 26 April 1978, A1, A17; "Wichita Repeals Homosexual Law," *NYT*, 10 May 1978, A18; "Voters in Eugene, Ore., Repeal Ordinance on Homosexual Rights," *NYT*, 24 May 1978, A18; "Governor Brown Wins Big in California, but His Running Mate May Be in Trouble," *Sun*, 8 November 1978, A7. For *Obergefell v. Hodges*, see "A Profound Ruling Delivers Justice on Gay Marriage," *NYT*, 26 June 2015, accessed 29 July 2015, http://www.nytimes.com/2015/06/27/opinion/a-profound-ruling-delivers-justice-on-gay-marriage.html. For a vote on citizens' rights in Texas, see "Opponents of Houston Rights Measure Focused on Bathrooms, and Won," *NYT*, 4 November 2015, accessed 8 November 2015, http://www.nytimes.com/2015/11/05/us/houston-anti-discrimination-bathroom-ordinance.html?_r=0; "Watch: Houston Mayor Annise Parker Delivers Awesomely Hard-Hitting and Honest HERO Concession Speech," The New Civil Rights Movement, 4 November 2015, accessed 8 November 2015, http://www.thenewcivilrightsmovement.com/davidbadash/watch_houston_mayor_annise_parker_delivers_awesomely_honest_hero_concession_speech.

28. GR, interview with JRF, 20 March 2004; Richardson, "Energy of the People Passing through Me," 296; "Supreme Court Invalidates Key Part of Voting Rights Act," *NYT*, 25 June 2013, accessed 13 January 2014, http://www.nytimes.com/2013/06/26/us/supreme-court-ruling.html?pagewanted=all. Also see "A Dream Undone: Inside the 50-Year Campaign to Roll Back the Voting Rights Act,"

NYT Magazine, 29 July 2015, accessed 29 July 2015, http://www.nytimes
.com/2015/07/29/magazine/voting-rights-act-dream-undone.html?_r=0; Martin
Gilens and Benjamin I. Page, "Testing Theories of American Politics: Elites, Interest
Groups, and Average Citizens," *Perspectives on Politics* 12, no. 3 (September 2014):
564–81; "Small Pool of Rich Donors Dominates Election Giving," *NYT*, 1 August
2015, accessed 3 August 2015, http://www.nytimes.com/2015/08/02/us/small
-pool-of-rich-donors-dominates-election-giving.html?_r=0.

29. GR, interview with Robert Penn Warren; GR, interview with JRF, 20 March
2004.

30. Ibid.; Richardson, "Energy of the People Passing through Me," 294.

31. Richardson, "Energy of the People Passing through Me," 294.

Conclusion

1. GR, interview with Ja A. Jahannes; GR, interviews with JRF, 17 August 2002,
20 March 2004, 17 July 2010.

2. Donna Richardson, interview with JRF; Casey Hayden, preface to *Freedom
Song: A Personal Story of the 1960s Civil Rights Movement*, by Mary King (New York:
William Morrow, 1987), 7; GR, email to JRF, 16 August 2015.

3. GR, interview with JRF, 20 March 2004; GR, interview with Dick Gordon.

4. "Program: George Washington's Birthday Convocation," Washington College
(Chestertown, MD), 22 February 2008; "Commencement Program," Morgan State
University, 18 May 2008, 14; "Minutes," Cambridge City Council, 9 June 2008,
accessed 6 August 2008, http://www.ci.cambridge.md.us/minutes/2008/06-09-08
_minutes.htm; "Cambridge Honors Gloria Richardson," *Dorchester Star*, 15 August
2008, accessed 15 September 2010, http://www.dorchesterstar.com/articles
/2008/08/15/news/44219.txt; "Program: Twenty-Eighth Annual Founders' Day
Observance," Riverside Club of New York City (part of the National Association of
Negro Business and Professional Women's Clubs Inc.), 29 March 2009; "Ivy Young
Willis & Martha Willis Dale Award," Cabrini University (Radnor, PA), 8 April 2015,
accessed 7 August 2015, http://www.cabrini.edu/Academics/Academic-Departments
/History-and-Political-Science-Department/Ivy-Young-Willis-Award; "Living History," *Dorchester Star* (Easton, MD), 24 July 2017, accessed 24 July 2017, http://www
.myeasternshoremd.com/dorchester_star/news/article_6ce3d55d-4b9f
-58fd-b863-2db19d2077a3.html.

For the mural and heritage sites, see "Dorchester County Mural Dedication,"
WMDT (Salisbury, MD), 21 July 2017, accessed 22 July 2017, http://www.wmdt
.com/news/maryland/dorchester-county-mural-dedication-1/591141891; "Maryland's African-American Heritage Guide," Maryland Office of Tourism, n.d., 29,
accessed 23 August 2010, http://viewer.zmags.com/publication/6631b929#/66
31b929/1; "Maryland Women's Heritage Trail," Maryland Women's History Project,
Sylvan Learning Foundation, and Maryland State Teachers Association, n.d., accessed
20 March 2011, http://mdwomensheritagecenter.org/pdf/Heritage_Poster.pdf.

Richardson was also included in "The Long Walk to Freedom: Portraits of Civil
Rights, Then and Now," Brooklyn Public Library, 2001; see advertisement, *NYT*, 23

February 2001, B3. In addition, she was profiled in an *Ebony* article on women civil rights activists; see "3 Unsung Feminist Civil Rights Leaders: Rosa Parks Wasn't Hardly the Only Sister Making Moves during 'the Movement,'" Ebony.com, 25 March 2014, accessed 27 March 2014, http://www.ebony.com/news-views/3 -unsung-feminist-civil-rights-leaders-405#axzz2xC3j80Z9. For the March on Washington anniversary, see "The Rampant Sexism at March on Washington," The Root.com, 22 August 2013, accessed 5 August 2015, http://www.theroot.com /articles/culture/2013/08/the_rampant_sexism_at_the_march_on_washington.ht ml#storify/e45b3ae3554217045f8d221636da11b4; "Civil Rights Pioneer Gloria Richardson, 91, on How Women Were Silenced at 1963 March on Washington," Democracy Now! 27 August 2013, accessed 28 August 2013, http://www.democra cynow.org/2013/8/27/civil_rights_pioneer_gloria_richardson_91.

For other profiles of Richardson, see "Unsung Hero: Gloria Richardson, Now 92, Led Rights Battle in Md.," *Philadelphia Inquirer*, 10 April 2015, B1, B5; "Fighting for Equality in 1963 Small-Town America," BBC.com, 17 June 2015, accessed 17 June 2015, http://www.bbc.com/news/magazine-33135521; "The Defiant One: Why You Should Know Civil Rights Icon Gloria Richardson," The Root.com, 7 July 2015, accessed 7 July 2015, http://www.theroot.com/articles/history/2015/07 /why_you_should_know_civil_rights_icon_gloria_richardson.1.html.

5. "Civil Rights Champion Gloria Richardson Dandridge Returns to Cambridge for 'Reflections on Pine,'" *Dorchester Banner*, 18 July 2017, accessed 20 July 2017, http://www.dorchesterbanner.com/dorchester/civil-rights-champion-gloria -richardson-dandridge-returns-cambridge-reflections-pine/.

6. "Cambridge Mayor Wins Second Term," *Star Democrat* (Easton, MD), 11 July 2012, accessed 7 August 2015, http://www.stardem.com/news/local_news /article_44641fd6-cb0d-11e1-abf6-001a4bcf887a.html; "Cambridge Public Housing Agreement Will Be Signed," *Dorchester Banner*, 10 April 2015, accessed 30 July 2015, http://www.dorchesterbanner.com/dorchester/cambridge-public-housing -agreement-will-be-signed/; "Cambridge Council Approves $21M in Upgrades to Housing Projects," WBOC.com, 15 April 2015, accessed 30 July 2015, http://www .wboc.com/story/28804963/cambridge-council-approves-21-million-in-upgrades -to-housing-projects; "Cambridge OKs Agreement to Privatize Public Housing," *Star Democrat* (Easton, MD), 1 May 2015, accessed 7 August 2015, http://www .stardem.com/news/local_news/article_befea09a-60ea-54b2-bf39-a7cfed7363de .html; GR, emails to JRF, 31 July 2015, 2 August 2015.

7. GR, interview with JRF, 20 March 2004; GR, email to JRF, 4 August 2015; "Program," LawForBlackLives.org, accessed 29 July 2015, http://www.law4black lives.org/program/; United for a Fair Economy, http://www.faireconomy.org/; Dream Defenders, http://www.dreamdefenders.org/; Black Youth Project 100, http://byp100.org/; "Moral Mondays: Religious Progressives Protest North Carolina Policies," Time.com, 1 July 2013, accessed 29 July 2015, http://swampland .time.com/2013/07/01/moral-mondays-religious-progressives-protest-north-car olina-policies/.

8. Richardson participated in "Conversations in Black Freedom Studies: Honoring the Legacy of Black Women Radicals Gloria Richardson and Mae Mallory," 1 December 2016; GR, email to SNCC listserv, 9 December 2016. For an article that

makes the same point as Richardson, see "What Those Who Studied Nazis Can Teach Us about the Strange Reaction to Donald Trump," *Huffington Post*, 19 December 2016, accessed 24 December 2016, http://www.huffingtonpost.com/entry/donald -trump-nazi-propaganda-coordinate_us_58583b6fe4b08debb78a7d5c.

9. "Conversations in Black Freedom Studies: The Biography of Global Black Power Politics: Stokely Carmichael and Walter Rodney," Schomburg Center for Research in Black Culture, New York City, 1 May 2014, accessed 1 May 2014, http://schomburgcenter.tumblr.com/post/83639045099/thursday-may-1-2014-6 -8-pm-conversations-in.

Bibliography

Archives and Document Collections

Cambridge Nonviolent Action Committee Papers, State Historical Society of Wisconsin, Madison. "The Negro Ward of Cambridge, Maryland: A Study in Social Change." September 1963.

Civil Rights during the Kennedy Administration, 1961–63. Part 2, *The Papers of Burke Marshall, Assistant Attorney General for Civil Rights*. Microfilm ed. Reel 26. Frederick, MD: University Publications of America, 1986.

Clarence Logan. Notes and clippings file. Partial copy in author's possession.

Andrew Moursund. Notes and clippings file. Partial copy in author's possession.

Southern Christian Leadership Conference Papers, King Center, Atlanta, GA.

Student Nonviolent Coordinating Committee Papers, King Center, Atlanta, GA.

Oral Histories and Interviews (by the author unless otherwise noted)

James Boardley, telephone interview, 25 June 2014.

Leo Branton Jr., telephone interview, 3 September 2009.

John H. Britton, telephone interview, 8 July 2005.

Edward Brooke, telephone interviews, 9 August 2007 and 23 February 2010.

Edward Brooke, interview with the National Visionary Leadership Project, n.d. Accessed 24 November 2012. http://www.visionaryproject.org/brookeedward/.

Virginia Brown-Nolan, telephone interview, 25 February 2010.

Larry Chester, 8 January 2007.

Lemuel Chester, 8 January 2007.

Dwight Cromwell, interview with Sandy Harney, 27 August 1997 (copy in author's possession).

Charles Ensley, telephone interview, 21 December 2004.

Jacqueline Fassett, telephone interview, 3 May 2012.

Arnie Goldwag, telephone interview, 3 February 2004.

Dick Gregory, telephone interview, 21 July 2008.

Enez Grubb, interview with Sandy Harney, 27 August 1997 (copy in author's possession).

William Hall, telephone interview, 22 February 2004.

Purcell Jeter, telephone interview, 27 June 2008.

John Kady, telephone interview, 10 December 2005.

Dorie Ladner, telephone interview, 19 May 2009.
Joyce Ladner, telephone interview, 30 March 2005.
Barbara Wesley Lassiter, 28 October 2004.
Jonathan Lubell, telephone interview, 17 September 2009.
Don Lundy, telephone interview, 16 September 2004.
Charlene Mitchell, telephone interview, 17 February 2004.
Faye Moore, telephone interview, 26 January 2004.
Diane Nash, telephone interview, 29 April 2010.
Margaret Willis Reynolds, telephone interview, 16 April 2005.
Donna Richardson, telephone interview, 31 January 2008.
Gloria Richardson, interview with Robert Penn Warren, 2 March 1964. Robert Penn Warren Center for the Humanities, Vanderbilt University, Nashville, TN.
Gloria Richardson, interview with John Britton, 11 October 1967. Civil Rights Documentation Project, Howard University, Washington, DC (copy in author's possession).
Gloria Richardson, interview with Peter Goldman, 18 May 1969 (copy in author's possession).
Gloria Richardson, interview with Ja A. Jahannes, 8 April 1988 (copy in author's possession).
Gloria Richardson, 2002–2015.
Gloria Richardson, radio interview with Dick Gordon, 16 January 2009.
Gloria Richardson, radio interview with Dan Rodricks, 13 June 2013.
Tamara Richardson, telephone interview, 13 June 2009.
Anthony Sagona, telephone interview, 24 March 2004.
Cleveland Sellers, telephone interview, 24 February 2004.
Virginia Hayes Shields and Calvin K. Shields Sr., telephone interview, 10 February 2005.
Max Stanford (aka Muhammad Ahmad), telephone interview, 24 February 2010.
Mark Suckle, 26 December 2013.
C. T. Vivian, telephone interview, 23 March 2011.
Walter Washington, interview with the National Visionary Leadership Project, n.d. Accessed 24 November 2012. http://www.visionaryproject.org/washingtonwalter/.
Mary Annetta St. Clair Wesley, 28 October 2004.
Lois Wiley, telephone interview, 21 July 2010.
Russell E. Wroten, telephone interview, 2 August 2009.

Articles, Books, and Other Sources

"About the Order of the Eastern Star." General Grand Chapter of the Eastern Star. Accessed 20 September 2011. http://www.easternstar.org/about_oes.html.
Alexander, Michelle. *The New Jim Crow: Mass Incarceration in the Age of Colorblindness*. New York: New Press, 2012.
Allen, Norm R., ed. *African-American Humanism: An Anthology*. Buffalo, NY: Prometheus Books, 1991.

"The American Race Problem as Reflected in American Literature." *Journal of Negro Education* 8, no. 3 (July 1939): 275–90.

Anderson, James D. *The Education of Blacks in the South, 1860–1935.* Chapel Hill: University of North Carolina Press, 1988.

Argersinger, Jo Ann E. *Toward a New Deal in Baltimore: People and Government in the Great Depression.* Chapel Hill: University of North Carolina Press, 1988.

Baldwin, James. *The Fire Next Time.* New York: Vintage International, 1993.

Barrett, Samuel. "A Plea for Unity." *Colored American Magazine* 7 (1904): 49.

Bartlett, Bruce. *Wrong on Race: The Democratic Party's Buried Past.* New York: Palgrave Macmillan, 2009.

Barusch, Amanda. *Foundations of Social Policy: Social Justice in Human Perspective.* 3rd ed. Belmont, CA: Brooks/Cole, 2009.

"Be Registered to Vote, Congressman Tells Protesters." *Jet,* 14 May 1964, 14–16.

Beal, Frances. "Double Jeopardy: To Be Black and Female." In *The Black Woman: An Anthology,* edited by Toni Cade Bambara, 90–100. New York: Mentor, 1970.

"Behold the Hatred, Resentment, and Mockery Aimed at Anti-Iraq War Protesters." *Atlantic,* 21 March 2013. Accessed 24 July 2015. http://www.theatlantic.com /politics/archive/2013/03/behold-the-hatred-resentment-and-mockery-aimed -at-anti-iraq-war-protesters/274230/.

Berman, Ari. *Give Us the Ballot: The Modern Struggle for Voting Rights in America.* New York: Picador, 2015.

Biondi, Martha. *To Stand and Fight: The Struggle for Civil Rights in Postwar New York City.* Cambridge, MA: Harvard University Press, 2003.

Borchert, James. *Alley Life in Washington: Family, Community, Religion, and Folklife in the City, 1850–1970.* Urbana: University of Illinois Press, 1980.

Boyd, Herb. *Baldwin's Harlem: A Biography of James Baldwin.* New York: Atria Books, 2008.

Bracey, Susan L. *Life by the Roaring Roanoke: A History of Mecklenburg County, Virginia.* Mecklenburg, VA: Mecklenburg County Bicentennial Commission, 1977.

Breitman, George, ed. *Malcolm X Speaks: Selected Speeches and Statements.* New York: Grove Press, 1990.

"Brief History of Howard University." Howard University. Accessed 29 August 2011. http://www.howard.edu/explore/history.htm.

"Brief History of Morgan State University." Morgan State University. Accessed 22 September 2011. http://www.morgan.edu/About_MSU/University_History.html.

Brilliant, Mark. *The Color of America Has Changed: How Racial Diversity Shaped Civil Rights Reform in California, 1941–1978.* New York: Oxford University Press, 2012.

Britton, John H. "Woman behind Cambridge Racial Revolt: Female Dynamo Had City at Point of Explosion before Truce." *Jet,* 8 August 1963, 14–20.

Brock, Annette K. "Gloria Richardson and the Cambridge Movement." In *Women in the Civil Rights Movement: Trailblazers and Torchbearers, 1941–1965,* edited by Vicki L. Crawford, Jacqueline Anne Rouse, and Barbara Woods, 121–44. Bloomington: Indiana University Press, 1990.

Brooke, Edward. *Bridging the Divide: My Life.* New Brunswick, NJ: Rutgers University Press, 2007.

Brown, C. Christopher. "Chapter Twelve: Cambridge at Early 20th Century." Unpublished manuscript.

———. "One Step Closer to Democracy: African American Voting in Late Nineteenth-Century Cambridge." *Maryland Historical Magazine* 95, no. 4 (2000): 428–37.

Brown, Elaine. *A Taste of Power: A Black Woman's Story.* New York: Anchor Books, 1993.

Brown, Fahamisha Patricia. "And I Owe It All to Sterling Brown: The Theory and Practice of Black Literary Studies." *African American Review* 31, no. 3 (1997): 449–53.

Brown, Rachel. "A Summer in Cambridge." *Horn Book Magazine* 40, no. 3 (June 1964): 315–19.

Brown, Sterling. "Folk Literature." In *The Negro Caravan,* edited by Sterling A. Brown, Arthur P. Davis, and Ulysses Lee, sec. 4. New York: Dryden Press, 1941.

Bruchey, Eleanor S. "The Development of Baltimore Business, 1880–1914." *Maryland Historical Society Magazine* 64, no. 1 (1969): 18–42.

———. "The Industrialization of Maryland: 1860–1914." In *Maryland: A History, 1632–1974,* edited by Richard Walsh and William Lloyd Fox, 396–498. Baltimore: Maryland Historical Society, 1974.

Brugger, Robert J. *Maryland: A Middle Temperament, 1634–1980.* Baltimore: Johns Hopkins University Press, 1988.

Buni, Andrew. *The Negro in Virginia Politics, 1902–1965.* Charlottesville: University Press of Virginia, 1967.

Burrell, William Patrick, and D. E. Johnson Sr. *Twenty-Five Years History of the Grand Fountain of the United Order of True Reformers: 1881–1905.* Richmond, VA: Grand Fountain, United Order of True Reformers, 1909.

"Cambridge Baby Dies in Troopers' Tear Gas Mist." *Jet,* 28 May 1964, 8–9.

"Cambridge Leader Quits Rights Role for Marriage." *Jet,* 17 September 1964, 23.

"Cambridge, Maryland, 'City of Progress' for Rich." *New America,* 31 August 1963, 4.

"Cambridge Seeks Leader to Replace Mrs. Richardson." *Jet,* 18 June 1964, 9.

Campbell, James. *Talking at the Gates: A Life of James Baldwin.* Berkeley: University of California Press, 1991.

Camper, Joyce A. A. "Sterling Brown: Maker of Community in Academia." *African American Review* 31, no. 3 (1997): 437–41.

Cannato, Vincent. *The Ungovernable City: John Lindsay and His Struggle to Save New York.* New York: Basic Books, 2001.

Canton, David A. *Raymond Pace Alexander: A New Negro Lawyer Fights for Civil Rights in Philadelphia.* Jackson: University Press of Mississippi, 2010.

Carmichael, Stokely (Kwame Ture). "Interview." In *The Price of Dissent: Testimonies to Political Repression in America,* edited by Bud Schultz and Ruth Schultz, 212. Berkeley: University of California Press, 2001.

Carmichael, Stokely, and Charles V. Hamilton. *Black Power: The Politics of Liberation in America.* New York: Random House, 1967.

Carmichael, Stokely, and Ekwueme Michael Thelwell. *Ready for Revolution: The Life and Struggles of Stokely Carmichael (Kwame Ture).* New York: Scribner, 2005.

Carson, Clayborne. *In Struggle: SNCC and the Black Awakening of the 1960s.* Cambridge, MA: Harvard University Press, 1995.

Carson, Clayborne, Emma J. Lapsansky-Werner, and Gary B. Nash. *African American Lives: The Struggle for Freedom.* Vol. 2. New York: Pearson Longman, 2005.

Cary, Francine Curro, ed. *Washington Odyssey: A Multicultural History of the Nation's Capital.* Washington, DC: Smithsonian Books, 2003.

"A Cauldron of Hate." *Time,* 19 July 1963. Accessed 9 August 2007. http://www.time.com/time/magazine/article/0,9171,896863,00.html.

Cecelski, David S. *Along Freedom Road: Hyde County, North Carolina, and the Fate of Black Schools in the South.* Chapel Hill: University of North Carolina Press, 1994.

Chafe, William Henry. *Civilities and Civil Rights: Greensboro, North Carolina, and the Black Struggle for Equality.* New York: Oxford University Press, 1980.

Cha-Jua, Sundiata Keita, and Clarence Lang. "The 'Long Movement' as Vampire: Temporal and Spatial Fallacies in Recent Black Freedom Studies." *Journal of African American History* 92, no. 2 (Spring 2007): 265–88.

Chappell, Marisa, Jenny Hutchinson, and Brian Ward, "'Dress Modestly, Neatly . . . as if You Were Going to Church': Respectability, Class and Gender in the Montgomery Bus Boycott and the Early Civil Rights Movement." In *Gender and the Civil Rights Movement,* edited by Peter J. Ling and Sharon Monteith, 69–100. New Brunswick, NJ: Rutgers University Press, 2004.

Charron, Katherine Mellen. *Freedom's Teacher: The Life of Septima Clark.* Chapel Hill: University of North Carolina Press, 2009.

"Chester Cases Voided Seven Years Later." *Crisis* 78, no. 3 (April–May 1971): 100.

Churchill, Ward, and Jim Vander Wall. *The COINTELPRO Papers: Documents from the FBI's Secret Wars against Dissent in the United States.* Boston: South End Press, 1990.

"Civil Rights: A Zealot's Stand." *Time,* 11 October 1963. Accessed 20 June 2011. http://www.time.com/time/magazine/article/0,9171,873084,00.html.

"Civil Rights Pioneer Gloria Richardson, 91, on How Women Were Silenced at 1963 March on Washington." *Democracy Now!* 27 August 2013. Accessed 28 August 2013. http://www.democracynow.org/2013/8/27/civil_rights_pioneer_gloria_richardson_91.

Cleage, Albert B., Jr. *Black Christian Nationalism: New Directions for the Black Church.* New York: William Morrow, 1971.

Cleaver, Kathleen Neal. "Racism, Civil Rights, and Feminism." In *Critical Race Feminism,* edited by Adrien Katherine Wing, 35–43. New York: NYU Press, 1997.

Cleaver, Kathleen, and George Katsiaficas, eds. *Liberation, Imagination, and the Black Panther Party: A New Look at the Panthers and Their Legacy.* New York: Routledge/Taylor & Francis, 2001.

Cobb, Charles E., Jr. *On the Road to Freedom: A Guided Tour of the Civil Rights Trail.* Chapel Hill, NC: Algonquin Books, 2008.

———. *This Nonviolent Stuff'll Get You Killed: How Guns Made the Civil Rights Movement Possible.* New York: Basic Books, 2014.

Cohen, Cathy J. *Democracy Remixed: Black Youth and the Future of American Politics.* New York: Oxford University Press, 2010.

"Commencement Program." Morgan State University, 18 May 2008.

Countryman, Matthew J. *Up South: Civil Rights and Black Power in Philadelphia.* Philadelphia: University of Pennsylvania Press, 2007.

Crosby, Emilye. *A Little Taste of Freedom: The Black Freedom Struggle in Claiborne County, Mississippi.* Chapel Hill: University of North Carolina Press, 2005.

Cruse, Harold. *Rebellion or Revolution?* Minneapolis: University of Minnesota Press, 2009.

Curtin, Philip D. *The Atlantic Slave Trade: A Census.* Madison: University of Wisconsin Press, 1969.

Dailey, June. "Deference and Violence in the Postbellum Urban South: Manners and Massacres in Danville, Virginia." *Journal of Southern History* 63, no. 3 (1997): 553–90.

Davis, Arthur P. "E. Franklin Frazier (1894–1962): A Profile." *Journal of Negro Education* 31, no. 4 (Autumn 1962): 429–35.

Davis, Thulani. "It's Time to Call for New Black Leadership, We Need You." *Village Voice,* 18–24 February 2004, 32–34, 37.

"The Defiant One: Why You Should Know Civil Rights Icon Gloria Richardson." TheRoot.com, 7 July 2015. Accessed 7 July 2015. http://www.theroot.com /articles/history/2015/07/why_you_should_know_civil_rights_icon_gloria _richardson.1.html.

Desantis, John. *For the Color of His Skin: The Murder of Yusuf Hawkins and the Trial of Bensonhurst.* New York: St. Martin's Press, 1991.

Desmond-Harris, Jenée. "What Young Activists Could Teach Jay Z." The Root.com, 26 July 2013. Accessed 9 June 2015. http://www.theroot.com/articles /culture/2013/07/jay_zs_response_to_belafonte_criticism_what_young_activists _could_teach_him.html.

"Detroit Slates 'Black Summit' for Northern Leaders." *Jet,* 14 November 1963, 4.

De Veaux, Alexis. *Warrior Poet: A Biography of Audre Lorde.* New York: W. W. Norton, 2004.

Dillard, Angela D. *Faith in the City: Preaching Radical Social Change in Detroit.* Ann Arbor: University of Michigan Press, 2007.

Dittmer, John. *The Good Doctors: The Medical Committee for Human Rights and the Struggle for Social Justice in Health Care.* New York: Bloomsbury, 2009.

———. *Local People: The Struggle for Civil Rights in Mississippi.* Chicago: University of Illinois Press, 1995.

"Dr. King, Others Forecast Violence in Rights Struggle." *Jet,* 21 November 1963, 6–7.

Drake, St. Clair, and Horace R. Cayton. *Black Metropolis: A Study of Negro Life in a Northern City.* Chicago: University of Chicago Press, 1970.

Du Bois, W. E. B. "The Negro College." *Crisis* 41 (August. 1933): 175–77.

———. "A Negro Nation within a Nation." In *Ripples of Hope: Great American Civil Rights Speeches,* edited by Josh Gottheimer, 170–73. New York: Basic Civitas Books, 2003.

———. "The Negroes of Farmville, Virginia: A Social Study." In *W. E. B. Du Bois: A Reader by William Edward Burghardt Du Bois,* edited by David L. Lewis, 231–36. New York: Henry Holt, 1995.

"E. Franklin Frazier, 1894–1962: Sociologist, Educator, Author, Scholar—A Bio-Bibliography." Howard University. Accessed 24 October 2012. http://www.howard.edu/library/social_work_library/Franklin_Frazier.htm.

Elfenbein, Jessica I. *The Making of a Modern City: Philanthropy, Civic Culture, and the Baltimore YMCA.* Gainesville: University Press of Florida, 2001.

Estes, Steve. *I Am a Man! Race, Manhood, and the Civil Rights Movement.* Chapel Hill: University of North Carolina Press, 2005.

Farrison, W. Edward. "Negro Scholarship." *Crisis* 41 (February 1934): 33–34.

"The Federalist Papers: No. 51." The Avalon Project: Documents in Law, History and Diplomacy, Lillian Goldman Law Library, Yale Law School. Accessed 19 October 2017. http://avalon.law.yale.edu/18th_century/fed51.asp.

Ferguson, Karen. *Top Down: The Ford Foundation, Black Power, and the Reinvention of Racial Liberalism.* Philadelphia: University of Pennsylvania Press, 2013.

"The Fierce Urgency of Now: Why Young Protesters Bum-Rushed the Mic." The Root.com, 14 December 2014. Accessed 26 July 2015. http://www.theroot.com/articles/culture/2014/12/the_fierce_urgency_of_now_why_young_protesters_bum_rushed_the_mic.html.

"Fighting for Equality in 1963 Small-Town America." British Broadcasting Company, 17 June 2015. Accessed 17 June 2015. http://www.bbc.com/news/magazine-33135521.

Fleming, Cynthia Griggs. *Soon We Will Not Cry: The Liberation of Ruby Doris Smith Robinson.* Lanham, MD: Rowman & Littlefield, 1998.

Foeman, Anita K. "Gloria Richardson: Breaking the Mold." *Journal of Black Studies* 26 (May 1996): 604–15.

Foner, Eric. *Free Soil, Free Labor, Free Men: The Ideology of the Republican Party before the Civil War.* New York: Oxford University Press, 1995.

Ford, Tanisha C. *Liberated Threads: Black Women, Style, and the Global Politics of Soul.* Chapel Hill: University of North Carolina Press, 2015.

Forman, Jim. *The Making of Black Revolutionaries.* Seattle, WA: Open Hand Publishing, 1985.

"40 Years on, Newark Re-examines Painful Riot Past." National Public Radio, 14 July 2007. Accessed 11 April 2015. http://www.npr.org/templates/story/story.php?storyId=11966375.

Fountain, Charles. *Another Man's Poison: The Life and Writings of Columnist George Frazier.* Chester, CT: Globe Pequot Press, 1984.

Franklin, John Hope, and Alfred Moss. *From Slavery to Freedom: A History of African Americans.* 7th ed. New York: McGraw-Hill, 1994.

Franklin, Sekou M. *After the Rebellion: Black Youth, Social Movement Activism, and the Post–Civil Rights Generation.* New York: NYU Press, 2014.

Fraser, Clara, and Richard S. Fraser. *Crisis and Leadership.* Seattle, WA: Red Letter Press, 2000.

Frazier, E. Franklin. *The Negro Family in Chicago.* Chicago: University of Chicago Press, 1932.

———. "A Note on Negro Education." *Opportunity*, March 1924, 75–77.

———. "The Pathology of Race Prejudice." *Forum*, June 1927, 856–61.

Frazier, George. "Be Like a Buddhist." *Boston Herald*, 25 July 1963, 12.

———. "Mrs. Richardson: True Segregationist." *Boston Herald*, 19 June 1963, 12.

"From the Deep South to the Midwest, a Generation Demands Justice." *Nation*, 23 July 2013. Accessed 9 June 2015. http://www.thenation.com/blog/175353/deep-south-midwest-generation-demands-justice.

"From the RFK Memorial Poverty Tour: Fields Ripe with Injustice." Robert F. Kennedy Memorial Center for Human Rights. Accessed 23 February 2014. http://rfkcenter.org/from-the-rfk-memorial-poverty-tour-fields-ripe-with-injustice.

Gal, Susan. "Between Speech and Silence: The Problems of Research on Language and Gender." In *Gender at the Crossroads of Knowledge: Feminist Anthropology in the Postmodern Era*, edited by Micaela di Leonardo, 175–203. Berkeley: University of California Press, 1991.

Gallen, David. *Malcolm X: As They Knew Him*. New York: Carroll & Graf, 1992.

Gardner, Michael R. *Harry Truman and Civil Rights: Moral Courage and Political Risks*. Carbondale: Southern Illinois University Press, 2003.

Garland, Phyl. "Builders of a New South." *Ebony*, August 1966, 27–30, 34, 36–37.

Gasman, Marybeth, et al. "Unearthing Promise and Potential: Our Nation's Historically Black Colleges and Universities." In *Association for the Study of Higher Education Report 35, no. 5*, 5–9. Somerset, NJ: John Wiley & Sons, 2010.

Gatewood, Willard B. *Aristocrats of Color: The Black Elite, 1880–1920*. Bloomington: Indiana University Press, 1990.

Gault, Charlayne Hunter. "Heirs to a Legacy of Struggle: Charlayne Hunter Integrates the University of Georgia." In *Sisters in the Struggle: African-American Women in the Civil Rights–Black Power Movement*, edited by Bettye Collier-Thomas and V. P. Franklin, 75–84. New York: NYU Press, 2001.

Giddings, Paula. *When and Where I Enter: The Impact of Black Women on Race and Sex in America*. New York: Quill, 1984.

Gilmore, Glenda Elizabeth. *Gender and Jim Crow: Women and the Politics of White Supremacy in North Carolina, 1896–1920*. Chapel Hill: University of North Carolina Press, 1996.

Gitlin, Todd. *Occupying Wall Street: The Inside Story of an Action that Changed America*. Chicago: Haymarket Books, 2012.

———. *The Sixties: Years of Hope, Days of Rage*. New York: Bantam, 1993.

Glazer, Nathan, and Daniel P. Moynihan. *Beyond the Melting Pot: The Negroes, Puerto Ricans, Jews, Italians, and Irish of New York City*. Cambridge, MA: MIT Press, 1970.

"Gloria Richardson." *Newsweek*, 5 August 1963.

"Gloria Richardson Explains Cambridge, Maryland to N.Y." *New York Amsterdam News*, 24 August 1963, 18.

"Gloria Richardson: Lady General of Civil Rights." *Ebony*, July 1964, 23–26, 28, 30–31.

Goldberg, Louis C. "Ghetto Riots and Others: The Faces of Civil Disorder in 1967." *Journal of Peace Research* 5, no. 2 (1968): 116–32.

Goldman, Peter. *The Death and Life of Malcolm X*. Champaign: University of Illinois Press, 1979.

Goosman, Stuart L. *Group Harmony: The Black Urban Roots of Rhythm & Blues*. Philadelphia: University of Pennsylvania Press, 2005.

Gore, Dayo F., Jeanne Theoharis, and Komozi Woodard, eds. *Want to Start a Revolution? Radical Women in the Black Freedom Struggle.* New York: NYU Press, 2009.

Grant, George C. "Desegregation in Maryland since the Supreme Court Decision." *Journal of Negro Education* 24, no. 3 (Summer 1955): 275–86.

Grant, Joanne. *Ella Baker: Freedom Bound.* New York: Wiley, 1998.

Green, Constance McLaughlin. *The Secret City: A History of Race Relations in the Nation's Capital.* Princeton, NJ: Princeton University Press, 1967.

Green, Susanne E. "Black Republicans on the Baltimore City Council, 1890–1931." *Maryland Historical Magazine* 74 (September 1979): 203–22.

Gregory, Dick. *Up from Nigger.* New York: Stein & Day, 1976.

"Gregory, SNCC Get Action in Ga. Restaurant Blitz." *Jet,* 16 January 1964, 5.

Griffin, Susan. "The Way of All Ideology." *Signs: Journal of Women in Culture and Society* 7, no. 3 (1982): 641–60.

Guralnick, Peter. *Dream Boogie: The Triumph of Sam Cooke.* New York: Little, Brown, 2005.

Hahn, Steven. *A Nation under Our Feet: Black Political Struggles in the Rural South from Slavery to the Great Migration.* Cambridge, MA: Belknap, 2003.

Haines, Herbert. *Black Radicalism and the Civil Rights Mainstream.* Knoxville: University of Tennessee Press, 1988.

Halisi, Clyde, and James Mtume, eds. *The Quotable Karenga.* Los Angeles: US Organization, 1967.

Hall, Jacquelyn Dowd. "The Long Civil Rights Movement and the Political Uses of the Past." *Journal of American History* 91, no. 4 (March 2005): 1233–63.

Hamlin, Françoise N. *Crossroads at Clarksdale: The Black Freedom Struggle in the Mississippi Delta after World War II.* Chapel Hill: University of North Carolina Press, 2012.

A Handbook of Virginia. 7th ed. Richmond: Department of Agriculture and Immigration of the State of Virginia, 1919.

Handlin, Oscar, and Mary Handlin. "Origins of Southern Labor System." *William and Mary Quarterly* 7, no. 2 (1950): 199–222.

Harding, Vincent, et al. *We Changed the World: African Americans, 1945–1970.* New York: Oxford University Press, 1997.

"Harlem History: Twenty Two West ('22 West')." *Harlem World Magazine,* 25 September 2011. Accessed 24 September 2012. http://harlemworldmag.com/2011/09/25/harlem-history-twenty-two-west-22-west/.

Harley, Sharon. "Chronicle of a Death Foretold." In *Sisters in the Struggle: African-American Women in the Civil Rights–Black Power Movement,* edited by Bettye Collier-Thomas and V. P. Franklin, 174–96. New York: NYU Press, 2001.

Harris, Leonard, and Charles Molesworth. *Alain L. Locke: The Biography of a Philosopher.* Chicago: University of Chicago Press, 2008.

Harris, Richard E. *Politics and Prejudice: A History of Chester (Pa) Negroes.* Apache Junction, AZ: Relmo Publishers, 1991.

Hart, George L. *Official Report of the Proceedings of the Twentieth Republican National Convention, Held in Chicago, Illinois, June 14, 15 and 16, 1932.* New York: Tenny Press, 1932.

Hartshorn Memorial College Catalog, 1920–1921. Richmond: Virginia Union University and Hartshorn Memorial College, 1921.

Hayden, Casey. Preface to *Freedom Song: A Personal Story of the 1960s Civil Rights Movement*, by Mary King. New York: William Morrow, 1987.

Hayden, Casey, and Mary King. "Sex and Caste: A Kind of Memo from Casey Hayden and Mary King to a Number of Other Women in the Peace and Freedom Movements." University of Illinois at Chicago, 1965. Accessed 18 February 2014. http://uic.edu/orgs/cwluherstory/CWLUArchive/memo.html.

Henry, David. *Up Pine Street: A Pictorial History of the African American Community of Cambridge, Maryland 1884–1951*. Vol. 1. Woodstock, MD: David Henry, 2003.

Hicks, Helena Sorrell. "The Black Apprentice in Maryland Court Records from 1661 to 1865." Dissertation, University of Maryland, 1988.

Hill, Herbert. "Black Workers, Organized Labor, and Title VII of the 1964 Civil Rights Act: Legislative History and Litigation Record." In *Race in America: The Struggle for Equality*, edited by Herbert Hill and James E. Jones Jr., 263–341. Madison: University of Wisconsin Press, 1993.

Hill, Laura Warren, and Julia Rabig, eds. *The Business of Black Power: Community Development, Capitalism, and Corporate Responsibility in Postwar America*. Rochester, NY: University of Rochester Press, 2012.

"History of Highland Beach." Town of Highland Beach, MD. Accessed 13 December 2011. http://highlandbeachmd.org/.

"History of the Knights of Pythias." The Pythians: The Order of the Knights of Pythias. Accessed 12 August 2011. http://www.pythias.org/about/pythstory.html.

Hoffecker, Carol, and Annette Woolard. "Black Women in Delaware's History." In *A History of African Americans of Delaware and Maryland's Eastern Shore*, edited by Carole Marks. University of Delaware, 1997. Accessed 29 August 2010. http://www.udel.edu/BlackHistory/blackwomen.html.

Hogan, Wesley. "How Democracy Travels: SNCC, Swarthmore Students, and the Growth of the Student Movement in the North, 1961–1964." *Pennsylvania Magazine of History and Biography* 126, no. 3 (July 2002): 437–70.

Holloway, Jonathan Scott. *Confronting the Veil: Abram Harris Jr., E. Franklin Frazier, and Ralph Bunche, 1919–1941*. Chapel Hill: University of North Carolina Press, 2001.

Holsaert, Faith. "Resistance U." In *Hands on the Freedom Plow: Personal Accounts by Women in SNCC*, edited by Faith Holsaert et al., 181–95. Urbana: University of Illinois Press, 2010.

hooks, bell. *Feminist Theory from Margin to Center*. Boston: South End Press, 1984.

"Howard U. Conference." *Negro Digest*, March 1964, 78–91.

Howard University: Alumni Today, 2010. Brewster, NY: Harris Connect, 2010.

Howard University Bulletin: Annual Catalogue 1938–1939. Vol. 18, 30 April 1939.

Howard University Bulletin: Annual Catalogue 1939–1940. Vol. 19, 15 May 1940.

Howard University Bulletin: Annual Catalogue 1940–1941. Vol. 20, 15 May 1941.

Howard University Bulletin: Annual Catalogue 1941–1942. Vol. 21, 15 May 1942.

Hughes, Langston. "Cowards from the Colleges." *Crisis* 41 (August 1934): 226–28.

"Ivy Young Willis & Martha Willis Dale Award." Cabrini University, 8 April 2015. Accessed 7 August 2015. http://www.cabrini.edu/Academics/Academic-Depart ments/History-and-Political-Science-Department/Ivy-Young-Willis-Award.

Jackson, Robert L., and Emerson C. Walden. "A History of Provident Hospital, Baltimore, Maryland." *Journal of the National Medical Association* 59, no. 3 (May 1967): 157–65.

James, Joy. *Shadow Boxing.* New York: St. Martin's Press, 1999.

Janken, Kenneth Robert. *Rayford W. Logan and the Dilemma of the African-American Intellectual.* Amherst: University of Massachusetts, 1993.

Jeffries, Hasan Kwame. *Bloody Lowndes: Civil Rights and Black Power in Alabama's Black Belt.* New York: NYU Press, 2010.

Johnson, Cedric. *Revolutionaries to Race Leaders: Black Power and the Making of African American Politics.* Minneapolis: University of Minnesota Press, 2007.

Johnson, Nicholas. *Negroes and the Gun: The Black Tradition of Arms.* Amherst, NY: Prometheus Books, 2014.

Jonathan L. "Tales from a Black Filled Childhood: Who Will Lead My Black Generation . . . No One?" Black Youth Project, 26 April 2013. Accessed 28 April 2013. http://www.blackyouthproject.com/2013/04/tales-from-a-black-filled -childhood-who-will-lead-my-black-generation-no-one/#more-32306.

Jones, Charles E., ed. *The Black Panther Party [Reconsidered].* Baltimore: Black Classic Press, 2005.

Jones, Patrick T. *The Selma of the North: Civil Rights Insurgency in Milwaukee.* Cambridge, MA: Harvard University Press, 2009.

Jordan, Ervin L., Jr. *Black Confederates and Afro-Yankees in Civil War Virginia.* Charlottesville: University of Virginia Press, 1995.

Joseph, Peniel E. *Waiting 'til the Midnight Hour: A Narrative History of Black Power in America.* New York: Henry Holt, 2006.

Kahlenberg, Richard D. *Tough Liberal: Albert Shanker and the Battles over Schools, Unions, Race, and Democracy.* New York: Columbia University Press, 2009.

Kahn, Tom, and August Meier. "Recent Trends in the Civil Rights Movement." *New Politics* 3 (Spring 1964): 34–53. Reprint.

Kempton, Murray. "Gloria, Gloria." *New Republic,* 16 November 1963, 15.

Kerr, Audrey Elisa. *The Paper Bag Principle: Class, Colorism, and Rumor and the Case of Black Washington, D.C.* Knoxville: University of Tennessee Press, 2006.

Kimmel, Ross M. "Free Black People in Seventeenth Century Maryland." *Maryland Historical Magazine* 71, no. 1 (1976): 19–25.

King, Mary. *Freedom Song: A Personal Story of the 1960s Civil Rights Movement.* New York: William Morrow, 1987.

LaFrance, Marianne. *Why Smile: The Science behind Facial Expressions.* New York: W. W. Norton, 2013.

Lee, Chana Kai. "Anger, Memory, and Personal Power: Fannie Lou Hamer and Civil Rights Leadership." In *Sisters in the Struggle: African-American Women in the Civil Rights–Black Power Movement,* edited by Bettye Collier-Thomas and V. P. Franklin, 139–70. New York: NYU Press, 2001.

————. *For Freedom's Sake: The Life of Fannie Lou Hamer.* Urbana: University of Illinois Press, 1999.

Leeming, David Adams. *James Baldwin: A Biography.* New York: Knopf, 1994.

Levy, Peter B. *Civil War on Race Street: The Civil Rights Struggle in Cambridge, Maryland.* Gainesville: University Press of Florida, 2003.

Lewis, David Levering. *King: A Biography.* Urbana: University of Illinois Press, 1978.

————. *W. E. B. Du Bois: Biography of a Race, 1868–1919.* New York: Henry Holt, 1993.

————. *W. E. B. Du Bois: The Fight for Equality and the American Century, 1919–1963.* New York: Henry Holt, 2000.

Lewis, John. "A Trend toward Aggressive Nonviolent Action." In *Black Protest Thought in the Twentieth Century,* 2nd ed., edited by August Meier, Elliott M. Rudwick, and Francis L. Broderick, 352–60. Indianapolis: Bobbs-Merrill, 1971.

————. *Walking with the Wind: A Memoir of the Movement.* New York: Simon & Schuster, 1998.

Lewis-Colman, David M. *Race against Liberalism: Black Workers and the UAW in Detroit.* Urbana: University of Illinois Press, 2008.

Lincoln University Catalogue, 1922–1923. Hampton, VA: Hampton Institute Press, 1923.

Ling, Peter J., and Sharon Monteith, eds. *Gender and the Civil Rights Movement.* New Brunswick, NJ: Rutgers University Press, 2004.

"A Literary Tribute to Sterling A. Brown." Howard University Libraries. Accessed 22 October 2012. http://www.howard.edu/library/reference/guides/Sterling Brown.htm.

Locke, Alain L. *The New Negro, an Interpretation.* New York: Albert & Charles Boni, 1925.

Lomax, Louis E. *The Negro Revolt.* New York: Harper & Row, 1962.

Lorde, Audre. "The Uses of Anger: Women Responding to Racism." In *Sister Outsider: Essays and Speeches.* Freedom, CA: Crossing Press, 1984.

Mace, Darryl C. *In Remembrance of Emmett Till: Regional Stories and Media Responses to the Black Freedom Struggle.* Lexington: University Press of Kentucky, 2014.

Malcolm X. "The Ballot or the Bullet," 12 April 1964. Accessed 5 March 2013. http://americanradioworks.publicradio.org/features/blackspeech/mx.html.

————. "Interview with A. B. Spellman," 19 March 1964. *Monthly Review* 16, no. 1 (May 1964). Accessed 5 March 2009. http://www.monthlyreview.org/564mx .htm.

————. "Message to Grassroots," 10 November 1963. TeachingAmericanHistory .org. Accessed 10 May 2014. http://teachingamericanhistory.org/library /document/message-to-grassroots/.

Marsh, Clifton E. *The Lost-Found Nation of Islam in America.* Lanham, MD: Scarecrow Press, 2000.

Maryland Advisory Committee to the United States Commission on Civil Rights. *Report on Maryland: Employment.* February 1964.

"Maryland Women's Hall of Fame: Verda Welcome." Maryland State Archives, 2001. Accessed 7 June 2012. http://www.msa.md.gov/msa/educ/exhibits /womenshall/html/welcome.html.

"Maryland Women's Heritage Trail." Maryland Women's History Project et al., n.d. Accessed 20 March 2011. http://mdwomensheritagecenter.org/pdf/Heritage _Poster.pdf.

"Maryland's African-American Heritage Guide." Maryland Office of Tourism, n.d. Accessed 23 August 2010. http://viewer.zmags.com/publication/6631b929# /6631b929/1.

May, Gary. *Bending toward Justice: The Voting Rights Act and the Transformation of American Democracy.* New York: Basic Books, 2013.

McConnell, Roland C., ed. *Three Hundred and Fifty Years: A Chronology of the Afro-Am in Maryland, 1634–1984.* Annapolis: Maryland Commission on Afro-Am History and Culture for the Maryland State Department of Economic and Community Development, 1985.

McDougall, Harold. *Black Baltimore: A New Theory of Community.* Philadelphia: Temple University Press, 1993.

McElvey, Kay Kajiyyah. "Early Black Dorchester, 1776–1870: A History of the Struggle of African-Americans in Dorchester County, Maryland, to Be Free to Make Their Own Choices." Dissertation, University of Maryland, College Park, 1991.

McFadden, Robert D., et al. *Outrage: The Story behind the Tawana Brawley Hoax.* New York: Bantam, 1990.

McGirr, Lisa. *Suburban Warriors: The Origins of the New American Right.* Princeton, NJ: Princeton University Press, 2001.

McGuinn, Henry J. "Equal Protection of the Law and Fair Trials in Maryland." *Journal of Negro History* 24, no. 2 (April 1939): 143–66.

McGuinn, Henry J., and Tinsley Lee Spraggins. "Negro in Politics in Virginia." *Journal of Negro Education* 26, no. 3 (1957): 378–89.

McGuire, Danielle L. *At the Dark End of the Street: Black Women, Rape, and Resistance—A New History of the Civil Rights Movement from Rosa Parks to the Rise of Black Power.* New York: Vintage, 2010.

McKay, Claude. "If We Must Die." In *Let Nobody Turn Us Around: Voices of Resistance, Reform, and Renewal,* edited by Manning Marable and Leith Mullings, 246. New York: Rowman & Littlefield, 2000.

Meier, August, and Elliott M. Rudwick. *CORE: A Study in the Civil Rights Movement, 1942–1968.* New York: Oxford University Press, 1973.

Meyerowitz, Joanne, ed. *Not June Cleaver: Women and Gender in Postwar America, 1945–1960.* Philadelphia: Temple University Press, 1994.

"Milestones." *Time,* 11 September 1964. Accessed 31 March 2008. http://www .time.com/time/printout/0,8816,830688,00.html.

Millner, Sandra Y. "Recasting Civil Rights Leadership: Gloria Richardson and the Cambridge Movement." *Journal of Black Studies* 26 (July 1996): 668–87.

Mills, Kay. *This Little Light of Mine: The Life of Fannie Lou Hamer.* New York: Plume, 1993.

Moore, James T. "Black Militancy in Readjuster Virginia, 1879–1883." *Journal of Southern History* 41, no. 2 (1975): 167–86.

Morales, Leslie Anderson, and Beverly Pierce, eds. *Virginia Slave Births Index, 1853–1865.* Vol. 3, *H–L.* Westminster, MD: Heritage Books, 2007.

Morgan, Philip D., and Michael L. Nicholls. "Slaves in Piedmont Virginia, 1720–1790." *William and Mary Quarterly* 46, no. 2 (1989): 211–51.

Muse, Clifford L., Jr. "Howard University and the Federal Government during the Presidential Administrations of Herbert Hoover and Franklin Delano Roosevelt, 1928–1945." *Journal of Negro History* 76, no. 1 (Winter–Autumn 1991): 1–20.

———. "The Howard University Players." Howard University, February 2001. Accessed 16 December 2009. http://www.huarchivesnet.howard.edu/howarcor Sketch1.htm.

Nadasen, Premilla. *Rethinking the Welfare Rights Movement.* New York: Routledge, 2012.

———. *Welfare Warriors: The Welfare Rights Movement in the United States.* New York: Routledge, 2004.

"The Negro Family: The Case for National Action." US Department of Labor, Office of Policy Planning and Research, March 1965. Accessed 20 May 2015. http://web.stanford.edu/~mrosenfe/Moynihan%27s%20The%20Negro%20Family.pdf.

"Negro Leaders Give Their Views: Prospects for '64 in the Civil Rights Struggle." *Negro Digest,* January 1964, 9, 12–13.

"Negroes Threat 'To Close Town' Backs Gregory." *Jet,* 11 June 1964, 7.

Nelson, Bruce. *Divided We Stand: American Workers and the Struggle for Black Equality.* Princeton, NJ: Princeton University Press, 2002.

Newton, Huey P. "A Letter from Huey P. Newton to the Revolutionary Brothers and Sisters about the Women's Liberation and Gay Liberation Movements." *Black Panther,* 21 August 1970, 5.

"The 1973 Fire, National Personnel Records Center." National Archives. Accessed 17 November 2011. http://www.archives.gov/st-louis/military-personnel/fire-1973.html.

"Nonviolence/Violence." *Howard Magazine,* January 1966, 5–8.

Ogbar, Jeffrey O. G. *Black Power: Radical Politics and African American Identity.* Baltimore: Johns Hopkins University Press, 2004.

Olson, Karen. "Old West Baltimore: Segregation, African-American Culture, and the Struggle for Equality." In *The Baltimore Book: New Views of Local History,* edited by Elizabeth Fee, Linda Shopes, and Linda Zeidman, 57–80. Philadelphia: Temple University Press, 1991.

Olson, Lynne. *Freedom's Daughters: The Unsung Heroines of the Civil Rights Movement from 1830 to 1970.* New York: Scribner, 2001.

"Patricia Harris Co-Chairman of Powerful Rights Lobby." *Jet,* 25 July 1963, 8–9.

Payne, Charles M. *I've Got the Light of Freedom: The Organizing Tradition and the Mississippi Freedom Struggle.* Berkeley: University of California Press, 1995.

Pernoud, Regine, and Narue-Veronique Clin. *Joan of Arc: Her Story.* Translated by Jeremy Duquesnay Adams. New York: St. Martin's Press, 1998.

Perry, Bruce. *Malcolm: The Life of a Man Who Changed America.* Barrytown, NY: Station Hill, 1991.

Pinn, Anthony B. *African American Humanist Principles: Living and Thinking Like the Children of Nimrod.* New York: Palgrave Macmillan, 2004.

Piri, Thomas. *Down These Mean Streets.* New York: Knopf, 1967.

Press release. Lincoln University, Office of Marketing. Accessed 9 March 2010. http://www.lincoln.edu/marketing/pr/news0429043.html.

Princess Anne Academy Catalogue, 1935–1936. Princess Anne, MD, 1935.

Pritchett, Wendell E. *Robert Clifton Weaver and the American City: The Life and Times of an Urban Reformer.* Chicago: University of Chicago Press, 2008.

"Professional News: In Memoriam: Hayes." *Journal of the National Medical Association* 39, no. 5 (September 1947): 220.

Program: George Washington's Birthday Convocation. Washington College, 22 February 2008.

Program: LawForBlackLives.org. Accessed 29 July 2015. http://www.law4black lives.org/program/.

Program: Twenty-Eighth Annual Founders' Day Observance. Riverside Club of New York City, 29 March 2009.

Purdum, Todd. *An Idea Whose Time Has Come: Two Presidents, Two Parties, and the Battle for the Civil Rights Act of 1964.* New York: Henry Holt, 2014.

Purnell, Brian. "'Drive Awhile for Freedom': Brooklyn CORE's 1964 Stall-in and Public Discourses on Protest Violence." In *Groundwork: Local Black Freedom Movements in America,* edited by Jeanne Theoharis and Komozi Woodard, 45–75. New York: NYU Press, 2005.

———. *Fighting Jim Crow in the County of Kings: The Congress of Racial Equality in Brooklyn.* Lexington: University Press of Kentucky, 2013.

Rahman, Ahmad. *The Regime Change of Kwame Nkrumah: Epic Heroism in Africa and the Diaspora.* Basingstoke, UK: Palgrave Macmillan, 2007.

"The Rampant Sexism at March on Washington." The Root.com, 22 August 2013. Accessed 5 August 2015. http://www.theroot.com/articles/culture/2013/08 /the_rampant_sexism_at_the_march_on_washington.html#storify/e45b3ae355 4217045f8d221636da11b4.

Ransby, Barbara. *Ella Baker and the Black Freedom Movement: A Radical Democratic Vision.* Chapel Hill: University of North Carolina Press, 2003.

Ravitch, Diane. *The Great School Wars: New York City, 1805–1973.* New York: Basic Books, 1974.

"Raymond Pace Alexander, Biographical Sketch." University of Pennsylvania Archives and Records Center. Accessed 18 December 2011. http://www.archives.upenn .edu/faids/upt/upt50/alexander_rpa.html.

Report of the National Advisory Commission on Civil Disorders, Summary of Report. 1968. Accessed 2 September 2010. http://www.eisenhowerfoundation.org /docs/kerner.pdf.

Richardson, Gloria. "Cambridge, Maryland, 'City of Progress' for Rich." *New America,* 31 August 1963, 4.

———. "The Energy of the People Passing through Me." In *Hands on the Freedom Plow: Personal Accounts by Women in SNCC,* edited by Faith Holsaert et al., 273–97. Urbana: University of Illinois Press, 2010.

———. "Focus on Cambridge." *Freedomways* 4, no. 1 (1964): 28–34.

———. Letter to the editor. *Ebony,* May 1974, 18.

Ritterhouse, Jennifer. *Growing up Jim Crow: How Black and White Children Learned Race.* Chapel Hill: University of North Carolina Press, 2006.

Robbins, Jhan, and June Robbins. "Why Didn't They Hit Back?" *Redbook*, July 1963. CORE reprint, n.d. Civil Rights Movement Veterans (CRMVET). Accessed 1 July 2012. http://www.crmvet.org/info/core_nv_redbook.pdf.

Robeson, Paul. *Here I Stand*. Boston: Beacon Press, 1958.

Robnett, Belinda. *How Long? How Long? African American Women in the Struggle for Civil Rights*. New York: Oxford University Press, 1997.

———. "Women in the Student Non-Violent Coordinating Committee: Ideology, Organizational Structure, and Leadership." In *Gender and the Civil Rights Movement*, edited by Peter J. Ling and Sharon Monteith, 131–68. New Brunswick, NJ: Rutgers University Press, 2004.

Rollins, Avon, Sr. "August 28th 1963—The March on Washington." Civil Rights Movement Veterans (CRMVET), 14 June 2008. Accessed 17 July 2011. http://www.crmvet.org/info/mowrolin.htm.

"Sadie Tanner Mossell Alexander, Biographical Sketch." University of Pennsylvania Archives and Records Center. Accessed 18 December 2011. http://www.archives.upenn.edu/faids/upt/upt50/alexander_stma.html.

Sales, William W., Jr. *From Civil Rights to Black Liberation: Malcolm X and the Organization of Afro-America Unity*. Boston: South End Press, 1994.

Schechter, Patricia A. *Ida B. Wells-Barnett & American Reform 1880–1930*. Chapel Hill: University of North Carolina Press, 2001.

Schultz, Bud, and Ruth Schultz, eds. *The Price of Dissent: Testimonies to Political Repression in America*. Berkeley: University of California Press, 2001.

Schweinitz, Rebecca de. *If We Could Change the World: Young People and America's Long Struggle for Racial Equality*. Chapel Hill: University of North Carolina Press, 2009.

Scott, Lynn Orilla. "Challenging the American Conscience, Re-imagining American Identity: James Baldwin and the Civil Rights Movement." In *A Historical Guide to James Baldwin*, edited by Douglas Field, 141–76. New York: Oxford University Press, 2009.

Scurlock, George C., et al. "Additional Information and Corrections in Reconstruction Records." *Journal of Negro History* 5, no. 2 (1920): 235–48.

Seale, Bobby. "Bobby Seale Explains Panther Politics." *Guardian*, 21 February 1970, 10.

———. *Seize the Time*. Baltimore: Black Classic Press, 1991.

Sellers, Cleveland. *The River of No Return*. New York: William Morrow, 1973.

Smith, C. Fraser. *Here Lies Jim Crow: Civil Rights in Maryland*. Baltimore: Johns Hopkins University Press, 2008.

Sonnie, Amy, and James Tracy. *Hillbilly Nationalists, Urban Race Rebels, and Black Power: Community Organizing in Radical Times*. New York: Melville House, 2011.

Spencer, Herbert. *Social Statics: Or, the Conditions Essential to Human Happiness Specified*. London: John Chapman, 1851.

Springer, Kimberly. *Living for the Revolution: Black Feminist Organizations, 1968–1980*. Durham, NC: Duke University Press, 2005.

Stevenson, Brenda E. *Life in Black and White: Family and Community in the Slave South*. New York: Oxford University Press, 1997.

Streator, George. "Negro College Radicals." *Crisis* 41 (February 1934): 47.

Streff, Jonathan Beirne. "Reading Race: The Roots of the Chester, Pennsylvania, Race Riot of 1917." Master's thesis, Temple University, 1999.

"Strong Women Were Pillars behind Civil Rights Movement." *USA Today*, 19 August 2013. Accessed 22 August 2013. http://www.usatoday.com/story/news/nation/2013/08/19/march-on-washington-women/2648011/.

Student Nonviolent Coordinating Committee. "Founding Statement," 15–17 April 1960. Civil Rights Movement Veterans (CRMVET). Accessed 6 July 2017. http://www.crmvet.org/docs/sncc1.htm.

"Surveillance under the USA PATRIOT Act." American Civil Liberties Union. Accessed 24 July 2015. https://www.aclu.org/surveillance-under-usa-patriot-act.

Szabo, Peter S. "An Interview with Gloria Richardson Dandridge." *Maryland Historical Magazine* 89, no. 3 (1994): 347–58.

"Talk Is of a Revolution—Complete with Mixed Blood." *Jet*, 28 November 1963, 14–19.

Taylor, A. A. "The Negro an Efficient Laborer." *Journal of Negro History* 11, no. 2 (1926): 363–78.

"Ten Things to Know about the March on Washington." Teaching Tolerance, 28 August 2012. Accessed 22 August 2013. http://www.tolerance.org/blog/ten-things-know-about-march-washington.

Theoharis, Jeanne. *The Rebellious Life of Mrs. Rosa Parks.* Boston: Beacon Press, 2013.

Theoharis, Jeanne, and Komozi Woodard, eds. *Freedom North: Black Freedom Struggles Outside of the South, 1940–1980.* New York: Palgrave Macmillan, 2003.

———. *Groundwork: Local Black Freedom Movements in America.* New York: NYU Press, 2005.

"3 Unsung Feminist Civil Rights Leaders." *Ebony*, 25 March 2014. Accessed 27 March 2014. http://www.ebony.com/news-views/3-unsung-feminist-civil-rights-leaders 405#axzz2xC3j80Z9.

Tolnay, Stewart E. *The Bottom Rung: African American Family Life on Southern Farms.* Urbana: University of Illinois Press, 1999.

Trever, Edward. "Gloria Richardson and the Cambridge Civil Rights Movement, 1962–1964." Master's thesis, Morgan State University, 1994.

Tyler, Gus. *Look for the Union Label: A History of the International Ladies Garment Workers Union.* Armonk, NY: M. E. Sharpe, 1995.

Tyson, Cyril deGrasse. *Power and Politics in Central Harlem, 1862–1964: The HARYOU Experience.* New York: Jay Street Publishers, 2004.

Tyson, Timothy B. *Radio Free Dixie: Robert F. Williams and the Roots of Black Power.* Chapel Hill: University of North Carolina Press, 1999.

Umoja, Akinyele Omowale. *We Will Shoot Back: Armed Resistance in the Mississippi Freedom Movement.* New York: NYU Press, 2013.

"Uninvited Guest." *Time*, 22 May 1964. Accessed 9 August 2007. http://www.time.com/time/printout/0,8816,871094,00.html.

"Unite with Whites, Leaders Urge; Guard Unit Mixed." *Jet*, 4 June 1964, 8–9.

"Universal Declaration of Human Rights." United Nations, 10 December 1948. Accessed 2 August 2017. http://www.ohchr.org/EN/UDHR/Documents /UDHR_Translations/eng.pdf.

Urquhart, Brian. *Ralph Bunche: An American Life.* New York: W. W. Norton, 1993.

Van Deburg, William L. *New Day in Babylon.* Chicago: University of Chicago Press, 1992.

"Viewpoint: Why Was the Biggest Protest in World History Ignored?" Time.com, 15 February 2013. Accessed 24 July 2015. http://world.time.com/2013/02/15 /viewpoint-why-was-the-biggest-protest-in-world-history-ignored/.

Virginia Union University Catalog, 1910–1911. Richmond, VA: Williams Printing Company, 1911.

Von Eschen, Donald, Jerome Kirk, and Maurice Pinard. "The Disintegration of the Negro Non-Violent Movement." *Journal of Peace Research* 6, no. 3 (1969): 215–34.

Walker, Jenny. "The 'Gun-Toting' Gloria Richardson: Black Violence in Cambridge, Maryland." In *Gender and the Civil Rights Movement,* edited by Peter J. Ling and Sharon Monteith, 169–86. New Brunswick, NJ: Rutgers University Press, 2004.

Ward, Brian. *Just My Soul Responding: Rhythm and Blues, Black Consciousness and Race Relations.* Berkeley: University of California Press, 1998.

Washington, Cynthia. "We Started from Different Ends of the Spectrum." *Southern Exposure* 9, no. 4 (Winter 1977): 14.

Watkinson, James D. "William Washington Browne and the True Reformers of Richmond, Virginia." *Virginia Magazine of History and Biography* 97 (1989): 375–98.

Watts, Dan. "Mrs. Richardson's Revolt." *Liberator,* November 1963, 2.

"What Ever Happened to . . . Gloria Richardson: Civil Rights Leader Now Works with NCNW." *Ebony,* February 1974, 138.

"What Those Who Studied Nazis Can Teach Us about the Strange Reaction to Donald Trump." HuffingtonPost.com, 19 December 2016. Accessed 24 December 2016. http://www.huffingtonpost.com/entry/donald-trump-nazi-propaganda -coordinate_us_58583b6fe4b08debb78a7d5c.

White, Deborah Gray. *Too Heavy a Load: Black Women in Defense of Themselves, 1894–1994.* New York: W. W. Norton, 1999.

White, Edmund. *City Boy: My Life in New York during the 1960s and '70s.* New York: Bloomsbury USA, 2009.

White, Walter Francis. *A Man Called White: The Autobiography of Walter White.* Athens: University of Georgia Press, 1995.

"Why Do Women Always Have to Smile?" Slate.com, 18 June 2013. Accessed 23 June 2013. http://www.slate.com/articles/double_x/doublex/2013/06/bitchy _resting_face_and_female_niceness_why_do_women_have_to_smile_more.html.

Wilkerson, Cathy. "'It Was All Men Talking:' Cathy Wilkerson on 1960s Campus Organizing." History Matters: The U.S. Survey Course on the Web. George Mason University. Accessed 21 July 2017. http://historymatters.gmu.edu/d /6913.html.

Wilkerson, Isabel. *The Warmth of Other Suns: The Epic Story of America's Great Migration*. New York: Random House, 2010.

"William Beverly Carter (1921–1982)." Office of the Historian, Bureau of Public Affairs, United States Department of State. Accessed 4 November 2012. http://history.state.gov/departmenthistory/people/carter-william-beverly.

Williams, Patricia J. "Spirit-murdering the Messenger: The Discourse of Finger-pointing as the Law's Response to Racism." In *Critical Race Feminism*, edited by Adrien Katherine Wing, 229–36. New York: NYU Press, 1997.

Williams, Rhonda Y. *Concrete Demands: The Search for Black Power in the 20th Century*. New York: Routledge, 2014.

———. *The Politics of Public Housing: Black Women's Struggles against Urban Inequality*. New York: Oxford University Press, 2005.

Women of Triumph II. Everett L. Marshburn, executive producer. Baltimore: Maryland Public Television, 1998. Videocassette.

Woodard, Komozi. "It's Nation Time in NewArk: Amiri Baraka and the Black Power Experiments in Newark, New Jersey." In *Freedom North: Black Freedom Struggles Outside the South, 1940–1980*, edited by Jeanne Theoharis and Komozi Woodard, 287–311. New York: Palgrave Macmillan, 2003.

———. "Message from the Grassroots: The Black Power Experiment in Newark, New Jersey." In *Groundwork: Local Black Freedom Movements in America*, edited by Jeanne Theoharis and Komozi Woodard, 77–96. New York: NYU Press, 2005.

Woodson, Carter G. *The Mis-education of the Negro*. Trenton, NJ: Africa World Press, 1990.

Woodward, C. Vann. *Origins of the New South, 1877–1913*. Baton Rouge: Louisiana State University Press, 1951.

Wynes, Charles E. *Race Relations in Virginia, 1870–1902*. Charlottesville: University of Virginia Press, 1961.

Yanow, Scott. *Classic Jazz*. San Francisco: Backbeat Books, 2001.

Zinn, Howard. *SNCC: The New Abolitionists*. Cambridge, MA: South End Press, 2002.

Index

34–35; family's support of her self-respect, 39–40, 53; father's opposition to her joining the WAAC, 58; FBI file, 278; finding work after her divorce from Dandridge, 214; firing guns, 109; "Freedom Now" rally speech printed in *New America* newspaper, 88; *Freedomways* essay, 207; gender and her activism, 163, 166–67; growing national influence, 164; at Howard University, 50; influence on Malcolm X, 196–97; inherits father's pharmacy, 62; intellect, 165, 282; jobs since leaving the civil rights movement, 216–18; leadership, 116, 169; leadership abilities and intellect, 165; leadership skills, 153, 168, 217–18; leadership style, 9, 88, 145; leadership traits, 165; limits of voting, 134–35, 223; love of theater, 54; on Malcolm X's assassination, 196; marriage and divorce from Frank Dandridge, 159, 194, 213, 214; marriage and divorce from Harry Richardson, 59–60, 62–63, 67; maternal grandfather's death, 62; maternal grandfather's influence on her attitude about religion, 39; organizing philosophy, 85, 226, 230; on parenting, 60; parenting style, 61; personality traits, 226; philosophies, 70, 176, 228; on President Kennedy's assassination, 143; as president of the Howard Players, 54, 257; protesting Howard University's dean of women, 53; protesting racial discrimination during college, 52; racial pride, 4, 33, 41–42; reason for leaving the civil rights movement, 195; reasons for boycotting referendum, 104, 108, 118, 134, 136; reasons for joining CNAC, 79–81; receives Richard Allen Foundation Award, 164; rejection of politics of respectability, 5, 95, 125; relationship with Malcolm X, 175–78, 182–83, 195; resigning from SNCC's

executive committee, 194; as role model to younger activists, 168; secular humanism, 5, 8, 10, 39, 46, 49, 54, 65, 80, 122, 165, 166, 195, 207, 218, 228; self-actualization, 225; social conformity and resistance, 29–30, 33–35, 53, 58–60, 62–63, 67; support of self-defense, 190–91; supporting Malcolm X, 177, 282, 286, 291, 296; threat of being lynched, 101; trip to Québec, Canada, 64; trips to California, 120–21, 184; unease with public speaking, 30, 40, 133; as union delegate, 218; university professors, 44–48; use of silence, 89, 102, 228; use of sociological training, 153; view on communism, 49; view on religion, 39; on voter education and registration, 85; voting as a tactic, 136, 182, 191; at the White House, 119; work with SAFE, 150
Richardson, Harry, 59–60, 62–63, 66
Richardson, Tamara, 60–62, 64, 83–84, 194–95, 200, 214
Richmond, VA, 20, 22
Rimpo, Maurice, 141
Ringold, John W., 75
Robeson, Paul, 131, 166
Robinson, Reginald "Reggie," 72–74, 81, 101–2, 104–5, 107, 111–12, 114, 131, 150
Robnett, Belinda, 6, 167
Rob Roy factory, Cambridge, MD, 89
Rockefeller, Nelson, 179, 186
Rockland Palace, Harlem, 183
Rodney, Walter, 307
Rogers, Morton, 191
Rogers, Nahaz, 180, 182, 185
Rollins, Avon, Sr., 122
Roosevelt, Franklin D., 48
Royal Theater, Baltimore, MD, 26
Rustin, Bayard, 124, 127, 166

Sagona, Anthony, 276n4, 310
Salem Methodist Church, Harlem, 122
Salisbury, MD, 13, 36–37, 91, 94

Civil Rights and the Struggle for Black Equality in the Twentieth Century

Series Editors

Steven F. Lawson, Rutgers University
Cynthia Griggs Fleming, University of Tennessee

Freedom's Main Line: The Journey of Reconciliation and the Freedom Rides
Derek Charles Catsam

Gateway to Equality: Black Women and the Struggle for Economic Justice in St. Louis
Keona K. Ervin

The Chicago Freedom Movement: Martin Luther King Jr. and Civil Rights Activism in the North
edited by Mary Lou Finley, Bernard LaFayette Jr., James R. Ralph Jr., and Pam Smith

The Struggle Is Eternal: Gloria Richardson and Black Liberation
Joseph R. Fitzgerald

Subversive Southerner: Anne Braden and the Struggle for Racial Justice in the Cold War South
Catherine Fosl

Constructing Affirmative Action: The Struggle for Equal Employment Opportunity
David Hamilton Golland

River of Hope: Black Politics and the Memphis Freedom Movement, 1865–1954
Elizabeth Gritter

The Dream Is Lost: Voting Rights and the Politics of Race in Richmond, Virginia
Julian Maxwell Hayter

Sidelined: How American Sports Challenged the Black Freedom Struggle
Simon Henderson

Becoming King: Martin Luther King Jr. and the Making of a National Leader
Troy Jackson

Civil Rights in the Gateway to the South: Louisville, Kentucky, 1945–1980
Tracy E. K'Meyer

In Peace and Freedom: My Journey in Selma
Bernard LaFayette Jr. and Kathryn Lee Johnson

Democracy Rising: South Carolina and the Fight for Black Equality since 1865
Peter F. Lau

Civil Rights Crossroads: Nation, Community, and the Black Freedom Struggle
Steven F. Lawson

Selma to Saigon: The Civil Rights Movement and the Vietnam War
Daniel S. Lucks

In Remembrance of Emmett Till: Regional Stories and Media Responses to the Black Freedom Struggle
Darryl Mace

Freedom Rights: New Perspectives on the Civil Rights Movement
edited by Danielle L. McGuire and John Dittmer

This Little Light of Mine: The Life of Fannie Lou Hamer
Kay Mills

After the Dream: Black and White Southerners since 1965
Timothy J. Minchin and John A. Salmond

Faith in Black Power: Religion, Race, and Resistance in Cairo, Illinois
Kerry Pimblott

Fighting Jim Crow in the County of Kings: The Congress of Racial Equality in Brooklyn
Brian Purnell

Roy Wilkins: The Quiet Revolutionary and the NAACP
Yvonne Ryan

James and Esther Cooper Jackson: Love and Courage in the Black Freedom Movement
Sara Rzeszutek

Thunder of Freedom: Black Leadership and the Transformation of 1960s Mississippi
Sue [Lorenzi] Sojourner with Cheryl Reitan

For a Voice and the Vote: My Journey with the Mississippi Freedom Democratic Party
Lisa Anderson Todd

Art for Equality: The NAACP's Cultural Campaign for Civil Rights
Jenny Woodley

For Jobs and Freedom: Race and Labor in America since 1865
Robert H. Zieger